Y0-CAV-379

Reframing Politics in the Hebrew Bible

A New Introduction with Readings

Reframing Politics in the Hebrew Bible

A New Introduction with Readings

Edited, with Introduction and Notes,
by Mira Morgenstern

Hackett Publishing Company, Inc.
Indianapolis/Cambridge

Copyright © 2017 by Hackett Publishing Company, Inc.

All rights reserved
Printed in the United States of America

20 19 18 17   1 2 3 4 5 6 7

For further information, please address
Hackett Publishing Company, Inc.
P.O. Box 44937
Indianapolis, Indiana 46244-0937

www.hackettpublishing.com

Cover design by Brian Rak
Interior design by Laura Clark
Composition by Aptara, Inc.

Library of Congress Cataloging-in-Publication Data

Names: Morgenstern, Mira, editor.
Title: Reframing politics in the Hebrew Bible : a new introduction with
    readings / edited, with introduction and notes, by Mira Morgenstern.
Description: Indianapolis ; Cambridge : Hackett Publishing Company, [2017] |
    Includes bibliographical references and index.
Identifiers: LCCN 2017018594 | ISBN 9781624664618 (pbk.) | ISBN
    9781624664625 (cloth)
Subjects: LCSH: Politics in the Bible. | Bible. Old Testament—Political
    aspects. | Bible. Old Testament—Criticism, interpretation, etc.
Classification: LCC BS1199.P6 R44 2017 | DDC 221.8/32—dc23
LC record available at https://lccn.loc.gov/2017018594

The paper used in this publication meets the minimum requirements of
American National Standard for Information Sciences—Permanence of
Paper for Printed Library Materials, ANSI Z39.48–1984.

∞

CONTENTS

Contents

ACKNOWLEDGMENTS

Writing a book about political theory in the Hebrew Bible is a difficult undertaking. Many people will say it cannot be done; others will argue that it should not be done. Both groups view the Hebrew Bible as containing messages mainly of religious import that have no place in the discourse of political theory.

In many ways, this book has been years in the making. It has been lurking, unperceived, in my own mind as I have written on Rousseau and his relation to texts of the Hebrew Bible, and on the development of political discourse in the texts of the Hebrew Bible. I thank Brian Rak for having the vision to perceive the scholarly and academic need for a book that utilizes the texts of the Hebrew Bible to demonstrate that the Bible contains texts of political theory central to the development of political theory and its discourse. Working with Brian has been a demanding joy: his respect for the text and his determination to oversee a book with multiple audiences that still makes its arguments fairly and firmly helped keep in mind the larger dimensions of this project.

I would also like to thank Laura Clark for expertly shepherding this work through production, as well as Harbour Fraser Hodder and Mireidys Garcia for their own exacting editorial work on it.

Writing a book creates many debts of gratitude, which are a pleasure to acknowledge here. My childhood family of origin was always a place in which texts, both biblical and secular, were furiously debated; this activity continues to dominate the family meals even now at our family of creation. Studies with my teachers have given me the skills to navigate texts, both ancient and modern, with fierce questioning: I acknowledge with gratitude the lessons learned from Rabbi Dr. Isaac Suna ob'm and from Rabbi Dr. Walter Orenstein. Conversations with colleagues and friends Dr. Susan Weissman and Dr. Shoshana Rybak have also been of singular importance.

On the political science side of the academic aisle, there are similar debts of gratitude and friendship: I thank Professor Michael Walzer for his willingness to spend time with me in conversation on many of the topics that have found their way into this book. Likewise, I thank Professor Gordon Schochet for his pithy comments, his wise advice, and his unstinting support of this academic project. Our conversations about political theory and the Hebrew Bible have sustained me over the years of this project.

Finally, this book is dedicated to the memory of Marshall Berman. Through the years, in the contexts of our teacher-student conversations and subsequently in our dialogues as colleagues, we debated texts both in political theory and in the Bible; disagreement on textual implications always took a back seat to the intense love for these texts that dominated our conversations. Marshall believed in this project even though he did not live to see its completion. I offer this book with the hope that we all continue to analyze texts so that we can create a world in which discourse furthers understanding and not belligerence.

INTRODUCTION

The Hebrew Bible is a collection of texts[1] that was both formed within, and helped to form, the ancient Near East. But strangely enough for a work of such antiquity, the Hebrew Bible has also played an important role in the development of the modern world. Since early modern times, it has been mined not just for religious and moral dicta but also for any theoretical light its texts may shed on the organization and values of a just political regime appropriate to the modern era.[2] This process of political interpretation and discovery continues in our own day, if usually on a less theoretically ambitious scale: advocates on all sides of controversial political issues are still quick to call on select passages from the Hebrew Bible to buttress their particular point of view. Both supporters and opponents of the 2015 Supreme Court decision legalizing same-sex marriage, for example, seized upon Hebrew biblical passages to bolster their own viewpoints.[3] In such cases, texts from the Hebrew Bible are marshaled as crucial components of a potent political argument in the service of practical objectives, as well as—often implicitly—part of a theoretical argument about the nature and achievement of justice.

In the academy, the Hebrew Bible continues to figure in more self-consciously theoretical debates regarding the nature and achievements of justice. In highlighting questions of moral significance presented in its texts, some recent scholarly works have claimed that the Hebrew Bible presents an intellectual project commensurate with that of the ancient Greek philosophers and, consequently, advocates for a dialogue between these two kinds

---

1. The Hebrew Bible, whose traditional canonized form is often referred to as the Masoretic text, is customarily held to contain its books within three major divisions:

    I. Torah (or Pentateuch): Genesis, Exodus, Leviticus, Numbers, Deuteronomy

    II. Prophets: Joshua, Judges, Samuel, Kings, Isaiah, Jeremiah, Ezekiel, Hosea, Joel, Amos, Obadiah, Jonah, Micah, Nahum, Habakkuk, Zephaniah, Haggai, Zechariah, Malachi

    III. Writings: Chronicles, Psalms, Job, Proverbs, Ruth, Song of Songs, Ecclesiastes, Lamentations, Esther, Daniel, Ezra/Nehemiah

2. See Gordon Schochet, Fania Oz-Sulzberger, and Meirav Jones, eds., *Political Hebraism: Judaic Sources in Early Modern Political Thought* (Jerusalem: Shalem Press, 2008); also see Frank E. Manuel, *The Broken Staff: Judaism through Christian Eyes* (Cambridge, MA: Harvard University Press, 1992).

3. Samuel G. Freedman, "Push within Religions for Gay Marriage Gets Little Attention," *New York Times*, July 25, 2015.

of discourse.[4] Other scholarly examinations of the Hebrew Bible focus on finding interpretational "space" for believers and unbelievers alike as they search for their own versions of spiritual and philosophical meaning in the modern world.[5]

Unlike the first approach, I tend to focus in this volume on the perspectives of those living in the modern world. Thus, I do not privilege the ancient Greek philosophical tradition as normative for modern morality or politics. And unlike the second approach, I do not analyze the Hebrew Bible as a roadmap for attaining a sense of spiritual or philosophical purpose. Instead, I emphasize more practical aspects of Hebrew biblical political discourse and narrative, such as its representation of the concrete challenges of constructing the polity depicted in its pages.

This anthology examines the texts of the Hebrew Bible in order to show how its voices, though from faraway lands and times, continue to speak to the fundamental human aspirations of today's readers as these have evolved within the changing realities of political structures and circumstances of twenty-first-century life. In this context, it presents the Hebrew biblical texts within a self-consciously modern frame that highlights their keen investigations of the human condition as experienced through the warp and woof of politics. One example is the Hebrew Bible's evolving representation of cities—from the murderous inhospitality of Sodom (Genesis 18:17–33), to the shelter of dedicated Cities of Refuge for perpetrators of manslaughter (Exodus 21:12–14 and Deuteronomy 4:41–43), to the wickedness of Nineveh (Jonah 1:2), to the magnificence of Solomon's Jerusalem (I Kings 6, 7, 10)—and the ways in which cities' physical and social structures help shape the lives of their denizens, a topic that has long resonated in political thought and continues to do so today.[6]

---

4. Perhaps not surprisingly, such studies are often undertaken with Platonic presuppositions and priorities and are often influenced by the approach and preoccupations of the influential twentieth-century political theorist Leo Strauss. Cf. Thomas Pangle, *Political Philosophy and the God of Abraham* (Baltimore: Johns Hopkins University Press, 2003), esp. 1–16.

5. Leon Kass, *The Beginning of Wisdom* (Chicago: University of Chicago Press, 2003), esp. the introduction.

6. The topic of cities and their relations to their citizens occupies a prime place in the history of political theory, from the teachings of Socrates, to Plato's *Republic*, to the essays of Rousseau, to the writings of Marx. A more recent (if less theoretically explicit) example of the complexities of this topic is seen in an article in the June 5, 2016, Sunday edition of the *New York Times Magazine* called simply "The High Life Issue." Its vertigo-inducing presentation of text and high-altitude photos, together with its focus on the experience of building as well as living within a New York City rising above eight hundred feet, foregrounds the verticality and "feel" of this new aspect of urban architecture—and in the process, illuminates aspects of its impact on various stakeholders, workers, and people living in the city.

In examining the wide-ranging themes of the Hebrew Bible, this volume focuses on contributions to political theory represented in its texts.[7] Evaluating these contributions to political theory is undertaken by carefully attending to the narrative strategies, linguistic expressions, and literary genres and devices found in the Hebrew Bible. (In this formalistic sense, with its emphasis on the literary tools by which the Hebrew biblical texts express themselves, this study may be said to bear certain similarities to some of the literary or philosophical studies noted above.) The textual examinations that undergird this volume utilize these characteristics of the Hebrew biblical texts specifically to highlight their nuanced and sometimes counterintuitive arguments about politics and the institutions of political life represented in its pages. For example, this volume highlights the support for monarchy among the Israelites as it surveys the prolonged conversation about self-rule held among the Israelites, Samuel, and God (I Samuel 8, 10).[8]

In thus exploring the Hebrew Bible's contribution to political theory, this volume highlights the distinctively human and even tragic issues involved in settling questions of the dominion and organization of society. The institutionalization of politics, as the Hebrew Bible demonstrates, does not come without its price. This sobering vision is a crucial link between the narrative trajectory of the Hebrew Bible and modern efforts to attain security within a complex world whose intricate composition indicates, but often masks, complicated power realities.

Still, the very act of reading ancient texts in attempting to chart their relevance to political issues of the modern and postmodern world raises complex questions about the historical quality of these texts. For the purposes of many, it seems logical to treat ancient texts and the political themes they contain in a consciously historical manner, one that tries to account for the actual world of the ancient Near East in which these texts were generated, even if a disproportionate emphasis on historical consideration might obscure other aspects of those texts.

For my purposes, a different approach seems necessary. I view the Hebrew biblical texts highlighted in this study as representing a web of values with a great deal to say about politics, not just as these are presented in the narratives of the Hebrew Bible but also as they help formulate the

---

7. At the same time, it is important to note that this volume is not a work of comparative politics, biblical archaeology, philology, or history and thus does not aim to identify "original inspirations" or "influences" among ancient Near Eastern texts bearing on politics.

8. Conventionally enough, this anthology, like the Hebrew Bible itself, represents politics not as a realm to which both Divine and human actors are subject but as a realm of distinctively—and thus exclusively—human activity to which God is no more subject than He is to other, more natural, constraints upon human life (even if He does, as in I Samuel, interact with those who are subject to them).

political values that have enabled modern democracies to emerge since the Enlightenment. Reflecting this perspective, this volume emphasizes the political qualities and theoretical insights of the Hebrew biblical texts without delving into the historical realities of the ancient Near East.

Despite this political emphasis, this volume does not take a hortatory approach to what a revolutionary politics based on Hebrew biblical texts might accomplish, as do modern viewpoints that are allied with varieties of political theology or liberation theology. The aim of this volume is neither to present faith-based teachings nor to do theology. Instead, it highlights how the texts of the Hebrew Bible contribute to the modern awareness of what politics can accomplish and how political discourse can help change the practical arrangements of power.

In presenting these aspects of politics to us, the Hebrew Bible itself first confronts us as a kind of unity, even if its structure reveals itself to be a work composed of many books, books that are themselves composed of different parts. I have thus chosen to treat the Hebrew Bible essentially as a unitary work—that is, one that can be made sense of when considered as a whole. This approach is atypical of most modern biblical scholarship in the academy (which tends not to bracket concerns of historical provenance, as I have done),[9] yet allows for a sharper focus on specific themes—in this case, politics and the values upon which coherent political systems may be based.

Even in our historically conscious age, this prioritization of valuative coherence over historical provenance can be seen as in keeping with an approach often taken to fundamental political texts. While the U.S. Constitution, for example, may be considered the product of different hands over multiple generations, the text itself is often read as a unitary work in terms of its political structure and values as well as its articulation of its citizens' rights and responsibilities.[10] In taking a similar approach to the Hebrew Bible, I am far from denying its textual or historical complexity. Indeed, as we shall see later, my reading, while leaving aside questions of historicity as well as authorial and editorial provenance, utilizes the very heterogeneity

---

9. Many literary approaches to the Hebrew biblical texts do go beyond the exclusive concerns of historical provenance highlighted by some proponents of theories such as the Documentary Hypothesis. The Documentary Hypothesis analyzes the Hebrew biblical texts—and particularly the Pentateuch—as a function of what its proponents consider to be the different literary, authorial, and editorial streams in texts customarily considered by more traditional scholars to be unitary creations. On this point, see the analysis of Susan A. Handelman, *The Slayers of Moses* (Albany: SUNY Press, 1983).

10. It is this understanding—the consideration of the Hebrew Bible as a whole (see note 1 above)—that informs this volume's sense of the text when speaking of the Hebrew Bible's approach to particular issues or themes. This may be said to be in keeping with the notion of constitutionality when interpreting the approach of the U.S. Constitution to matters of legal or political import.

of the Hebrew Bible—its plethora of literary forms and voices—to demonstrate the coherence of its political (and arguably its philosophical) vision of freedom and dignity for all human beings.

Challenges of Reading the Hebrew Bible Politically

The Hebrew Bible is a difficult text to read, for many reasons. Not the least of these is that its texts cover an unusually long narrative trajectory, presenting themselves as a history of the world starting from its creation, followed by the account of God's choice of one line of Abraham's clan to become a nation (the Israelites) that would eventually inhabit their Promised Land. In the course of its descriptions of the formation and development of the Israelite nation, the Hebrew Bible chronicles the Israelites' travails of slavery in, and liberation from, Egypt, highlighting the Israelites' acceptance of the commandments of the Torah at Mount Sinai and their subsequent conquest of their Promised Land.

But the story of the Israelites does not end there. Subsequent books of the Hebrew Bible describe the unstable nature of the Israelites' sojourn in their Promised Land, due to the enmity of the surrounding nations and even, as the Hebrew biblical texts themselves attest, to the Israelites' predilection for idolatry, particularly as practiced by the neighboring nation-states and empires. Eventually, the Israelites adapt these nations' methods of governance as well, as reflected in the Israelite request for a king (to replace the judges that had never successfully or permanently unified the Israelite tribes under their sway).

As described by the texts in the Hebrew Bible, monarchical governance does not achieve the security anticipated by the Israelites who had clamored for it. In fact, the Solomonic kingdom of ancient Israel winds up splitting into two kingdoms: the Northern Kingdom and the Southern Kingdom. Eventually, the Israelites of the Southern Kingdom are conquered by King Nebuchadnezzar of the Babylonian Empire and exiled to Babylonia (the Northern Kingdom by then had effectively been scattered by King Sennacherib of the Assyrian Empire). But, in a development that is conventionally unimaginable, particularly in the ancient world depicted in the Hebrew Bible, the Israelites (of the Southern Kingdom) do manage to return to their ancestral homeland—this by permission of King Cyrus of Persia, who by then ruled "all the kingdoms of the earth" (Ezra 1:1–4)—and establish their Second Commonwealth.[11]

---

11. To be sure, the narrative of the Hebrew Bible does not end "happily ever after": in their Second Commonwealth, the Israelites remain a client state of Persia and of other empires that subsequently dominate the Ancient Near East.

This complicated background is only one reason why readers can find the Hebrew Bible's texts to be an obscure—as well as obscuring—scrim through which to attempt to clarify the implications of politics and of political situations. Another is that the texts of the Hebrew Bible are often approached, whether consciously or unconsciously, from perspectives other than those reflected in the texts themselves. For many readers, the Hebrew Bible is just another name for the Old Testament. Such readers fail to take account of the real differences in content between different versions of the Old Testament stemming from various Christian (e.g., Catholic, Protestant, Orthodox) versions of the canon. Of more relevance to the present study, however (and setting aside questions arising from the relationship of the Old Testament to the New), they overlook the fact that various Christian canons of the Old Testament differ significantly from the canon of the Hebrew Bible.

From an interpretive standpoint, this leads to real differences in how the various texts of any given Bible are read, since different canons necessarily present different hermeneutical contexts, and hence different accounts, of the messages that can be drawn from the texts. When reading a Bible from a particular perspective—for example, the standpoint of politics, as in this volume—the significance of canonical differences can become commensurately magnified. This becomes especially apparent when books of obvious political import—the Books of Maccabees, for example (which are not included in the Hebrew biblical canon)—are among the key differences between canons. It is the particularity of a canon that allows—and, some would argue, even requires—the reader to approach it as an integrated whole.

But coming to grips with the Hebrew Bible even on its own terms poses great challenges, since it is composed of so many different kinds of texts—ranging from legalistic texts (e.g., Leviticus) to narratives that are poetic (e.g., Psalms), novelistic (e.g., Ruth, Esther), didactic (e.g., Proverbs), and even historical (e.g., the Book of Judges) in nature. Each of these textual forms requires different hermeneutical techniques to lay bare its own meanings and implications. This means that interpreting the Hebrew biblical texts is a complex enterprise, particularly as we read these nuanced texts through the lens of politics. Making things yet more challenging, the texts of the Hebrew Bible highlight a wide range of political experiences and their impact on the people who form the communities in which these events take place. By including both the shadows and sunshine of nation formation and leadership, the Hebrew Bible presents difficult situations whose ambiguities seem both to derive from and reflect the complications of real life.

Two episodes from the Hebrew Bible suffice to illustrate its keen perception of the complexities of human nature and national identity—and of the terrible burdens and ironic privileges of leadership. Moses, as the Hebrew Bible tells us, is ready to sacrifice everything for his people. In the wake of the Israelites' idolatrous construction of the Golden Calf, he even rejects God's announcement that He will wipe out the Israelite nation and restart it from Moses alone. Instead, Moses insists that the Israelites be forgiven: "If not, please erase me from Your book" (Exodus 32:32). At the same time, Moses relays and oversees the implementation of Divine directives that wipe out thousands of Israelites (Exodus 32:27–28). In a later era, David establishes Israel as a unified polity by launching his monarchy over the united Israelite tribes (II Samuel 5:1–3). At the same time, he abuses his royal authority by taking Batsheva, another man's wife, and causing that man's death (II Samuel 11:1–21). As it turns out, David's self-involved actions in embarking upon his relationship with Batsheva have implications for the succession of the Davidic monarchy that David himself does not envision. Leadership, as the Hebrew Bible points out, often involves inner conflict, as well as reconciliation, with the often momentous and unforeseen consequences of decisions.

As mentioned above, this volume avoids approaching the Hebrew Bible from either historical or specifically religious viewpoints. But the new context utilized here should not be seen as presenting an exclusivist challenge to these more conventional approaches to elucidating the texts of the Hebrew Bible. The Hebrew Bible has been read in many ways over the years, and the ever-changing questions and frameworks within which we read these ancient texts is one thing that keeps them perennially relevant, even exciting. As we will see later, this ability of its texts to adapt to new frameworks of interpretation has also contributed to the Hebrew Bible's strong relationship to the genesis of modern democracy.

Importantly, differentiating political from traditionally religious or historical approaches to interpreting the texts of the Hebrew Bible does not involve ignoring the reality of the influence of religious beliefs on political life. Rather, reading the texts of the Hebrew Bible politically means first of all engaging in a close reading of the biblical texts' representation of the emergence of the Israelites as a people whose collective identity is based on monotheistic worship and on particular practices, both religious and social, that sharply differentiate them from their neighbors.

Additionally, reading the Hebrew Bible politically means taking the Israelites seriously as a people facing concrete problems of political survival: they live in a homeland surrounded by militarily strong nations that do not particularly like the Israelite presence in the region and that periodically war with them. The enmity of these neighboring monarchies and empires may stem from cultural and political discomfort with the novel monotheistic worldview of the Israelites, along with its revolutionary political and social implications (as we will see in the various selections on the City in Part I, Chapter 1, monotheism forms part of the context for the strained relations between the Israelites and their warlike neighbors in the Promised Land in the deliberations leading up to the request for a king).

Also, or alternatively, the recurrent wars between the Israelites and their neighbors may be symptoms of political and military expansionism on the part of these neighbors (or even, at certain junctures in history as presented by these texts, of the Israelites themselves). In any case, the practical fact remains that the Israelites living in this inhospitable situation must formulate effective responses in order to ensure their physical survival. They must learn how to fight; they must develop military strategy; and they must effectively govern themselves. All of these are distinctively political questions, and the texts that treat issues such as these are the focus of this anthology.[12]

But these politically themed texts do more than comment on the past development of the Israelite nation as presented in the Hebrew Bible. In addition, these narratives highlight the more specific challenges of reading the Hebrew Bible as political theory.

Does the Hebrew Bible Count as Political Theory?

The query posed in this heading itself raises a prior question: just how does one define political theory?

Finding an answer to this question is not simple—for one thing, doing so with precision requires distinguishing political theory from other closely related terms. Much ink has been spilled on the differences between political theory, political philosophy, and political thought. The introduction to Sheldon Wolin's *Politics and Vison*, which has long been cited as authoritative on this matter, offers several suggestions for distinguishing between these terms and the endeavors that they designate. In the context of this discussion, we will focus on his understanding of political theory. Wolin's claims (which are in fact not always easy to reconcile with one another) offer nuanced interpretations of the aims of political theory and the process of its engagement.

---

12. The approach of this volume to its texts does suggest that I am not persuaded by theological arguments to the effect that the religious character of the Hebrew Bible requires that no text within it (particularly in the Torah, traditionally considered to be the direct word of God) be interpreted in any way that is not only or primarily theological in intent and implication. I mention this contention not to refute it at length but merely to note that it fails on its own merits to do justice to the texts of the Hebrew Bible inasmuch as it ignores their literary complexity and multilayered referential richness. As commentators on the Hebrew Bible have long realized, recognition of the sacred nature of a text does not implicitly justify an a priori circumscription of the range of themes or subject matter to which it can refer.

To a large extent, Wolin toggles between what he views as the practical aspects of political theory, on one hand, and its larger, philosophical implications, on the other. Thus, for Wolin, political theory is not exclusively concerned with philosophical matters: it is linked to the practical affairs of politics, although distinct from them. But Wolin also insists that while political theory is linked to practice,[13] theory itself is not constrained by the limits of what is practicable.[14] And when Wolin does suggest that political theory is primarily concerned with the larger issues evoked by the establishment of a polity, he takes special care to link these higher aims to the attempt to think about the empirical roles that power and its ramifications play in the ability of human beings to conceive of and build a polity as their conscious response to the current order of their environment. Wolin sums up his concept of political theory with the suggestion that its practice is much more concerned with the larger questions of meaning, focusing on the "goals . . . proper to a political society."[15]

By Wolin's various criteria, then, what the Hebrew Bible has to say about politics would seem to fit squarely within the framework of political theory, even though neither "political" nor "theory" is a biblical term: the Hebrew biblical texts deal with human behavior regarding order; they refer to institutionalized practices even if they do not focus on their mechanisms; and they certainly promote a view of human life and society with a notion of an elevated—perhaps even consciously transcendent—meaning at their center.

But there is another conception of what political theory ought to encompass. This approach highlights institutional arrangements as fundamental to the enterprise of political theory. In this context, the Hebrew Bible's lack of emphasis on the orders of institutional procedure and constitutional structure—so central to ancient Greek political thought and to the notions expressed by American political thinkers regarding the maintenance of political democracy[16]—has been conventionally viewed as portraying a lack of proper theorizing about politics on the part of the authors of

---

13. "What is important for political theory is that these institutionalized practices ["regularly used for handling public matters," p. 7] play a fundamental role in ordering and directing human behavior and in determining the character of events." *Politics and Vision: Continuity and Innovation in Western Political Thought* (Princeton, NJ: Princeton University Press, [1960] 2004), 7.

14. "Political theory is not so much interested in political practices, or how they operate, but rather in their meaning" (Ibid., 7).

15. Ibid., 10.

16. See in this connection *The Federalist*, particularly nos. 10 and 51, by James Madison, ed. J. R. Pole (Indianapolis: Hackett, 2005).

the Hebrew Bible. In effect, this argument goes, the Israelites do not really develop for themselves writings that conform to conventional expectations for traditional political texts. Where are their systematic, reasoned considerations of government structure, of political deliberation, or of political decision making?

Michael Walzer highlights these questions in his brilliantly written *In God's Shadow: Politics in the Hebrew Bible*. In this book, he argues that although the texts of the Hebrew Bible are "engaged with politics," they are in fact not very interested in it. In Walzer's view, whatever raw materials the Hebrew biblical texts may offer for the construction of a properly theoretical political discourse, the Hebrew Bible itself presents us with no well-developed analyses of the aims, processes, and institutions of politics commensurate with those evident in the ancient Greek texts that form a central part of our political heritage as well. They are just not there. For Walzer, there is no political theory in the Hebrew Bible.[17]

Still, despite these very real differences in understanding what is entailed in identifying a text as part of the discourse of political theory, neither Wolin nor Walzer takes account of the difference between constructing a theoretical discourse on the basis of the raw materials in a text, on the one hand, and recognizing the theoretical discourse that is implicit in the text, on the other. While one traditional understanding of political theory, focusing on political institutionalization (in the way that Aristotle formulates it in his *Politics*, for example), is largely absent from the Hebrew Bible, that point alone does not take account of all the ways in which political theory may manifest itself in its texts.[18]

The concept of political theory put forth in this volume emphasizes the *implicit* nature of its exposition in the Hebrew Bible, where it is found not on the surface of the text but woven into its fabric. This exposition can be brought to light by paying close attention to what are often considered to be mere matters of literary presentation, whether these be themes, narratives, strategies, contrasts, ironies, oblique comments, or even silence. Doing so allows us to notice the breadth and rich variety of political life as presented in the Hebrew Bible, highlighting the differences between what one may call the institutionalization of politics—that is, the obvious trade in power plays as these find institutional form in the public domain—and what may be classified as thinking about and participating in the shaping of power relations, whether in the public or private spheres.

---

17. Michael Walzer, *In God's Shadow: Politics in the Hebrew Bible* (New Haven, CT: Yale University Press, 2012), xii.

18. On this point, see Wolin, *Politics and Vision*, 7–8. The implications of this lack of focus on the details of institutionalization are considered below, toward the end of this introduction.

Applying this distinction between "official" and "sideline" activities in or near the political sphere, whether done consciously or not, has consequences. Utilizing the conventional categories of ancient Greek political thought, such as constitutional structure, or institutionalization, to assess the political implications and theoretical "heft" of Hebrew biblical texts often boils down to applying arbitrarily narrow conceptions of what is to be understood as political theory—and what is therefore considered to belong to the field of politics—and what, by implication, does not partake of these lofty endeavors. When these traditional understandings, together with analyses of institutional development that are then privileged as markers of what "counts" as political theory, are subsequently—even automatically—read back into Hebrew biblical texts, its writings are necessarily assumed to have little or no importance for political theory.

For political theory as conventionally construed, the effects of this demarcation of its scope are inherently conservative, if not stultifying. Making systematic analysis of political institutionalization the sine qua non of political theory chokes its vital life force and denudes it of the revolutionary, unsettling characteristics that can make it a crucial tool for changing society and history. This is precisely the role that political theory has consciously assumed in modern times—as we see, for example, in the writings of Rousseau—and it is a fundamental part of what political theory has come to mean in the context of modern life, highlighting the immediate relevance of political theory to people who may not be accustomed to viewing themselves as the authors of political change.[19]

But in fact, as even the following examples, drawn from the great variety of Hebrew biblical texts, suggest, the Hebrew Bible is not devoid of even the more conventional understandings of institutional analysis and concerns. The books of Esther and Daniel offer robust representations of the high stakes of political maneuvering and the processes of choosing which techniques to use in order to ensure the best outcomes for the different agendas of power that are in play. How one engages in political discourse, and how one must negotiate the often Byzantine byways of political bureaucracies, are presented in Hebrew biblical texts as crucial elements for ensuring both one's own survival and the achievement of particular political goals.[20]

---

19. For a more detailed analysis of Rousseau as a political thinker (despite his unique approaches to expressing his sense of political themes), see my *Rousseau and the Politics of Ambiguity* (University Park: Penn State University Press, 1996).

20. In this context, the subtext of the Hebrew biblical books of Esther and Daniel evokes some of the practical concerns of managing politics that are at the forefront of Machiavelli's *The Prince* (written in 1513).

In addition, the Hebrew Bible recognizes that talking to and about the people who embody political or social institutions often serves as a short path to evaluating and to participating in those institutions. For example, in the conversation that takes place between Esther and Mordecai upon their learning of Haman's genocidal plot (Esther 4:4–17), it is possible to trace through Esther's weighted answers her evolving consideration of which plan of political appeal and stratagem might prove most effective; in the end, it is her analysis and strategy that prevail, and not Mordecai's.[21]

A more protracted example of a dialogue presented in the context of a personal relationship that also functions as a representation of political analysis may be found when the Hebrew biblical text describes conversations between David and Jonathan on the management of King Saul's homicidal hatred of David (I Samuel 20:1–42). While on the surface this discussion seems to revolve around David's presence or absence at a royal court celebration, David's calibrated answers make it clear that he is aware of the need to prepare himself for the future challenges of managing court life when he himself would take the throne.[22] In this context, one in which political concerns are depicted as being disguised within seemingly banal considerations of court etiquette, focusing on institutional development as an exclusive (or even preponderant) criterion for assessing the presence or quality of theoretical considerations implicit in a text can cause one to lose sight of—if not suppress—the legitimate substance and aims of political theory as a whole.

Importantly, the topics in which the Hebrew Bible engages—the uniqueness of urban life and its effect on its denizens, the nature of justice, the paradoxes of violence, the demands of leadership, the challenges of nation formation and national survival—indicate a convergence of subject matter between its texts and the concerns of traditional political theory. As we will see in this volume, the rich treatment of these various topics in the texts of the Hebrew Bible makes a compelling case for the recognition of Hebrew biblical texts as important writings for the study of political theory.

Expanding the Circle: From "Politics" to "the Political"

In addition to noting the various nuances of the term "theory," it is important to consider the important differences between various uses and meanings of the term "politics" as well as its (usually merely) adjectival form, "political." On the one hand, "politics" has been understood to refer narrowly to public

---

21. See Esther 4:4–17.

22. See I Samuel 20:1–42.

and institutional power struggles and their power relations. But "politics" can also signify something broader, encompassing power relations within much wider frames of reference, ranging from public life to private life and in between these arenas. Often—and particularly in much of ancient Greek political thought—distinctions between what is and what is not considered to be part of the domain of politics are utilized as one way of justifying existing power structures.

At issue is the differentiation of decision-making processes and institutions dominated by elite individuals or groups from the dull, often messy, and therefore downgraded quotidian practices that underlie the physical realities supporting social and political structures. (Marx would later refer to these social and political structures as the "superstructure.") As it happens, these unsung functions that are conventionally taken for granted were traditionally relegated in the ancient world to women and slaves. In this dualistic view of life, whose realms were conventionally viewed as mutually exclusive, appraisals of certain groups such as women, who were traditionally preoccupied with the physical minutiae of childbirth and household activities, tended to view them as naturally unfit for, and therefore to be excluded from, the domain of power and public affairs—that is, politics (in the narrow sense).

Conventional understandings of political theory—whether those of Plato or Aristotle in the ancient Greek world or those shown in classical American democratic writings that focus on the importance of ensuring that political institutions prevent the tyranny that results from the centralization of power in one place[23]—contrast with and thus highlight this volume's new approach to the contributions of the Hebrew Bible to political theory. As we have already noted, the Hebrew Bible implicitly distinguishes between descriptions of concrete institutionalization of politics (in the narrow sense), on the one hand, and, on the other, the involvement of people from spheres not traditionally considered part of that domain, who, transgressively or not, take part in the discussions regarding power relations and who thereby play important roles in influencing and determining events within that domain. In short, the Hebrew Bible shows itself to be quite interested in the phenomena designated by this broader sense of our term, denoting a realm that can be described as "the political."

Seen in this broader context of the political, the selections included in this volume allow us to appreciate the importance of these political actors not only for the concerns and makeup of political theory in our own day but also, as we shall see, for the historical development of

---

23. This structural definition of tyranny is highlighted in *The Federalist*, particularly nos. 10 and 51, by James Madison.

political thought during the era of the Enlightenment, a period crucial to the development of the United States in particular and of modern democracy in general. This connection, while seemingly novel today, was already was well understood by many eighteenth-century political thinkers,[24] including those playing central roles in the political founding of the United States.

Understanding the connection between "politics" (in the narrow sense) and the "political" (in its broader context), and taking into account the implications of the realities of everyday life for the larger theoretical concerns of politics as they develop in the modern world, Enlightenment thinkers are particularly engaged with the focus of the Hebrew Bible on just these matters. Consequently, they consciously interpret the texts of the Hebrew Bible with a view to elucidating the implications of its texts for both politics and the political[25] as they justify their arguments for revolutionary political change.

---

24. One argument that has been advanced to explain this phenomenon—the interest in the texts of the Hebrew Bible exhibited by many Enlightenment thinkers—is that linking the new revolutionary aims of the early modern era to the Hebrew biblical texts worked, in effect, to justify the goals of these Enlightenment thinkers and, therefore, could serve as a source of advancing support for these revolutionary goals among the larger public. Leo Strauss, in his *Natural Right and History* (Chicago: University of Chicago Press, repr. 1963), esp. 186–218, may be read as one example of this approach (Strauss goes on to argue that these biblical proof texts were, in effect, utilized not as a function of faith in these texts but rather prophylactically to ward off the potential ire of the political censors).

But it is important to note that this is not the only way to interpret the Enlightenment interest in the Hebrew biblical texts as a means to support revolutionary change. Central to their strategy of close reading of Hebrew biblical texts is what Enlightenment thinkers view as the immense contradiction between the absolute rulers' use of selected Hebrew biblical texts to justify their overweening power (via theories such as the Divine Right of Kings) and the contrary implications of those same Hebrew biblical texts when forcefully interpreted by more liberal-leaning members of the reading public. Many Enlightenment thinkers who utilize the texts of the Hebrew Bible to support their revolutionary aims view their own readings of it as exemplifying the triumph of reason (i.e., what they consider to be clear readings of various Hebrew biblical texts) over what they deemed superstition (i.e., what they identified with conventional readings supporting the political status quo).

25. The Hebrew Bible's foregrounding of the links between activity that we have described as political, on the one hand, and the institutions of politics, on the other, finds parallels in writings of the Enlightenment age. These include many of Rousseau's works, especially *The Discourse on Inequality, Émile*, and his prose poem *The Levite of Ephraim* (see the analysis in "Women, Power, and the Politics of Everyday Life" in my *Rousseau* for a more complete discussion of this issue).

As we see in this volume, these connections between politics and everyday life are evident in the texts of the Hebrew Bible as well; one example of this is its setting of political discourse in places (e.g., granaries, fields) not typically viewed as locations where institutional

The Hebrew Bible and the Enlightenment Reader

The connections that Enlightenment thinkers establish between their own innovations in modern political thought and the texts of the Hebrew Bible are especially crucial to what we have come to identify as the birth of modern democracy. Many of the Enlightenment's novel ideas about establishing the sort of polity in which power would be shared among larger numbers of people occur within an intellectual culture that consciously pays a new kind of attention to these Hebrew biblical texts.

Particularly innovative about the intellectual consideration of the Hebrew Bible during the Enlightenment is that, for the most part, it takes place outside of traditional religious contexts. An obvious early example is Spinoza's writings on the Hebrew Bible.[26] While Spinoza does not, as some Enlightenment thinkers do, regard the Hebrew Bible as Divinely sourced, he does recognize its texts as a basis for limited executive or governmental power over the individual (chap. 17 of *A Theological-Political Treatise*). In chapter 18 of that same work, Spinoza arguably reads the Hebrew Bible as enabling a de facto absence of political-institutional enforcement of religion;[27] like Hobbes, Spinoza distinguishes between matters of faith and issues of religious practice.

---

politics are practiced. Importantly, these Hebrew biblical texts are seriously studied as part of the intellectual and political agendas of the Enlightenment era.

To be sure, parallelism is not, in and of itself, a proof of influence. Still, the similarity of thematic juxtapositions in the writings of these widely disparate historical eras suggests a closer logical relationship than mere happenstance of literary style. Expressing her own desire for the political aims of the American Revolution to be grounded in the concrete reality of everyday life (particularly as experienced in marriage, the locus of gender relations for most adults of her own era), Abigail Adams has this to say: "Remember the Ladies.... Do not put such unlimited power into the hands of the Husbands. Remember, all Men would be tyrants if they could" (Letter to John Adams, March 31, 1776; in Alice S. Rossi, ed., *The Feminist Papers* [Boston: Northeastern University Press, 1988], 10). In the run-up to the American Revolutionary War, Abigail Adams' understanding of *political* tyranny as rooted in the injustices promoted in *everyday life* similarly reflects the linkages between institutional-based *politics*, on the one hand, and the more pervasive *political* practices and discourses of daily life, on the other.

26. Although Spinoza (1632–1677) technically antedates what is usually referred to as the Enlightenment (which tends to be identified with the eighteenth century), the quality of his thought and writings places him squarely within its range. See Jonathan Israel's contention, in *Radical Enlightenment: Philosophy and the Making of Modernity* (New York: Oxford University Press, 2001), that Dutch thought is at the core of Enlightenment theory.

27. This is a contentious point and represents a vexed issue in the interpretation of Spinoza's text. On the one hand, Spinoza claims (without historical or textual backing) that, with respect to the relationship between the religion and polity of the ancient Israelites, "he who forsook his religion ceased to be a citizen" (*Theological-Political Treatise*, trans. Samuel Shirley, 2nd ed. [Indianapolis: Hackett, 1991; repr. 1998], 189). On the other hand, Spinoza acknowledges

After Spinoza, the aim of most Enlightenment thinkers who consult texts of the Hebrew Bible in the process of composing their political critiques and essays supporting revolutionary change is not to discover any theologically based view of God's directives for establishing a just polity. Such doctrinal viewpoints, in and of themselves, often held no particular importance for many Enlightenment writers.[28] Rather, their new reading of Hebrew biblical texts was undertaken with the explicit purpose of establishing a rational, individual-centered basis for obedience to government.

Central to Enlightenment evaluations of morally justified political and social institutions are the themes and values expressed by Hebrew biblical

---

nearly immediately afterward that "all this was a matter of theory rather than fact" (189–90). Further still, Spinoza goes on to conflate the religious structure of the Tabernacle (and its successor, the Temple) with the political government of the Israelites (even though these developments are described in the Hebrew Bible as occurring historically in different periods and for distinctive reasons) and describes a confederate-like structure in the Israelite political framework, such that each tribe is governed locally by "captains" first chosen by Moses (193; subsequent methods for choosing these local leaders are not discussed determinatively by Spinoza). While Spinoza's notion of division of powers (195–200) holds much interest for theoretical discussions of the development of federalism (see Daniel J. Elazar, *Covenant and Polity in Biblical Israel* [New Brunswick, NJ: Transaction, 1995], 75–93), of greater relevance to the central argument of this anthology is his discussion of the relationship between religious practice and belief and the consequences of that relationship. Spinoza's implicit acknowledgment that the Israelites did not want to be subjugated to a theocracy manned by an elite class (whether political or religious) lies at the core of his understanding of the motives behind Israelite disobedience to Hebrew biblical edicts. In the end, Spinoza's argument (shared with Hobbes) that the political ruler may control outward religious practice but literally cannot control matters of internal belief (224–25, 227, 229) neatly severs matters of faith (belief) from matters of power (religious practice). It insists, as a consequence, that religious elites should have no part in the system of political power (Spinoza says outright, "How disastrous it is for both religion and state to grant to religious functionaries any right to issue decrees or to concern themselves with state business" [ibid., 208]).

This conclusion may not strike twenty-first-century readers as a great achievement in terms of personal freedom, but it does eliminate hypocrisy from the standard equation of actual religious practice with ideal moral right, a major step forward that arguably contributes to the eventual separation of church and state in modern times.

28. Enlightenment philosophes such as Voltaire and Diderot even amuse themselves by writing scathing reviews of discrete biblical narratives they consider to be outrageous examples of the irrational beliefs advocated by faith institutions; indeed, many of their critiques of the Hebrew Bible were considered heretical and (at least by some of their Jewish readers) anti-Semitic. While Voltaire and Diderot, like Spinoza, do not believe in the Divine roots of the Hebrew Bible, Voltaire's and Diderot's propensity for poking fun at the Hebrew Bible differs from Spinoza's more serious approach to its texts, perhaps because, like Hobbes, Spinoza differentiates between matters of faith (which are for him matters of individual choice) and issues of religious observance (which he insists should lie outside the province of government; *Theological-Political Treatise*, chap. 20).

texts. These concerns are utilized during the Enlightenment by believers and nonbelievers alike as well as by both the formally religious and the more freethinking Deists to structure their arguments about both politics and freedom. These critical voices take seriously those texts of the Hebrew Bible mandating justice for all, fairness for the worker, and equity in the judicial system. They utilize these concepts to justify rebellion against contemporary political institutions that support hierarchies of power based on the traditional grounds of influence, ancestry, or wealth. For these eighteenth-century critics, the moral messages of the Hebrew Bible remove the traditional obligations of obedience that nonaristocratic members of these societies might normally have felt towards these traditional institutions, whose myriad violations of justice now belied their demand for the people's submission to them. Many of Rousseau's writings, particularly the *Social Contract*, advance this viewpoint.

This approach to political theory includes new ideas regarding the mutual responsibilities of the government and the governed. It also highlights a new view of the government's limited mandate, which is understood to be focused on achieving goals for the greater happiness and development of its citizens, and not for the self-aggrandizement of their rulers. In this context, the purpose of consulting texts of the Hebrew Bible is primarily to clarify the nature, and to justify the existence, of the kind of polity that could harness the new social, economic, and technological forces that were unsettling traditional arrangements of power. In the process, these thinkers articulate what we have come to recognize as a set of democratic values.

The revolutionary thinkers of the eighteenth century utilize texts of the Hebrew Bible in various ways. In some cases, as we have seen above, the critique in terms of goals and values is straightforward (even if its application in practice might prove more complex). In other cases, the analysis is more intricate—to the point that it is not even apparent, at first glance, that a particular Hebrew biblical text in question actually functions as a critique at all. One example of this is found in Rousseau's *The Levite of Ephraim*, a prose poem that reimagines the Hebrew Bible's text in Judges 19–21 (see the relevant selections in this volume). In this work, Rousseau interrogates the links between alienation, violence, and nationhood, rethinking the connections among these ideas in terms of the political crises of his own era.[29] Another example of the complexities involved in utilizing Hebrew biblical texts to support revolution can be seen in the biblical citation "proclaiming liberty" (Leviticus 25:10) engraved on Philadelphia's Liberty Bell. In the

---

29. Mira Morgenstern, "Strangeness, Violence, and the Establishment of Nationhood in Rousseau's *Lévite d'Ephraïm*," *Eighteenth-Century Studies* 41, no. 3 (2008): 359–81.

Hebrew biblical context, these words arguably refer more directly to ensuring economic equity than to increasing political liberties. Yet many revolutionary political thinkers almost certainly viewed the former prospect much more critically than the latter.[30]

The influence of Hebrew biblical texts on political theory, and on bringing about political changes in self-government in the eighteenth century, can be viewed in both narrow and wide contexts. In the narrower framework, the utilization of Hebrew biblical texts in the debates leading up to the American Revolution can account for the substantial participation of clergy in the American colonies in these discussions. In that context, these contributions could be viewed as sociological reflections of the identity of participants in colonial political debates.

But the utilization of Hebrew biblical texts in interpreting and shaping political events, and the actual contexts in which these events are understood, go beyond the political discourses regarding support for, or opposition to, the American Revolution delivered by many eighteenth-century clergy. Rather, the close attention paid to the texts of the Hebrew Bible by eighteenth-century political writers and actors points to a more fundamental change in the context of political discourse itself.

In this era of revolution, changes in political ideas and theory were generated in discourses that were both embedded in Hebrew biblical narratives and rooted in what we have come to identify as the "standard political canon." Varying and shifting interpretations of Hebrew biblical political texts, as well as those texts normally considered to be part of the canon of political theory, are central to this process. For example, many people are familiar with the broadly ranging readings of John Locke in which proponents and opponents of the American Revolution engaged while publishing their widely varying tracts on the American Revolution. But far fewer realize that these eighteenth-century partisans also held fiercely opposing views on the appropriateness and legitimacy of monarchy as a form of political organization, based precisely on their wide-ranging interpretations of a fixed number of Hebrew biblical texts. Specifically, the different readings of I Samuel 8 both determine and reflect the stances of American colonists toward their own British monarch.[31]

---

30. Increasing political liberties is a professed aim of most American revolutionaries—ensuring economic equity, not quite as much. See Charles A. Beard, *An Economic Interpretation of the Constitution of the United States* (New York: Macmillan, 1914, repr. Dover, 2004).

31. See, for example, Jonathan Boucher's "On Civil Liberty, Passive Obedience, and Non-Resistance" (1774) as opposed to Thomas Paine's "Common Sense" (1776), both of which examine the writings of John Locke as well as the Hebrew biblical narrative of I Samuel 8 to reach dramatically opposite conclusions.

Another instance in which divergent readings of Hebrew biblical texts shape the political discourse is found when the United States attempts to deal with the moral horror of slavery. Many churches in the nineteenth-century American South, in their simplistic claims that slavery was biblically mandated,[32] refused to take account of the plethora of rules in the Hebrew Bible that carefully regulated the treatment of indentured servants as well as of bound servants and slaves. As we will see in Chapter 7, "Justice," the Hebrew biblical demands regarding fair treatment of slaves—for example, the concrete prohibitions against harming or killing them (with severe legal consequences for this violation) and the absolute prohibitions against returning escaped slaves to their erstwhile masters—underscore its acknowledgement of the fundamental humanity of slaves.

The Hebrew Bible's emphasis on slaves' humanity—their right to plan and effect changes in their own lives—provides a stark contrast to the system of chattel slavery practiced in the nineteenth-century American South. To be sure, the Hebrew Bible does permit a form of slavery to be exercised under strict conditions—and with specific requirements placed on the masters regarding their responsibilities to safeguard the well-being of their slaves. But this can hardly be seen as an unequivocal vindication of the practice of slavery. The Hebrew Bible's imposition of so many rules on slaveholders arguably even indicates the taking of a tactically abolitionist approach to the institution as a whole—namely, to regulate it out of existence (notably, this is how Lincoln reads the intent of the American Founders regarding slavery in the United States).[33]

Yet another example of the Hebrew Bible's influence on political discourse is feminism. Already in the eighteenth century, feminist thinkers insisted that some conventional understandings of "Eve's sin" as bringing death and destruction upon humanity is a misrepresentation of the actual text as written in the Hebrew Bible. Letters written in the eighteenth century by Judith Sargent Murray[34] and in the nineteenth century by Angelina

---

32. For a critical discussion of such claims, see Larry R. Morrison, "The Religious Defense of American Slavery Before 1830," *Journal of Religious Thought* 37, no. 2 (1980).

33. Lincoln, "Address at the Cooper Institute," in *The Portable Abraham Lincoln*, ed. Andrew Delbanco (New York: Viking/Penguin, 1992; repr. 1993), 167–87. This speech was given in New York City on February 27, 1860.

34. "The same breath of God animates, enlivens, and invigorates us. . . . It does not appear that she was governed by any one sensual appetite. . . . Adam could not plead the same deception . . . as he had proof positive of the fallacy of the [serpent's] argument . . . he had received the command *immediately* from the mouth of the Deity" (1780; "Essay on the Equality of the Sexes" in *Selected Letters and Essays of Judith Sargent Murray*, ed. Sharon M. Harris [New York: Oxford University Press, 1995], 12; emphasis in original).

Grimké[35] make explicit reference to the Hebrew Bible not only to solidify their bona fides in a society that took Hebrew biblical texts seriously but also to affirm a position regarding justice for women that resonates with arguments both sacred and secular. Similarly, Elizabeth Cady Stanton's *The Woman's Bible*,[36] while not promoting the Divine origins of the Bible as such, implicitly acknowledges the Hebrew Bible's importance by attempting what can be viewed as a rewrite for this ancient text that embraces justice for all people, including women.

As noted before, references to Hebrew biblical texts do more than influence eighteenth-century revolutionary values and goals, affecting their ideas and actions (even if the full implementation of the ideas outlined by the Hebrew Bible remained partial at best). In addition, the political import of the Hebrew biblical texts affects the basis of political arrangements, which in turn enable the future expansion of democratic rights to more and more groups within the polities in which these debates take place. Even now, as the expansion of democratic rights, especially in putatively democratic nations, remains an ongoing process, the texts of the Hebrew Bible, in similar fashion, continually reveal themselves anew to their engaged readers.

Democracy and Political Equality in the Hebrew Bible: The Case of Korah

Many twenty-first-century readers of the Hebrew Bible wonder whether it is possible to talk about the democratic values enshrined in the Hebrew Bible while acknowledging the largely closed system of leadership that dominates its texts. This question comes to the fore in the narrative concerning Korah, his contentions regarding the nature of Moses' and Aaron's leadership of the Israelites, and his untimely demise (Numbers 16:32–33; see the relevant selections in this volume).

As we will see later in this volume, Korah demands equality for all Israelites, including, most tellingly, equal participation in the service in the Tabernacle, the portable Temple in the wilderness in which Korah and his followers aim to bring the *Ketoret* (incense), whose offering is reserved for the priests (*Cohanim*). Calls for equality resonate well in the twenty-first century, and many readers fail to comprehend why Korah comes to his ignominious end.

---

35. "Let us examine the account of her creation . . . not placed under his [i.e., man's] authority as a *subject*, but by his side . . . under the government of God only." Sarah Grimké and Angelina Grimké, *On Slavery and Abolitionism: Essays and Letters* (New York: Penguin, 2014), letter 12; Angelina Grimké to Catherine Beecher, 1836, 319.

36. Seattle: Pacific Publishing Studio, [1895] 1898; repr. 2014.

But some critics contend that the image of Korah as a disinterested democrat does not quite work. According to this reading, what makes the argument of Korah ring false is the gap between the reasons Korah gives for his challenge to Moses and Aaron and the textual evidence as to what actually motivates him.

In this view, Korah's proclaimed interest in having everyone join in the Temple/Tabernacle service rings false in terms of Korah's own position in the hierarchy: as a highly placed Levite, he and his family retained the signal honor of transporting the holy vessels of the Tabernacle on the Israelite journeys in the wilderness (Numbers 3:31, 4:3–15). According to this reading, the clue to the true motivation of Korah's request is found in the citation of Korah's genealogy. While seemingly an innocuous notation, the recitation of this genealogy here is textually problematic, because the same genealogy had already appeared in Numbers 3; in a laconic text such as the Hebrew Bible, apparent redundancies point to an issue in the text that requires further examination.

In this understanding, what bothers Korah is centered in his genealogy: Korah is disturbed by the fact that he has not been chosen to perform priestly functions in the Tabernacle, because according to his genealogical calculations, the priesthood should have devolved to him. Korah's reasoning is based on the fact that Kehath (Jacob's grandson and Levi's son) himself had four sons: Amram (Moses' and Aaron's father); Yitzhar (Korah's father); Hebron; and Uziel (tellingly, Hebron and Uziel, the last two sons, do not figure in this controversy). In Korah's reasoning, if one son of Amram (Moses) is the political leader, the religious leadership (priesthood) should go to the son of Levi's second-born son, Yitzhar (i.e., himself). Korah felt that his branch of the family was being slighted. He perceives this as unjust.

According to this view, although Korah uses the language of democracy for all, his real goal is to grasp the privileged position of priesthood for himself. It is noteworthy that while this argument does impugn his motives, it does not suggest that the Hebrew biblical text claims that democratic arguments in themselves are essentially false, or even self-seeking.

One thing that becomes evident in examining Korah's words is that he makes claims that he cannot substantiate. He hints that Moses and Aaron are power hungry: "Why do you *raise yourselves up* above the congregation of the Lord?" (Numbers 16:3; emphasis mine). But the Hebrew biblical texts themselves make a different case: they repeat that Moses and Aaron did not seek power; indeed, Moses consistently refuses power and asks repeatedly to be released from his leadership tasks (see the passages in "The Leader Refuses His Job" and also Exodus 3:1 to 4:13). Korah thus essentially weakens his case by making outlandish claims for it.

And yet, a flawed advocate is not the same thing as a bad case; at any rate, Korah's argument should be evaluated on its merits. Little noticed by most critics is that the very fact that the Hebrew Bible devotes some of its laconic text to Korah's pronouncements suggests that it (implicitly, at least) gives a certain amount of credence to some of his general points. For example, Korah's most general assertions about the (holy) nature of the Israelite community are never disputed, certainly not by either Moses or Aaron, whose leadership Korah challenges.

In addition, many of the claims of Korah and his cohorts regarding the dangers of untrammeled leadership are taken seriously by the Hebrew Bible. A close examination of the text about the position of the monarch makes this clear: in Deuteronomy 17:14–20, the monarch is enjoined from raising himself above his people (even in his own heart); he may not enlarge his personal wealth or entourage; and the monarch must always remember that he is a human being in the service of the people and God. Likewise, the essential point from which Korah's argument departs, the equality and holiness of the Israelite people, is never disputed; the Hebrew biblical text acknowledges this at the Theophany on Mount Sinai, when God refers to all the Israelites as "a kingdom of priests and a holy nation" (Exodus 19:6). At issue is Korah's ascription specifically to Moses and to Aaron of a willful desire to exercise all power by themselves.

Following this train of thought, a major contribution of the Korah narrative for some readers is hermeneutical, focusing on the challenges of applying a general truth to a particular case. The Korah narrative thus functions as a kind of metatext, interrogating the difference between the plausibility of an argument in theory and the limits of its applicability to a particular set of circumstances. As this argument has it, Korah has much of value to say about the dangers of leadership, a position elsewhere defended in the Hebrew Bible, as we have seen. But his argument does not hold in the specific cases of Moses and Aaron, whose leadership Korah challenges.

The Hebrew Bible, Human Rights, and Democracy

The linkages between democratic developments and the interpretation of Hebrew biblical texts are not always acknowledged because often they are not completely understood. In our own day, the Hebrew Bible makes a central thematic contribution to the understanding of what it means to be a human being and regarding the social and political entitlements due any and every individual as a consequence of their human identity.[37] One might even go further and argue that the Hebrew Bible articulates a conception of human rights in a form that is recognizable to its modern readers.

---

37. Emphasizing this point is the cogent *Exodus and Revolution* by Michael Walzer (New York: Basic Books, 1985).

Although it is true that the term "human rights" does not appear in the Hebrew Bible, the absence of this expression does not mean that the concept itself is not manifest there. In fact, many of the Hebrew biblical texts are so solicitous of the welfare of the marginalized persons evoked in their pages that their care can be seen as a major theme of the Hebrew Bible as a whole.

Yet despite this emphasis on human welfare, certain Hebrew biblical texts promote values that seem to hollow out the concrete understanding of human rights that, in its modern incarnation, roots certain basic liberties and entitlements in the very concept of humanity. One such example is the texts mandating the destruction of Amalek (Exodus 17:8–17; see also Deuteronomy 25:17–18); another focuses on what appears to be the Hebrew Bible's toleration (although not unconditional support) of slavery.

The call to destroy Amalek has aroused different reactions on the part of readers of the Hebrew Bible. Some see it as an act of quid pro quo political balancing: according to the account in Exodus 17:8, Amalek starts the war against the Israelites and therefore must be prepared to accept its consequences. But other readers claim that the Hebrew biblical call to destroy Amalek is symptomatic of a broader bloodthirstiness on the part of the Hebrew Bible and the Israelites whose ethos it prescribes.[38]

But both these assertions are without merit. If the latter contention were true, bloodthirstiness and violence would be expected leitmotifs of Israelite warfare and history as presented in the Hebrew Bible. In fact, they are not. The Hebrew Bible does not represent the Israelites as being vindictive (which disposes of the quid pro quo analysis), not even against their former taskmasters and ongoing imperial power, the ancient Egyptians.[39] Unlike the ancient Greeks, the Israelites do not valorize warfare and acts of glory in battle as crucial to realizing peaks of individual greatness; they do not establish alliances predicated on vanquishing traditional enemies.

A more serious objection that bears particularly on the Amalek narrative with its accompanying call for destruction of the Amalekites is that even if the Amalek narrative is an outlier example, an anomaly that never comes to actual historical realization in the pages of the Hebrew Bible (and indeed one that Saul explicitly disobeys in I Samuel 15), it still represents

---

38. Regina M. Schwartz, *The Curse of Cain: The Violent Legacy of Monotheism* (Chicago: University of Chicago Press, 1997).

39. It is telling that in the Hebrew biblical texts, with the exception of the case of the Egyptians, the reciprocal courtesy of conceding national survival is not extended by other nations to the Israelites, whether the Israelites are living in their own homeland (as reflected in the reasons that the Israelites ask for a king in the first place) or in exile within a large multinational empire (as evident in the genocide proposed by Haman in the Book of Esther).

a moral defect in what might otherwise be considered the Hebrew Bible's admirable effort (especially in the context of an intolerant ancient world) to promote human rights for all people, even the dispossessed and the marginalized. For these contemporary readers, the exception (to tolerance) does not prove the rule; rather, it destroys the moral coherence of that rule.[40]

But if the Hebrew Bible is read in accordance with what might be identified as its own (implicit) line of reasoning, as opposed to a particular understanding of Kantian rationale, other interpretative possibilities emerge. While the Hebrew Bible operates according to well-defined moral rules (the emphasis on kindness and fairness among the disparate members of society represents just one example of this attitude), it tends to avoid ruminating on the ideal structure that moral rules ought to take.[41] For the most part, the Hebrew Bible focuses its attention on evaluating the interaction among personages and the moral dilemmas that they face. This has important practical consequences for eliciting the active participation of readers in fashioning their moral responses to the exigencies of their own lives. Rather than imposing a monolithic view of precisely how duties toward others—and, by implication, the rights of others—are to be observed, the Hebrew Bible draws its readers into the ongoing narrative of its text. By participating in the text's open-endedness,[42] the readers themselves figuratively engage with its personages and issues in their own processes of moral resolution.

This moral dexterity on the part of the Hebrew Bible makes all the difference with regard to evaluating its strictures against Amalek. Amalek is one nation, although not the only one (see Chapter 10, "Violence"), that is marked for annihilation in the Hebrew Bible. Importantly, that directive emerges out of a narrative demonstrating that the annihilating impulse attaches first to the Amalekites.[43] In the face of this ongoing enmity, what is the proper national response for the Israelites? This question should not be

---

40. This approach fits in well with the notion of Kant's categorical imperative: once the category is breached, one (the idea, the principle) stands outside of ideal, coherent moral discourse. *Groundwork of the Metaphysics of Morals* (New York: Harper Collins, repr. 2009), I.2.

41. In *Not in God's Name: Confronting Religious Violence* (New York: Schocken, 2015), 171, Jonathan Sacks puts it this way, "It [i.e., the Book of Genesis but by extension perhaps the Hebrew Bible itself] represents truth-as-story rather than truth-as-system."

42. "and you shall meditate upon it [i.e., the Torah] day and night" (Joshua 1:8; JPS translation: "thou shalt meditate therein day and night").

43. This is highlighted in Deuteronomy's recapitulation of the incident that, in the Hebrew biblical presentation, takes place right after the Israelites are liberated from Egypt: "Remember what Amalek did unto thee by the way as ye came forth out of Egypt; how he met thee by the way, and smote the hindmost of thee, all that were enfeebled in thy rear, when thou wast faint and weary; and he feared not God" (Deuteronomy 25:17–18). Note the emphasis on smiting "the hindmost" of a "faint and weary" group of people.

mischaracterized as reducing moral analysis to a blame game: there is more to the moral justification of responses to aggression than the consideration of "who started it."

As the text presents it, neither do the Israelites at this juncture choose to start a fight (for the sake of demonstrating their prowess), nor do they specifically pick the Amalekites as their target in battle. Rather, the Hebrew biblical text depicts the Amalekites as going out of their way to combat this group of enervated (former) slaves. The Hebrew Bible views this action on the part of the Amalekites as ruthless brutality, and it is this element that the Hebrew biblical text condemns for eternity, rather than just emphasizing the directive to destroy the Amalekites. In fact, the Hebrew Bible depicts God, not the Israelites, as vowing to destroy this nation (Exodus 17:14, 17). This point is highlighted in the Deuteronomic text: it is the "memory" of Amalek—what they did and what they somehow eternally represent—that is the focus of the Hebrew biblical command to the Israelites.[44] The attack on the Israelites by Amalek—an attack on civilians from behind, by picking on the weakest stragglers among them—represents wanton cruelty neither tolerated nor considered tolerable by the Hebrew Bible.

Arguments regarding the imperfect extension of human rights to all on the part of the Hebrew Bible have also been raised against what is perceived as the Hebrew Bible's embrace of slavery. But it is important to remember that the mere existence of this claim does not imply its justification. Nor is the substance of the American slave owners' self-interested reading of the texts of the Hebrew Bible[45] as promoting the chattel slavery that existed in the nineteenth-century American South borne out as a correct reading of the text. It is notable that the slavery-fighting Grimké sisters in the nineteenth-century American South repeatedly insist that the word in the Hebrew Bible that traditionally and incorrectly had been translated as "slavery" and used to justify slavery in the American South refers in most cases *not* to ownership of another human being (as in the American South) but to a system of indentured servitude. As set forth in the Hebrew Bible, this system requires manumission after a finite period, as well as establishing the erstwhile servant with the means to earn a living on his or her own (see further the section on concrete social justice in Chapter 7, "Justice").[46]

---

44. "thou shalt blot out the *remembrance* of Amalek from under heaven; thou shalt not forget" (Deuteronomy 25:19; emphasis mine).

45. See note 32 above.

46. The standard term for this type of indentured servitude was six years (Exodus 21:2–3; Deuteronomy 15:12–15). Admittedly, prisoners of war captured as a result of military victories might represent a small, but significant, exception to this rule. Regarding the Grimké sisters' understanding of servitude as expounded in the Hebrew Bible, see "Appeal to the Christian Women of the South" in Grimké and Grimké, *On Slavery and Abolitionism*.

While some may argue that the system of indentured servitude applies largely to Hebrew bondsmen or -women, it is noteworthy that non-Israelite slaves[47] are also presented as persons possessing their own dignity, which is carefully guarded by affirmative Hebrew biblical commands. For example, all servants or slaves must keep the Sabbath; that is, no work may be demanded of them on that day (Exodus 20:8–11). Also, all servants (irrespective of origin) are to participate in all festivals, including the consumption of the Passover sacrifice, which by Hebrew biblical law was forbidden to the uncircumcised (Exodus 12:48). This meant that all male slaves, including non-Israelite ones, had to be circumcised. As described by the Hebrew biblical text, this circumcision was accompanied by the consequent acceptance of the basic tenets of monotheistic belief, which implies that even non-Israelite slaves shared in communal life. A non-Israelite slave owned by a priest could even eat of the priestly gifts (known in the Hebrew Bible as *Terumah*), which are specifically forbidden to any other Israelites who are not priests (Leviticus 22:11, 13).

It is easy, of course, to dismiss these points as concerning, at best, matters of ritualistic observance; and no one could argue that, with respect even to these, the practices sanctioned reflect anything like the ideals of religious liberty now accepted in the West. In the context of the Hebrew biblical world, however, they are important parts of a central argument pointing to a recognition of the personhood of the slave. That personhood is why the life of the slave is not taken for granted, and why she or he participates in the central rituals that define Israelite communal existence in the Hebrew Bible. Since all human beings are considered by the Hebrew Bible to be made in God's image (Genesis 1:27), it makes sense, in that context, to insist upon the personhood of all, and especially of slaves.

Still, the passages in the Hebrew Bible dealing with slavery bring up another issue regarding its approach to human rights. In the Hebrew Bible, evidence of the human rights of slaves may be seen in the rules specifying largely what the master is forbidden to do to them: how, for example, the master may not wound them or kill them. But these negatively styled directives raise an issue regarding the Hebrew Bible's extension of human rights to slaves: how seriously can such an extension of human rights be taken when expressed not in positive terms but rather as the mere consequence of a negative command or warning?

One response to that question is to note that the warnings directed to the masters regarding the treatment of their Canaanite slaves, although expressed as negative prohibitions, do compel positive directives pertaining

---

47. That is to say, a "servant from the nations surrounding you" (Leviticus 25:44). The Israelites are represented in the Hebrew Bible as having both Israelite and non-Israelite slaves.

to the behavior of the masters regarding the treatment of their slaves; for example, if a slave is wounded at the hand of the master, the master must immediately free the slave. In these cases, the purported differences between the positive and negative conceptualizations of these rights arguably become a matter of linguistic preference, rather than substantive concern.

Also, from both the philosophical and the politically pragmatic points of view, one may contend that it is in fact the negative delineation of rights—the demarcation of where the more powerful party may not interfere, even and especially concerning the rights of those less powerful (which historically was often considered an accepted consequence of "might" determining "right")—that is substantively the more vital guarantee of those rights.[48] Notably in the American Constitution, those rights most cherished as the essence of freedom are couched in negative terms.[49]

The Hebrew Bible advances an understanding of human beings in which even normally overlooked members of society have rights, including the dispossessed, the servant, the orphan, and the widow, to name just a few of the socially marginalized. In essence, all people, even those who are on the sidelines of society and who are conventionally treated (even in our own more "enlightened" day) as people without the same claims to equality that "regular people" enjoy, are to be handled fairly in court (e.g., Exodus 18:24; Deuteronomy 1:16–18, 16:19); are to have access to all gleanings and leavings of the farmer so that they do not starve (Deuteronomy 24:19–22; Ruth 2:2–3); and are not to be deprived at night of the wraps that they have been forced to leave as a surety for outstanding loans if that is all they have with which to cover themselves (Deuteronomy 24:10–13).

To be sure, the Hebrew Bible acknowledges manifestations of social inequality. At the same time, it insists that the presence of hierarchical inequalities, and even inequities, do not obviate the overwhelming moral imperative to treat all human beings, including slaves, as people with equal claims

---

48. See Isaiah Berlin, who says, "The defence of liberty consists in the 'negative' goal of warding off interference." "Two Concepts of Liberty" in Berlin, *Liberty*, ed. Henry Hardy (New York: Oxford University Press, repr. 2002), 174. Although one may argue that Berlin goes on to critique this notion (which he attributes to John Stuart Mill), in the end he concedes it is at the very nub—although not necessarily encompassing the entire extent—of liberty: "The essence of the notion of liberty, in both the 'positive' and the 'negative' senses, is the *holding off* of something or someone. . . . Every interpretation of the word 'liberty,' however unusual, must include a minimum of what I have called 'negative' liberty. . . . The freedom of a society, or a class or a group, in this sense of freedom, is measured by the strength of these barriers [i.e., protecting negative liberty]" (ibid., 204, 207, 211; my emphasis).

49. The liberties of the First Amendment, to give just one example, are framed as instances of what Congress may *not* do.

to human dignity (see further the section on concrete social justice in Chapter 7, "Justice").[50] It insists, in short, on distinguishing matters of social inequality from issues concerning the moral treatment of other human beings. In a move that seems difficult for the twenty-first-century reader to accept, the Hebrew Bible can accommodate the reality of a hierarchical society with a call for human dignity.

While some readers may view this adjustment as an example of "bad faith," other readers may recognize the insistence on human dignity for each person and each stratum within society as a way of fostering a concrete recognition of essential equality, even among social unequals. It signals this essential equality most clearly precisely when conditions are themselves least equal. The Hebrew Bible implicitly recognizes that it is easy to insist on essential equality in an ideal world; the challenge is to recognize others' equality when conditions are actually unequal and thus militate against extending dignity to social "inferiors." In that situation, the recognition of and the appropriate response to equality require a conscious act of will that arguably indicates a determination to work toward equality's more complete realization.

The Hebrew Bible, Human Rights, and Covenant

While some twenty-first-century readers may wonder whether the texts of the Hebrew Bible truly recognize human rights for all, other readers take a different tack. This group argues that what some people read as human rights in the Hebrew Bible can best be understood not as extending to all human beings but rather as a function of membership in a covenant that is based on belief and worship of the Divinity. For our purposes, the question is which approach is better reflected in the texts of the Hebrew Bible and which approach is favored by the Enlightenment writings that ground the modern development of democracy.

At first glance, it may seem obvious that the Hebrew Bible would base its justification of human rights on a covenantal approach; after all, the Hebrew Bible's first example of covenant is the one with Noah that applies

---

50. For different nuances of the philosophical implications of human dignity, see Jeremy Waldron's *Dignity, Rank, and Rights* (New York: Oxford, 2015); esp. "that is my hypothesis: the modern notion of *human* dignity involves an upward equalization of rank . . . that was formerly accorded to nobility" (33). Waldron does not see huge differences between his approach and what he characterizes as the Judeo-Christian notion of "the dignity of humanity as such" (ibid., 31); he approvingly cites the notion of the "narrower" and "wider" concepts of dignity to prove a linkage between the two approaches (ibid., 44, note 69). On the political level, however, these two defining imageries regarding the extent of human dignity may yield differing juridical implications, whose elaboration is beyond the scope of this introduction.

to all of humankind, guaranteeing them safety from universal destruction.[51] With an understanding of survival as the most basic human right of all, this rationale would seem to be self-justifying.

But this approach presents several problems. It ignores the more embracing notion of human rights as they are directly expressed by various texts of the Hebrew Bible. This point refers, for example, to major prophets like Isaiah (1:17) and later prophets like Micah (esp. 2, 3, 6:11–16, 7), who describe the enactment of human rights (resulting from fulfilling the Hebrew biblical dicta to be charitable, fair, equitable, etc.) as transcending group affiliation. Furthermore, these Hebrew biblical prophets present the honoring of human rights as an obligation required of all human beings and benefiting all people, regardless of covenantal membership.[52]

This larger understanding of human rights is consistent with the concept of Natural Law as it is understood by many Enlightenment theorists,[53] precisely as their approach locates rights within the broader understanding of what it means to be human.[54] In this view, rights involve *both* entitlements *and* responsibilities that extend beyond particular group association.[55] This

---

51. The covenant with Noah is Daniel J. Elazar's paradigm for the covenant between God and humanity in the Hebrew Bible (see "Obligations and Rights in the Jewish Political Tradition: Some Preliminary Observations" [*Jewish Political Studies Review* 3: 3–4, Fall 1991]; many of his arguments in that essay also appear in his *Covenant and Polity*, esp. 35–97). The text itself of the Hebrew Bible, and the substance of the covenant with Noah, evoke violence and destruction as elements that will be avoided by both parties, the human and the Divine (Genesis 6:11, 8:21, 9:11–17). But Elazar then shifts from the narrower understanding of the covenant with Noah as supported by the plain text of the Hebrew Bible to its wider gloss as interpreted by the Talmud and the Midrash (BT Sanhedrin 56a; Genesis Rabbah 34:8). Elazar's insistent references to the wider understanding of the underpinnings of the Noahide Covenant to include the seven Noahide laws, with the attendant claim that the Hebrew Bible bases human rights on covenantal obligations, contends that the Hebrew Bible extends human rights *only* to those people who keep the seven Noahide laws. To be sure, these Noahide laws may appear unobjectionable to many readers of the Hebrew Bible: they include positive requirements like monotheistic worship and upholding civil laws as well as prohibitions against idol worship, animal cruelty, etc. But Elazar's linkage of the observance of these laws to the enjoyment of human rights contains troubling implications (for a detailed evaluation, see the appendix).

52. See the appendix.

53. An extended discussion of Natural Law is beyond the scope of this introduction. A thumbnail sketch: in its Enlightenment incarnation, Natural Law refers to the law of God, Who is viewed as having created the world, and extends to basic moral rules that (should) regulate human society as well.

54. As Thomas Jefferson notes in his Declaration of Independence, these "inalienable rights" are "self-evident," which is to say, they require no additional proof regarding their substantive or logical foundation.

55. See "The Hebrew Bible and the Enlightenment Reader," xxxi ff. above, esp. xxxv.

separation of human rights from specific group membership is important: it generalizes human rights at the same time as it avoids the slippery slope of "awarding" human rights only to those with whom a (moral) connection is felt. With its generalization of justice, this approach also avoids linking a particular understanding of God to one's political and personal autonomy (in other words, one's religious affiliation is separated from one's liberty and self-expression). In due course, this approach would contribute to the development known as "separation of church and state." To be sure, not all Enlightenment thinkers necessarily endorse every moral dictum expressed in the texts of the Hebrew Bible. Still, the Hebrew Bible provides many Enlightenment thinkers with support for their justification of individual rights vis-à-vis the government, which in turn vindicates their writings on revolution.

In this connection, it is important to emphasize that the various references to God made by many Enlightenment thinkers (including Jefferson) in describing the State of Nature and the basic human rights established there should not be interpreted as a backhanded acceptance of covenantal theory on their part, an approach that links the expression of human rights to belief in God. Enlightenment *philosophes* in general, many of whom also subscribed to the notion of political justification expressed by social contract theorists, utilize their various conception(s) of God to justify a concept of equality among human beings that, at least in theory, pertains to all.[56] In this understanding, God is not a party to structuring ongoing political obligations since, by social contract definition (accepted by most Enlightenment political theorists), political obligations (e.g., obedience to a government or ruler) are justified only by the people's (ongoing) consent.

Thus, the social contract theorists' invocation of God does not play the role that covenantal theorists ascribe to it.[57] For social contract and Enlightenment thinkers, political obligations take place within a sphere that is separate from religious devotion and/or expression. God is invoked by Enlightenment thinkers to establish the basis of human equality and (by implication) the nonnegotiable nature of its existence; for these thinkers, the political implications of this point belong to the sphere of *political* (as opposed to covenantal) obligations.

---

56. For a reading of the U.S. Declaration of Independence that views (political) equality as the basis of (political) liberty, see Danielle Allen's *Our Declaration: A Reading of the Declaration of Independence in Defense of Equality* (New York: Norton, 2014).

57. Even Locke, who invokes God in passing when he denies toleration to atheists, does not argue that obedience to God underlies obedience to the monarch (*Letter Concerning Toleration*). Locke argues the contrary point, as his *First Treatise* amply shows. See, among other citations, par. 85 of "First Treatise" in *Locke's Two Treatises of Government*, ed. Peter Laslett (New York: Cambridge University Press, repr. 2003), 204, par. 95, 211.

This is not to say that God has no role to play in social contract theory or in Enlightenment political thought or even in Hebrew biblical concepts of the community. Quite the contrary, as our discussions of the repeated citations and analyses of the Hebrew biblical texts by Enlightenment thinkers have shown. In essence, as we shall also see in the next section, the separation of God from political life does not mean that He is absent from communal life. This holds true for the contexts of both Hebrew biblical texts and Enlightenment political writings. Importantly, this is where the notion of covenant can become a significant part of the communal conversation. To be sure, the tone of the texts of the Hebrew Bible, as well as those of liberal Enlightenment political thinkers, marks human rights as a political issue whose scope is not limited just to covenantal participants. At the same time, the values of the covenant can—and arguably are encouraged to—structure the understandings of the communal sphere regarding the political arena and the expression of human rights.

This understanding can mitigate the concern, expressed by many covenantal (and communitarian) theorists, that a communal sense of moral obligation is necessary to support a shared political vision; without this communal moral sense, they fear, there is little concrete basis for social cohesion.[58] Importantly, this idea is not a strange one for many Enlightenment thinkers. Jefferson himself, no great advocate of religion in the public square, points out that linking public actions to matters of belief injures the very faith that one claims to be supporting.[59] It is well known that Jefferson held no particular brief for encouraging religious faith; his concern in this context for the integrity of religious principle points to his practical recognition that religious beliefs nevertheless play an important role in the communal life of the people. However, Jefferson cautions against these beliefs becoming politically exclusionary markers; in that case, their role as social glue inevitably disintegrates and is more conducive to social vice and turmoil than to virtue and stability.

---

58. Michael Sandel expresses this concern in *Democracy's Discontent* (Cambridge, MA: Harvard University Press, 1996).

59. "that therefore the proscribing any citizen as unworthy the public confidence by laying upon him an incapacity of being called to offices of trust and emolument, unless he profess or renounce this or that religious opinion, is depriving him injuriously of those privileges and advantages to which, in common with his fellow citizens, he has a natural right; that it tends also to corrupt the principles of that *very* religion it is meant to encourage, by bribing, with a monopoly of worldly honours and emoluments, those who will externally profess and conform to it; that though indeed these are criminal who do not withstand such temptation, yet neither are those innocent who lay the bait in their way; *that the opinions of men are not the object of civil government, nor under its jurisdiction.*" "Draft of the Virginia Statute for Religious Freedom, 1777–1779," in Lenni Brenner, ed., *Jefferson and Madison on Separation of Church and State* (Fort Lee, NJ: Barricade, 2004), 49.

What the modern invocation of Natural Law adds to the notion of society as linked by a communal moral enterprise is the ability to view the political sphere as an inclusive arena. To be sure, that can involve extending rights to people with whom one may have severe disagreements. Given that this volume does not analyze the historical realities of the eras depicted by the Hebrew biblical texts, we will not speculate as to whether nonbelievers, for example, actually exercised their full range of political rights in the time frames portrayed by these writings. Nor does the notion of an open political sphere implicitly recognized by the Hebrew Bible imply that its texts incorporate twenty-first-century conceptions of human rights. But it does acknowledge the presence of the deep and powerful roots of the contemporary discourse of human rights in this ancient text.

While some presentations of covenantal theories of human rights seem to make the argument that a system of human rights following this justification would still be enjoyed by "most" people,[60] readers of the Hebrew Bible should be aware of the real danger to human rights implicit in such an approach. This is not just a matter of semantics. In practical terms, making recognition of human rights conditional upon membership within a particular covenant (however extensive one might deem that covenant to be) means that political rights are subject to what amounts to a religious test, one that easily ends up transporting people down the morally slippery slope of "awarding" human rights to specific designees. While this condition has in fact historically obtained in many times and places, that linkage is not articulated or approved by the Hebrew Bible. As we argue in a later section of this introduction, the Hebrew Bible's narrative trajectory is one in which matters of religious belief are presented as distinguishable from action in the political sphere (see "State and Religion" below).

This point—regarding the relationship of Hebrew biblical values to the arguments implicit in biblical texts—merits consideration. It is worthwhile for us, the twenty-first-century readers of the Hebrew Bible, to reflect on just why the Hebrew Bible chooses to include topics such as covenant, and (implicitly) human rights, without clearly delineating an originary connection between them. The nuanced complexities of the Hebrew biblical text support an inclusive understanding of human rights without forgetting the moral values (like equality, justice, and fairness) that must underlie these rights so that they retain a coherent, substantive content (see "The Hebrew Bible, Human Rights, and Democracy" above) and do not become just empty husks of verbiage without concrete significance. Equally important, the Hebrew Bible is

---

60. It is important to note that this volume analyzes the Hebrew Bible and its contribution to political theory; it makes no argument concerning the Talmudic or later historical contributions of Jewish political thought to this issue.

alert to the potential dangers in openly ascribing human rights to particular groups or "covenants." Also, the Hebrew Bible takes care to underline the inclusive nature of human rights, and the human obligation to extend them as far as they may go, without confusing the exercise of human rights with a callous disregard of the rights of others—for example, doing whatever one feels like doing and justifying it with a self-serving "moral" rationale.

In the end, it may not be possible, or even desirable, to identify the Hebrew Bible's approach to human rights with its twenty-first-century articulation. However, it is important to acknowledge that the Hebrew Bible's understanding of human dignity is profoundly based on an underlying notion of human equality,[61] which becomes explicitly evident in the writings of later prophets such as Amos (esp. chaps. 5, 6, 8) and Malachi (esp. chap. 3), among others. For the Hebrew Bible, human rights first and foremost include the rights to dignity and to possessing a fair stake in society. The Hebrew Bible makes its points by enumerating the liminal members of Israelite society at that time; twenty-first-century readers may consider whether our ability in the current day to itemize additional groups deserving of human rights is the same thing as actually extending equal human rights to them, and to all.

State and Religion

It is natural to wonder who enforces religion in the political society described in the Hebrew Bible. This statement itself prompts a query: which point in the political development of the Israelite nation (as this process is represented in the Hebrew Bible) is at issue here? The Hebrew Bible describes the Israelites passing through many different stages in their political development: starting as an ill-assorted group of slaves with little shared identity beyond their common slave experience and monotheistic heritage, the Israelites undertake the long journey in the wilderness during which they are beset by many trials and tribulations. Finally, they settle into their Promised Land, where they take on the challenges of forming a cohesive society. It would seem logical to twenty-first-century eyes that these different stages of communal and political development might evoke different responses to the relationship between political power and religious observance.[62] In fact,

---

61. See note 56 (Danielle Allen).

62. It is instructive that Jean-Jacques Rousseau, an Enlightenment political theorist whose works articulate a rights-based and individually focused vision of the world that we have come to recognize as central to modernity, explicitly departs from an idealized vision of one perfect leadership model. Rousseau insists that different periods in a people's development require different approaches to leadership (see note 63 for the Hebrew biblical expression of this concept with regard to Moses); for Rousseau, this enables the people to express their own "General Will," which is Rousseau's way of identifying the people's articulation of their own true best interest. For more on this topic, see my *Rousseau*, esp. 170–79.

the Hebrew Bible does seem to present different models of the relationship between political power and religious observance as these are reflected in the Hebrew Bible's narrative history, along with a nuanced sense of norms that change with historical circumstance and the varying needs of the people.

But this is not obvious to every reader of the Hebrew Bible. In this context, some readers interpret Moses' leadership as one of unified religious and political power, leaving the Israelites no real choice to be politically or religiously disobedient. For this group, a dominant image that typifies the Hebrew Bible's approach to leadership as a whole is exemplified by the account of the worshippers of the Golden Calf being killed by the Levites at Moses' behest, which the Hebrew Bible describes as a command relayed from God (Exodus 32:27). Many contend, as a result, that the Hebrew Bible favors a unified political-religious axis, or what can be called a theocracy. In this reading, the leadership of Moses represents organizational unification of religion and state, along with its inevitable moral outcome: no true freedom of choice to deviate from the set path of religious actions and worship (because punishment for malefactors is so swift).

But there is another way to read the texts, both in terms of the organizational structures of the relations between religion and state and the degree of moral autonomy vouchsafed to the Israelites. Utilizing the analytic model that connects the stage of a people's political development to the kind of leader best suited to direct them allows us to view the possibilities of the state-religion relationship in a new way. In this view, the early stages of the relationship between religious observance and political organization need not—and should not—be seen as defining the normative relationship between these two domains. According to this approach, the union of religious and political power in the figure of Moses is remarkable largely for being presented by the Hebrew Bible as unique in Israelite history;[63] in Rousseau's terms, the first leader of a nation may prove to be an outlier in terms of later institutional development. In effect, the union of religious and political power at this point of Israelite political proto-nationhood is the exception that proves the rule of the state-religion connection that would later ensue in the Hebrew biblical texts' narrative of future Israelite political development.

The presentation of the subsequent phases of the state-religion connection occurs once the Hebrew biblical text describes the establishment of the monarchy. At this point, a different set of considerations comes into play. Unlike the Near Eastern potentates of ancient times, the Israelite monarch is warned against misunderstanding the nature of his position. According to the Hebrew biblical text, the monarch is not fundamentally different from

---

63. "And there hath not arisen a prophet since in Israel like unto Moses, whom the LORD knew face to face" (Deuteronomy 34:10).

any other Israelite—thus, he may not have too many wives or horses and he may not be prideful (Deuteronomy 17:15). By the same token, he may not proclaim himself to be Divine. To guard against that equation (common in the world in which kings often construed themselves as priests or deities), the king must keep a copy of the Torah—which the Israelites recognized as God's Divine writ—with him at all times and read from it always; that is to say, the monarch must recognize that he is bound by the Divine word as is any other Israelite and must not confuse his possession of political power with being Divine (Deuteronomy 17:18–20).[64] This is a direct consequence of Hebrew biblical monotheism: belief in the one God that reigns supreme means that no political ruler can be confused—or be allowed to confuse himself—with God.

The ruler's lack of identification with God raises another question: once a human ruler is charged with governing the people, what is the place of God in the system of governance? Within the Hebrew biblical texts, there is the open recognition that the advent of institutionalized political power generally means that God will no longer play the traditional role that He had played in the early stages of the political life of the Israelites.

This point is made clear in the dialogue between the (prophet and judge) Samuel and God as depicted in I Samuel 8:7: Samuel interprets the Israelite request for a king (with its attendant assumption that Samuel's own sons are not acceptable to the Israelites as leaders) as a personal rejection of him. God hastens to correct Samuel: "For they have not rejected thee, but they have rejected Me, that I should not *be king* over them" (my emphasis). While this dialogue has often been interpreted as a sort of "lamentation contest" (who is really the more aggrieved: Samuel or God?), its textual context makes it clear that God is commenting on an inevitable consequence of establishing a centralized government that will necessarily dominate the local tenor of life that had previously obtained. The introduction of a complex polity concomitantly implies that for the most part, God will withdraw His palpable presence from the daily life of the political sphere.

---

64. Another point about the separation between, and the presumption against confusing, the power of a king and the nature of the Divine is that, for the Hebrew Bible, the Divinity is understood as more than just a great power (in the manner of the Phoenician gods Ba'al or Molech, whose names derive from the Semitic roots connoting power and dominion). Throughout the Hebrew Bible, God is depicted as absolutely powerful but also as choosing to be connected to the human beings in the world that He created: He speaks with people (Noah); He argues with them (Abraham); and He instructs them (Moses). For more on this topic, see Abraham Joshua Heschel's *God in Search of Man* (New York: Farrar, Straus & Giroux, [1955] repr. 1983) and the various essays of Rabbi Dr. Joseph B. Soloveitchik, e.g., *The Lonely Man of Faith* (New York: Random House, [1965] repr. 2006); *Halakhic Man* (Philadelphia: Jewish Publication Society, [1953] 1981).

Some readers of the Hebrew Bible have interpreted this development as completely negative. But it is important to note that this is not precisely the way the Hebrew Bible presents it. Readers of the Hebrew Bible may recall that when God does judge the actions of the Israelites to be evil, severe consequences ensue almost immediately (as exemplified by the Hebrew biblical text's depiction of the various punishments suffered by the Israelites during their wilderness sojourn on the way to their Promised Land; see Numbers 11:31–34). Since God does not immediately urge punishment or predict negative outcomes in this situation for the Israelites, readers understand that the text is not judging the Israelites' choice as evil on its face. After all, God does immediately order Samuel to anoint a king (ibid., 8), which means that God accedes to His own withdrawal from politics. But this choice involves difficult consequences.

The Hebrew Bible depicts these complications historically. In its drawn-out descriptions of the history of the Israelite monarchy, with both elevated and lowly political practitioners, the Hebrew Bible notes the price for that development, as both monarchies (in the Southern and Northern kingdoms) inevitably deteriorate. Contemporary readers of the Hebrew Bible might wonder about the logical reasons for Israel's politically troubled history at this stage of the monarchy.

The Hebrew Bible's account of the political challenges experienced by the Israelites in their historical development makes it evident that their political deterioration is multiply determined. The biblical narrative itself blames the Israelite predilection for idolatry (leading to the removal of Divine protection from the Israelites) for causing their subjugation by their neighbors.[65] But these texts also depict increasing corruption on the part of the monarchy, including murder of individuals in connection with matters of faith that are viewed as antimonarchical (or as inconvenient for a particular monarch) as well as linked to court intrigues that end in civil war.[66]

---

65. This pattern is present in the texts of the Hebrew Bible even before the onset of the monarchy, as seen in Judges 2:11, 3:5–15. For instances of this type of account linking (national) punishment of the Israelites to idolatry also after the monarchy is established, see I Kings 11:1–11, 33–35, 12:26–32.

66. Some of these civil wars might be seen as wars between communities, as when the Hebrew Bible takes note of the ongoing wars between Israelite and Judahite kings (see, for example, I Kings 14:30, 15:16, 15:32). But the Hebrew Bible also describes more contained battles within each of the Israelite kingdoms that reflect political instability. One such text narrates the bloody coup of Zimri, co-leader of the royal chariots, against the Israelite king Ela; according to the text, Zimri is himself toppled by a military coup one week later (I Kings 16:10–19), which leads to a four-year civil war (ibid., 21–23). An example of a text that narrates the instance of a leader killing her own people is when Jezebel methodically murders all the monotheistic priests (except for a handful who are successfully hidden; see I Kings 18).

The acme of the corrupt monarchy that harms the very people for whose protection it was originally established (I Samuel 8) is highlighted in the story of Naboth and his vineyard (I Kings 21). Ahab, the king of the Northern kingdom, is encouraged by Queen Jezebel (and the corrupt members of the royal bureaucracy/judiciary) to concoct a court case against Naboth in order to take possession of Naboth's vineyard, which Ahab deeply covets (and with which Naboth had refused to part because the vineyard was part of his family legacy that, according to Hebrew biblical law, had to remain within the family). The false accusation to which Naboth is subjected ends in his execution and in the king's usurpation of Naboth's vineyard. Thus, with his (multiply) illegal action, Ahab manages to disregard, in one fell swoop, the sixth, eighth, and ninth (and arguably also the tenth) commandments, for which he is roundly chastised by the prophet Elijah.

The backdrop against which this famous example of royal corruption plays out is the gradual disorder of political life. The Hebrew Bible presents an ongoing account of the widening gap between the haves and the have-nots of Israelite society, even as Israelite political autonomy (in both kingdoms) is portrayed as increasingly compromised. One such example (although usually cited as an instance of the prophet's ability to cure) is the story of the Aramean general Na'aman, whose wife is noted, in passing, as having in her service an Israelite maid (II Kings 7:20). In the Hebrew biblical narrative, this maid is credited with giving the advice that leads to Na'aman's cure (he seeks the advice of the Israelite prophet Elisha to heal his *tza'ra'at*, "leprosy"). The additional political implication of this story is that Israelite borders are no longer secure (in itself a diminution of Israelite political autonomy) and that the poorer among the Israelites are already living a life with exilic markers: they no longer reside in autonomous communities organized by Israelite law or custom but are instead subject to people and rules of the surrounding societies that seek to conquer them.

As the texts of the Hebrew Bible present it, this period exhibits a progressive dismantling of Israelite control over the wider surrounding areas that had originally been established by Solomon (see, e.g., II Kings 8:20ff., 17:13–25; also see, e.g., Amos 8:6; Isaiah 26, 28). This point also serves as another example of the Israelite kingdoms' increasing political dysfunction. To be sure, all of these components can be seen as inextricably linked. In this understanding, the rejection of monotheism and the embrace of idolatry promote disregard of the religious and moral practices that had previously defined Israelite society and supported their social comity—that is, the basic values of equality and respect for all individuals regardless of their social or economic origins. For this interpretation, the neglect of those values inevitably results in the weakening of social bonds, leading to the conquest and exile of Israelites from their land.

Readers of the Hebrew Bible might wonder why similar instances of idol worship in other periods of history depicted by the Hebrew Bible—notably, the period portrayed in the Book of Judges—do not result in the kind of political dysfunction depicted in the biblical Book of Kings. Analyses of the Hebrew biblical narratives that present these accounts highlight distinctive patterns to explain such disparate political outcomes. In the account presented in the Book of Judges, a negative cyclical pattern is evident: the Israelites worship idols, are politically subjugated, repent, and are rescued. By contrast, most of the narratives in Kings describe a different configuration, one in which the Israelites' idol worship leads to increasingly negative spirals of political dysfunction: from internal battles to bloody border raids to conquest and exile (II Kings 24–25).

Identifying patterns of negative cycles as opposed to negative spirals may seem to fixate on distinctions without real differences. But it is important to note that cycles, while repetitive, do not necessarily worsen the situation; the cycles return more or less to their previous starting point (Judges 2:11–23, 3:5–15). But negative spirals, by definition, result in ever-worsening consequences. Consequently, while negative cycles and negative spirals both have deleterious effects, the resurgence of Israelite autonomous political life is depicted as far less likely after the series of worsening maelstroms depicted in Kings (II Kings 24–25). Still, acknowledging differences in narrative models to describe various instances of idol worship and their dissimilar outcomes merely underlines the primary question: why do similar actions (idol worship) lead to different results (temporary subjugation as opposed to exile)?

One way of answering this question is to note the Hebrew Bible's depiction of the different contexts of the various systems of political organizations experienced by the Israelites during these disparate eras. The Book of Judges depicts the period in which judges lead various combinations of Israelite tribes into battle against their enemies as less stable in organizational terms, but also as providing various pathways to experiment with different techniques to achieve their political goals. Sometimes this involves negotiation (e.g., Gideon); other times it calls for stealth fighting (e.g., Samson); and sometimes all-out war is the only recourse (e.g., the general Barak under the leadership of Deborah). As depicted in the Book of Kings, however, the era of monarchs exhibits sclerotic tendencies on the part of rulers who view their positions as platforms for achieving personal desires rather than for ensuring the safety of the people whose welfare they are pledged to secure. During these more troublesome periods, the structural difference in governance—powerful, centralized monarchy—allows wrongdoings in Israelite society to become inescapable spirals of self-destruction, devastation, and subsequent exile.

Why does the monarchy enable these permanently negative consequences? The overwhelming characteristic of monarchy in the time periods depicted by the Hebrew Bible is its propensity for grasping at absolute power. This presents not only personal and political inconvenience to the Israelites in terms of individual freedoms that a monarch may easily revoke (see the arguments of Samuel [I Samuel 8:11–18] later in this volume) but a real spiritual danger to them as well: the monarch's (near-)absolute power could easily force the Israelites to reject (on a more permanent basis) their traditional monotheistic belief and practices (e.g., I Kings 12:26–32, 13:33–34, 14:22–26; see also below pp. lx ff. "bad bargain"). As depicted in the Hebrew biblical texts, this is what in fact occurs (I Kings 15:30).

The Hebrew Bible introduces the changes that would occur with the advent of monarchy with the suggestion that the presence of God would no longer be evident in the political sphere. As noted above, the withdrawal itself is not presented as a necessarily unmitigated evil. But it is a change—and a challenge—that the Israelites are portrayed as being unable to withstand and still maintain their existence as an autonomous group in their own land. Assessing the differences in these different periods in the context of the structural institutions of governance is one way to account for this phenomenon. Doing so also raises the possibility of a structurally based alternative vision: arguably, if the Israelites had been able to establish a monarchical system in which the people (or some association within the population) were able to maintain a base of power that could withstand monarchical overreach (as in the oft-mentioned matter of idolatry, for example), the negative spiral of "moral corruption—political corruption—social disorder—conquest—exile" might have been averted.

The Hebrew Bible's depiction of history, of course, is not the same as a narrative of what might have been. But it is important to note that the texts of the Hebrew Bible do accede (even if, on some readings, reluctantly) to the separation of God from the political sphere. At the same time, the separation of the two spheres involves complications of their own, since the respective existences of the political and the religious realms inevitably highlight the relationship between those arenas. Does the separation of political power from Divinity extend to the enforcement of Divine writ? In more contemporary terms, to what extent is the enforcement of religious observances separate from—or alternatively, a function of—the political realm in the Hebrew Bible?

Analyzing the Hebrew biblical texts in order to answer this question brings us to the discovery—surprising in so ancient a work—of the consequences for moral autonomy enabled by the distinctive state-religion relationship sketched by the Hebrew Bible. The form of this innovation is no less remarkable than its content: it is presented in the text through the silences of the Hebrew Bible itself, particularly in places where it might have been expected that the Hebrew Bible would comment in detail on this relationship.

The Hebrew Bible presents no text commanding or even suggesting that a political official be charged with policing the people's religious observance.[67] It mentions God often, but politically based institutions of religious enforcement not at all.[68] There are Elders, to be sure; there are even priests and judges. But they are not presented as embedded in the political corridors of power and as charged with carrying out political directives to enforce religious dicta (although some of these religious/judicial authorities—e.g., Samuel—are at times portrayed as exercising immense political influence). In effect, these officials are not even mentioned when the Hebrew Bible talks about the consequences for the Israelites if they choose the path of religious disobedience.[69]

This omission is significant: in texts replete with detailed regulations for a wide range of activities, the absence of institutionally based enforcement of religious orders is striking. It highlights an important value for the

---

67. This point refers specifically to the question of whether the Hebrew Bible demands enforcement of religious law by courts charged with the adjudication of civil law. That the Hebrew Bible recognizes a realm of civil law may come as a surprise to its casual readers. That it does so is a central thesis of Simon Federbush's *Mishpat HaMelukha BeYisrael* ([The Rule of Kingship in Israel], ed. Ben-Tzion Rosenfeld [Jerusalem: Mossad haRav Kook, (1973) 2005] [in Hebrew]), in which he demonstrates the implied "doubledness"—or duality—of civil/political and religious law as depicted in the Hebrew Bible. Federbush cites copious biblical evidence for a dual system of courts: regular civil courts (for example, those dealing with monetary judgments) and priestly courts (for the identification of phenomena such as *tza'ra'at* [the skin disease cited by the Hebrew Bible as punishment for certain types of illicit speech]; see the episode in which Miriam is punished for speaking against Moses [Numbers 12:1–16]). These dual structures are mentioned in the historical section of the Prophets (II Kings, for example) as well as in II Chronicles 19 (concerning the courts established by King Yehoshafat). According to Federbush, this doubled system is evident both in legislation and in the adjudication of law: there are corresponding legislative bodies (the king, the Sanhedrin) as well as parallel court systems (religious courts at all levels leading up to the Sanhedrin and courts established by the king leading up to the royal court in the king's palace); I Kings 7:7–8 highlights Solomon's activity in this regard.

68. Even when comments in the Mishna and the Talmud, documents composed in the centuries toward the end of and just after the biblical era, allude to the Sanhedrin (the national religious supreme court in Ancient Israel) as it functioned in biblical times, the references are to a judicial body deciding questions of law and adjudicating cases, not to a religious body whose judicial decisions were automatically enforced by the political state. In dealing with the texts of the Hebrew Bible, it is important not to confuse biblical dicta with historical analysis.

69. The Hebrew Bible's understanding of God as the all-powerful controller of life seems to make the notion of the need for human enforcement of Divine commands redundant. As noted above (in connection with popular enforcement of justice in some high-profile cases described by the Hebrew Bible as occurring during the Israelites' desert journey after their liberation from Egyptian slavery), the presence of human "enforcers" is an exceptional occurrence that arguably precedes the Israelites' entry into the more "mature" phase of political self-realization.

Hebrew biblical texts: that religious observance remains the responsibility of each individual and is not a political token to be bartered or even compelled. For the Hebrew Bible, the moral dimension of individual freedom is not subject to political coercion.

It is worthwhile noting that just as religious functionaries are not presented as embedded in the political hierarchy, the political arm—as exemplified by the monarch—is not portrayed as being in charge of regulating the religious arena or of making mandatory the subjects' religious observances, either. This is not to say that the monarch is deprived of religious influence: as depicted in the Hebrew Bible, the monarch was supposed to be a model figure for the Israelite community (see the description of Solomon as he celebrates the dedication of the Temple in Jerusalem in I Kings 8).

Even taking into account the king's wide range of influence in various arenas of life, however,[70] the Hebrew Bible insists that the king is just that: a king. That gives him a lot of political power. Still, the king is not God, and he is not the High Priest. As the Hebrew biblical texts detail the large amount of conflict among kings, priests, and prophets, that awareness underlies a significant sense of separation between the political and the religious realms. The Hebrew biblical texts seem persuaded that the Israelites would recognize the need to obey their religious laws without state-enforced or perennial strong-armed duress.[71] As noted below, the presence of charismatic events and people that seem to indicate a kind of social enforcement of religious codes is not the same thing as political-institutional enforcement of religious codes.[72]

As described in the Hebrew Bible, the kind and extent of religious liberty experienced by the Israelites is itself a double-edged sword.[73] The Hebrew

---

70. In any society, including the one depicted in the pages of the Hebrew Bible, it is difficult to construct institutions that are completely impermeable to each other.

71. Technically speaking, as presented in the Hebrew biblical texts, the state did not exist at the time that the Israelites are presented with and accept the range of religious directives upon and after their departure from Egypt, as seen in Exodus 19:5–8, the texts normally adduced as evidence for a theocracy.

72. See note 73 and the end of 69 (above).

73. Deuteronomy 30:19 highlights this nuanced point by strategically switching from the plural to the singular in describing the moral imperatives and stakes of making choices. The verse begins by stating that all of you (second person, plural) have the "options of good and evil, life and death, placed before you." The responsibility for deciding among the options, however, and the advice of the Bible, is specifically given to each individual and is indicated in the text by switching to the second-person singular grammatical form. To be sure, the personal decision may well be rendered even more fraught with the realization that this private decision carries with it crucial communal implications. Importantly, however, even this text does not describe either religious institutionalization or religious enforcement by the state.

Bible makes that point elliptically when it describes how the Israelites are censured throughout their history by prophet after prophet who scold them for having abandoned the monotheistic worship of God to follow the idolatrous practices of their neighbors. Despite these negative repercussions, the ability of the Israelites to flout the central tenet of their religious ordinances as noted in the Hebrew biblical text does indicate that the Israelites experienced a certain amount of religious autonomy, even if the kind of autonomy invoked is not congruent with various conceptions of contemporary (twenty-first-century) notions of individually sourced systems of morality.[74] In this connection, it is noteworthy that when the Israelites, under the influence of a righteous king, do repent and again take up their monotheistic practices, this event is depicted as resulting from an act of persuasion, and not compulsion, on the part of the king.[75]

The conclusion that emerges is that the resounding silence of the Hebrew Bible concerning institutional enforcement of religious life winds up functioning as a tacit allowance, or even approval, of the separation of political power and religious authority. To be sure, the separation between religious

---

74. Though the large number of Hebrew biblical regulations mandating draconian punishments for varieties of behavior that are today considered matters of personal choice is frequently noted, it is important to remember that the textual mention of religious laws and their mandated punishments in and of itself does not imply that cases of this sort were rampant in real life. Indeed, textual references to instances involving punishments such as stoning are rare enough in the Hebrew Bible to be treated as exceptional events (e.g., the case of the individual who gathered wood on the Sabbath—a fundamental violation of the Sabbath law—who was stoned to death; see Numbers 15:32–36). Law, as H. L. A. Hart has noted (*The Concept of Law* [Oxford: Oxford University Press, (1961) repr. 1994, 2012]), may often have a prescriptive function—setting a moral standard—that differs from a historical description of fact. Although the aim of the present volume is not to recover the history of Hebrew biblical texts but rather to examine their foundational nature as political texts, it is notable that the Mishna (a compendium of legal and philosophical texts edited by Rabbi Judah the Prince in the second century CE) remarks in one of its historical observations that capital cases were so rare in biblical Israel that the court that issued the death penalty even once in seventy years was (ignominiously) labeled a "bloody court" (Makkot 1:10). The fact that the Mishna lays the onus of frequent capital punishment (even once in seventy years!) on the court as opposed to blaming the "sinfulness" of the people anticipates Montesquieu's remark (in *The Spirit of the Laws*, book VI) that the need to punish people excessively reflects more on the corruption of political institutions than on what many construe as the evil in human nature. In VI.11 of *The Spirit of the Laws*, Montesquieu remarks, "The Romans were a people of integrity. . . . It was enough to give them counsels instead of ordinances" (Montesquieu, *The Spirit of the Laws*, ed. Anne Cohler, Basia Wilmer, and Harold Stone [Cambridge, UK: Cambridge University Press, 1989], 84). By the same token, Montesquieu notes, "If you see other countries in which men are restrained only by cruel punishments, . . . this arises largely from the violence of government" (ibid., 85).

75. See the narrative in II Kings 23 in which King Josiah reads the scroll of the Torah to the Israelites, who then renew the covenant.

and political power depicted in the Hebrew Bible does not approach what twenty-first-century standards would qualify as separation between church and state.[76] Nonetheless, its significance is remarkable.

The Hebrew Bible's differentiation between political and religious power remains an overlooked development within the traditional canon of political theory. It signals a significant degree of freedom within the domain of faith and, as we shall see below, a strong determination to limit the political powers of the state. As already noted, much of the Hebrew Bible's implicit distinctions between political and religious power are accepted by various Enlightenment thinkers, many of whom, as already indicated, were also avid readers of the Hebrew Bible. As we have already seen, this is particularly evident in writings[77] by the founders of the American republic and is realized constitutionally in the anti-Establishment clause of its Constitution's First Amendment. Whether or not these Enlightenment thinkers are consciously aware in every instance of the effect that the texts of the Hebrew Bible have on particular elements of their own political theory, the contributions that these Hebrew biblical texts, as understood by these Enlightenment thinkers, offer in this regard do influence the debate over the proper aims and scope of politics.

An important part of this new understanding is the limited extent of the political realm. This concept is directly linked to the Hebrew Bible's insistence that the monarch cannot be equated with God. The upshot of this point is that, as opposed to the Hebrew Bible's understanding of the infinitude of God's powers, the power of the human monarch—and thus of the state that he represents or embodies—is limited. Enlightenment political thought takes this perception of the Hebrew Bible seriously: it mandates limited government based on its own conception of the origin of power—the people's consent—and, in the case of the American founders, ensures that the power of government is itself divided and hence less likely to devolve into tyranny.[78]

The separation between the religious and the political realms as countenanced by the Hebrew Bible—if only by its resounding silence on their

---

76. The incipient separation of religion and politics, and the implicit (latent) secularization of the political sphere of the Israelites as presented in the Hebrew Bible, are far more limited and less explicit than contemporary expressions of "separation of church and state" (as the American principle of secularism is formulated), to say nothing of the less formally "neutral" doctrine of secularism existing in some modern countries today.

77. For example, see Thomas Jefferson's *Bill for Establishing Religious Freedom* (1777) and "Query 17" in his *Notes on the State of Virginia* (1784; both in *Notes on the State of Virginia* [New York: Penguin, 1999]). Locke counsels against embedding religion in political life (*A Letter Concerning Toleration* [Indianapolis: Hackett, (1689) 1983]).

78. See in this connection *The Federalist*, particularly nos. 10 and 51, by James Madison.

(expected, albeit unfulfilled) union in its texts—is not trivial.[79] It also points forward to an understanding of the political realm as requiring an aura of secularism (since in the texts of the Hebrew Bible, citizens' political rights and powers are not specifically linked to individual religious obedience) and hence legitimation, particularly vis-à-vis its citizenry. It is important to note in this regard, at least in the Hebrew biblical presentation of the early coronations of Israelite monarchs, that Israelite monarchs are given their authority not only through prophetic installation and anointment (1 Samuel 10:1, 16:12–13) but also by popular acclaim (I Samuel 11:15; II Samuel 2:4, 5:1–3).

Beyond the philosophical justification of the Hebrew Bible's separation of religious from political power lies a more practical concern. Most of the texts of the Hebrew Bible that portray the Israelites as forsaking their unique monotheistic belief system depict this development as taking place under the rule of Israelite kings who (taking their cue from the neighboring absolute despots who combine both religious and political power under their auspices) are portrayed as leading the Israelites into idol worship. Thus, from the viewpoint of the Hebrew Bible, the union of political and religious power is a bad bargain; more often than not, this combination results in situations that undermine the transcendent values enshrined in its texts.

Interestingly enough, the narratives of the Hebrew Bible foreshadow Tocqueville's observation, in *Democracy in America*, that people living in countries without state-enforced religion are themselves more religiously observant.[80] The Hebrew Bible endorses this basic argument, demonstrating in its historical narratives that making religion a function of political power

---

79. See Hobbes again: the liberties of subjects depend (among other things) on "the silence of the Law" (*Leviathan*, ed. C. B. Macpherson [New York: Penguin, repr. 1986], II.21.271).

80. "Upon my arrival in the United States, it was the religious aspect of the country which first struck me. As I extended my stay, I perceived the large political consequences which flowed form these new facts.

"I have seen among us the spirit of religion and the spirit of liberty almost always march in opposite directions. Here, I found them intimately united with each other; they reign together on the same soil.

"Each day I felt my desire grown to know the cause of this phenomenon.

"In order to learn it, I questioned the faithful of each denomination; above all, I sought out the company of clergy. . . . All attributed the peaceful empire that religion exercises in their country principally to the complete separation of church and state.

" . . . The American clergy . . . saw that it was necessary to give up religious influence if they wished to acquire any political power, and they have preferred to lose the support of power than to share in its vicissitudes.

"In America, religion is perhaps less powerful than it has been at certain times and among certain peoples, but its influence is more durable. . . . It acts only within a single sphere, but it covers it completely and dominates it effortlessly. . . . It is loved, affirmed, and honored."

(as occurred with the advent of a variety of powerful monarchs in ancient Israel) winds up subordinating religious practice to the whims of the holder of political power.

An additional interesting point about the Hebrew Bible's championing of a God-centered public, or communal, life without institutionalized religious compulsion is that it parallels the early modern desacralization of politics, including the desacralization of the king, that occurs in France in the century leading up to the French Revolution.[81] As Roger Chartier points out, religious feeling becomes politicized throughout the eighteenth century, but this is a result, and not the cause, of the changes in religious beliefs, which had already started to become deinstitutionalized (from the political realm) in the seventeenth century. Chartier's argument is that a certain amount of secularization is needed if religious feeling is to become voluntarily embedded in people's hearts and minds. Secularization, in that view, actually expands the locus of spiritual belief, by generalizing it from strictures of state-enforced religious practice to a looser and more inclusive ability to relate to more people in different social and political spaces and to use spiritual beliefs in ways that promote unity rather than exacerbate violence.

Freedom without Systematization: Metatextual Discourse in the Hebrew Bible

The opprobrium attached by some contemporary critics of the Hebrew Bible to the seeming lack of a systemwide, or universal, approach in the Hebrew Bible to issues like human rights (which today is officially considered to apply to all human beings, excluding the exceptions that are conveniently swept out of view), seems to parallel the conventional disparagement of the Hebrew Bible's lack of institutional detail. This omission, as we have already seen, is taken as proof of the Hebrew Bible's inadequacy as a text of political theory. Within the context of the Hebrew Bible, however, it may be more productive to consider these textually viewed deficiencies—the lack of institutional detail as well as the dearth of "universal" moral systemic generalizations—in terms of the hermeneutical self-understandings of the different texts making up the Hebrew Bible. This approach reads the Hebrew Bible as proffering a metatextual discourse about the processes of human moral and political choice at the same time that it points its readers

---

Alexis de Tocqueville, "The Principal Causes That Make Religion Powerful in America" in *Democracy in America*, trans. Stephen D. Grant (Indianapolis: Hackett, 2000), 136–41.

81. Roger Chartier, *Cultural Origins of the French Revolution* (Durham, NC: Duke University Press, 1991), esp. 100–110.

to what it considers to be the correct moral approach. Indeed, it reads the Hebrew Bible as being concerned not only with highlighting the practice of ethical living but also with enabling the moral freedom to arrive at this choice.

The Hebrew Bible eschews the rigidities of systemization, even if these can provide its readers with logical certainties and even moral confidence. Instead, it prefers to challenge its readers to apply to their own lives the inferences that they themselves derive from its texts. The resulting open-ended quality of the texts of the Hebrew Bible is reflected in the many genres in which it is written. In distributing its moral and political messages among all of these sorts of texts, the Hebrew Bible engages in a kind of textual imitation of reasoning in real life, in which people attempt, through recourse to different ways of thinking about issues (ranging from scientific research to anecdotal evidence), to formulate a coherent and satisfactory approach to ethical and political dilemmas.

By considering issues in different kinds of texts from all angles—and not relying upon a predigested, systemic approach—the Hebrew Bible models an empirical approach to moral choice that is dynamic and engaged. Similarly, its depiction of political spaces and institutions suggests that moral and political deliberation actively function not only in official places of public congregation (such as the Greek agora) but beyond them as well. Thus, matters of political import are not limited to the narrow conventional understandings of that classification. By addressing the general reader, as opposed to focusing on particular elites within privileged groups, the Hebrew Bible performatively opens up the consideration of political matters to anyone who wants to engage in these issues.

The challenges of modernity have made readers of the twenty-first century more reluctant to adopt the conventional assumptions of identifying political theory texts exclusively with writings that focus on the details of institutional function. In the modern world, we are aware that, as presented in texts of the Hebrew Bible, practices not officially attached to political processes often have deeply political implications. This is a central insight of early modern political thought: in his *Confessions*, Rousseau declares that everything, in essence, is political.[82] This perception has likewise been enshrined by the feminist catchphrase "the personal is political."[83] In this context, the Hebrew Bible's lack of emphasis on constitutional and

---

82. "Tout tenoit radicalement à la politique." *Confessions* book 9, p. 404 in (Paris: Gallimard, 1959) OC I.404.

83. This phrase appeared in Carol Hanisch's 1969 essay titled "The Personal Is Political" in the anthology edited by Shulamith Firestone, *Notes from the Second Year: Women's Liberation* (New York: Radical Feminists, 1970).

institutional structures can be seen as representing more than just the dearth of robust institutional political development and imagination on the part of the ancient Israelites.

Rather, this silence on institutional particulars may be viewed as manifesting a point of view that, given the ancient provenance of the Hebrew Bible, is surprisingly welcoming to the more modern understanding of "the political" as connecting issues of real political import to areas of life that are not manifestly tied to the warp and woof of politics. Thus, for example, when the Hebrew Bible charts David's rise to political power through his relationships with women, and the ultimate breakup of Solomon's kingdom due to the same issue, the takeaway lesson is not just the rueful, if traditionally dismissive, referral to "cherchez la femme." The larger point is that women know about the inner workings of political dynasty making (see the communications between Batsheva and David in I Kings 1:11–30) and are instrumental in the political negotiations central to survival in estranging constructions of empire (Esther 4:11–17). In the context of the Hebrew Bible's lack of emphasis on the particulars of institutional arrangements, the concept of the political extends beyond the lines of established institutions to include areas of life in which all human beings participate. Issues regarding power are not the sole purview of people formally involved in recognized public institutions. In the Hebrew Bible, politics really does (or at least can) belong to the people.

A Note on the Presentation of Biblical Texts

Readers of this volume will notice that in some cases, a given biblical text is presented more than once. This is not an editorial oversight but rather a focus on the multiple meanings of a text when viewed in different contexts.

A Note on the Translation

There are several translations of the Hebrew Bible into English. To be sure, no translation is perfect, and individual preferences regarding style and cadence may differ. Due to a combination of practical issues as well as the wish to mark fidelity to the language of the original biblical Hebrew text, this volume utilizes the 1917 Jewish Publication Society version (JPS 1917). Instances in which I have incorporated a divergent translation are clearly indicated in the notes. The spelling of some proper names adopted by the JPS 1917 version diverges slightly from more commonly used present-day spellings; such names appear unrevised in the biblical selections, though I typically adopt the more familiar modern spelling and transliteration in the editorial apparatus.

Appendix: A Response to Elazar on Human Rights and Covenant in the Hebrew Bible

Daniel J. Elazar's argument in "Obligations and Rights in the Jewish Political Tradition: Some Preliminary Observations (*Jewish Political Studies Review* 3: 3–4, Fall 1991) is essentially that what one might think of in the Hebrew Bible as "human rights" do not inhere in a group or individual *as* rights, but are at best safeguarded through a kind of functional equivalent: the "obligations" placed upon others who are in a position to give (in an empirical sense) to the group or individual in question. In Elazar's words, "it is not that the widows, orphans and strangers have rights [but rather that, in order to have their basic needs fulfilled] ... they can call upon their fellow Israelites to live up to their obligations" (ibid.; many of his arguments in that essay appear also in *Covenant and Polity in Biblical Israel* [New Brunswick, NJ: Transaction, 1995, especially pp. 35-97]).

But what can this mean in concrete terms? Elazar seems to posit a division between the source of obligation (in the context of the Torah, that is God) and the (social or political) rationale for adhering to the commandments at issue here, which Elazar bases on being a party to the covenant. But that distinction only begs the question of what actually occurs when people in the category of the needy (to take just one example) are construed as not having rights of their own; or, more precisely, as not having the right to food, shelter, etc., which on a practical level prevents them from taking their equal place in society as citizens of the Israelite polity.

There are several problems with Elazar's locating the rationale for the kind of political obligation that obtains within a covenantal society exclusively in being a party to the covenant. Counterintuitively for a theory propounded by a political scientist, Elazar's understanding that an obligation on the part of the rich does not create a parallel right on behalf of the poor leaves virtually no (political) space for the poor to advocate on their own behalf. The argument that the only way for a poor person to enjoy basic rights is by depending on the kindness of strangers also requires reliance upon others' automatic assumption of their charitable obligations. But without established political mechanisms that enforce these requirements, how likely is it that these obligations will be actually and actively fulfilled?[84] Trusting that third parties will fulfill their obligations without these requirements being actively enforced makes for a distinctly weak political argument—as when

---

84. This question calls to mind a literary treatment by Jane Austen of a kind of obligation even closer to home: in *Sense and Sensibility*, Austen satirizes the early nineteenth-century English convention of requiring the needy to rely upon the charity of relatives. This is evident in the novel's pointed description of the younger Mrs. Dashwood coaxing her husband out of any notion of responsibility for his newly impoverished stepmother and stepsisters upon the passing of their husband and father, respectively.

Elazar argues, by implication, that it is up to the prophet (or other kinds of leader) to advocate for people without these rights (1995, 339–40).

But Elazar's move—focusing on obligation rather than rights—leads to theoretical murkiness, if not self-contradiction. On a fundamental level, he does not approve of the notion of rights inhering in individuals at all, in any society, because he sees this as leading to "the vulgar modern conception of rights as the individual's right to do whatever he [*sic*] pleases" (1995, 90). Yet he implicitly acknowledges that in a covenantal society rights do inhere in certain groups or individuals when he states that, in such a society, some people may have no rights at all (Elazar seems to claim that this status would apply mainly to people who adhere to no covenant at all, yet does not specify what conditions would fulfill the basic requirements of a covenant that he might find acceptable) or rights of a very different sort (e.g., referring to the "rights" of the poor). And he explicitly states the following: "Covenants . . . make possible differentiation in rights among those who are covenant partners or those who are partners to different covenants" (ibid., 87). In trying to articulate this idea in a theoretically precise manner, Elazar invokes a category of rights he variously styles as "fundamental" or "covenantal" rights (ibid., 89–90)—rights of a kind that most people today would think of as tantamount to human rights (at least with respect to the values such rights attempt to safeguard). In effect, when it comes to rights he wants to have his cake and eat it too.

Theoretically, it would be possible to construct a polity that operates in this way, by differentiating between the rights held by parties to different covenants—although one might have concerns about the concrete realization of human rights thereby achieved (see Elazar's suggestion above [1995, 87]). But even so, Elazar must deal with the second objection to what he claims is the Hebrew biblical approach to his theory of (truncated) human rights. For what Elazar claims on behalf of the Hebrew Bible is counter to what the Hebrew Bible itself has to say about the rights of people in general (who by definition may not be covenantal members). What about the stranger at the gates?[85] How do you treat the person whose covenantal affiliation is not known to you? Elazar has two answers for this issue: at some points, he simply avoids the discussion (deeming it an "open question" [ibid.]). Later in the same paragraph, he does agree that the "stranger at the gates" has "the same rights as Israelites" although he does suggest that there may be some "outer limits to those basic rights" (ibid., 88).

In his discussion of what he terms "covenantal obligation" overshadowing "rights" in the *political* context, Elazar seems to forget the importance placed by the Hebrew Bible on the consent and opinion of the average person, the "regular individual." This point comes to the fore with the Hebrew Bible's

---

85. This expression appears in Exodus 20:10 and in Deuteronomy 24:14.

description of a major political change for the Israelites: the installation of a monarchy. Despite the vast powers employed by the monarch even in the narratives presented in the Hebrew Bible, the drive to establish a monarchy is portrayed as originating in the Israelite populace, which the narrative portrays as inherently justifying the nature of the request (I Samuel 8:7).

The fundamental role of consent on the part of the people is presented not just as a unique and systemic occurrence at this early juncture of Israelite history but as including the popular approval of particular kings as well (particularly the early ones); the people's consent is required both for inaugurating the monarchy as a system of government and for establishing the rule of specific monarchs (see the discussion in the introduction to this volume [pp. lx ff.]). Thus, in the political sense, government and its (even coercive) powers do operate within the structure of the people's consent (however that concept may be particularly construed), which logically includes the (enforceable) rights of the objects of obligation (i.e., to the widows and orphans as cited by Elazar). To argue the contrary would mean claiming that the request for a monarch is limited to the structural form of government alone with no implications for the concerns of the people that, as described by the Hebrew Bible, originally motivate this request (I Samuel 8). That mistaken reading curiously overlooks the evidence of the Hebrew biblical text, which specifies that the Israelites mention the military and judicial functions of the king that they request (I Samuel 8:20).

The same critique applies to Elazar's notion of the rights, or lack of rights, of particular population groups: here, the needy. To argue that the obligation of the well-off to ensure that the poor do not lack basic needs, such as food and clothing, itself creates no right on the part of the poor to receive this charity is logically perverse: it vitiates the empirical demands of these obligations and also politically enervates the notion of the responsibilities of government. It ignores the importance of "average citizens" not only in having a voice in structuring their political circumstances, but also in ensuring their economic ability to participate meaningfully in these political institutions. To be sure, in the context of the Hebrew Bible, this right from which the poor may benefit does not entitle them to insist on getting a fixed amount from a particular person: the Hebrew Bible allows the wealthy person to choose the particular objects of his charity. But the Hebrew Bible does insist on aspects of obligation that, since legally enforceable (particularly once centralized institutions exist), may also be construed as rights.

Beyond avoiding the expressed values of the Hebrew biblical text that is itself directed to all of humanity and not just to specific covenantal members (see the texts in Isaiah 1:17 and in Micah, esp. 2, 3, 6:11–16, 7] referenced above), Elazar also ignores the values implicit in some of the touchstone narratives of the Hebrew Bible. Ironically enough, one of these texts centers on the very question of neediness and obligation that Elazar insists does not create particular rights on behalf of the needy: the story of Ruth, whose practical resolution begins with a conversation—curiously theoretical in nature—centering on the asymmetric nature of the relationship between needs and obligation. This conversation takes place in the granary at night between Ruth—a penniless widow—and Boaz, in whose fields she had been gleaning leftover stalks of grain in order to feed herself and her mother-in-law, Naomi. In this conversation, Boaz specifically praises Ruth, since "your later kindness is greater than your first" (Ruth 3:10, my translation; JPS version: "thou hast shown more kindness in the end than at the beginning"). What does Boaz mean by citing these first and subsequent kindnesses? On one level, these can refer to distinct activities on the part of Ruth: the "early kindness" can recall Ruth's care in looking after her elderly mother-in-law through the hard work of gleaning in the fields, while the "later kindness" may allude to Boaz's appreciation that Ruth has chosen to marry him rather than some of the younger men that she may have met in the field.

But taking into account the context of this conversation, which occurs in the granary after Ruth has made clear to Boaz the complex material and legal situation in which she finds herself and Boaz's ability to ease these intricate situations, the "later kindness" may also refer to Boaz's gratitude that Ruth has made him aware of his moral obligations (see my *Conceiving a Nation*, esp. pp. 84–92, for more on this issue). This interchange between Ruth and Boaz is a complicated dialogue because, in the text of Ruth, moral obligations devolve upon many different personages at different points throughout the narrative. In our context here, the point is that the receiver of kindness also has a moral role to play that may be (ontologically) prior to the other person's act of giving, even if the performance of the act of receiving the particular kindness is (historically) subsequent to the action of the person who performs the kindness. The texts of the Hebrew Bible view asymmetric relationships as partaking of different obligations, although these may be of equally important moral value. In the Hebrew Bible, obligations are multiple and simultaneous—and so are human rights.

CHAPTER 1

CITIES

The Hebrew Bible refers to the first city as the result of passion and violence, stemming from the fratricide of Abel by Cain. In this context, establishing the city is a matter of security for Cain; the subsequent developments of husbandry, music, and tools may be viewed as elements providing for his autarkic autonomy. It is a small step from autarky to autocracy, as exemplified by Nimrod, the first monarch located in ancient Babylonia. The background to the Tower of Babel narrative is thus well established, along with the moral decline exemplified by Sodom and the Cities of the Plain. But the Hebrew Bible has other uses for the city: it can be used to provide justice (Cities of Refuge) and can exemplify justice (as in the Redeemed City).

A. The City as a Locus of Power

It is worth reflecting on the different uses to which urban centers are put, even in the beginning chapters of the Hebrew Bible.[1] The city of Babel and its tower could arguably be said to furnish (even if autocratically) places of stability and safety in an unsafe world. By the time we come to the Sodom narrative, however, the conditions are utterly changed. Here, the city is strong, yet the people cry out, and there is none to save them. (Sophocles' words, on the "city that mourns for this girl" [*Antigone* 1.644–45], seem to echo these emotions.) In this connection, it is instructive to see the different reactions of Abraham and Lot after sojourning in the courts of Egypt, one of the world's great powers at that time: once back in Canaan, Abraham returns to the altar that he had previously constructed (Genesis 13:14), while Lot focuses on superintending his increased wealth, and chooses to move to a city that would come to exemplify evil-doing.

---

1. Emphasizing the variety and complexity of the Hebrew Bible's allusions to the city, my approach contrasts with the comparatively monochromatic reading preferred by Yoram Hazony in *The Philosophy of Hebrew Scripture* (New York: Cambridge University Press, 2012), which presents the city as the harbinger of empire, with all of its accompanying social and moral associations (see especially chapter 4, "The Ethics of a Shepherd," pp. 103–39).

1. The First Founding

As the Hebrew Bible tells it, the first city is founded by Cain, after he has killed his brother, Abel, in a violent stew of passion and disappointment. Is this act of human destruction linked with urban construction? Is the city inevitably tainted by sin? Or does the city represent a point of civic pride, a new form of community that allows for more complex political awareness, as the ancient Greeks visualized? What is the connection between the Hebrew Bible's enumeration of the arts of animal husbandry, metallurgy, agriculture, music, and technology that develop at this juncture, and living in the city? On a deeper level, does the Hebrew Bible invite the reader to consider whether the (moral) essence of a development is determined by its roots or its consequences?

Genesis 4:16–22

16 And Cain went out from the presence of the LORD, and dwelt in the land of Nod, on the east of Eden. 17 And Cain knew his wife; and she conceived, and bore Enoch; and he builded a city, and called the name of the city after the name of his son Enoch.

18 And unto Enoch was born Irad; and Irad begot Mehujael; and Mehujael begot Methushael; and Methushael begot Lamech. 19 And Lamech took unto him two wives; the name of one was Adah, and the name of the other Zillah.

20 And Adah bore Jabal; he was the father of such as dwell in tents and have cattle. 21 And his brother's name was Jubal; he was the father of all such as handle the harp and pipe.

22 And Zillah, she also bore Tubal-cain, the forger of every cutting instrument of brass and iron; and the sister of Tubal-cain was Naamah.

2. The City as Seed of Empire

After a series of "begots" offering genealogical information, the Hebrew Bible recounts the increasing depravity of mankind, resulting in the Flood. After this cataclysm, human life is reconstituted from the immediate family of Noah; animal life is likewise reestablished from the animals that Noah had stowed with his family on the ark. In the middle of the new genealogical accounts, an interesting fact is slipped in: Nimrod establishes the first monarchy, and with it, the desire for empire-building takes hold.

Genesis 10:6–14

6 And the sons of Ham: Cush, and Mizraim, and Put, and Canaan. 7 And the sons of Cush: Seba, and Havilah, and Sabtah, and Raamah, and Sabteca; and the sons of Raamah: Sheba, and Dedan.

8 And Cush begot Nimrod; he began to be a mighty one in the earth. 9 He was a mighty hunter before the LORD; wherefore it is said: 'Like Nimrod a mighty hunter before the LORD.' 10 And the beginning of his kingdom was Babel, and Erech, and Accad, and Calneh, in the land of Shinar.

11 Out of that land went forth Asshur, and builded Nineveh, and Rehoboth-ir, and Calah, 12 and Resen between Nineveh and Calah—the same is the great city.

13 And Mizraim begot Ludim, and Anamim, and Lehabim, and Naphtuhim, 14 and Pathrusim, and Casluhim—whence went forth the Philistines—and Caphtorim.

3. The City and the Tower

It is not happenstance that the center of Nimrod's empire, Babel, is itself the focal point of the next narrative. Why is the building of this tower, a would-be architectural wonder of the ancient world, presented in the biblical text as a political issue, expressed in images of unity and dispersal? As the narrative concludes, is the diffusion of people from Babel, which can arguably be figured as an "exile" of its own, entirely negative in its implication? By inference, is "one language" for all people to speak inevitably a good thing? How does this narrative relate to Nimrod's establishment of unitary authority in the previous chapter in Genesis?

Genesis 11:1–9

1 And the whole earth was of one language and of one speech. 2 And it came to pass, as they journeyed east, that they found a plain in the land of Shinar; and they dwelt there.

3 And they said one to another: 'Come, let us make brick, and burn them thoroughly.' And they had brick for stone, and slime had they for mortar.

4 And they said: 'Come, let us build us a city, and a tower, with its top in heaven, and let us make us a name; lest we be scattered abroad upon the face of the whole earth.'

5 And the LORD came down to see the city and the tower, which the children of men builded.

6 And the LORD said: 'Behold, they are one people, and they have all one language; and this is what they begin to do; and now nothing will be withholden from them, which they purpose to do. 7 Come, let us go down, and there confound their language, that they may not understand one another's speech.'

8 So the LORD scattered them abroad from thence upon the face of all the earth; and they left off to build the city. 9 Therefore was the name of it called Babel; because the LORD did there confound the language of all the earth; and from thence did the LORD scatter them abroad upon the face of all the earth.

4. City of Evil

If the Tower of Babel presents an ambiguous, even ambivalent, representation of the city and its propensity for corruption and power schemes, the city of Sodom is portrayed as unequivocally evil and, equally important, as unredeemable (cf. Genesis 18:25, Abraham's dialogue with God about justice). In reading the three-part selection offered below, it is worth thinking about Lot's choice of Sodom as his domicile, the series of events leading up to its destruction, and the interaction between Lot and his daughters in the cave of Zo'ar subsequent to their flight from Sodom.

Other issues are raised as well: Are there differences among these texts in accounting for Sodom's wickedness? Why is Lot's wife punished? Is the Hebrew Bible really concerned with angles of peeking, or is there another moral concern latent in the text? Is there a difference between the evil done in the city and the evil done on the outskirts? Is there something about urban life that heightens the moral stakes of individual and communal actions? What is the significance of Lot, the urban man of importance who ends up in a cave? How does the kind of "knowledge" exhibited in this cave contrast with that of Plato's cave in *The Republic*?

Genesis 13:1–13

1 And Abram[2] went up out of Egypt, he, and his wife, and all that he had, and Lot with him, into the South. 2 And Abram was very rich in cattle, in silver, and in gold. 3 And he went on his

---

2. At this point in the text, Abram's name has not yet been changed to Abraham. This change is noted in Genesis 17:5.

journeys from the South even to Beth-el, unto the place where his tent had been at the beginning, between Beth-el and Ai; 4 unto the place of the altar, which he had made there at the first; and Abram called there on the name of the LORD. 5 And Lot also, who went with Abram, had flocks, and herds, and tents.

6 But³ the land was not able to bear them, that they might dwell together; for their substance was great, so that they could not dwell together. 7 And there was a strife between the herdmen of Abram's cattle and the herdmen of Lot's cattle. And the Canaanite and the Perizzite dwelt then in the land.

8 And Abram said unto Lot: 'Let there be no strife, I pray thee, between me and thee, and between my herdmen and thy herdmen; for we are brethren. 9 Is not the whole land before thee? separate thyself, I pray thee, from me; if thou wilt take the left hand, then I will go to the right; or if thou take the right hand, then I will go to the left.'

10 And Lot lifted up his eyes, and beheld all the plain of the Jordan, that it was well watered every where, before the LORD destroyed Sodom and Gomorrah, like the garden of the LORD, like the land of Egypt, as thou goest unto Zoar. 11 So Lot chose him all the plain of the Jordan; and Lot journeyed east; and they separated themselves the one from the other. 12 Abram dwelt in the land of Canaan, and Lot dwelt in the cities of the Plain, and moved his tent as far as Sodom. 13 Now the men of Sodom were wicked and sinners against the LORD exceedingly.

In the next selection, Abraham pleads with God to act fairly and with patience, even toward a city or cities of evildoers. By the Hebrew Bible's laconic standards, this is a long conversation: Abraham does not give up easily. Even God, Abraham argues, is not exempt from the requirements of justice.⁴

Genesis 18:16–33

16 And the men rose up from thence, and looked out toward Sodom; and Abraham went with them to bring them on the way.

---

3. JPS 1917: "And."

4. In this context, readers may recall Aristotle's digression on "equity which corrects the deficiencies of legal justice" (*Ethics*, "Justice," [chap. 5] Part X, 11372a; trans. J. A. K. Thomson; rev. by Hugh Tredennick; Introduction by Jonathan Barnes; New York: Penguin, repr. 2004; pp. 139–41).

17 And the LORD said: 'Shall I hide from Abraham that which I am doing; 18 seeing that Abraham shall surely become a great and mighty nation, and all the nations of the earth shall be blessed in him? 19 For I have known him, to the end that he may command his children and his household after him, that they may keep the way of the LORD, to do righteousness and justice; to the end that the LORD may bring upon Abraham that which He hath spoken of him.'

20 And the LORD said: 'Verily, the cry of Sodom and Gomorrah is great, and, verily, their sin is exceeding grievous. 21 I will go down now, and see whether they have done altogether according to the cry of it, which is come unto Me; and if not, I will know.'

22 And the men turned from thence, and went toward Sodom; but Abraham stood yet before the LORD.

23 And Abraham drew near, and said: 'Wilt Thou indeed sweep away the righteous with the wicked? 24 Peradventure there are fifty righteous within the city; wilt Thou indeed sweep away and not forgive the place for the fifty righteous that are therein? 25 That be far from Thee to do after this manner, to slay the righteous with the wicked, that so the righteous should be as the wicked; that be far from Thee; shall not the judge of all the earth do justly?' 26 And the LORD said: 'If I find in Sodom fifty righteous within the city, then I will forgive all the place for their sake.'

27 And Abraham answered and said: 'Behold now, I have taken upon me to speak unto the Lord, who am but dust and ashes. 28 Peradventure there shall lack five of the fifty righteous; wilt Thou destroy all the city for lack of five?' And He said: 'I will not destroy it, if I find there forty and five.'

29 And he spoke unto Him yet again, and said: 'Peradventure there shall be forty found there.' And He said: 'I will not do it for the forty's sake.'

30 And he said: 'Oh, let not the Lord be angry, and I will speak. Peradventure there shall thirty be found there.' And He said: 'I will not do it, if I find thirty there.'

31 And he said: 'Behold now, I have taken upon me to speak unto the Lord. Peradventure there shall be twenty found there.' And He said: 'I will not destroy it for the twenty's sake.'

32 And he said: 'Oh, let not the Lord be angry, and I will speak yet but this once. Peradventure ten shall be found there.' And He said: 'I will not destroy it for the ten's sake.'

33 And the LORD went His way, as soon as He had left off speaking to Abraham; and Abraham returned unto his place.

The next section describes the actions that occur immediately before Sodom's destruction, ending with the (to twenty-first-century ears, incestuous) circumstances that lead to the conception of Ammon and Moab, who would themselves eventually develop into neighboring nations with important influences on Israelite history.

Readers may question the "hospitality" that Lot shows, particularly as it involves his offering his daughters to the violence of the Sodom townspeople who surround his house. At what point does excessive hospitality become cruelty?

Genesis 19

1 And the two angels came to Sodom at evening;[5] and Lot sat in the gate of Sodom; and Lot saw them, and rose up to meet them; and he fell down on his face to the earth; 2 and he said: 'Behold now, my lords, turn aside, I pray you, into your servant's house, and tarry all night, and wash your feet, and ye shall rise up early, and go on your way.' And they said: 'Nay; but we will abide in the broad place all night.' 3 And he urged them greatly; and they turned in unto him, and entered into his house; and he made them a feast, and did bake unleavened bread, and they did eat.

4 But before they lay down, the men of the city, even the men of Sodom, compassed the house round, both young and old, all the people from every quarter. 5 And they called unto Lot, and said unto him: 'Where are the men that came in to thee this night? bring them out unto us, that we may know them.'

6 And Lot went out unto them to the door, and shut the door after him. 7 And he said: 'I pray you, my brethren, do not so wickedly. 8 Behold now, I have two daughters that have not known man; let me, I pray you, bring them out unto you, and do ye to them as is good in your eyes; only unto these men do nothing; forasmuch as they are come under the shadow of my roof.' 9 And they said: 'Stand back.' And they said: 'This one fellow came in to

---

5. JPS 1917: "at even."

sojourn, and he will needs play the judge; now will we deal worse with thee, than with them.' And they pressed sore upon the man, even Lot, and drew near to break the door.

10 But the men put forth their hand, and brought Lot into the house to them, and the door they shut. 11 And they smote the men that were at the door of the house with blindness, both small and great; so that they wearied themselves to find the door.

12 And the men said unto Lot: 'Hast thou here any besides? son-in-law, and thy sons, and thy daughters, and whomsoever thou hast in the city; bring them out of the place; 13 for we will destroy this place, because the cry of them is waxed great before the LORD; and the LORD hath sent us to destroy it.'

14 And Lot went out, and spoke unto his sons-in-law, who married his daughters, and said: 'Up, get you out of this place; for the LORD will destroy the city.' But he seemed unto his sons-in-law as one that jested.

15 And when the morning arose, then the angels hastened Lot, saying: 'Arise, take thy wife, and thy two daughters that are here; lest thou be swept away in the iniquity of the city.' 16 But he lingered; and the men laid hold upon his hand, and upon the hand of his wife, and upon the hand of his two daughters; the LORD being merciful unto him. And they brought him forth, and set him without the city. 17 And it came to pass, when they had brought them forth abroad, that he said: 'Escape for thy life; look not behind thee, neither stay thou in all the Plain; escape to the mountain, lest thou be swept away.'

18 And Lot said unto them: 'Oh, not so, my lord; 19 behold now, thy servant hath found grace in thy sight, and thou hast magnified thy mercy, which thou hast shown unto me in saving my life; and I cannot escape to the mountain, lest the evil overtake me, and I die. 20 Behold now, this city is near to flee unto, and it is a little one; oh, let me escape thither—is it not a little one?—and my soul shall live.' 21 And he said unto him: 'See, I have accepted thee concerning this thing also, that I will not overthrow the city of which thou hast spoken. 22 Hasten thou, escape thither; for I cannot do any thing till thou be come: thither.'—Therefore the name of the city was called Zoar.— 23 The sun was risen upon the earth when Lot came unto Zoar.

24 Then the LORD caused to rain upon Sodom and upon Gomorrah brimstone and fire from the LORD out of heaven; 25 and He overthrow those cities, and all the Plain, and all the inhabitants of the cities, and that which grew upon the ground. 26 But his wife looked back from behind him, and she became a pillar of salt.

27 And Abraham got up early in the morning to the place where he had stood before the LORD. 28 And he looked out toward Sodom and Gomorrah, and toward all the land of the Plain, and beheld, and, lo, the smoke of the land went up as the smoke of a furnace. 29 And it came to pass, when God destroyed the cities of the Plain, that God remembered Abraham, and sent Lot out of the midst of the overthrow, when He overthrew the cities in which Lot dwelt.

30 And Lot went up out of Zoar, and dwelt in the mountain, and his two daughters with him; for he feared to dwell in Zoar; and he dwelt in a cave, he and his two daughters. 31 And the first-born said unto the younger: 'Our father is old, and there is not a man in the earth to come in unto us after the manner of all the earth. 32 Come, let us make our father drink wine, and we will lie with him, that we may preserve seed of our father.'

33 And they made their father drink wine that night. And the first-born went in, and lay with her father; and he knew not when she lay down, nor when she arose. 34 And it came to pass on the morrow, that the first-born said unto the younger: 'Behold, I lay yesternight with my father. Let us make him drink wine this night also; and go thou in, and lie with him, that we may preserve seed of our father.' 35 And they made their father drink wine that night also. And the younger arose, and lay with him; and he knew not when she lay down, nor when she arose. 36 Thus were both the daughters of Lot with child by their father. 37 And the first-born bore a son, and called his name Moab—the same is the father of the Moabites unto this day. 38 And the younger, she also bore a son, and called his name Ben-ammi—the same is the father of the children of Ammon unto this day.

In the Hebrew Bible, the image of Sodom as the epitome of the evil city remains in use long after Sodom itself is destroyed. Ezekiel uses the trope of Sodom to warn the Israelites that their evil is likewise approaching the point of destructive punishment.

49 Behold, this was the iniquity of thy sister Sodom: pride, fulness of bread, and careless ease was in her and in her daughters; neither did she strengthen the hand of the poor and needy. 50 And they were haughty, and committed abomination before Me; therefore I removed them when I saw it.

B. The City as Refuge

The Hebrew Bible presents the cities of Ancient Israel as more than just economic or political centers. In addition, certain cities (including those that were also part of the Levite landholding) functioned as places of refuge for people who feared a miscarriage of justice, namely, being murdered by the relative of a person whose death they had inadvertently caused. The Hebrew Bible's provision of entire cities for the protection of those who have killed another human being inadvertently and without malice underscores both its profound realism about the dangers of blood vengeance in the context of civic life, and its commitment, even at the level of civic planning, to the imperatives of justice.

In reading these texts, it is useful to think about why entire cities, rather than designated sections of cities or particular buildings, are set aside in the Hebrew Bible as safe havens for people whose otherwise benign actions culminate in the death of a bystander. Additionally, why is there an overlap among Cities of Refuge and those cities designated as residential locations for the Levites? Also, consider the differences among the several Hebrew biblical texts that focus on the Cities of Refuge, particularly as reflecting the distinctive nuances emphasized by each of these texts.

1. Cities of Refuge for Perpetrators of Inadvertent Manslaughter

12 He that smiteth a man, so that he dieth, shall surely be put to death. 13 And if a man lie not in wait, but God cause it to come to hand; then I will appoint thee a place whither he may flee.

14 And if a man come presumptuously upon his neighbour, to slay him with guile; thou shalt take him from Mine altar, that he may die.

Near the beginning of Deuteronomy, the text details the process by which, historically, the Cities of Refuge were set aside.

Deuteronomy 4:41–43

41 Then Moses set aside[6] three cities beyond the Jordan toward the sunrising; 42 that the manslayer might flee thither, that slayeth his neighbour unawares, and hated him not in time past; and that fleeing unto one of these cities he might live: 43 Bezer in the wilderness, in the table-land, for the Reubenites; and Ramoth in Gilead, for the Gadites; and Golan in Bashan, for the Manassites.

Later in Deuteronomy, the text expands upon the details and rationale of constructing the Cities of Refuge, and of their potential uses.

Deuteronomy 19:1–13

1 When the LORD thy God shall cut off the nations, whose land the LORD thy God giveth thee, and thou dost succeed them, and dwell in their cities, and in their houses; 2 thou shalt separate three cities for thee in the midst of thy land, which the LORD thy GOD giveth thee to possess it. 3 Thou shalt prepare thee the way, and divide the borders of thy land, which the LORD thy God causeth thee to inherit, into three parts, that every manslayer may flee thither.

4 And this is the case of the manslayer, that shall flee thither and live: whoso killeth his neighbour unawares, and hated him not in time past; 5 as when a man goeth into the forest with his neighbour to hew wood, and his hand fetcheth a stroke with the axe to cut down the tree, and the head slippeth from the helve, and lighteth upon his neighbour, that he die; he shall flee unto one of these cities and live; 6 lest the avenger of blood pursue the manslayer, while his heart is hot, and overtake him, because the way is long, and smite him mortally; whereas he was not deserving of death, inasmuch as he hated him not in time past.

7 Wherefore I command thee, saying: 'Thou shalt separate three cities for thee.' 8 And if the LORD thy God enlarge thy border, as He hath sworn unto thy fathers, and give thee all the land which He promised to give unto thy fathers— 9 if thou shalt keep all this commandment to do it, which I command thee this day, to love the LORD thy God, and to walk ever in

---

6. JPS 1917: "separated."

His ways—then shalt thou add three cities more for thee, beside these three; 10 that innocent blood be not shed in the midst of thy land, which the LORD thy God giveth thee for an inheritance, and so blood be upon thee.

11 But if any man hate his neighbour, and lie in wait for him, and rise up against him, and smite him mortally that he die; and he flee into one of these cities; 12 then the elders of his city shall send and fetch him thence, and deliver him into the hand of the avenger of blood, that he may die. 13 Thine eye shall not pity him, but thou shalt put away the blood of the innocent from Israel, that it may go well with thee.

The Levites were given no landholdings in the Promised Land; their domiciles were forty-eight cities given over to their use, together with some outside lots for their subsistence agriculture and husbandry.

The cities of the Levites were traditionally also utilized as Cities of Refuge; importantly, the availability of refuge was not extended to those implicated in cases of premeditated murder.

2. Levitical Cities

Numbers 35:1–34

1 And the LORD spoke unto Moses in the plains of Moab by the Jordan at Jericho, saying: 2 'Command the children of Israel, that they give unto the Levites of the inheritance of their possession cities to dwell in; and open land round about the cities shall ye give unto the Levites. 3 And the cities shall they have to dwell in; and their open land shall be for their cattle, and for their substance, and for all their beasts. 4 And the open land about the cities, which ye shall give unto the Levites, shall be from the wall of the city and outward a thousand cubits round about. 5 And ye shall measure without the city for the east side two thousand cubits, and for the south side two thousand cubits, and for the west side two thousand cubits, and for the north side two thousand cubits, the city being in the midst. This shall be to them the open land about the cities.

6 And the cities which ye shall give unto the Levites, they shall be the six cities of refuge, which ye shall give for the manslayer to flee thither; and beside them ye shall give forty and two cities. 7 All the cities which ye shall give to the Levites shall be forty and

eight cities: them shall ye give with the open land about them. 8 And concerning the cities which ye shall give of the possession of the children of Israel, from the many ye shall take many, and from the few ye shall take few; each tribe according to its inheritance which it inheriteth shall give of its cities unto the Levites.'

9 And the LORD spoke unto Moses, saying: 10 'Speak unto the children of Israel, and say unto them: When ye pass over the Jordan into the land of Canaan, 11 then ye shall appoint you cities to be cities of refuge for you, that the manslayer that killeth any person through error may flee thither. 12 And the cities shall be unto you for refuge from the avenger, that the manslayer die not, until he stand before the congregation for judgment. 13 And as to the cities which ye shall give, there shall be for you six cities of refuge. 14 Ye shall give three cities beyond the Jordan, and three cities shall ye give in the land of Canaan; they shall be cities of refuge. 15 For the children of Israel, and for the stranger and for the settler among them, shall these six cities be for refuge, that every one that killeth any person through error may flee thither.

16 But if he smote him with an instrument of iron, so that he died, he is a murderer; the murderer shall surely be put to death. 17 And if he smote him with a stone in the hand, whereby a man may die, and he died, he is a murderer; the murderer shall surely be put to death. 18 Or if he smote him with a weapon of wood in the hand, whereby a man may die, and he died, he is a murderer; the murderer shall surely be put to death. 19 The avenger of blood shall himself put the murderer to death; when he meeteth him, he shall put him to death. 20 And if he thrust him of hatred, or hurled at him any thing, lying in wait, so that he died; 21 or in enmity smote him with his hand, that he died; he that smote him shall surely be put to death: he is a murderer; the avenger of blood shall put the murderer to death when he meeteth him.

22 But if he thrust him suddenly without enmity, or hurled upon him any thing without lying in wait, 23 or with any stone, whereby a man may die, seeing him not, and cast it upon him, so that he died, and he was not his enemy, neither sought his harm; 24 then the congregation shall judge between the smiter and the avenger of blood according to these ordinances; 25 and the congregation shall deliver the manslayer out of the hand of

the avenger of blood, and the congregation shall restore him to
his city of refuge, whither he was fled; and he shall dwell therein
until the death of the high priest, who was anointed with the
holy oil.

26 But if the manslayer shall at any time go beyond the border
of his city of refuge, whither he fleeth; 27 and the avenger of
blood find him without the border of his city of refuge, and the
avenger of blood slay the manslayer; there shall be no bloodguiltiness for him; 28 because he must remain in his city of refuge
until the death of the high priest; but after the death of the high
priest the manslayer may return into the land of his possession.
29 And these things shall be for a statute of judgment unto you
throughout your generations in all your dwellings.

30 Whoso killeth any person, the murderer shall be slain at the
mouth of witnesses; but one witness shall not testify against any
person that he die. 31 Moreover ye shall take no ransom for the
life of a murderer, that is guilty of death; but he shall surely be
put to death. 32 And ye shall take no ransom for him that is fled
to his city of refuge, that he should come again to dwell in the
land, until the death of the priest. 33 So ye shall not pollute the
land wherein ye are; for blood, it polluteth the land; and no expi-
ation can be made for the land for the blood that is shed therein,
but by the blood of him that shed it. 34 And thou shalt not defile
the land which ye inhabit, in the midst of which I dwell; for I the
LORD dwell in the midst of the children of Israel.'

For further reading, see also Joshua 20:1–9, 21:1–3, and I Chronicles 6:42.

C. Cosmopolitan Cities, Corrupted Cities, Redeemed Cities

Cities in the Hebrew Bible are not inevitably uniform in nature: they may be
corrupt, but they may also redeem themselves. In Solomon's time, Jerusalem
is presented (not unproblematically) as a city of commercial movement and
cultural plurality: Jerusalem is enriched by the trade stimulated by Solomon's
building of the Temple and of his own palace.

At first glance, these texts may appear to focus less on a city than on
the man at its center, King Solomon, who transforms his father David's
besieged kingdom into a center of commerce and empire. King Solomon is
the middleman for much of the area's trade (see I Kings 10:29); the description of his throne and his wisdom signals power felt well beyond the person

of King Solomon himself. The splendor of his court implies the existence of a city cognizant of its magnificence and costs; note the text's careful record of the palaces that Solomon builds for his foreign wives (I Kings 9:24, for example).

The text of the Hebrew Bible seems to imply that Israel's commercial and cultural expansion under Solomon comes at a price: the cultural pluralism of Solomon's wives introduces idolatry into Jerusalem, which betokens the eventual diminution of his kingdom.

I Kings 9:10–28

10 And it came to pass at the end of twenty years, wherein Solomon had built the two houses, the house of the LORD and the king's house—11 now Hiram the king of Tyre had furnished Solomon with cedar-trees and cypress-trees, and with gold, according to all his desire—that then king Solomon gave Hiram twenty cities in the land of Galilee. 12 And Hiram came out from Tyre to see the cities which Solomon had given him: and they pleased him not. 13 And he said: 'What cities are these which thou hast given me, my brother?' And they were called the land of Cabul, unto this day. 14 And Hiram sent to the king sixscore talents of gold.

15 And this is the account of the levy which king Solomon raised; to build the house of the LORD, and his own house, and Millo, and the wall of Jerusalem, and Hazor, and Megiddo, and Gezer. 16 Pharaoh king of Egypt had gone up, and taken Gezer, and burnt it with fire, and slain the Canaanites that dwelt in the city, and given it for a portion unto his daughter, Solomon's wife. 17 And Solomon built Gezer, and Beth-horon the nether, 18 and Baalath, and Tadmor in the wilderness, in the land, 19 and all the store-cities that Solomon had, and the cities for his chariots, and the cities for his horsemen, and that which Solomon desired to build for his pleasure in Jerusalem, and in Lebanon, and in all the land of his dominion. 20 All the people that were left of the Amorites, the Hittites, the Perizzites, the Hivites, and the Jebusites, who were not of the children of Israel; 21 even their children that were left after them in the land, whom the children of Israel were not able utterly to destroy, of them did Solomon raise a levy of bondservants, unto this day. 22 But of the children of Israel did Solomon make no bondservants; but they were the men of war, and his servants, and his princes, and his captains, and rulers of his chariots and of his horsemen.

23 These were the chief officers that were over Solomon's work, five hundred and fifty, who bore rule over the people that wrought in the work.

24 But Pharaoh's daughter came up out of the city of David unto her house which [Solomon] had built for her; then did he build Millo.

25 And three times in a year did Solomon offer burnt-offerings and peace-offerings upon the altar which he built unto the LORD, offering thereby, upon the altar that was before the LORD. So he finished the house. 26 And king Solomon made a navy of ships in Ezion-geber, which is beside Eloth, on the shore of the Red Sea, in the land of Edom. 27 And Hiram sent in the navy his servants, shipmen that had knowledge of the sea, with the servants of Solomon. 28 And they came to Ophir, and fetched from thence gold, four hundred and twenty talents, and brought it to king Solomon.

I Kings 10:11–29

11 And the navy also of Hiram, that brought gold from Ophir, brought in from Ophir great plenty of sandal-wood and precious stones. 12 And the king made of the sandal-wood pillars for the house of the LORD, and for the king's house, harps also and psalteries for the singers; there came no such sandal-wood, nor was seen, unto this day. 13 And king Solomon gave to the queen of Sheba all her desire, whatsoever she asked, beside that which Solomon gave her of his royal bounty. So she turned, and went to her own land, she and her servants.

14 Now the weight of gold that came to Solomon in one year was six hundred threescore and six talents of gold, 15 beside that which came of the merchants, and of the traffic of the traders, and of all the kings of the mingled people and of the governors of the country. 16 And king Solomon made two hundred targets of beaten gold: six hundred shekels of gold went to one target. 17 And he made three hundred shields of beaten gold: three pounds of gold went to one shield; and the king put them in the house of the forest of Lebanon.

18 Moreover the king made a great throne of ivory, and overlaid it with the finest gold. 19 There were six steps to the throne, and the top of the throne was round behind; and there were arms on

either side by the place of the seat, and two lions standing beside the arms. 20 And twelve lions stood there on the one side and on the other upon the six steps; there was not the like made in any kingdom.

21 And all king Solomon's drinking-vessels were of gold, and all the vessels of the house of the forest of Lebanon were of pure gold; none were of silver; it was nothing accounted of in the days of Solomon. 22 For the king had at sea a navy of Tarshish with the navy of Hiram; once every three years came the navy of Tarshish, bringing gold, and silver, ivory, and apes, and peacocks.

23 So king Solomon exceeded all the kings of the earth in riches and in wisdom. 24 And all the earth sought the presence of Solomon, to hear his wisdom, which God had put in his heart. 25 And they brought every man his present, vessels of silver, and vessels of gold, and raiment, and armour, and spices, horses, and mules, a rate year by year.

26 And Solomon gathered together chariots and horsemen; and he had a thousand and four hundred chariots, and twelve thousand horsemen, that he bestowed in the chariot cities, and with the king at Jerusalem. 27 And the king made silver to be in Jerusalem as stones, and cedars made he to be as the sycamore-trees that are in the Lowland, for abundance. 28 And the horses which Solomon had were brought out of Egypt; also out of Keveh, the king's merchants buying them of the men of Keveh at a price. 29 And a chariot came up and went out of Egypt for six hundred shekels of silver, and a horse for a hundred and fifty; and so for all the kings of the Hittites, and for the kings of Aram, did they bring them out by their means.

I Kings 3:1

1 And Solomon became allied to Pharaoh king of Egypt by marriage, and took Pharaoh's daughter, and brought her into the city of David, until he had made an end of building his own house, and the house of the LORD, and the wall of Jerusalem round about.

I Kings 11:1–8

1 Now king Solomon loved many foreign women, besides the daughter of Pharaoh, women of the Moabites, Ammonites,

Edomites, Zidonians, and Hittites; 2 of the nations concerning which the LORD said unto the children of Israel: 'Ye shall not go among them, neither shall they come among you; for surely they will turn away your heart after their gods'; Solomon did cleave unto these in love. 3 And he had seven hundred wives, princesses, and three hundred concubines; and his wives turned away his heart.

4 For it came to pass, when Solomon was old, that his wives turned away his heart after other gods; and his heart was not whole with the LORD his God, as was the heart of David his father. 5 For Solomon went after Ashtoreth the goddess of the Zidonians, and after Milcom the detestation of the Ammonites.

6 And Solomon did that which was evil in the sight of the LORD, and went not fully after the LORD, as did David his father. 7 Then did Solomon build a high place for Chemosh the detestation of Moab, in the mount that is before Jerusalem, and for Molech the detestation of the children of Ammon. 8 And so did he for all his foreign wives, who offered and sacrificed unto their gods.

1. *The Idolatrous City*

The Hebrew biblical narrative describes the moral dissolution that arrives at the end of Solomon's reign and is exemplified in its cities, especially Jerusalem.

In the following selection, the Hebrew Bible takes up the case of a city that has completely abandoned the Israelite monotheistic faith.

Deuteronomy 13:13–19

13 If thou shalt hear tell concerning one of thy cities, which the LORD thy God giveth thee to dwell there, saying: 14 'Certain base fellows are gone out from the midst of thee, and have drawn away the inhabitants of their city, saying: Let us go and serve other gods, which ye have not known';

15 then shalt thou inquire, and make search, and ask diligently; and, behold, if it be truth, and the thing certain, that such abomination is wrought in the midst of thee; 16 thou shalt surely smite the inhabitants of that city with the edge of the sword, destroying it utterly, and all that is therein and the cattle thereof, with the edge of the sword.

17 And thou shalt gather all the spoil of it into the midst of the broad place thereof, and shall burn with fire the city, and all the spoil thereof every whit, unto the LORD thy God; and it shall be a heap for ever; it shall not be built again. 18 And there shall cleave nought of the devoted thing to thy hand, that the LORD may turn from the fierceness of His anger, and show thee mercy, and have compassion upon thee, and multiply thee, as He hath sworn unto thy fathers; 19 when thou shalt hearken to the voice of the LORD thy God, to keep all His commandments which I command thee this day, to do that which is right in the eyes of the LORD thy God.

2. Jerusalem: The Abandoned City

In various texts of the Hebrew Bible, warnings are given regarding the consequences of abandoning monotheism: if you abandon God, God will abandon you. This trope is often presented as the image of the abandoned city, particularly Jerusalem.

Lamentations 1:1–22

א[7]

1 HOW DOTH the city sit solitary,
That was full of people!
How is she become as a widow!
She that was great among the nations,
And princess among the provinces,
How is she become a vassal city![8]

ב

2 She weepeth sore in the night,
And her tears are on her cheeks;
She hath none to comfort her
Among all her lovers;
All her friends have dealt treacherously with her,
They are become her enemies.

---

7. Following the traditional presentation of the JPS 1917 translation, I have retained the designation of Hebrew letters before each verse of this selection, pointing to the alphabetical ordering of the verses (i.e., which follows the order of the Hebrew alphabet).

8. Here, the New Revised Standard Version "vassal" is used as a more comprehensible term than the more ambiguous JPS 1917 rendering of it as "tributary"; I have added the noun "city" to clarify the referent to which the word "vassal" alludes.

ג

3   Judah is gone into exile because of affliction,
    And because of great servitude;
    She dwelleth among the nations,
    She findeth no rest;
    All her pursuers overtook her
    Within the straits.

ד

4   The ways of Zion do mourn,
    Because none come to the solemn assembly;
    All her gates are desolate,
    Her priests sigh;
    Her virgins are afflicted,
    And she herself is in bitterness.

ה

5   Her adversaries are become the head,
    Her enemies are at ease;
    For the LORD hath afflicted her
    For the multitude of her transgressions;
    Her young children are gone into captivity
    Before the adversary.

ו

6   And gone is from the daughter of Zion
    All her splendour;
    Her princes are become like harts
    That find no pasture,
    And they are gone without strength
    Before the pursuer.

ז

7   Jerusalem remembereth
    In the days of her affliction and of her anguish
    All her treasures that she had
    From the days of old;
    Now that her people fall by the hand of the adversary,
    And none doth help her,
    The adversaries have seen her,
    They have mocked at her desolations.

ח

8 Jerusalem hath grievously sinned,
  Therefore she is become as one unclean;
  All that honoured her despise her,
  Because they have seen her nakedness;
  She herself also sigheth,
  And turneth backward.

ט

9 Her filthiness was in her skirts,
  She was not mindful of her end;
  Therefore is she come down wonderfully,
  She hath no comforter.
  'Behold, O LORD, my affliction,
  For the enemy hath magnified himself.'

י

10 The adversary hath spread out his hand
   Upon all her treasures;
   For she hath seen that the heathen
   Are entered into her sanctuary,
   Concerning whom Thou didst command
   That they should not enter into Thy congregation.

כ

11 All her people sigh,
   They seek bread;
   They have given their pleasant things for food
   To refresh the soul.
   'See, O LORD, and behold,
   How abject I am become.'

ל

12 'Let it not come unto you, all ye that pass by!
   Behold, and see
   If there be any pain like unto my pain,
   Which is done unto me,
   Wherewith the LORD hath afflicted me
   In the day of His fierce anger.

מ

13 From on high hath He sent fire
   Into my bones, and it prevaileth against them;

He hath spread a net for my feet,
He hath turned me back;
He hath made me desolate
And faint all the day.

נ

14 The yoke of my transgressions is impressed by His hand;
They are knit together,
They are come up upon my neck;
He hath made my strength to fail;
The Lord hath delivered me into their hands,
Against whom I am not able to stand.

ס

15 The Lord hath set at nought
All my mighty men in the midst of me;
He hath called a solemn assembly against me
To crush my young men;
The Lord hath trodden as in a winepress
The virgin the daughter of Judah.'

ע

16 'For these things I weep;
Mine eye, mine eye runneth down with water;
Because the comforter is far from me,
Even he that should refresh my soul;
My children are desolate,
Because the enemy hath prevailed.'

פ

17 Zion spreadeth forth her hands;
There is none to comfort her;
The LORD hath commanded concerning Jacob,
That they that are round about him should be his adversaries;
Jerusalem is among them
As one unclean.

צ

18 'The LORD is righteous;
For I have rebelled against His word;
Hear, I pray you, all ye peoples,
And behold my pain:
My virgins and my young men
Are gone into captivity.

ק

19 I called for my lovers,
    But they deceived me;
    My priests and mine elders
    Perished in the city,
    While they sought them food
    To refresh their souls.

ר

20 Behold, O LORD, for I am in distress,
    Mine inwards burn;
    My heart is turned within me,
    For I have grievously rebelled.
    Abroad the sword bereaveth,
    At home there is the like of death.

שׁ

21 They have heard that I sigh,
    There is none to comfort me;
    All mine enemies have heard of my trouble, and are glad,
    For Thou hast done it;
    Thou wilt bring the day that Thou hast proclaimed,
    And they shall be like unto me.

ת

22 Let all their wickedness come before Thee;
    And do unto them,
    As Thou hast done unto me
    For all my transgressions;
    For my sighs are many
    And my heart is faint.'

In contrast to the elegiac tone of Lamentations, the words of Isaiah exhibit a reflective tone: how can Jerusalem, the city of justice, have sunk so low?

Isaiah 1:21–23

21 How is the faithful city
Become a harlot!
She that was full of justice,
Righteousness lodged in her,
But now murderers.
22 Thy silver is become dross,
Thy wine mixed with water.
23 Thy princes are rebellious,

And companions of thieves;
Every one loveth bribes,
And followeth after rewards;
They judge not the fatherless,
Neither doth the cause of the widow come unto them.

3. Jerusalem: The Redeemed City

Jerusalem is not portrayed as a perennial victim. The city is seen as a dynamic actor fashioning her own destiny, not merely as a foil for the ambitions of other nations. This aspect of the city's identity will receive additional emphasis later in the Hebrew Bible (see Chapter 7, "Justice").

Zechariah 8:4–8

4 Thus saith the LORD of hosts: There shall yet old men and old women sit in the broad places of Jerusalem, every man with his staff in his hand for very age. 5 And the broad places of the city shall be full of boys and girls playing in the broad places thereof.

6 Thus saith the LORD of hosts: If it be marvellous in the eyes of the remnant of this people in those days, should it also be marvellous in Mine eyes? saith the LORD of hosts.

7 Thus saith the LORD of hosts: Behold, I will save My people from the east country, and from the west country; 8 And I will bring them, and they shall dwell in the midst of Jerusalem; and they shall be My people, and I will be their God, in truth and in righteousness.

Importantly, the Hebrew biblical texts suggest that redemption involves more than just autonomy. Redemption for Jerusalem means that the city will return to its vocation, as the seat of justice—and thus, by implication, as the abode of God, the center of international justice, and the place of unity and joy.

Isaiah 1:16–17, 26–28

16 Wash you, make you clean,
Put away the evil of your doings
From before Mine eyes,
Cease to do evil;
17 Learn to do well;
Seek justice, relieve the oppressed,
Judge the fatherless, plead for the widow.
. . . .

26 And I will restore thy judges as at the first,
And thy counsellors as at the beginning;
Afterward thou shalt be called The city of righteousness,
The faithful city.
27 Zion shall be redeemed with justice,
And they that return of her with righteousness.
28 But the destruction of the transgressors and the sinners shall
    be together,
And they that forsake the LORD shall be consumed.

Jeremiah 3:17–18

17 At that time they shall call Jerusalem The throne of the
LORD; and all the nations shall be gathered unto it, to the name
of the LORD, to Jerusalem; neither shall they walk any more
after the stubbornness of their evil heart. 18 In those days the
house of Judah shall walk with the house of Israel, and they shall
come together out of the land of the north to the land that I have
given for an inheritance unto your fathers.

Zechariah 8:20–23

20 Thus saith the LORD of hosts: It shall yet come to pass, that
there shall come peoples, and the inhabitants of many cities; 21
and the inhabitants of one city shall go to another, saying: Let us
go speedily to entreat the favour of the LORD, and to seek the
LORD of hosts; I will go also. 22 Yea, many peoples and mighty
nations shall come to seek the LORD of hosts in Jerusalem, and
to entreat the favour of the LORD. 23 Thus saith the LORD of
hosts: In those days it shall come to pass, that ten men shall take
hold, out of all the languages of the nations, shall even take hold
of the skirt of him that is a Jew, saying: We will go with you, for
we have heard that God is with you.

Isaiah 2:2–4

2 And it shall come to pass in the end of days,
That the mountain of the LORD'S house
Shall be established as the top of the mountains,
And shall be exalted above the hills;
And all nations shall flow unto it.
3 And many peoples shall go and say:
'Come ye, and let us go up to the mountain of the LORD,

To the house of the God of Jacob;
And He will teach us of His ways,
And we will walk in His paths.'
For out of Zion shall go forth the law,
And the word of the LORD from Jerusalem.
4 And He shall judge between the nations,
And shall decide for many peoples;
And they shall beat their swords into plowshares,
And their spears into pruninghooks;
Nation shall not lift up sword against nation,
Neither shall they learn war any more.

Isaiah 56:7

7 Even them will I bring to My holy mountain,
And make them joyful in My house of prayer;
Their burnt-offerings and their sacrifices
Shall be acceptable upon Mine altar;
For My house shall be called
A house of prayer for all peoples.

For further reading, see Isaiah 62:12, 66:10, and 60:4.

CHAPTER 2
DREAMS

The Hebrew Bible presents dreams not just as personal expressions but also as sources of information about issues of political importance. Note the similarities and differences between Joseph's and Daniel's dreams, and consider how these dreamers envision—or don't envision—the realities of power politics, as well as how the text presents the audiences that hear (willingly or not) their dreams and interpretations.

A. Dreams at the Start of Israelite Communal Existence: Fractured Narratives

The imagery in Joseph's dreams clues in the reader of the Hebrew Bible that these dreams reflect more than just the perplexities of social family dynamics: the image of bowing, which appears in both dreams recounted in Genesis 37, is as politically significant as it is domestically charged. Joseph's relaying of this image sets off his brothers' anger and jealous rage. Their hostile questioning appears to invoke an important distinction in biblical Hebrew pertinent to kingship: "*HaMaLoKH? HaMaSHoL?*" translates as "Shalt thou indeed reign over us? Or shall thou have dominion over us?" Genesis 37:8.[1]

The Hebrew Bible highlights the way that Joseph's awareness of other people grows through his experiences of dream interpretation. This is especially relevant to Joseph's interpretations of dreams in Egypt, whether these are of his fellow prisoners or of the Pharaoh himself. Essentially, the experiences both of having and of interpreting dreams prepare Joseph to

---

1. Readers will notice further on, in the notes to the first section of Chapter 5, "Women," a slightly different configuration of the Hebrew verb translated here as "to have dominion over." This is due to the fact that biblical Hebrew verbs are structured with a two- or three-letter root (*m'l'kh* for "to reign" [or "to rule"], *m'sh'l* for "to have dominion over" in this instance; cf. the commentary by Malbim mentioned in Chapter 5), whose form changes depending on the number and gender of the person who is either the subject or object of the verb. Malbim interprets *m'l'kh* as ruling with people's (or citizens') consent, and *m'sh'l* as implying rule that is imposed upon a group (that accepts the fact of this dominion, but unwillingly).

navigate through the complexities of the Egyptian court, influencing how he phrases his interpretations and suggestions for managing the coming famine through the implementation of revolutionary centralized economic planning.

In reading these texts, it is worthwhile to consider how Joseph is able to grow through his experiences with dreams. What actually changes for Joseph? Are his circumstances in Egypt when interpreting dreams more or less friendly than they had been while living with his family in his ancestral land of Canaan? Do Joseph's roles in these narratives differ in a way that might be accounted for by his moral, psychological, or social growth? What is the difference between dreaming and dream interpretation? Do the tools of modern psychoanalysis help the modern reader better analyze these narratives?

Genesis 37

וישב[2]

1 And Jacob dwelt in the land of his father's sojournings, in the land of Canaan.

2 These are the generations of Jacob. Joseph, being seventeen years old, was feeding the flock with his brethren, being still a lad even with the sons of Bilhah, and with the sons of Zilpah, his father's wives; and Joseph brought evil report of them unto their father. 3 Now Israel loved Joseph more than all his children, because he was the son of his old age; and he made him a coat of many colours. 4 And when his brethren saw that their father loved him more than all his brethren, they hated him, and could not speak peaceably unto him.

5 And Joseph dreamed a dream, and he told it to his brethren; and they hated him yet the more. 6 And he said unto them: 'Hear, I pray you, this dream which I have dreamed: 7 for, behold, we were binding sheaves in the field, and, lo, my sheaf arose, and also stood upright; and, behold, your sheaves came round about, and bowed down to my sheaf.' 8 And his brethren said to him: 'Shalt thou indeed reign over us? or shalt thou indeed have dominion over us?' And they hated him yet the more for his dreams, and for his words.

---

2. In keeping with the traditional presentation of the JPS 1917 translation, I have retained the names of the weekly synagogue Torah readings, as included in the Hebrew.

9 And he dreamed yet another dream, and told it to his brethren, and said: 'Behold, I have dreamed yet a dream: and, behold, the sun and the moon and eleven stars bowed down to me.' 10 And he told it to his father, and to his brethren; and his father rebuked him, and said unto him: 'What is this dream that thou hast dreamed? Shall I and thy mother and thy brethren indeed come to bow down to thee to the earth?' 11 And his brethren envied him; but his father kept the saying in mind.

12 And his brethren went to feed their father's flock in Shechem. 13 And Israel said unto Joseph: 'Do not thy brethren feed the flock in Shechem? come, and I will send thee unto them.' And he said to him: 'Here am I.' 14 And he said to him: 'Go now, see whether it is well with thy brethren, and well with the flock; and bring me back word.' So he sent him out of the vale of Hebron, and he came to Shechem. 15 And a certain man found him, and, behold, he was wandering in the field. And the man asked him, saying: 'What seekest thou?' 16 And he said: 'I seek my brethren. Tell me, I pray thee, where they are feeding the flock.' 17 And the man said: 'They are departed hence; for I heard them say: Let us go to Dothan.' And Joseph went after his brethren, and found them in Dothan.

18 And they saw him afar off, and before he came near unto them, they conspired against him to slay him. 19 And they said one to another: 'Behold, this dreamer cometh. 20 Come now therefore, and let us slay him, and cast him into one of the pits, and we will say: An evil beast hath devoured him; and we shall see what will become of his dreams.' 21 And Reuben heard it, and delivered him out of their hand; and said: 'Let us not take his life.' 22 And Reuben said unto them: 'Shed no blood; cast him into this pit that is in the wilderness, but lay no hand upon him'—that he might deliver him out of their hand, to restore him to his father.

23 And it came to pass, when Joseph was come unto his brethren, that they stripped Joseph of his coat, the coat of many colours that was on him; 24 and they took him, and cast him into the pit—and the pit was empty, there was no water in it. 25 And they sat down to eat bread; and they lifted up their eyes and looked, and, behold, a caravan of Ishmaelites came from Gilead, with their camels bearing spicery and balm and ladanum, going to carry it down to Egypt.

26 And Judah said unto his brethren: 'What profit is it if we slay our brother and conceal his blood? 27 Come, and let us sell him to the Ishmaelites, and let not our hand be upon him; for he is our brother, our flesh.' And his brethren hearkened unto him. 28 And there passed by Midianites, merchantmen; and they drew and lifted up Joseph out of the pit, and sold Joseph to the Ishmaelites for twenty shekels of silver. And they brought Joseph into Egypt.

29 And Reuben returned unto the pit; and, behold, Joseph was not in the pit; and he rent his clothes. 30 And he returned unto his brethren, and said: 'The child is not; and as for me, whither shall I go?' 31 And they took Joseph's coat, and killed a he-goat, and dipped the coat in the blood; 32 and they sent the coat of many colours, and they brought it to their father; and said: 'This have we found. Know now whether it is thy son's coat or not.' 33 And he knew it, and said: 'It is my son's coat; an evil beast hath devoured him; Joseph is without doubt torn in pieces.'

34 And Jacob rent his garments, and put sackcloth upon his loins, and mourned for his son many days. 35 And all his sons and all his daughters rose up to comfort him; but he refused to be comforted; and he said: 'Nay, but I will go down to the grave to my son mourning.' And his father wept for him. 36 And the Medanites sold him into Egypt unto Potiphar, an officer of Pharaoh's, the captain of the guard.

The following selection describes Joseph's experiences in interpreting dreams from the bowels of an Egyptian prison.

Genesis 40

1 And it came to pass after these things, that the butler of the king of Egypt and his baker offended their lord the king of Egypt. 2 And Pharaoh was wroth against his two officers, against the chief of the butlers, and against the chief of the bakers. 3 And he put them in ward in the house of the captain of the guard, into the prison, the place where Joseph was bound. 4 And the captain of the guard charged Joseph to be with them, and he ministered unto them; and they continued a season in ward. 5 And they dreamed a dream both of them, each man his dream, in one night, each man according to the interpretation of his dream, the butler and the baker of the king of Egypt, who were bound in the prison.

6 And Joseph came in unto them in the morning, and saw them, and, behold, they were sad. 7 And he asked Pharaoh's officers that were with him in the ward of his master's house, saying: 'Wherefore look ye so sad to-day?' 8 And they said unto him: 'We have dreamed a dream, and there is none that can interpret it.' And Joseph said unto them: 'Do not interpretations belong to God? tell it me, I pray you.'

9 And the chief butler told his dream to Joseph, and said to him: 'In my dream, behold, a vine was before me; 10 and in the vine were three branches; and as it was budding, its blossoms shot forth, and the clusters thereof brought forth ripe grapes, 11 and Pharaoh's cup was in my hand; and I took the grapes, and pressed them into Pharaoh's cup, and I gave the cup into Pharaoh's hand.'

12 And Joseph said unto him: 'This is the interpretation of it: the three branches are three days; 13 within yet three days shall Pharaoh lift up thy head, and restore thee unto thine office; and thou shalt give Pharaoh's cup into his hand, after the former manner when thou wast his butler. 14 But have me in thy remembrance when it shall be well with thee, and show kindness, I pray thee, unto me, and make mention of me unto Pharaoh, and bring me out of this house. 15 For indeed I was stolen away out of the land of the Hebrews; and here also have I done nothing that they should put me into the dungeon.'

16 When the chief baker saw that the interpretation was good, he said unto Joseph: 'I also saw in my dream, and, behold, three baskets of white bread were on my head; 17 and in the uppermost basket there was of all manner of baked food for Pharaoh; and the birds did eat them out of the basket upon my head.'

18 And Joseph answered and said: 'This is the interpretation thereof: the three baskets are three days; 19 within yet three days shall Pharaoh lift up thy head from off thee, and shall hang thee on a tree; and the birds shall eat thy flesh from off thee.'

20 And it came to pass the third day, which was Pharaoh's birthday, that he made a feast unto all his servants; and he lifted up the head of the chief butler and the head of the chief baker among his servants. 21 And he restored the chief butler back unto his butlership; and he gave the cup into Pharaoh's hand. 22 But he hanged the chief baker, as Joseph had interpreted to

them. 23 Yet did not the chief butler remember Joseph, but forgot him.

In the next selection, Joseph is equal to the challenge of interpreting Pharaoh's dream in a way that satisfies both Pharaoh's overt and hidden questions: he provides Pharaoh with a sense of closure that also incorporates the country's future trajectory.

Genesis 41

1 And it came to pass at the end of two full years, that Pharaoh is dreaming:[3] and, behold, he stood by the river.[4]

2 And, behold, there came up out of the river seven kine, well-favoured and fat-fleshed; and they fed in the reed-grass. 3 And, behold, seven other kine came up after them out of the river, ill-favoured and lean-fleshed; and stood by the other kine upon the brink of the river. 4 And the ill-favoured and lean-fleshed kine did eat up the seven well-favoured and fat kine. So Pharaoh awoke. 5 And he slept and dreamed a second time: and, behold, seven ears of corn came up upon one stalk, rank and good. 6 And, behold, seven ears, thin and blasted with the east wind, sprung up after them. 7 And the thin ears swallowed up the seven rank and full ears. And Pharaoh awoke, and, behold, it was a dream.

8 And it came to pass in the morning that his spirit was troubled; and he sent and called for all the magicians of Egypt, and all the wise men thereof; and Pharaoh told them his dream; but there was none that could interpret them unto Pharaoh.

9 Then spoke the chief butler unto Pharaoh, saying: 'I make mention of my faults this day: 10 Pharaoh was wroth with his servants, and put me in the ward of the house of the captain of

---

3. JPS 1917: "that Pharaoh dreamed." In this case, I have chosen to use the present continuous form of the verb as most directly reflecting the actual verb tense employed by the Hebrew Bible. The Midrash, sensitive to the nuances of language and vocabulary in the Hebrew biblical text, focuses on the seeming dissonant use of this tense (after all, the Hebrew Bible is relating a story that already happened, and all of the other verbs in the story are constructed in the past tense) and points out that the strange use of the present continuous form of the verb "to be" (i.e., "is dreaming") highlights one aspect of what was disturbing to Pharaoh about the dream: that it was neither a past nor a merely unfinished event, but had an emphatically recurrent and ongoing quality; Pharaoh is dreaming a dream that he has been continuously dreaming for two years (i.e., "at the end of two full years, Pharaoh was [still] dreaming"). For more on this issue, see my *Conceiving a Nation*, esp. pp. 18–24.

4. [[That is, the Nile.—JPS 1917 eds.]]

the guard, me and the chief baker. 11 And we dreamed a dream in one night, I and he; we dreamed each man according to the interpretation of his dream. 12 And there was with us there a young man, a Hebrew, servant to the captain of the guard; and we told him, and he interpreted to us our dreams; to each man according to his dream he did interpret.

13 And it came to pass, as he interpreted to us, so it was: I was restored unto mine office, and he was hanged.' 14 Then Pharaoh sent and called Joseph, and they brought him hastily out of the dungeon. And he shaved himself, and changed his raiment, and came in unto Pharaoh.

15 And Pharaoh said unto Joseph: 'I have dreamed a dream, and there is none that can interpret it; and I have heard say of thee, that when thou hearest a dream thou canst interpret it.' 16 And Joseph answered Pharaoh, saying: 'It is not in me; God will give Pharaoh an answer of peace.'

17 And Pharaoh spoke unto Joseph: 'In my dream, behold, I stood upon the brink of the river. 18 And, behold, there came up out of the river seven kine, fat-fleshed and well-favoured; and they fed in the reed-grass. 19 And, behold, seven other kine came up after them, poor and very ill-favoured and lean-fleshed, such as I never saw in all the land of Egypt for badness. 20 And the lean and ill-favoured kine did eat up the first seven fat kine. 21 And when they had eaten them up, it could not be known that they had eaten them; but they were still ill-favoured as at the beginning. So I awoke. 22 And I saw in my dream, and, behold, seven ears came up upon one stalk, full and good. 23 And, behold, seven ears, withered, thin, and blasted with the east wind, sprung up after them. 24 And the thin ears swallowed up the seven good ears. And I told it unto the magicians; but there was none that could declare it to me.'

25 And Joseph said unto Pharaoh: 'The dream of Pharaoh is one; what God is about to do He hath declared unto Pharaoh. 26 The seven good kine are seven years; and the seven good ears are seven years: the dream is one. 27 And the seven lean and ill-favoured kine that came up after them are seven years, and also the seven empty ears blasted with the east wind; they shall be seven years of famine. 28 That is the thing which I spoke unto Pharaoh: what God is about to do He hath shown unto Pharaoh. 29 Behold, there come seven years of great plenty throughout

all the land of Egypt. 30 And there shall arise after them seven years of famine; and all the plenty shall be forgotten in the land of Egypt; and the famine shall consume the land; 31 and the plenty shall not be known in the land by reason of that famine which followeth; for it shall be very grievous. 32 And for that the dream was doubled unto Pharaoh twice, it is because the thing is established by God, and God will shortly bring it to pass.

33 Now therefore let Pharaoh look out a man discreet and wise, and set him over the land of Egypt. 34 Let Pharaoh do this, and let him appoint overseers over the land, and take up the fifth part of the land of Egypt in the seven years of plenty. 35 And let them gather all the food of these good years that come, and lay up corn under the hand of Pharaoh for food in the cities, and let them keep it. 36 And the food shall be for a store to the land against the seven years of famine, which shall be in the land of Egypt; that the land perish not through the famine.'

37 And the thing was good in the eyes of Pharaoh, and in the eyes of all his servants. 38 And Pharaoh said unto his servants: 'Can we find such a one as this, a man in whom the spirit of God is?' 39 And Pharaoh said unto Joseph: 'Forasmuch as God hath shown thee all this, there is none so discreet and wise as thou. 40 Thou shalt be over my house, and according unto thy word shall all my people be ruled; only in the throne will I be greater than thou.' 41 And Pharaoh said unto Joseph: 'See, I have set thee over all the land of Egypt.'

42 And Pharaoh took off his signet ring from his hand, and put it upon Joseph's hand, and arrayed him in vestures of fine linen, and put a gold chain about his neck. 43 And he made him to ride in the second chariot which he had; and they cried before him: 'Abrech'; and he set him over all the land of Egypt. 44 And Pharaoh said unto Joseph: 'I am Pharaoh, and without thee shall no man lift up his hand or his foot in all the land of Egypt.' 45 And Pharaoh called Joseph's name Zaphenath-paneah; and he gave him to wife Asenath the daughter of Poti-phera priest of On. And Joseph went out over the land of Egypt.—

46 And Joseph was thirty years old when he stood before Pharaoh king of Egypt.—And Joseph went out from the presence of Pharaoh, and went throughout all the land of Egypt. 47 And in the seven years of plenty the earth brought forth in heaps. 48 And he gathered up all the food of the seven years which were

in the land of Egypt, and laid up the food in the cities; the food of the field, which was round about every city, laid he up in the same. 49 And Joseph laid up corn as the sand of the sea, very much, until they left off numbering; for it was without number.

50 And unto Joseph were born two sons before the year of famine came, whom Asenath the daughter of Potiphera priest of On bore unto him. 51 And Joseph called the name of the first-born Manasseh:[5] 'for God hath made me forget all my toil, and all my father's house.' 52 And the name of the second called he Ephraim:[6] 'for God hath made me fruitful in the land of my affliction.' 53 And the seven years of plenty, that was in the land of Egypt, came to an end. 54 And the seven years of famine began to come, according as Joseph had said; and there was famine in all lands; but in all the land of Egypt there was bread. 55 And when all the land of Egypt was famished, the people cried to Pharaoh for bread; and Pharaoh said unto all the Egyptians: 'Go unto Joseph; what he saith to you, do.' 56 And the famine was over all the face of the earth; and Joseph opened all the storehouses, and sold unto the Egyptians; and the famine was sore in the land of Egypt. 57 And all countries came into Egypt to Joseph to buy corn; because the famine was sore in all the earth.

B. Dreams as Structuring Political Understanding

The Hebrew Bible presents dreams as experiential "texts" that can help their protagonists work through anticipated challenges in ruling (e.g., Solomon, Nebuchadnezzar). Dreams that need decoding provide opportunities for their interpreters to improve their own or their communities' standing at the royal court (Daniel and, as we have previously seen, Joseph). The dream that Daniel interprets, centering on the rise and fall of empires, and the implied political and moral closure of history, recalls similar themes adumbrated in Abraham's Covenant Between the Pieces (see Chapter 3; Genesis 15:1–21). Historical closure is also presented in the dreams that are harbingers of the Redemptive Apocalypse (see Chapter 2; Jeremiah 24:1–10).

In reading these texts, consider how dream interpretation varies with circumstances of time and place (for Nebuchadnezzar's dream, see Chapter 2. C.: Royal Dream Interpretation in Exile, below). Daniel, like Joseph,

---

5. [[That is, Making to forget.—JPS 1917 eds.]]

6. [[From a Hebrew word signifying to be fruitful.—JPS 1917 eds.]]

interprets as an exiled captive (see further, chapter 1 of the Book of Daniel), but the circumstances of these two interpreters differ significantly, as Daniel is depicted as more subjected to the vagaries of court infighting than is Joseph. How are Nebuchadnezzar's character and reaction to his own dream portrayed in comparison to the description of Pharaoh and his approach to the interpretation of his dream?

1. Solomon's Dream

I Kings 3:5–15

5 In Gibeon the LORD appeared to Solomon in a dream by night; and God said: 'Ask what I shall give thee.' 6 And Solomon said: 'Thou hast shown unto Thy servant David my father great kindness, according as he walked before Thee in truth, and in righteousness, and in uprightness of heart with Thee; and Thou hast kept for him this great kindness, that Thou hast given him a son to sit on his throne, as it is this day. 7 And now, O LORD my God, Thou hast made Thy servant king instead of David my father; and I am but a little child; I know not how to go out or come in. 8 And Thy servant is in the midst of Thy people which Thou hast chosen, a great people, that cannot be numbered nor counted for multitude.

9 Give Thy servant therefore an understanding heart to judge Thy people, that I may discern between good and evil; for who is able to judge this Thy great people?' 10 And the speech pleased the LORD, that Solomon had asked this thing.

11 And God said unto him: 'Because thou hast asked this thing, and hast not asked for thyself long life; neither hast asked riches for thyself, nor hast asked the life of thine enemies; but hast asked for thyself understanding to discern justice; 12 behold, I have done according to thy word: lo, I have given thee a wise and an understanding heart; so that there hath been none like thee before thee, neither after thee shall any arise like unto thee. 13 And I have also given thee that which thou hast not asked, both riches and honour—so that there hath not been any among the kings like unto thee—all thy days. 14 And if thou wilt walk in My ways, to keep My statutes and My commandments, as thy father David did walk, then I will lengthen thy days.'

15 And Solomon awoke, and, behold, it was a dream; and he came to Jerusalem, and stood before the ark of the covenant of the LORD, and offered up burnt-offerings, and offered peace-offerings, and made a feast to all his servants.

2. Royal Dream Interpretation in Exile

Daniel's experience with dream interpretation in exile is no less fraught than Joseph's. Indeed, one could argue that, as a member of an exiled nation with built-in political and ethnic enemies at the Babylonian court, Daniel stood in greater personal danger than Joseph, whose own danger, at the time of his dream interpretation to Pharaoh, seemed to consist mainly in being remanded back to prison. Daniel must perform a nearly magical act: to both reveal and interpret a hidden dream of the unpredictable king, Nebuchadnezzar.

Daniel 2

1 And in the second year of the reign of Nebuchadnezzar, Nebuchadnezzar dreamed dreams; and his spirit was troubled, and his sleep broke from him. 2 Then the king commanded to call the magicians, and the enchanters, and the sorcerers, and the Chaldeans, to tell the king his dreams. So they came and stood before the king. 3 And the king said unto them: 'I have dreamed a dream, and my spirit is troubled to know the dream.' 4 Then spoke the Chaldeans to the king in Aramaic: 'O king, live for ever! tell thy servants the dream, and we will declare the interpretation.' 5 The king answered and said to the Chaldeans: 'The thing is certain with me; if ye make not known unto me the dream and the interpretation thereof, ye shall be cut in pieces, and your houses shall be made a dunghill. 6 But if ye declare the dream and the interpretation thereof, ye shall receive of me gifts and rewards and great honour; only declare unto me the dream and the interpretation thereof.' 7 They answered the second time and said: 'Let the king tell his servants the dream, and we will declare the interpretation.' 8 The king answered and said: 'I know of a truth that ye would gain time, inasmuch as ye see the thing is certain with me, 9 that, if ye make not known unto me the dream, there is but one law for you; and ye have agreed together to speak before me lying and corrupt words, till the time be changed; only tell me the dream, and I shall know that ye can declare unto me

the interpretation thereof.' 10 The Chaldeans answered before the king, and said: 'There is not a man upon the earth that can declare the king's matter; forasmuch as no great and powerful king hath asked such a thing of any magician, or enchanter, or Chaldean. 11 And it is a hard thing that the king asketh, and there is none other that can declare it before the king, except the gods, whose dwelling is not with flesh.' 12 For this cause the king was angry and very furious, and commanded to destroy all the wise men of Babylon. 13 So the decree went forth, and the wise men were to be slain; and they sought Daniel and his companions to be slain.

14 Then Daniel returned answer with counsel and discretion to Arioch the captain of the king's guard, who was gone forth to slay the wise men of Babylon; 15 he answered and said to Arioch the king's captain: 'Wherefore is the decree so peremptory from the king?' Then Arioch made the thing known to Daniel. 16 Then Daniel went in, and desired of the king that he would give him time, that he might declare unto the king the interpretation.

17 Then Daniel went to his house, and made the thing known to Hananiah, Mishael, and Azariah, his companions; 18 that they might ask mercy of the God of heaven concerning this secret; that Daniel and his companions should not perish with the rest of the wise men of Babylon. 19 Then was the secret revealed unto Daniel in a vision of the night. Then Daniel blessed the God of heaven. 20 Daniel spoke and said:

Blessed be the name of God
From everlasting even unto everlasting;
For wisdom and might are His;
21 And He changeth the times and the seasons;
He removeth kings, and setteth up kings;
He giveth wisdom unto the wise,
And knowledge to them that know understanding;
22 He revealeth the deep and secret things;
He knoweth what is in the darkness,
And the light dwelleth with Him.
23 I thank Thee, and praise Thee,
O Thou God of my fathers,
Who hast given me wisdom and might,

And hast now made known unto me what we desired of Thee;
For Thou hast made known unto us the king's matter.

24 Therefore Daniel went in unto Arioch, whom the king
had appointed to destroy the wise men of Babylon; he went
and said thus unto him: 'Destroy not the wise men of Babylon;
bring me in before the king, and I will declare unto the king the
interpretation.'

25 Then Arioch brought in Daniel before the king in haste,
and said thus unto him: 'I have found a man of the children of
the captivity of Judah, that will make known unto the king the
interpretation.' 26 The king spoke and said to Daniel, whose
name was Belteshazzar: 'Art thou able to make known unto me
the dream which I have seen, and the interpretation thereof?' 27
Daniel answered before the king, and said: 'The secret which the
king hath asked can neither wise men, enchanters, magicians,
nor astrologers, declare unto the king; 28 but there is a God
in heaven that revealeth secrets, and He hath made known to
the king Nebuchadnezzar what shall be in the end of days. Thy
dream, and the visions of thy head upon thy bed, are these: 29
as for thee, O king, thy thoughts came [into thy mind] upon thy
bed, what should come to pass hereafter; and He that revealeth
secrets hath made known to thee what shall come to pass. 30 But
as for me, this secret is not revealed to me for any wisdom that I
have more than any living, but to the intent that the interpretation may be made known to the king, and that thou mayest know
the thoughts of thy heart.

31 Thou, O king, sawest, and behold a great image. This image,
which was mighty, and whose brightness was surpassing, stood
before thee; and the appearance thereof was terrible. 32 As for
that image, its head was of fine gold, its breast and its arms of
silver, its belly and its thighs of brass, 33 its legs of iron, its feet
part of iron and part of clay. 34 Thou sawest till that a stone was
cut out without hands, which smote the image upon its feet
that were of iron and clay, and broke them to pieces. 35 Then
was the iron, the clay, the brass, the silver, and the gold, broken
in pieces together, and became like the chaff of the summer
threshing-floors; and the wind carried them away, so that no
place was found for them; and the stone that smote the image
became a great mountain, and filled the whole earth. 36 This

is the dream; and we will tell the interpretation thereof before the king.

37 Thou, O king, king of kings, unto whom the God of heaven hath given the kingdom, the power, and the strength, and the glory; 38 and wheresoever the children of men, the beasts of the field, and the fowls of the heaven dwell, hath He given them into thy hand, and hath made thee to rule over them all; thou art the head of gold. 39 And after thee shall arise another kingdom inferior to thee; and another third kingdom of brass, which shall bear rule over all the earth. 40 And the fourth kingdom shall be strong as iron; forasmuch as iron breaketh in pieces and beateth down all things; and as iron that crusheth all these, shall it break in pieces and crush. 41 And whereas thou sawest the feet and toes, part of potters' clay, and part of iron, it shall be a divided kingdom; but there shall be in it of the firmness of the iron, forasmuch as thou sawest the iron mixed with miry clay. 42 And as the toes of the feet were part of iron, and part of clay, so part of the kingdom shall be strong, and part thereof broken. 43 And whereas thou sawest the iron mixed with miry clay, they shall mingle themselves by the seed of men; but they shall not cleave one to another, even as iron doth not mingle with clay. 44 And in the days of those kings shall the God of heaven set up a kingdom, which shall never be destroyed; nor shall the kingdom be left to another people; it shall break in pieces and consume all these kingdoms, but it shall stand for ever. 45 Forasmuch as thou sawest that a stone was cut out of the mountain without hands, and that it broke in pieces the iron, the brass, the clay, the silver, and the gold; the great God hath made known to the king what shall come to pass hereafter; and the dream is certain, and the interpretation thereof sure.' 46 Then the king Nebuchadnezzar fell upon his face, and worshipped Daniel, and commanded that they should offer an offering and sweet odours unto him. 47 The king spoke unto Daniel, and said: 'Of a truth it is, that your God is the God of gods, and the Lord of kings, and a revealer of secrets, seeing thou hast been able to reveal this secret.' 48 Then the king made Daniel great, and gave him many great gifts, and made him to rule over the whole province of Babylon, and to be chief prefect over all the wise men of Babylon. 49 And Daniel requested of the king, and he appointed Shadrach, Meshach, and Abed-nego, over the affairs of the province of Babylon; but Daniel was in the gate of the king.

C. Dreams as a Function of Hope: The Pre-Redemption Apocalypse

In the next reading, dreams utilize natural symbols to predict the final redemption as a hopeful and fruitful experience. This dream reverses the expected doom of history, and instead views the future as the source of hope and joy.

Jeremiah 24

1 The LORD showed me, and behold two baskets of figs set before the temple of the LORD; after that Nebuchadrezzar king of Babylon had carried away captive Jeconiah the son of Jehoiakim, king of Judah, and the princes of Judah, with the craftsmen and smiths, from Jerusalem, and had brought them to Babylon. 2 One basket had very good figs, like the figs that are first-ripe; and the other basket had very bad figs, which could not be eaten, they were so bad. 3 Then said the LORD unto me: 'What seest thou, Jeremiah?' And I said: 'Figs; the good figs, very good; and the bad, very bad, that cannot be eaten, they are so bad.'

4 And the word of the LORD came unto me, saying: 5 'Thus saith the LORD, the God of Israel: Like these good figs, so will I regard the captives of Judah, whom I have sent out of this place into the land of the Chaldeans, for good. 6 And I will set Mine eyes upon them for good, and I will bring them back to this land; and I will build them, and not pull them down; and I will plant them, and not pluck them up. 7 And I will give them a heart to know Me, that I am the LORD; and they shall be My people, and I will be their God; for they shall return unto Me with their whole heart. 8 And as the bad figs, which cannot be eaten, they are so bad; surely thus saith the LORD: So will I make Zedekiah the king of Judah, and his princes, and the residue of Jerusalem, that remain in this land, and them that dwell in the land of Egypt; 9 I will even make them a horror among all the kingdoms of the earth for evil; a reproach and a proverb, a taunt and a curse, in all places whither I shall drive them. 10 And I will send the sword, the famine, and the pestilence, among them, till they be consumed from off the land that I gave unto them and to their fathers.'

For further reading, see Jeremiah 25:15–27.

CHAPTER 3

COVENANT

In the Hebrew biblical text, covenant is more than a simple exchange; rather, it signifies an agreement to a reciprocal set of activities or undertakings (a contract) that affects the identities and relationships of the parties to the covenant. These identity-bound exchanges are not always explicitly formulated; sometimes the exchange is implicit. In the covenant with Noah, when God promises not to destroy the world, the implied exchange (in the preceding verses Genesis 9:1–7) is that people shall no longer act with untrammeled violence towards one another.

In the case of the Covenant Between the Pieces, with Abraham (Genesis 15:1–21), the Hebrew biblical text essentially stipulates that Abraham already had demonstrated his ability to keep the terms of the covenant ("And he believed in the LORD; and He counted it to him for righteousness" [Genesis 15:6]). In return, God covenants that the sweep of history for Abraham's descendants would have moral (and political) closure and would not be merely a series of arbitrary events (Genesis 15:12–21); this section, specifying the historical account of what would befall Abraham's descendants, may be read as a second part of the Covenant Between the Pieces, whose first part (1–11), not included in this volume, focuses on Abraham's childlessness and the ritual aspects of the Covenant Between the Pieces. In addition, as reiterated often in Genesis and also in Exodus, Abraham is promised the land of Canaan for his descendants in perpetuity. The covenant of circumcision is likewise ongoing and projects forward into history: circumcision is a sign of belonging to the Abrahamic clan.

Finally, there is the national covenant at Sinai, in which the Israelites are taken as God's people and are consequently expected to observe the range of commandments given in the Torah. In the pages of the Hebrew Bible, the Israelites' frequent failure to keep their part of the national covenant forms a major theme of the Later Prophets, with the consequent punishments that occur for this breach. God's people are no longer beneficiaries of the promise of historical closure; they are driven from their Promised Land and thrown defenseless into exile. However, as the text in Amos 7 makes clear (see below in Chapter 15, "Standing up for the Israelites"), the fact of the covenant overrides the particular terms of the covenant: the relationship itself is never broken.

In reading these texts, note the differences among all these episodes of covenant. Who are the parties to each covenant? Who is affected by each covenant? What differences exist between the covenants with Abraham and the covenant with Noah? How does the expression of the national covenant change between the episode at Sinai/Horeb and the Israelites' entry to their Promised Land? To what can these differences be ascribed?

A. The Covenant with Noah

Genesis 9:9–17

9 'As for Me, behold, I establish My covenant with you, and with your seed after you; 10 and with every living creature that is with you, the fowl, the cattle, and every beast of the earth with you; of all that go out of the ark, even every beast of the earth. 11 And I will establish My covenant with you; neither shall all flesh be cut off any more by the waters of the flood; neither shall there any more be a flood to destroy the earth.' 12 And God said: 'This is the token of the covenant which I make between Me and you and every living creature that is with you, for perpetual generations: 13 I have set My bow in the cloud, and it shall be for a token of a covenant between Me and the earth. 14 And it shall come to pass, when I bring clouds over the earth, and the bow is seen in the cloud, 15 that I will remember My covenant, which is between Me and you and every living creature of all flesh; and the waters shall no more become a flood to destroy all flesh. 16 And the bow shall be in the cloud; and I will look upon it, that I may remember the everlasting covenant between God and every living creature of all flesh that is upon the earth.' 17 And God said unto Noah: 'This is the sign[1] of the covenant which I have established between Me and all flesh that is upon the earth.'

---

1. JPS 1917: "token."

B. The Covenant of History with Abraham

Genesis 15:7–21

7 And He said unto him: 'I am the LORD that brought thee out of Ur of the Chaldees, to give thee this land to inherit it.' 8 And he said: 'O Lord GOD, whereby shall I know that I shall inherit it?' 9 And He said unto him: 'Take Me a heifer of three years old, and a she-goat of three years old, and a ram of three years old, and a turtle-dove, and a young pigeon.' 10 And he took him all these, and divided them in the midst, and laid each half over against the other; but the birds divided he not. 11 And the birds of prey came down upon the carcasses, and Abram drove them away. 12 And it came to pass, that, when the sun was going down, a deep sleep fell upon Abram; and, lo, a dread, even a great darkness, fell upon him. 13 And He said unto Abram: 'Know of a surety that thy seed shall be a stranger in a land that is not theirs, and shall serve them; and they shall afflict them four hundred years; 14 and also that nation, whom they shall serve, will I judge; and afterward shall they come out with great substance. 15 But thou shalt go to thy fathers in peace; thou shalt be buried in a good old age. 16 And in the fourth generation they shall come back hither; for the iniquity of the Amorite is not yet full.' 17 And it came to pass, that, when the sun went down, and there was thick darkness, behold a smoking furnace, and a flaming torch that passed between these pieces. 18 In that day the LORD made a covenant with Abram, saying: 'Unto thy seed have I given this land, from the river of Egypt unto the great river, the river Euphrates; 19 the Kenite, and the Kenizzite, and the Kadmonite, 20 and the Hittite, and the Perizzite, and the Rephaim, 21 and the Amorite, and the Canaanite, and the Girgashite, and the Jebusite.'

C. The Covenant of Belonging

Genesis 17:1–14

1 And when Abram[2] was ninety years old and nine, the LORD appeared to Abram, and said unto him: 'I am God Almighty; walk before Me, and be thou wholehearted. 2 And I will make My

---

2. At this point in the text, Abram's name has not yet been changed to Abraham. This change is noted in Genesis 17:5.

covenant between Me and thee, and will multiply thee exceedingly.' 3 And Abram fell on his face; and God talked with him, saying: 4 'As for Me, behold, My covenant is with thee, and thou shalt be the father of a multitude of nations. 5 Neither shall thy name any more be called Abram, but thy name shall be Abraham; for the father of a multitude of nations have I made thee. 6 And I will make thee exceeding fruitful, and I will make nations of thee, and kings shall come out of thee. 7 And I will establish My covenant between Me and thee and thy seed after thee throughout their generations for an everlasting covenant, to be a God unto thee and to thy seed after thee. 8 And I will give unto thee, and to thy seed after thee, the land of thy sojournings, all the land of Canaan, for an everlasting possession; and I will be their God.' 9 And God said unto Abraham: 'And as for thee, thou shalt keep My covenant, thou, and thy seed after thee throughout their generations. 10 This is My covenant, which ye shall keep, between Me and you and thy seed after thee: every male among you shall be circumcised. 11 And ye shall be circumcised in the flesh of your foreskin; and it shall be a token of a covenant betwixt Me and you. 12 And he that is eight days old shall be circumcised among you, every male throughout your generations, he that is born in the house, or bought with money of any foreigner, that is not of thy seed. 13 He that is born in thy house, and he that is bought with thy money, must needs be circumcised; and My covenant shall be in your flesh for an everlasting covenant. 14 And the uncircumcised male who is not circumcised in the flesh of his foreskin, that soul shall be cut off from his people; he hath broken My covenant.'

D. The Covenant with the Land and the People Reiterated

Exodus 6:2–8

2 And God spoke unto Moses, and said unto him: 'I am the LORD;

3 and I appeared unto Abraham, unto Isaac, and unto Jacob, as God Almighty, but by My name[3] יהוה I made Me not known to them. 4 And I have also established My covenant with them,

---

3. [[The ineffable name, read *Adonai*, which means *the Lord*.—JPS 1917 eds.]]

to give them the land of Canaan, the land of their sojournings, wherein they sojourned. 5 And moreover I have heard the groaning of the children of Israel, whom the Egyptians keep in bondage; and I have remembered My covenant. 6 Wherefore say unto the children of Israel: I am the LORD, and I will bring you out from under the burdens of the Egyptians, and I will deliver you from their bondage, and I will redeem you with an outstretched arm, and with great judgments; 7 and I will take you to Me for a people, and I will be to you a God; and ye shall know that I am the LORD your God, who brought you out from under the burdens of the Egyptians. 8 And I will bring you in unto the land, concerning which I lifted up My hand to give it to Abraham, to Isaac, and to Jacob; and I will give it you for a heritage: I am the LORD.'

E. The National Covenant at Sinai

Exodus 24:3–8

3 And Moses came and told the people all the words of the LORD, and all the ordinances; and all the people answered with one voice, and said: 'All the words which the Lord hath spoken will we do.' 4 And Moses wrote all the words of the LORD, and rose up early in the morning, and builded an altar under the mount, and twelve pillars, according to the twelve tribes of Israel. 5 And he sent the young men of the children of Israel, who offered burnt-offerings, and sacrificed peace-offerings of oxen unto the LORD. 6 And Moses took half of the blood, and put it in basins; and half of the blood he dashed against the altar. 7 And he took the book of the covenant, and read in the hearing of the people; and they said: 'All that the LORD hath spoken will we do, and obey.' 8 And Moses took the blood, and sprinkled it on the people, and said: 'Behold the blood of the covenant, which the LORD hath made with you in agreement with all these words.'

F. The Covenant at Entry to the Promised Land

Deuteronomy 7:12–15

12 And it shall come to pass, because ye hearken to these ordinances, and keep, and do them, that the LORD thy God shall

keep with thee the covenant and the mercy which He swore unto thy fathers, 13 and He will love thee, and bless thee, and multiply thee; He will also bless the fruit of thy body and the fruit of thy land, thy corn and thy wine and thine oil, the increase of thy kine and the young of thy flock, in the land which He swore unto thy fathers to give thee. 14 Thou shalt be blessed above all peoples; there shall not be male or female barren among you, or among your cattle. 15 And the LORD will take away from thee all sickness; and He will put none of the evil diseases of Egypt, which thou knowest, upon thee, but will lay them upon all them that hate thee.

Deuteronomy 28:69, 29

69 These are the words of the covenant which the LORD commanded Moses to make with the children of Israel in the land of Moab, beside the covenant which He made with them in Horeb.

1 And Moses called unto all Israel, and said unto them:

Ye have seen all that the LORD did before your eyes in the land of Egypt unto Pharaoh, and unto all his servants, and unto all his land; 2 the great trials which thine eyes saw, the signs and those great wonders; 3 but the LORD hath not given you a heart to know, and eyes to see, and ears to hear, unto this day. 4 And I have led you forty years in the wilderness; your clothes are not waxen old upon you, and thy shoe is not waxen old upon thy foot. 5 Ye have not eaten bread, neither have ye drunk wine or strong drink; that ye might know that I am the LORD your God. 6 And when ye came unto this place, Sihon the king of Heshbon, and Og the king of Bashan, came out against us unto battle, and we smote them. 7 And we took their land, and gave it for an inheritance unto the Reubenites, and to the Gadites, and to the half-tribe of the Manassites. 8 Observe therefore the words of this covenant, and do them, that ye may make all that ye do to prosper.

נצבים

9 Ye are standing this day all of you before the LORD your God: your heads, your tribes, your elders, and your officers, even all the men of Israel, 10 your little ones, your wives, and thy stranger that is in the midst of thy camp, from the hewer of thy wood unto the drawer of thy water; 11 that thou shouldest enter into the covenant of the LORD thy God—and into His

oath—which the LORD thy God maketh with thee this day; 12 that He may establish thee this day unto Himself for a people, and that He may be unto thee a God, as He spoke unto thee, and as He swore unto thy fathers, to Abraham, to Isaac, and to Jacob. 13 Neither with you only do I make this covenant and this oath; 14 but with him that standeth here with us this day before the LORD our God, and also with him that is not here with us this day— 15 for ye know how we dwelt in the land of Egypt; and how we came through the midst of the nations through which ye passed; 16 and ye have seen their detestable things, and their idols, wood and stone, silver and gold, which were with them— 17 lest there should be among you man, or woman, or family, or tribe, whose heart turneth away this day from the LORD our God, to go to serve the gods of those nations; lest there should be among you a root that beareth gall and wormwood; 18 and it come to pass, when he heareth the words of this curse, that he bless himself in his heart, saying: 'I shall have peace, though I walk in the stubbornness of my heart—that the watered be swept away with the dry'; 19 the LORD will not be willing to pardon him, but then the anger of the LORD and His jealousy shall be kindled against that man, and all the curse that is written in this book shall lie upon him, and the LORD shall blot out his name from under heaven; 20 and the LORD shall separate him unto evil out of all the tribes of Israel, according to all the curses of the covenant that is written in this book of the law. 21 And the generation to come, your children that shall rise up after you, and the foreigner that shall come from a far land, shall say, when they see the plagues of that land, and the sicknesses wherewith the LORD hath made it sick; 22 and that the whole land thereof is brimstone, and salt, and a burning, that it is not sown, nor beareth, nor any grass groweth therein, like the overthrow of Sodom and Gomorrah, Admah and Zeboiim, which the LORD overthrew in His anger, and in His wrath; 23 even all the nations shall say 'Wherefore hath the LORD done thus unto this land? what meaneth the heat of this great anger?' 24 then men shall say: 'Because they forsook the covenant of the LORD, the God of their fathers, which He made with them when He brought them forth out of the land of Egypt; 25 and went and served other gods, and worshipped them, gods that they knew not, and that He had not allotted unto them; 26 therefore the anger of the LORD was kindled against this land, to bring upon it all the curse that is written in this book; 27 and the LORD rooted them out of their land in anger, and in wrath, and in great indignation, and cast them into another land, as it is this day'.— 28 The secret things belong unto the LORD our God; but the things that are revealed belong unto us and to our children for ever, that we may do all the words of this law.

CHAPTER 4

LEADERSHIP

In the pages of the Hebrew Bible, leadership is largely presented as a multilevel problem and not as an unproblematic reward. Few narratives of leadership in either world literature or history emphasize, as the Hebrew Bible does, the mutual, and even simultaneous, refusal of leadership by both leader and people. Few texts, certainly not of this vintage, examine the internal complexities of leadership and power-sharing.

In reading these texts, consider the following questions: How do leaders deal with rebellion? Is Korah a true democrat, or does he just utilize democratic words for his own benefit? How does the Korah narrative interrogate the difference between equality and sameness? In what way does the Hebrew Bible present leadership as estranged and estranging, and how do future Israelite leaders (for example, in the biblical Book of Judges) deal with this complexity?

A. The People Refuse Their Leaders: Indifference and Complaints

Perhaps inexplicably—considering their oppressed status in Egypt, and the absence of any recorded homegrown movements of protest to counter their beleaguered positions—the Israelites are not particularly impressed with Moses from the beginning, even though he comes explicitly to deliver them from Egyptian bondage. This attitude towards Moses continues throughout the miracles related in the Hebrew biblical text: the parting of the Re[e]d Sea, the Theophany at Mount Sinai, the miraculous manna food, and so on. In his forty years of leadership, Moses never takes permanent control of the situation; he even complains to God: "Am I a nursemaid, that I should carry them with me all the time?" (Numbers 11:12).[1]

---

1. My translation. JPS 1917 version: "Have I conceived all this people? have I brought them forth, that Thou shouldest say unto me: Carry them in thy bosom, as a nursing-father carrieth the sucking child, unto the land which Thou didst swear unto their fathers?"

1. The Israelites Show Indifference to Moses in Egypt

Exodus 6:9–13

9 And Moses spoke so unto the children of Israel; but they hearkened not unto Moses for impatience of spirit, and for cruel bondage.

10 And the LORD spoke unto Moses, saying: 11 'Go in, speak unto Pharaoh king of Egypt, that he let the children of Israel go out of his land.' 12 And Moses spoke before the LORD, saying: 'Behold, the children of Israel have not hearkened unto me; how then shall Pharaoh hear me, who am of uncircumcised lips?'

13 And the LORD spoke unto Moses and unto Aaron, and gave them a charge unto the children of Israel, and unto Pharaoh king of Egypt, to bring the children of Israel out of the land of Egypt.

2. The Israelites Complain at the Red Sea

This selection describes the Israelite reaction when the Egyptian army pursues them after their exit from Egypt.

Exodus 14:9–14

9 And the Egyptians pursued after them, all the horses and chariots of Pharaoh, and his horsemen, and his army, and overtook them encamping by the sea, beside Pi-hahiroth, in front of Baal-zephon. 10 And when Pharaoh drew nigh, the children of Israel lifted up their eyes, and, behold, the Egyptians were marching after them; and they were sore afraid; and the children of Israel cried out unto the LORD. 11 And they said unto Moses: 'Because there were no graves in Egypt, hast thou taken us away to die in the wilderness? wherefore hast thou dealt thus with us, to bring us forth out of Egypt? 12 Is not this the word that we spoke unto thee in Egypt, saying: Let us alone, that we may serve the Egyptians? For it were better for us to serve the Egyptians, than that we should die in the wilderness.' 13 And Moses said unto the people: 'Fear ye not, stand still, and see the salvation of the LORD, which He will work for you to-day; for whereas ye have seen the Egyptians to-day, ye shall see them again no more for ever. 14 The LORD will fight for you, and ye shall hold your peace.'

3. The Israelites Complain after the Splitting of the Red Sea

Exodus 16:1–3

1 And they took their journey from Elim, and all the congregation of the children of Israel came unto the wilderness of Sin, which is between Elim and Sinai, on the fifteenth day of the second month after their departing out of the land of Egypt. 2 And the whole congregation of the children of Israel murmured against Moses and against Aaron in the wilderness; 3 and the children of Israel said unto them: 'Would that we had died by the hand of the LORD in the land of Egypt, when we sat by the flesh-pots, when we did eat bread to the full; for ye have brought us forth into this wilderness, to kill this whole assembly with hunger.'

Exodus 17:1–4

1 And all the congregation of the children of Israel journeyed from the wilderness of Sin, by their stages, according to the commandment of the LORD, and encamped in Rephidim; and there was no water for the people to drink. 2 Wherefore the people strove with Moses, and said: 'Give us water that we may drink.' And Moses said unto them: 'Why strive ye with me? wherefore do ye try the LORD?' 3 And the people thirsted there for water; and the people murmured against Moses, and said: 'Wherefore hast thou brought us up out of Egypt, to kill us and our children and our cattle with thirst?' 4 And Moses cried unto the LORD, saying: 'What shall I do unto this people? they are almost ready to stone me.'

4. The Israelites Complain about the Manna

Numbers 11:1–15

1 And the people were as murmurers, speaking evil in the ears of the LORD; and when the LORD heard it, His anger was kindled; and the fire of the LORD burnt among them, and devoured in the uttermost part of the camp. 2 And the people cried unto Moses; and Moses prayed unto the LORD, and the fire abated. 3 And the name of that place was called Taberah, because the fire of the LORD burnt among them.

4 And the mixed multitude that was among them fell a lusting; and the children of Israel also wept on their part, and said: 'Would that we were given flesh to eat! 5 We remember the fish, which we were wont to eat in Egypt for nought; the cucumbers, and the melons, and the leeks, and the onions, and the garlic; 6 but now our soul is dried away; there is nothing at all; we have nought save this manna to look to.'—7 Now the manna was like coriander seed, and the appearance thereof as the appearance of bdellium. 8 The people went about, and gathered it, and ground it in mills, or beat it in mortars, and seethed it in pots, and made cakes of it; and the taste of it was as the taste of a cake baked with oil. 9 And when the dew fell upon the camp in the night, the manna fell upon it.—10 And Moses heard the people weeping, family by family, every man at the door of his tent; and the anger of the LORD was kindled greatly; and Moses was displeased.

11 And Moses said unto the LORD: 'Wherefore hast Thou dealt ill with Thy servant? and wherefore have I not found favour in Thy sight, that Thou layest the burden of all this people upon me? 12 Have I conceived all this people? have I brought them forth, that Thou shouldest say unto me: Carry them in thy bosom, as a nursing-father carrieth the sucking child, unto the land which Thou didst swear unto their fathers? 13 Whence should I have flesh to give unto all this people? for they trouble me with their weeping, saying: Give us flesh, that we may eat. 14 I am not able to bear all this people myself alone, because it is too heavy for me. 15 And if Thou deal thus with me, kill me, I pray Thee, out of hand, if I have found favour in Thy sight; and let me not look upon my wretchedness.'

5. The Israelites Complain Repeatedly and Want to Return to Egypt after the (Failed) Mission of the Spies

Numbers 14:1–4

1 And all the congregation lifted up their voice, and cried; and the people wept that night. 2 And all the children of Israel murmured against Moses and against Aaron; and the whole congregation said unto them: 'Would that we had died in the land of Egypt! or would we had died in this wilderness! 3 And wherefore

doth the LORD bring us unto this land, to fall by the sword? Our wives and our little ones will be a prey; were it not better for us to return into Egypt?' 4 And they said one to another: 'Let us make a captain, and let us return into Egypt.'

6. Israelite Complaints Continue Even as the Wilderness Sojourn Comes to an End

Numbers 20:1–9

1 And the children of Israel, even the whole congregation, came into the wilderness of Zin in the first month; and the people abode in Kadesh; and Miriam died there, and was buried there. 2 And there was no water for the congregation; and they assembled themselves together against Moses and against Aaron. 3 And the people strove with Moses, and spoke, saying: 'Would that we had perished when our brethren perished before the LORD! 4 And why have ye brought the assembly of the LORD into this wilderness, to die there, we and our cattle? 5 And wherefore have ye made us to come up out of Egypt, to bring us in unto this evil place? it is no place of seed, or of figs, or of vines, or of pomegranates; neither is there any water to drink.' 6 And Moses and Aaron went from the presence of the assembly unto the door of the tent of meeting, and fell upon their faces; and the glory of the LORD appeared unto them. 7 And the LORD spoke unto Moses, saying: 8 'Take the rod, and assemble the congregation, thou, and Aaron thy brother, and speak ye unto the rock before their eyes, that it give forth its water; and thou shalt bring forth to them water out of the rock; so thou shalt give the congregation and their cattle drink.' 9 And Moses took the rod from before the LORD, as He commanded him.

For further reading, see Numbers 21:1–7.

B. The Leader Refuses His Job: Struggling with the Burdens of Leadership

In the context of the anticipated and actual complaints, it is perhaps not surprising that Moses does not want the job of leadership (see Exodus 3 and

4:1–4). His authentic refusal of power is made clear by his delight in sharing the unique emblem of his power—his prophetic abilities—with the seventy Elders who are appointed to assist him (this, in addition to Jethro's accepted plan of judicial organization; see Exodus 18:12–26).

1. Moses Objects to His Commission

Exodus 4:1–4

1 And Moses answered and said: 'But, behold, they will not believe me, nor hearken unto my voice; for they will say: The lord hath not appeared unto thee.' 2 And the LORD said unto him: 'What is that in thy hand?' And he said: 'A rod.' 3 And He said: 'Cast it on the ground.' And he cast it on the ground, and it became a serpent; and Moses fled from before it. 4 And the LORD said unto Moses: 'Put forth thy hand, and take it by the tail' and he put forth his hand, and laid hold of it, and it became a rod in his hand.

2. Moses and Self-Doubt: Openness to Power-Sharing

Moses does not just doubt his ability to lead only in times of national crisis. He quickly recognizes that, for him at least, leadership itself inevitably involves a crisis of doubt (Numbers 11). The reader may wonder why this is so, as several personages in the Hebrew Bible evince no trouble at all exercising power (e.g., Nimrod and Pharaoh).

Several readings in this section speak to this issue. In one reading (Numbers 11:11–17), Moses clearly demonstrates an ongoing willingness to share power and communication with the Divine (which was considered a unique aspect of his leadership; see also Deuteronomy 1 and 5). But in a more famous dispute (Numbers 16), Korah insists that Moses in fact refuses to share power.

3. The Institution of Power-Sharing

Numbers 11:11–17

11 And Moses said unto the LORD: 'Wherefore hast Thou dealt ill with Thy servant? and wherefore have I not found favour

in Thy sight, that Thou layest the burden of all this people upon me? 12 Have I conceived all this people? have I brought them forth, that Thou shouldest say unto me: Carry them in thy bosom, as a nursing-father carrieth the sucking child, unto the land which Thou didst swear unto their fathers? 13 Whence should I have flesh to give unto all this people? for they trouble me with their weeping, saying: Give us flesh, that we may eat. 14 I am not able to bear all this people myself alone, because it is too heavy for me. 15 And if Thou deal thus with me, kill me, I pray Thee, out of hand, if I have found favour in Thy sight; and let me not look upon my wretchedness.'

16 And the LORD said unto Moses: 'Gather unto Me seventy men of the elders of Israel, whom thou knowest to be the elders of the people, and officers over them; and bring them unto the tent of meeting, that they may stand there with thee. 17 And I will come down and speak with thee there; and I will take of the spirit which is upon thee, and will put it upon them; and they shall bear the burden of the people with thee, that thou bear it not thyself alone.'

The text in Deuteronomy expands upon the procedure for choosing these Elders, and highlights their areas of responsibility.

Deuteronomy 1:9–17

9 And I spoke unto you at that time, saying: 'I am not able to bear you myself alone; 10 the LORD your God hath multiplied you, and, behold, ye are this day as the stars of heaven for multitude.—11 The LORD, the God of your fathers, make you a thousand times so many more as ye are, and bless you, as He hath promised you!—12 How can I myself alone bear your cumbrance, and your burden, and your strife? 13 Get you, from each one of your tribes, wise men, and understanding, and full of knowledge, and I will make them heads over you.' 14 And ye answered me, and said: 'The thing which thou hast spoken is good for us to do.' 15 So I took the heads of your tribes, wise men, and full of knowledge, and made them heads over you, captains of thousands, and captains of hundreds, and captains of fifties, and captains of tens, and officers, tribe by tribe. 16 And I charged your judges at that time, saying: 'Hear the causes between your brethren, and judge righteously between a man and his brother, and the stranger that is with him. 17 Ye shall not respect persons

in judgment; ye shall hear the small and the great alike; ye shall not be afraid of the face of any man; for the judgment is God's; and the cause that is too hard for you ye shall bring unto me, and I will hear it.'

4. Moses' Reaction to Power-Sharing

Moments of temporary fatigue often motivate arrangements of power-sharing. In such cases, the arrangements soon fall apart. Moses, by contrast, ascribes his response to the burden of leadership to its existential loneliness (Numbers 11:14; Deuteronomy 1:12). Consequently, he is happy to share.

In the Midrashic reading of the next selection, the prophecy of Eldad and Medad is traditionally said to be troublesome because of its disturbing content: predicting the death of Moses before the Israelites would enter their Promised Land. Moses' positive reaction to the fact of their prophesying—if only all the people could prophesy like that!—foregrounds Moses' account in Deuteronomy of the Theophany at Horeb.

Numbers 11:24–30

24 And Moses went out, and told the people the words of the LORD; and he gathered seventy men of the elders of the people, and set them round about the Tent. 25 And the LORD came down in the cloud, and spoke unto him, and took of the spirit that was upon him, and put it upon the seventy elders; and it came to pass, that, when the spirit rested upon them, they prophesied, but they did so no more. 26 But there remained two men in the camp, the name of the one was Eldad, and the name of the other Medad; and the spirit rested upon them; and they were of them that were recorded, but had not gone out unto the Tent; and they prophesied in the camp. 27 And there ran a young man, and told Moses, and said: 'Eldad and Medad are prophesying in the camp.' 28 And Joshua the son of Nun, the minister of Moses from his youth up, answered and said: 'My lord Moses, shut them in.' 29 And Moses said unto him: 'Art thou jealous for my sake? would that all the LORD's people were prophets, that the LORD would put His spirit upon them!' 30 And Moses withdrew into the camp, he and the elders of Israel.

In this next reading, Moses ascribes to all Israelites the unique ability, traditionally attributed just to Moses (Numbers 12:8), of being able to meet with God face to face.

Deuteronomy 5:1–5

1 And Moses called unto all Israel, and said unto them:

Hear, O Israel, the statutes and the ordinances which I speak in your ears this day, that ye may learn them, and observe to do them. 2 The LORD our God made a covenant with us in Horeb. 3 The LORD made not this covenant with our fathers, but with us, even us, who are all of us here alive this day. 4 The LORD spoke with you face to face in the mount out of the midst of the fire— 5 I stood between the LORD and you at that time, to declare unto you the word of the LORD; for ye were afraid because of the fire, and went not up into the mount.

C. Disputing the Uniqueness of Moses: The Challenge from His Siblings

The challenge to the uniqueness of Moses' abilities and right to lead comes first not from competition outside Moses' tribe but from inside Moses' own family: Miriam and Aaron take issue with Moses over the implications of his marriage. After all, the siblings reason, Moses is not the only one to have received prophecy from God: as members of the triumvirate leading the Israelites in the desert (cf. Micah 6:4), they had all received Divine prophecy.

In reading these sources, it is useful to reflect on both the talents for leadership and the fluctuating claims about the powers exercised by leaders. What makes some leaders open to arrangements of power-sharing while others are not? Is critiquing a leader the same as openly disrespecting him or her and refusing his or her leadership? Note that at the end of this narrative, Miriam's punishment does not depose her from the Triumvirate of Israelite leadership.

Numbers 12:1–15

1 And Miriam and Aaron spoke against Moses because of the Cushite woman whom he had married; for he had married a Cushite woman. 2 And they said: 'Hath the LORD indeed spoken only with Moses? hath He not spoken also with us?' And the LORD heard it.— 3 Now the man Moses was very meek, above all the men that were upon the face of the earth.— 4 And the LORD spoke suddenly unto Moses, and unto Aaron, and unto Miriam: 'Come out ye three unto the tent of meeting.' And they three came out. 5 And the LORD came down in a pillar of cloud, and stood at the door of the Tent, and called Aaron and

Miriam; and they both came forth. 6 And He said: 'Hear now My words: if there be a prophet among you, I the LORD do make Myself known unto him in a vision, I do speak with him in a dream. 7 My servant Moses is not so; he is trusted in all My house; 8 with him do I speak mouth to mouth, even manifestly, and not in dark speeches; and the similitude of the LORD doth he behold; wherefore then were ye not afraid to speak against My servant, against Moses?' 9 And the anger of the LORD was kindled against them; and He departed. 10 And when the cloud was removed from over the Tent, behold, Miriam was leprous, as white as snow; and Aaron looked upon Miriam; and, behold, she was leprous. 11 And Aaron said unto Moses: 'Oh my lord, lay not, I pray thee, sin upon us, for that we have done foolishly, and for that we have sinned. 12 Let her not, I pray, be as one dead, of whom the flesh is half consumed when he cometh out of his mother's womb.' 13 And Moses cried unto the LORD, saying: 'Heal her now, O God, I beseech Thee.'

14 And the LORD said unto Moses: 'If her father had but spit in her face, should she not hide in shame seven days? let her be shut up without the camp seven days, and after that she shall be brought in again.' 15 And Miriam was shut up without the camp seven days; and the people journeyed not till Miriam was brought in again.

D. Rebellion against Moses and Rejection of the Concept of Leadership: The Challenge from Korah

One traditional rationale for leadership is that it requires specialized training for which only some people show aptitude; this is one of Socrates' arguments in Plato's *Republic*.[2] Jethro makes a similar argument in terms of the efficient use of time (see the reading on Jethro's advice [Exodus 18:12–26], below).

---

2. "[T]he guardians of our state, then, inasmuch as their work is the most important of all, will need the most complete freedom from other occupations, and the greatest amount of skill and practice" (Cornford, p. 62; "skill and practice" is another way of talking about expertise). *The Republic of Plato*, translated by Francis Macdonald Cornford (New York: Oxford University Press, 1963). Cf. C. D. C. Reeve, *Plato's Republic*, which translates the passage in this way: "Then to the degree that the guardian's job is of greatest importance, it requires the most freedom from other things, as well as the greatest craft and practice" (375e; Indianapolis: Hackett, 2004, p. 53).

But some Israelites reject the notion of any specialization of function, as seen in the episode of Korah, whose narrative continues to evoke widespread controversy. (Various critical approaches to the substance of Korah's argument have already been presented in the Introduction to this volume—see "Democracy and Political Equality in the Hebrew Bible"—and will not be rehearsed here.) The reader of these texts is reminded that despite the judgment passed on the character and aspirations of Korah himself, his general arguments about the dangers of untrammeled power are taken quite seriously by the Hebrew Bible and are echoed, if only indirectly, elsewhere (Deuteronomy 17:14–20).

Numbers 16:1–35

1 Now Korah, the son of Izhar, the son of Kohath, the son of Levi, with Dathan and Abiram, the sons of Eliab, and On, the son of Peleth, sons of Reuben, took men;

2 and they rose up in face of Moses, with certain of the children of Israel, two hundred and fifty men; they were princes of the congregation, the elect men of the assembly, men of renown; 3 and they assembled themselves together against Moses and against Aaron, and said unto them: 'Ye take too much upon you, seeing all the congregation are holy, every one of them, and the LORD is among them; wherefore then lift ye up yourselves above the assembly of the LORD?' 4 And when Moses heard it, he fell upon his face. 5 And he spoke unto Korah and unto all his company, saying: 'In the morning the LORD will show who are His, and who is holy, and will cause him to come near unto Him; even him whom He may choose will He cause to come near unto Him. 6 This do: take you censors, Korah, and all his company; 7 and put fire therein, and put incense upon them before the LORD to-morrow; and it shall be that the man whom the LORD doth choose, he shall be holy; ye take too much upon you, ye sons of Levi.' 8 And Moses said unto Korah: 'Hear now, ye sons of Levi: 9 is it but a small thing unto you, that the God of Israel hath separated you from the congregation of Israel, to bring you near to Himself, to do the service of the tabernacle of the LORD, and to stand before the congregation to minister unto them; 10 and that He hath brought thee near, and all thy brethren the sons of Levi with thee? and will ye seek the priesthood also? 11 Therefore thou and all thy company that are gathered together against the LORD—; and

as to Aaron, what is he that ye murmur against him?' 12 And Moses sent to call Dathan and Abiram, the sons of Eliab; and they said: 'We will not come up; 13 is it a small thing that thou hast brought us up out of a land flowing with milk and honey, to kill us in the wilderness, but thou must needs make thyself also a prince over us? 14 Moreover thou hast not brought us into a land flowing with milk and honey, nor given us inheritance of fields and vineyards; wilt thou put out the eyes of these men? we will not come up.' 15 And Moses was very wroth, and said unto the LORD: 'Respect not thou their offering; I have not taken one ass from them, neither have I hurt one of them.' 16 And Moses said unto Korah: 'Be thou and all thy congregation before the LORD, thou, and they, and Aaron, to-morrow; 17 and take ye every man his fire-pan, and put incense upon them, and bring ye before the LORD every man his fire-pan, two hundred and fifty fire-pans; thou also, and Aaron, each his fire-pan.' 18 And they took every man his fire-pan, and put fire in them, and laid incense thereon, and stood at the door of the tent of meeting with Moses and Aaron. 19 And Korah assembled all the congregation against them unto the door of the tent of meeting; and the glory of the LORD appeared unto all the congregation.

20 And the LORD spoke unto Moses and unto Aaron, saying: 21 'Separate yourselves from among this congregation, that I may consume them in a moment.' 22 And they fell upon their faces, and said: 'O God, the God of the spirits of all flesh, shall one man sin, and wilt Thou be wroth with all the congregation?'

23 And the LORD spoke unto Moses, saying: 24 'Speak unto the congregation, saying: Get you up from about the dwelling of Korah, Dathan, and Abiram.' 25 And Moses rose up and went unto Dathan and Abiram; and the elders of Israel followed him. 26 And he spoke unto the congregation, saying: 'Depart, I pray you, from the tents of these wicked men, and touch nothing of theirs, lest ye be swept away in all their sins.' 27 So they got them up from the dwelling of Korah, Dathan, and Abiram, on every side; and Dathan and Abiram came out, and stood at the door of their tents, with their wives, and their sons, and their little ones. 28 And Moses said: 'Hereby ye shall know that the LORD hath sent me to do all these works, and that I have not done them of mine own mind. 29 If these men die the common death of

all men, and be visited after the visitation of all men, then the LORD hath not sent Me. 30 But if the LORD make a new thing, and the ground open her mouth, and swallow them up, with all that appertain unto them, and they go down alive into the pit, then ye shall understand that these men have despised the LORD.' 31 And it came to pass, as he made an end of speaking all these words, that the ground did cleave asunder that was under them. 32 And the earth opened her mouth and swallowed them up, and their households, and all the men that appertained unto Korah, and all their goods. 33 So they, and all that appertained to them, went down alive into the pit; and the earth closed upon them, and they perished from among the assembly. 34 And all Israel that were round about them fled at the cry of them; for they said: 'Lest the earth swallow us up.' 35 And fire came forth from the LORD, and devoured the two hundred and fifty men that offered the incense.

E. Moses Is Not Allowed to Complete His Task

After leading a fractious people, loyal to them even in the face of God's obvious displeasure (Moses refuses to go on as leader if God will not forgive the Israelites [Exodus 32:32]), it is puzzling why a seemingly minor infraction towards the end of the wilderness saga results in Moses' being relieved of his leadership, thus preventing his taking the Israelites into the Promised Land. Indeed, Moses may not even enter the Promised Land as a private individual. Alternate ways of reading this narrative yield many different approaches to this question.

Consider Aaron Wildavsky's comment on Moses' having been denied the completion of his task: "Moses teaches his people by leaving them.... The Hebrews were instructed to achieve their own salvation.... The great man is forbidden [to consummate his greatest projects] lest he come to worship his own work.... The leader disappears into the book."[3] In essence, Wildavsky argues that perhaps Moses' greatest legacy to his people is his self-effacing demonstration of leadership, achieved precisely by not exploiting the power and prerogatives of that position. (Recall George Washington's evocation of Cincinnatus on the occasion of Washington's refusal to enter into a third term of presidency.)

---

3. Aaron Wildavsky, *Moses as Political Leader* (Jerusalem: Shalem Press, 1984; repr. 2005), pp. 196, 198.

Although it is an ancient text, the Hebrew Bible exhibits reservations shared by many moderns about leadership's ability to constrain itself—stemming either from a leader's feeling of indispensability (a sentiment the Hebrew Bible does not ascribe to Moses), or from this feeling on the part of the people she or he guides—and thus offers a structural solution to the problem: leaders die.

1. Moses' Destiny Is Announced

Numbers 20:1–13

1 And the children of Israel, even the whole congregation, came into the wilderness of Zin in the first month; and the people abode in Kadesh; and Miriam died there, and was buried there. 2 And there was no water for the congregation; and they assembled themselves together against Moses and against Aaron. 3 And the people strove with Moses, and spoke, saying: 'Would that we had perished when our brethren perished before the LORD! 4 And why have ye brought the assembly of the LORD into this wilderness, to die there, we and our cattle? 5 And wherefore have ye made us to come up out of Egypt, to bring us in unto this evil place? it is no place of seed, or of figs, or of vines, or of pomegranates; neither is there any water to drink.' 6 And Moses and Aaron went from the presence of the assembly unto the door of the tent of meeting, and fell upon their faces; and the glory of the LORD appeared unto them. 7 And the LORD spoke unto Moses, saying: 8 'Take the rod, and assemble the congregation, thou, and Aaron thy brother, and speak ye unto the rock before their eyes, that it give forth its water; and thou shalt bring forth to them water out of the rock; so thou shalt give the congregation and their cattle drink.' 9 And Moses took the rod from before the LORD, as He commanded him. 10 And Moses and Aaron gathered the assembly together before the rock, and he said unto them: 'Hear now, ye rebels; are we to bring you forth water out of this rock?' 11 And Moses lifted up his hand, and smote the rock with his rod twice; and water came forth abundantly, and the congregation drank, and their cattle. 12 And the LORD said unto Moses and Aaron: 'Because ye believed not in Me, to sanctify Me in the eyes of the children of Israel, therefore ye shall not bring this assembly into the land which I have given them.' 13 These are the waters of Meribah, where the children of Israel strove with the LORD, and He was sanctified in them.

2. Moses Reflects on His Destiny and Disappointment

Deuteronomy 4:21–22

21 Now the LORD was angered with me for your sakes, and
swore that I should not go over the Jordan, and that I should not
go in unto that good land, which the LORD thy God giveth thee
for an inheritance; 22 but I must die in this land, I must not go
over the Jordan; but ye are to go over, and possess that good land.

F. Moses, Estrangement, and Leadership Style

Moses' leadership saga is plagued not only by frequent moments of rebellion
by the people that he tries to lead, but also by his own feelings of inadequacy.
An early glimpse into Moses' leadership style reveals a leader beset by problems of resource management—in this case, of time.

The solution recommended by Jethro, and that is forthwith implemented, involves a certain amount of estrangement on the part of Moses:
henceforth, Moses is no longer involved in adjudicating every dispute. In
reading the following texts, it is worth considering the role of estrangement
in establishing efficient modes of communal operation. To what extent does
one type of estrangement lead inevitably to another? At what point does
estrangement lead to a lack of sympathy between people and leader that can
result in alienation?[4]

It is soon apparent that just as the difficulties encountered in fulfilling one of Moses' communal roles, adjudication, lead to a kind of
organizational estrangement—notably presented as a solution, even an
administrative rescue—another undertaking, that of bringing down the
Ten Commandments from Mount Sinai, leads to a different sort of
estrangement. According to the Hebrew biblical text, after Moses writes
the second set of Tablets upon his second ascent on Mount Sinai, his face
shines so much that even Aaron, his own brother, is afraid to approach
him. This leads to Moses' covering his face with a veil (Exodus 34:30–33).
Moses subsequently removes his own tent from inside the Israelite/Levite
encampment.

The estrangement between Moses and his people is mirrored and
deepened by Moses' physical distance from them. This estrangement was

---

4. I am using the term "estrangement" here to signify disaffection of a more personal type;
"alienation," in this context, signifies a dissociation that is more structural (and hence more
difficult to uproot than a momentary estrangement).

already apparent when Moses ascended Mount Sinai to receive the (first) set of Tablets: the crisis leading to the sin of the Golden Calf was brought on by his absence. Similarly, the Midrashic reading (Sifrei s.v. Numbers 11:2) of the episode where Aaron and Miriam point out that they, too, are privy to God's prophetic word, highlights that the trigger to their comments is Moses' seclusion from the rest of the people (even from his wife). The Hebrew Bible sees the link between estrangement—even as a tactic in administrative strategy—and crisis; the issue is how to manage the interrelationship between the two in the context of evolving social and political dynamics.

1. Jethro's Advice

Exodus 18:12–26

12 And Jethro, Moses' father-in-law, took a burnt-offering and sacrifices for God; and Aaron came, and all the elders of Israel, to eat bread with Moses' father-in-law before God. 13 And it came to pass on the morrow, that Moses sat to judge the people; and the people stood about Moses from the morning unto the evening. 14 And when Moses' father-in-law saw all that he did to the people, he said: 'What is this thing that thou doest to the people? why sittest thou thyself alone, and all the people stand about thee from morning unto even?' 15 And Moses said unto his father-in-law: 'Because the people come unto me to inquire of God; 16 when they have a matter, it cometh unto me; and I judge between a man and his neighbour, and I make them know the statutes of God, and His laws.' 17 And Moses' father-in-law said unto him: 'The thing that thou doest is not good. 18 Thou wilt surely wear away, both thou, and this people that is with thee; for the thing is too heavy for thee; thou art not able to perform it thyself alone. 19 Hearken now unto my voice, I will give thee counsel, and God be with thee: be thou for the people before God, and bring thou the causes unto God. 20 And thou shalt teach them the statutes and the laws, and shalt show them the way wherein they must walk, and the work that they must do. 21 Moreover thou shalt provide out of all the people able men, such as fear God, men of truth, hating unjust gain; and place such over them, to be rulers of thousands, rulers of hundreds, rulers of fifties, and rulers of tens. 22 And let them judge the people at all seasons; and it shall be, that every great matter they shall

bring unto thee, but every small matter they shall judge themselves; so shall they make it easier for thee and bear the burden with thee. 23 If thou shalt do this thing, and God command thee so, then thou shalt be able to endure, and all this people also shall go to their place in peace.' 24 So Moses hearkened to the voice of his father-in-law, and did all that he had said. 25 And Moses chose able men out of all Israel, and made them heads over the people, rulers of thousands, rulers of hundreds, rulers of fifties, and rulers of tens. 26 And they judged the people at all seasons: the hard causes they brought unto Moses, but every small matter they judged themselves.

2. "Where Is Moses?"

Exodus 32:1–4

1 And when the people saw that Moses delayed to come down from the mount, the people gathered themselves together unto Aaron, and said unto him: 'Up, make us a god who shall go before us; for as for this Moses, the man that brought us up out of the land of Egypt, we know not what is become of him.' 2 And Aaron said unto them: 'Break off the golden rings, which are in the ears of your wives, of your sons, and of your daughters, and bring them unto me.' 3 And all the people broke off the golden rings which were in their ears, and brought them unto Aaron. 4 And he received it at their hand, and fashioned it with a graving tool, and made it a molten calf; and they said: 'This is thy god, O Israel, which brought thee up out of the land of Egypt.'

3. Moses Removes Himself from the Camp

Exodus 33:7–11

7 Now Moses used to take the tent and to pitch it without the camp, afar off from the camp; and he called it The tent of meeting. And it came to pass, that every one that sought the LORD went out unto the tent of meeting, which was without the camp. 8 And it came to pass, when Moses went out unto the Tent, that all the people rose up, and stood, every man at his tent door, and

looked after Moses, until he was gone into the Tent. 9 And it came to pass, when Moses entered into the Tent, the pillar of cloud descended, and stood at the door of the Tent; and [the LORD] spoke with Moses. 10 And when all the people saw the pillar of cloud stand at the door of the Tent, all the people rose up and worshipped, every man at his tent door. 11 And the LORD spoke unto Moses face to face, as a man speaketh unto his friend. And he would return into the camp; but his minister Joshua, the son of Nun, a young man, departed not out of the Tent.

Exodus 34:27–35

27 And the LORD said unto Moses: 'Write thou these words, for after the tenor of these words I have made a covenant with thee and with Israel.' 28 And he was there with the LORD forty days and forty nights; he did neither eat bread, nor drink water. And he wrote upon the tables the words of the covenant, the ten words. 29 And it came to pass, when Moses came down from mount Sinai with the two tables of the testimony in Moses' hand, when he came down from the mount, that Moses knew not that the skin of his face shone while He talked with him. 30 And when Aaron and all the children of Israel saw Moses, behold, the skin of his face shone; and they were afraid to come nigh him. 31 And Moses called unto them; and Aaron and all the rulers of the congregation returned unto him; and Moses spoke to them. 32 And afterward all the children of Israel came nigh, and he gave them in commandment all that the LORD had spoken with him in mount Sinai. 33 And when Moses had done speaking with them, he put a veil on his face. 34 But when Moses went in before the LORD that He might speak with him, he took the veil off, until he came out; and he came out; and spoke unto the children of Israel that which he was commanded. 35 And the children of Israel saw the face of Moses, that the skin of Moses' face shone;[5] and Moses put the veil back upon his face, until he went in to speak with Him.

G. Estranged Leaders in the Promised Land

The Hebrew Bible's illustration of the complex relationship between leadership and estrangement does not end with the period of Moses' guidance

---

5. JPS 1917: "sent forth beams."

of the Israelites. Even the era of the Judges (which occurs right after Joshua's conquest of the Promised Land) is depicted as being marked by estrangement between the Israelites and their leaders. In the successive narratives of this book, it becomes evident that no Judge can fully control or sway the populace: the arc of events is presented as one of recurring cycles of Israelite sin (idolatry), conquest by warlike nations surrounding the Israelites, and temporary salvation effected by particular judges. In the ongoing debates about the suitability of monarchy for the Israelites, Samuel, one of the most steadfast opponents of this form of government, winds up painting a picture of monarchy—urbanized, opulent—that, ironically enough, may be read as reinforcing the people's desire for this very form of government.

The following selections highlight the various types of estrangement among the Israelites as they lurch towards requesting a monarchy. In particular, it is worthwhile examining the backstories of the events related in Judges 11:4–28 and 12:1–6, as presented in Judges 10:6–18 and 11:1–3. How do these backstories influence the dialogue that takes place between Jephtah and the Elders of his tribe when they ask him to head the battle against the Ammonites? What is the connection between Jephtah's scorned social background and his ability, in his appeal to the Ammonites, to frame social and political history (the Ammonites descend from Lot's daughter, a great-niece of Abraham) in a way that makes peace a plausible option?

In these selections, it seems that while Jephtah is able to overlook personal discourtesies extended to him by members of his family and the Elders of his tribe, that sort of magnanimity is not available when it comes to dealing with members of other tribes that refuse to participate in the fight against Ammon (Judges 12:4–6). This kind of inter-tribal aloofness is problematic throughout the Book of Judges—Deborah makes reference to it in her Song of Victory (Judges 5:15–18)—and it is worth thinking about the connection between tribal disunity and the eventual desire for a monarch. To be sure, even Saul (after he has been privately anointed and publicly acclaimed as king [I Samuel 10:1; 24], but before his second and more decisive public acclamation at Gilgal [I Samuel 11:15]), is depicted as having problems exciting national passion when trying to raise an army to fight against the threatening Ammonite forces, and winds up employing graphic displays of violence before succeeding in raising an effective fighting force (see I Samuel 11:7–8; 11).

Please note that the selections here deliberately omit the more dramatic story of Jephtah's daughter, which comes in for fuller treatment further on in this anthology.

1. Jephtah and Familial/Tribal Estrangement

Judges 10:6–18

6 And the children of Israel again did that which was evil in the sight of the LORD, and served the Baalim, and the Ashtaroth, and the gods of Aram, and the gods of Zidon, and the gods of Moab, and the gods of the children of Ammon, and the gods of the Philistines; and they forsook the LORD, and served Him not. 7 And the anger of the LORD was kindled against Israel, and He gave them over into the hand of the Philistines, and into the hand of the children of Ammon. 8 And they oppressed and crushed the children of Israel that year; eighteen years [oppressed they] all the children of Israel that were beyond the Jordan in the land of the Amorites, which is in Gilead. 9 And the children of Ammon passed over the Jordan to fight also against Judah, and against Benjamin, and against the house of Ephraim, so that Israel was sore distressed. 10 And the children of Israel cried unto the LORD, saying: 'We have sinned against Thee, in that we have forsaken our God, and have served the Baalim.' 11 And the LORD said unto the children of Israel: "Did not I save you from the Egyptians, and from the Amorites, from the children of Ammon, and from the Philistines? 12 The Zidonians also, and the Amalekites, and the Maonites, did oppress you; and ye cried unto Me, and I saved you out of their hand. 13 Yet ye have forsaken Me, and served other gods; wherefore I will save you no more. 14 Go and cry unto the gods which ye have chosen; let them save you in the time of your distress.' 15 And the children of Israel said unto the LORD: 'We have sinned; do Thou unto us whatsoever seemeth good unto Thee; only deliver us, we pray Thee, this day.' 16 And they put away the strange gods from among them, and served the LORD; and His soul was grieved for misery of Israel.

17 Then the children of Ammon were gathered together, and encamped in Gilead. And the children of Israel assembled themselves together, and encamped in Mizpah. 18 And the people, the princes of Gilead, said to one another: 'What man is he that will begin to fight against the children of Ammon? He shall be head over all the inhabitants of Gilead.'

Judges 11:1–28

1 Now Jephthah the Gileadite was a mighty man of valour, and he was the son of a harlot; and Gilead begot Jephthah. 2 And Gilead's wife bore him sons; and when his wife's sons grew up, they drove out Jephthah, and said unto him: 'Thou shalt not inherit in our father's house; for thou art the son of another woman.' 3 Then Jephthah fled from his brethren, and dwelt in the land of Tob; and there were gathered vain fellows to Jephthah, and they went out with him.

4 And it came to pass after a while, that the children of Ammon made war against Israel. 5 And it was so, that when the children of Ammon made war against Israel, the elders of Gilead went to fetch Jephthah out of the land of Tob. 6 And they said unto Jephthah: 'Come and be our chief, that we may fight with the children of Ammon.' 7 And Jephthah said unto the elders of Gilead: 'Did not ye hate me, and drive me out of my father's house? and why are ye come unto me now when ye are in distress?' 8 And the elders of Gilead said unto Jephthah: 'Therefore are we returned to thee now, that thou mayest go with us, and fight with the children of Ammon, and thou shalt be our head over all the inhabitants of Gilead.' 9 And Jephthah said unto the elders of Gilead: 'If ye bring me back home to fight with the children of Ammon, and the LORD deliver them before me, I will be your head.' 10 And the elders of Gilead said unto Jephthah: 'The LORD shall be witness between us; surely according to thy word so will we do.' 11 Then Jephthah went with the elders of Gilead, and the people made him head and chief over them; and Jephthah spoke all his words before the LORD in Mizpah.

12 And Jephthah sent messengers unto the king of the children of Ammon, saying: 'What hast thou to do with me, that thou art come unto me to fight against my land?' 13 And the king of the children of Ammon answered unto the messengers of Jephthah: 'Because Israel took away my land, when he came up out of Egypt, from the Arnon even unto the Jabbok, and unto the Jordan; now therefore restore those cities peaceably.' 14 And Jephthah sent messengers again unto the king of the children of Ammon; 15 and he said unto him: 'Thus saith Jephthah: Israel took not away the land of Moab, nor the land of the children of Ammon. 16 But when they came up from

Egypt, and Israel walked through the wilderness unto the Red
Sea, and came to Kadesh; 17 then Israel sent messengers unto
the king of Edom, saying: Let me, I pray thee, pass through thy
land; but the king of Edom hearkened not. And in like manner
he sent unto the king of Moab; but he would not; and Israel
abode in Kadesh. 18 Then he walked through the wilderness,
and compassed the land of Edom, and the land of Moab, and
came by the east side of the land of Moab, and they pitched
on the other side of the Arnon; but they came not within the
border of Moab, for the Arnon was the border of Moab. 19 And
Israel sent messengers unto Sihon king of the Amorites, the
king of Heshbon; and Israel said unto him: Let us pass, we pray
thee, through thy land unto my place. 20 But Sihon trusted
not Israel to pass through his border; but Sihon gathered all
his people together, and pitched in Jahaz, and fought against
Israel. 21 And the LORD, the God of Israel, delivered Sihon
and all his people into the hand of Israel, and they smote them;
so Israel possessed all the land of the Amorites, the inhabitants of that country. 22 And they possessed all the border of
the Amorites, from the Arnon even unto the Jabbok, and from
the wilderness even unto the Jordan. 23 So now the LORD, the
God of Israel, hath dispossessed the Amorites from before His
people Israel, and shouldest thou possess them? 24 Wilt not
thou possess that which Chemosh thy god giveth thee to possess? So whomsoever the LORD our God hath dispossessed
from before us, them will we possess. 25 And now art thou any
thing better than Balak the son of Zippor, king of Moab? did
he ever strive against Israel, or did he ever fight against them?
26 While Israel dwelt in Heshbon and its towns, and in Aroer
and its towns, and in all the cities that are along by the side
of the Arnon, three hundred years; wherefore did ye not recover
them within that time? 27 I therefore have not sinned against
thee, but thou doest me wrong to war against me; the LORD, the
Judge, be judge this day between the children of Israel and the
children of Ammon.' 28 Howbeit the king of the children of
Ammon hearkened not unto the words of Jephthah which he
sent him.

Judges 12:1–6

1 And the men of Ephraim were gathered together, and passed
to Zaphon; and they said unto Jephthah: 'Wherefore didst thou

pass over to fight against the children of Ammon, and didst not call us to go with thee? we will burn thy house upon thee with fire.' 2 And Jephthah said unto them: 'I and my people were at great strife with the children of Ammon; and when I called you, ye saved me not out of their hand. 3 And when I saw that ye saved me not, I put my life in my hand, and passed over against the children of Ammon, and the LORD delivered them into my hand; wherefore then are ye come up unto me this day, to fight against me?' 4 Then Jephthah gathered together all the men of Gilead, and fought with Ephraim; and the men of Gilead smote Ephraim, because they said: 'Ye are fugitives of Ephraim, ye Gileadites, in the midst of Ephraim, and in the midst of Manasseh.' 5 And the Gileadites took the fords of the Jordan against the Ephraimites; and it was so, that when any of the fugitives of Ephraim said: 'Let me go over,' the men of Gilead said unto him: 'Art thou an Ephraimite?' If he said 'Nay'; 6 then said they unto him: 'Say now Shibboleth'; and he said 'Sibboleth'; for he could not frame to pronounce it right; then they laid hold on him, and slew him at the fords of the Jordan; and there fell at that time of Ephraim forty and two thousand.

For further reading, see Judges chapters 10, 11, and 12.

2. The Estranged Leader as Riddle

a. Samson and Estranging Riddles

With the advent of Samson, the last major Israelite judge before Samuel (and one who, moreover, is an important force in the political transition to monarchy), more complex forms of estrangement become apparent. Samson demands to marry a woman outside of his religious and national affiliation, and he consciously flirts with transgressive actions to save his people. For many of Samson's interlocutors, and even for Samson's own family, these types of interaction are needlessly estranging: Samson's fellow Israelites naturally fear the violent reactions of their Philistine conquerors, who are particularly cruel in exacting vengeance. In his dealings with the Philistines, Samson consciously seizes on his ability to disguise transgressive action as social pleasantry. These forces are epitomized in Samson's favored mode of verbal exchange: the riddle.[6]

---

6. For more on this topic, see my *Conceiving a Nation*, esp. pp. 132–64.

Judges 13:24–25

24 And the woman bore a son, and called his name Samson; and the child grew, and the LORD blessed him. 25 And the spirit of the LORD began to move him in Mahaneh-dan, between Zorah and Eshtaol.

Judges 14

1 And Samson went down to Timnah, and saw a woman in Timnah of the daughters of the Philistines. 2 And he came up, and told his father and his mother, and said: 'I have seen a woman in Timnah of the daughters of the Philistines; now therefore get her for me to wife.' 3 Then his father and his mother said unto him: 'Is there never a woman among the daughters of thy brethren, or among all my people, that thou goest to take a wife of the uncircumcised Philistines?' And Samson said unto his father: 'Get her for me; for she pleaseth me well.' 4 But his father and his mother knew not that it was of the LORD; for he sought an occasion against the Philistines. Now at that time the Philistines had rule over Israel.

5 Then went Samson down, and his father and his mother, to Timnah, and came to the vineyards of Timnah; and, behold, a young lion roared against him. 6 And the spirit of the LORD came mightily upon him, and he rent him as one would have rent a kid, and he had nothing in his hand; but he told not his father or his mother what he had done. 7 And he went down, and talked with the woman; and she pleased Samson well. 8 And after a while he returned to take her, and he turned aside to see the carcass of the lion; and, behold, there was a swarm of bees in the body of the lion, and honey. 9 And he scraped it out into his hands, and went on, eating as he went, and he came to his father and mother, and gave unto them, and they did eat; but he told them not that he had scraped the honey out of the body of the lion. 10 And his father went down unto the woman; and Samson made there a feast; for so used the young men to do. 11 And it came to pass, when they saw him, that they brought thirty companions to be with him. 12 And Samson said unto them: 'Let me now put forth a riddle unto you; if ye can declare it me within the seven days of the feast, and find it out, then I will give you thirty linen garments and

thirty changes of raiment; 13 but if ye cannot declare it me, then shall ye give me thirty linen garments and thirty changes of raiment.' And they said unto him: 'Put forth thy riddle, that we may hear it.' 14 And he said unto them:

Out of the eater came forth food,
And out of the strong came forth sweetness.
And they could not in three days declare the riddle.

15 And it came to pass on the seventh day, that they said unto Samson's wife: 'Entice thy husband, that he may declare unto us the riddle, lest we burn thee and thy father's house with fire; have ye called us hither to impoverish us?' 16 And Samson's wife wept before him, and said: 'Thou dost but hate me, and lovest me not; thou hast put forth a riddle unto the children of my people, and wilt thou not tell it me?' And he said unto her: 'Behold, I have not told it my father nor my mother, and shall I tell thee?' 17 And she wept before him the seven days, while their feast lasted; and it came to pass on the seventh day, that he told her, because she pressed him sore; and she told the riddle to the children of her people. 18 And the men of the city said unto him on the seventh day before the sun went down:

What is sweeter than honey?
And what is stronger than a lion?
And he said unto them:
If ye had not plowed with my heifer,
Ye had not found out my riddle.

19 And the spirit of the LORD came mightily upon him, and he went down to Ashkelon, and smote thirty men of them, and took their spoil, and gave the changes of raiment unto them that declared the riddle. And his anger was kindled, and he went up to his father's house. 20 But Samson's wife was given to his companion, whom he had had for his friend.

b. Samson: Estrangement and (Self-)Sacrifice

The relatively large (for the Hebrew Bible) number of incidents involving violence in the Samson narrative has led to the conventional evaluation of Samson as a lawless saboteur, a person who delights in force for its own sake. Samson is often presented as the Hebrew Bible's equivalent of the Hercules figure.

This largely simplistic reading of the Samson narrative overlooks Samson's complex relationship with estrangement. Unlike his parents, Samson views his deliberate social association with the Philistines (he marries the Timnite woman) as a way to carry the battle to Philistine precincts, a strategy that Samson could not openly employ because of the overwhelming nature of the Philistine domination of the Israelites. In effect, Samson employs the (guerrilla) tactics of a stealth revolution: he aims to achieve a conventional goal, his people's freedom, through non-conventional military techniques. For this, Samson sacrifices his own personal relationships and understandings, and even the favorable judgment of history.

In that context, the last verse of the Samson narrative can be seen as less a glorification of death than a comment on the partial achievement of Samson's own life. To be sure, the very incompleteness of his achievement can read as the greatest estrangement of all, as the fulfillment of the prophecy before Samson's birth that only Samson's mother comprehends: Samson will begin, but crucially not finish, the liberation of the Israelites. Is there anything more estranging than being part of, or even reading, a story that one does not finish? In evaluating the internal tension of Samson's life and works, modern readers may be reminded of the elusive nature of the psychotherapeutic cure, which Freud identifies with just such intellectual "closure."

Judges 15:1–14

1 But it came to pass after a while, in the time of wheat harvest, that Samson visited his wife with a kid; and he said: 'I will go in to my wife into the chamber.' But her father would not suffer him to go in. 2 And her father said: 'I verily thought that thou hadst utterly hated her; therefore I gave her to thy companion; is not her younger sister fairer than she? take her, I pray thee, instead of her.' 3 And Samson said unto them: 'This time shall I be quits with the Philistines, when I do them a mischief.' 4 And Samson went and caught three hundred foxes, and took torches, and turned tail to tail, and put a torch in the midst between every two tails. 5 And when he had set the torches on fire, he let them go into the standing corn of the Philistines, and burnt up both the shocks and the standing corn, and also the oliveyards. 6 Then the Philistines said: 'Who hath done this?' And they said: 'Samson, the son-in-law of the Timnite, because he hath taken his wife, and given her to his companion.' And the Philistines came up, and burnt her and her father with fire. 7 And Samson said unto

them: 'If ye do after this manner, surely I will be avenged of you, and after that I will cease.' 8 And he smote them hip and thigh with a great slaughter; and he went down and dwelt in the cleft of the rock of Etam.

9 Then the Philistines went up, and pitched in Judah, and spread themselves against Lehi. 10 And the men of Judah said: 'Why are ye come up against us?' And they said: 'To bind Samson are we come up, to do to him as he hath done to us.' 11 Then three thousand men of Judah went down to the cleft of the rock of Etam, and said to Samson: 'Knowest thou not that the Philistines are rulers over us? what then is this that thou hast done unto us?' And he said unto them: 'As they did unto me, so have I done unto them.' 12 And they said unto him: 'We are come down to bind thee, that we may deliver thee into the hand of the Philistines.' And Samson said unto them: 'Swear unto me, that ye will not fall upon me yourselves.' 13 And they spoke unto him, saying: 'No; but we will bind thee fast, and deliver thee into their hand; but surely we will not kill thee.' And they bound him with two new ropes, and brought him up from the rock. 14 When he came unto Lehi, the Philistines shouted as they met him; and the spirit of the LORD came mightily upon him, and the ropes that were upon his arms became as flax that was burnt with fire, and his bands dropped from off his hands.

Judges 16:4–30

4 And it came to pass afterward, that he loved a woman in the valley of Sorek, whose name was Delilah. 5 And the lords of the Philistines came up unto her, and said unto her: 'Entice him, and see wherein his great strength lieth, and by what means we may prevail against him, that we may bind him to afflict him; and we will give thee every one of us eleven hundred pieces of silver.' 6 And Delilah said to Samson: 'Tell me, I pray thee, wherein thy great strength lieth, and wherewith thou mightest be bound to afflict thee.' 7 And Samson said unto her: 'If they bind me with seven fresh bowstrings that were never dried, then shall I become weak, and be as any other man.' 8 Then the lords of the Philistines brought up to her seven fresh bowstrings which had not been dried, and she bound him with them. 9 Now she had liers-in-wait abiding in the inner chamber. And she said unto

him: 'The Philistines are upon thee, Samson.' And he broke the bowstrings as a string of tow is broken when it toucheth the fire. So his strength was not known. 10 And Delilah said unto Samson: 'Behold, thou hast mocked me, and told me lies; now tell me, I pray thee, wherewith thou mightest be bound.' 11 And he said unto her: 'If they only bind me with new ropes wherewith no work, hath been done, then shall I become weak, and be as any other man.' 12 So Delilah took new ropes, and bound him therewith, and said unto him: 'The Philistines are upon thee, Samson.' And the liers-in-wait were abiding in the inner chamber. And he broke them from off his arms like a thread. 13 And Delilah said unto Samson: 'Hitherto thou hast mocked me, and told me lies; tell me wherewith thou mightest be bound.' And he said unto her: 'If thou weavest the seven locks of my head with the web.' 14 And she fastened it with the pin, and said unto him: 'The Philistines are upon thee, Samson.' And he awoke out of his sleep, and plucked away the pin of the beam, and the web. 15 And she said unto him: 'How canst thou say: I love thee, when thy heart is not with me? thou hast mocked me these three times, and hast not told me wherein thy great strength lieth.' 16 And it came to pass, when she pressed him daily with her words, and urged him, that his soul was vexed unto death. 17 And he told her all his heart, and said unto her: 'There hath not come a razor upon my head; for I have been a Nazirite unto God from my mother's womb; if I be shaven, then my strength will go from me, and I shall become weak, and be like any other man.' 18 And when Delilah saw that he had told her all his heart, she sent and called for the lords of the Philistines, saying: 'Come up this once, for he hath told me all his heart.' Then the lords of the Philistines came up unto her, and brought the money in their hand. 19 And she made him sleep upon her knees; and she called for a man, and had the seven locks of his head shaven off; and she began to afflict him, and his strength went from him. 20 And she said: 'The Philistines are upon thee, Samson.' And he awoke out of his sleep, and said: 'I will go out as at other times, and shake myself.' But he knew not that the LORD was departed from him. 21 And the Philistines laid hold on him, and put out his eyes; and they brought him down to Gaza, and bound him with fetters of brass; and he did grind in the prison-house. 22 Howbeit the hair of his head began to grow again after he was shaven.

23 And the lords of the Philistines gathered them together to offer a great sacrifice unto Dagon their god, and to rejoice; for they said: 'Our god hath delivered Samson our enemy into our hand.' 24 And when the people saw him, they praised their god; for they said: 'Our god hath delivered into our hand our enemy, and the destroyer of our country, who hath slain many of us.' 25 And it came to pass, when their hearts were merry, that they said: 'Call for Samson, that he may make us sport.' And they called for Samson out of the prison-house; and he made sport before them; and they set him between the pillars. 26 And Samson said unto the lad that held him by the hand: 'Suffer me that I may feel the pillars whereupon the house resteth, that I may lean upon them.' 27 Now the house was full of men and women; and all the lords of the Philistines were there; and there were upon the roof about three thousand men and women, that beheld while Samson made sport. 28 And Samson called unto the LORD, and said: 'O Lord GOD, remember me, I pray Thee, and strengthen me, I pray Thee, only this once, O God, that I may be this once avenged of the Philistines for my two eyes.' 29 And Samson took fast hold of the two middle pillars upon which the house rested, and leaned upon them, the one with his right hand, and the other with his left. 30 And Samson said: 'Let me die with the Philistines.' And he bent with all his might; and the house fell upon the lords, and upon all the people that were therein. So the dead that he slew at his death were more than they that he slew in his life.

For further reading, see Judges chapters 13 through 16 in their entirety.

H. Requesting a New Kind of Leadership

Perceiving Samuel's sons as unfit to take over their father's position, the Israelites demand a king. Samuel is displeased when the Israelites ask him for a king; up till now, the tribes had been ruled (at times, sporadically) by judges, and matters of crises, by biblical report, had been appealed directly to God. While Samuel himself had fulfilled the role of battle commander when necessary (for further reading, see I Samuel 7), matters of justice are not best adjudicated by holders of excessive political power—as will become evident in the selections in the next section.

I Samuel 8:1–9

1 And it came to pass, when Samuel was old, that he made his sons judges over Israel. 2 Now the name of his first-born was

Joel; and the name of his second, Abijah; they were judges in Beer-sheba. 3 And his sons walked not in his ways, but turned aside after lucre, and took bribes, and perverted justice.

4 Then all the elders of Israel gathered themselves together, and came to Samuel unto Ramah. 5 And they said unto him: 'Behold, thou art old, and thy sons walk not in thy ways; now make us a king to judge us like all the nations.' 6 But the thing displeased Samuel, when they said: 'Give us a king to judge us.' And Samuel prayed unto the LORD. 7 And the LORD said unto Samuel: 'Hearken unto the voice of the people in all that they say unto thee; for they have not rejected thee, but they have rejected Me, that I should not be king over them. 8 According to all the works which they have done since the day that I brought them up out of Egypt even unto this day, in that they have forsaken Me, and served other gods, so do they also unto thee. 9 Now therefore hearken unto their voice; howbeit thou shalt earnestly forewarn them, and shalt declare unto them the manner of the king that shall reign over them.'

1. Samuel's Arguments against Monarchy

I Samuel 8:10–22

10 And Samuel told all the words of the LORD unto the people that asked of him a king. 11 And he said: 'This will be the manner of the king that shall reign over you: he will take your sons, and appoint them unto him, for his chariots, and to be his horsemen; and they shall run before his chariots. 12 And he will appoint them unto him for captains of thousands, and captains of fifties; and to plow his ground, and to reap his harvest, and to make his instruments of war, and the instruments of his chariots. 13 And he will take your daughters to be perfumers, and to be cooks, and to be bakers. 14 And he will take your fields, and your vineyards, and your oliveyards, even the best of them, and give them to his servants. 15 And he will take the tenth of your seed, and of your vineyards, and give to his officers, and to his servants. 16 And he will take your men-servants, and your maid-servants, and your goodliest young men, and your asses, and put them to his work. 17 He will take the tenth of your flocks; and ye shall be his servants. 18 And ye shall cry out in that day because of your king whom ye shall have chosen you; and the LORD will not answer you in that day.' 19 But the people refused to hearken unto the

voice of Samuel; and they said: 'Nay; but there shall be a king over us; 20 that we also may be like all the nations; and that our king may judge us, and go out before us, and fight our battles.' 21 And Samuel heard all the words of the people, and he spoke them in the ears of the LORD. 22 And the LORD said to Samuel: 'Hearken unto their voice, and make them a king.' And Samuel said unto the men of Israel: 'Go ye every man unto his city.'

2. Samuel Testifies to His Uncorrupted Leadership, but Accedes to Political Reality

I Samuel 12:1–5, 13–17

1 And Samuel said unto all Israel: 'Behold, I have hearkened unto your voice in all that ye said unto me, and have made a king over you. 2 And now, behold, the king walketh before you; and I am old and grayheaded; and, behold, my sons are with you; and I have walked before you from my youth unto this day. 3 Here I am; witness against me before the LORD, and before His anointed: whose ox have I taken? or whose ass have I taken? or whom have I defrauded? or whom have I oppressed? or of whose hand have I taken a ransom to blind mine eyes therewith? and I will restore it you.' 4 And they said: 'Thou hast not defrauded us, nor oppressed us, neither hast thou taken aught of any man's hand.' 5 And he said unto them: 'The LORD is witness against you, and His anointed is witness this day, that ye have not found aught in my hand.' And they said: 'He is witness.'

. . . .

13 Now therefore behold the king whom ye have chosen, and whom ye have asked for; and, behold, the LORD hath set a king over you. 14 If ye will fear the LORD, and serve Him, and hearken unto His voice, and not rebel against the commandment of the LORD, and both ye and also the king that reigneth over you be followers of the LORD your God—; 15 but if ye will not hearken unto the voice of the LORD, but rebel against the commandment of the LORD, then shall the hand of the LORD be against you, and against your fathers. 16 Now therefore stand still and see this great thing, which the LORD will do before your eyes. 17 Is it not wheat harvest to-day? I will call unto the LORD, that He may send thunder and rain; and ye shall know

and see that your wickedness is great, which ye have done in the sight of the LORD, in asking you a king.'

For further reading, see I Samuel 7:13–17, on Samuel's prowess as military leader.

I. The First Monarch: Insecurity and Depression

Leaders who inaugurate a new form of government for their countries are often heralded with complimentary titles such as "father of the country." Not so with Saul, who despite looking the part ("head and shoulders above the people," I Samuel 10:23) cannot stand up to the challenges of being a leader: Saul is afraid to greet the people as ruler ("hiding among the baggage," I Samuel 10:22); he vacillates in the face of popular displeasure (I Samuel 13:8–14); he masks his fear with overly rigid rules and impromptu decision-making, as in the narrative of Jonathan's mistaken tasting of honey while fighting the Philistines, when Saul had proclaimed a fast day (I Samuel 13:15–23, 14:1–23, 24–31, 37–48).

Another irony lurks in the text: when, after Divine displeasure with Saul becomes evident, Samuel is charged to anoint a new king, the initial pool of candidates omits the candidate who proves to be the Divine choice. In fact, when Samuel first sees David, he ignores him precisely because David does not look the part as Saul originally did (I Samuel 16:6–7, 11–12). The dissonance between looking the part of a ruler and fulfilling the demands of ruling is highlighted in contemporary studies of the American presidency that analyze the skills required for winning an election as opposed to those necessary for effective governing.[7]

For further reading, see I Samuel 13 to 14 (esp. verses 24–45).

1. The First King Loses His Kingdom

I Samuel 15:1–31

1 And Samuel said unto Saul: 'The LORD sent me to anoint thee to be king over His people, over Israel; now therefore

---

7. One example of this approach can be seen in Richard Ben Cramer's *What It Takes* (New York: Vintage, 1993), which understands George H. W. Bush's 1992 loss to Bill Clinton as resulting from Bush's failure to understand the importance of running an effective campaign, incorrectly relying instead on the public's ability to appreciate (as more valuable) the different set of skills involved in efficiently administering the government. Other studies have analyzed the different skill sets in winning the presidency as opposed to performing well in the job itself, as stemming from a candidate-centered (moral or intellectual) failure.

hearken thou unto the voice of the words of the LORD. 2 Thus saith the LORD of hosts: I remember that which Amalek did to Israel, how he set himself against him in the way, when he came up out of Egypt. 3 Now go and smite Amalek, and utterly destroy all that they have, and spare them not; but slay both man and woman, infant and suckling, ox and sheep, camel and ass.' 4 And Saul summoned the people, and numbered them in Telaim, two hundred thousand footmen, and ten thousand men of Judah. 5 And Saul came to the city of Amalek, and lay in wait in the valley. 6 And Saul said unto the Kenites: 'Go, depart, get you down from among the Amalekites, lest I destroy you with them; for ye showed kindness to all the children of Israel, when they came up out of Egypt.' So the Kenites departed from among the Amalekites. 7 And Saul smote the Amalekites, from Havilah as thou goest to Shur, that is in front of Egypt. 8 And he took Agag the king of the Amalekites alive, and utterly destroyed all the people with the edge of the sword. 9 But Saul and the people spared Agag, and the best of the sheep, and of the oxen, even the young of the second birth, and the lambs, and all that was good, and would not utterly destroy them; but every thing that was of no account and feeble, that they destroyed utterly.

10 Then came the word of the LORD unto Samuel, saying: 11 'It repenteth Me that I have set up Saul to be king; for he is turned back from following Me, and hath not performed My commandments.' And it grieved Samuel; and he cried unto the LORD all night. 12 And Samuel rose early to meet Saul in the morning; and it was told Samuel, saying: 'Saul came to Carmel, and, behold, he is setting him up a monument, and is gone about, and passed on, and gone down to Gilgal.' 13 And Samuel came to Saul; and Saul said unto him: 'Blessed be thou of the LORD; I have performed the commandment of the LORD.' 14 And Samuel said: 'What meaneth then this bleating of the sheep in mine ears, and the lowing of the oxen which I hear?' 15 And Saul said: 'They have brought them from the Amalekites; for the people spared the best of the sheep and of the oxen, to sacrifice unto the LORD thy God; and the rest we have utterly destroyed.' 16 Then Samuel said unto Saul: 'Stay, and I will tell thee what the LORD hath said to me this night.' And he said unto him: 'Say on.'

17 And Samuel said: 'Though thou be little in thine own sight, art thou not head of the tribes of Israel? And the LORD anointed thee king over Israel; 18 and the LORD sent thee on a journey,

and said: Go and utterly destroy the sinners the Amalekites, and fight against them until they be consumed. 19 Wherefore then didst thou not hearken to the voice of the LORD, but didst fly upon the spoil, and didst that which was evil in the sight of the LORD?' 20 And Saul said unto Samuel: 'Yea, I have hearkened to the voice of the LORD, and have gone the way which the LORD sent me, and have brought Agag the king of Amalek, and have utterly destroyed the Amalekites. 21 But the people took of the spoil, sheep and oxen, the chief of the devoted things, to sacrifice unto the LORD thy God in Gilgal.' 22 And Samuel said:

'Hath the LORD as great delight in burnt-offerings and sacrifices,
As in hearkening to the voice of the LORD?
Behold, to obey is better than sacrifice,
And to hearken than the fat of rams.
23 For rebellion is as the sin of witchcraft,
And stubbornness is as idolatry and teraphim.
Because thou hast rejected the word of the LORD, He hath also rejected thee from being king.'

24 And Saul said unto Samuel: 'I have sinned; for I have transgressed the commandment of the LORD, and thy words; because I feared the people, and hearkened to their voice. 25 Now therefore, I pray thee, pardon my sin, and return with me, that I may worship the LORD.' 26 And Samuel said unto Saul: 'I will not return with thee; for thou hast rejected the word of the LORD, and the LORD hath rejected thee from being king over Israel.' 27 And as Samuel turned about to go away, he laid hold upon the skirt of his robe, and it rent. 28 And Samuel said unto him: 'The LORD hath rent the kingdom of Israel from thee this day, and hath given it to a neighbour of thine, that is better than thou. 29 And also the Glory of Israel will not lie nor repent; for He is not a man, that He should repent.' 30 Then he said: 'I have sinned; yet honour me now, I pray thee, before the elders of my people, and before Israel, and return with me, that I may worship the LORD thy God.' 31 So Samuel returned after Saul; and Saul worshipped the LORD.

For further reading, see I Samuel 10:23–24, 13:15–23, 14:1–23, 24–31, and 37–48.

The Hebrew Bible does not specify a natural cause of Saul's "evil spirit" or, as Abraham Lincoln was wont to describe his own unhappy moods, his "melancholy." As presented in the text, however, Saul's depression is over-determined: it may be due specifically to David's (secret) anointment as king, which Saul manages somehow to deduce. It may also be due, in more general terms, to Saul's growing awareness of David as a potential political rival, whether from noticing the reaction of others to David's compelling personality, David's popularity among both the common people and the courtiers, or his celebrated victories in battle—especially his stunning defeat of Goliath.

2. The Anointing of David and Its Aftermath

I Samuel 16:1–13

1 And the LORD said unto Samuel: 'How long wilt thou mourn for Saul, seeing I have rejected him from being king over Israel? fill thy horn with oil, and go, I will send thee to Jesse the Beth-lehemite; for I have provided Me a king among his sons.' 2 And Samuel said: 'How can I go? if Saul hear it, he will kill me.' And the LORD said: 'Take a heifer with thee, and say: I am come to sacrifice to the LORD. 3 And call Jesse to the sacrifice, and I will tell thee what thou shalt do; and thou shalt anoint unto Me him whom I name unto thee.' 4 And Samuel did that which the LORD spoke, and came to Beth-lehem. And the elders of the city came to meet him trembling, and said: 'Comest thou peaceably?' 5 And he said: 'Peaceably; I am come to sacrifice unto the LORD; sanctify yourselves and come with me to the sacrifice.' And he sanctified Jesse and his sons, and called them to the sacrifice. 6 And it came to pass, when they were come, that he beheld Eliab, and said: 'Surely the LORD'S anointed is before Him.' 7 But the LORD said unto Samuel: 'Look not on his countenance, or on the height of his stature; because I have rejected him; for it is not as man seeth: for man looketh on the outward appearance, but the LORD looketh on the heart.' 8 Then Jesse called Abinadab, and made him pass before Samuel. And he said: 'Neither hath the LORD chosen this.' 9 Then Jesse made Shammah to pass by. And he said: 'Neither hath the LORD chosen this.' 10 And Jesse made seven of his sons to pass before Samuel. And Samuel said unto Jesse: 'The LORD hath not chosen these.' 11 And Samuel said unto Jesse: 'Are here all thy children?' And he said: 'There remaineth yet the youngest, and, behold, he keepeth the sheep.' And Samuel said unto Jesse: 'Send and fetch him; for we will not sit down till he come hither.' 12 And he sent, and brought him in. Now he was ruddy,

and withal of beautiful eyes, and goodly to look upon. And the LORD said: 'Arise, anoint him; for this is he.' 13 Then Samuel took the horn of oil, and anointed him in the midst of his brethren; and the spirit of the LORD came mightily upon David from that day forward. So Samuel rose up, and went to Ramah.

3. Political Stability and Psychological Debilitation: Dealing with a Ruler's Depression

I Samuel 16:14–23

14 Now the spirit of the LORD had departed from Saul, and an evil spirit from the LORD terrified him. 15 And Saul's servants said unto him: 'Behold now, an evil spirit from God terrifieth thee. 16 Let our lord now command thy servants, that are before thee, to seek out a man who is a skilful player on the harp; and it shall be, when the evil spirit from God cometh upon thee, that he shall play with his hand, and thou shalt be well.' 17 And Saul said unto his servants: 'Provide me now a man that can play well, and bring him to me.' 18 Then answered one of the young men, and said: 'Behold, I have seen a son of Jesse the Beth-lehemite, that is skilful in playing, and a mighty man of valour, and a man of war, and prudent in affairs, and a comely person, and the LORD is with him.' 19 Wherefore Saul sent messengers unto Jesse, and said: 'Send me David thy son, who is with the sheep.' 20 And Jesse took an ass laden with bread, and a bottle of wine, and a kid, and sent them by David his son unto Saul. 21 And David came to Saul, and stood before him; and he loved him greatly; and he became his armour-bearer. 22 And Saul sent to Jesse, saying: 'Let David, I pray thee, stand before me; for he hath found favour in my sight.' 23 And it came to pass, when the [evil] spirit from God was upon Saul, that David took the harp, and played with his hand; so Saul found relief, and it was well with him, and the evil spirit departed from him.

4. David Kills Goliath

I Samuel 17:1–11, 25–49, 54–58

1 Now the Philistines gathered together their armies to battle, and they were gathered together at Socoh, which belongeth

to Judah, and pitched between Socoh and Azekah, in Ephes-dammim. 2 And Saul and the men of Israel were gathered together, and pitched in the vale of Elah, and set the battle in array against the Philistines. 3 And the Philistines stood on the mountain on the one side, and Israel stood on the mountain on the other side; and there was a valley between them. 4 And there went out a champion from the camp of the Philistines, named Goliath, of Gath, whose height was six cubits and a span. 5 And he had a helmet of brass upon his head, and he was clad with a coat of mail; and the weight of the coat was five thousand shekels of brass. 6 And he had greaves of brass upon his legs, and a javelin of brass between his shoulders. 7 And the shaft of his spear was like a weaver's beam; and his spear's head weighed six hundred shekels of iron; and his shield-bearer went before him. 8 And he stood and cried unto the armies of Israel, and said unto them: 'Why do ye come out to set your battle in array? am not I a Philistine, and ye servants to Saul? choose you a man for you, and let him come down to me. 9 If he be able to fight with me, and kill me, then will we be your servants; but if I prevail against him, and kill him, then shall ye be our servants, and serve us.' 10 And the Philistine said: 'I do taunt the armies of Israel this day; give me a man, that we may fight together.' 11 And when Saul and all Israel heard those words of the Philistine, they were dismayed, and greatly afraid.

. . . .

25 And the men of Israel said: 'Have ye seen this man that is come up? surely to taunt Israel is he come up; and it shall be, that the man who killeth him, the king will enrich him with great riches, and will give him his daughter, and make his father's house free in Israel.'

26 And David spoke to the men that stood by him, saying: 'What shall be done to the man that killeth this Philistine, and taketh away the taunt from Israel? for who is this uncircumcised Philistine, that he should have taunted the armies of the living God?' 27 And the people answered him after this manner, saying: 'So shall it be done to the man that killeth him.' 28 And Eliab his eldest brother heard when he spoke unto the men; and Eliab's anger was kindled against David, and he said: 'Why art thou come down? and with whom hast thou left those few sheep in the wilderness? I know thy presumptuousness, and the naughtiness

of thy heart; for thou art come down that thou mightest see the battle.' 29 And David said: 'What have I now done? Was it not but a word?' 30 And he turned away from him toward another, and spoke after the same manner; and the people answered him after the former manner.

31 And when the words were heard which David spoke, they rehearsed them before Saul; and he was taken to him. 32 And David said to Saul: 'Let no man's heart fail within him; thy servant will go and fight with this Philistine.' 33 And Saul said to David: 'Thou art not able to go against this Philistine to fight with him; for thou art but a youth, and he a man of war from his youth.' 34 And David said unto Saul: 'Thy servant kept his father's sheep; and when there came a lion, or a bear, and took a lamb out of the flock, 35 I went out after him, and smote him, and delivered it out of his mouth; and when he arose against me, I caught him by his beard, and smote him, and slew him. 36 Thy servant smote both the lion and the bear; and this uncircumcised Philistine shall be as one of them, seeing he hath taunted the armies of the living God.' 37 And David said: 'The LORD that delivered me out of the paw of the lion, and out of the paw of the bear, He will deliver me out of the hand of this Philistine.' And Saul said unto David: 'Go, and the LORD shall be with thee.' 38 And Saul clad David with his apparel, and he put a helmet of brass upon his head, and he clad him with a coat of mail. 39 And David girded his sword upon his apparel, and he essayed to go[, but could not]; for he had not tried it. And David said unto Saul: 'I cannot go with these; for I have not tried them.' And David put them off him. 40 And he took his staff in his hand, and chose him five smooth stones out of the brook, and put them in the shepherd's bag which he had, even in his scrip; and his sling was in his hand; and he drew near to the Philistine.

41 And the Philistine came nearer and nearer unto David; and the man that bore the shield went before him. 42 And when the Philistine looked about, and saw David, he disdained him; for he was but a youth, and ruddy, and withal of a fair countenance. 43 And the Philistine said unto David: 'Am I a dog, that thou comest to me with staves?' And the Philistine cursed David by his god. 44 And the Philistine said to David: 'Come to me, and I will give thy flesh unto the fowls of the air, and to the beasts of the field.' 45 Then said David to the Philistine: 'Thou comest to me with a sword, and with a spear, and with a javelin; but I

come to thee in the name of the LORD of hosts, the God of the armies of Israel, whom thou hast taunted. 46 This day will the LORD deliver thee into my hand; and I will smite thee, and take thy head from off thee; and I will give the carcasses of the host of the Philistines this day unto the fowls of the air, and to the wild beasts of the earth; that all the earth may know that there is a God in Israel; 47 and that all this assembly may know that the LORD saveth not with sword and spear; for the battle is the LORD'S, and He will give you into our hand.' 48 And it came to pass, when the Philistine arose, and came and drew nigh to meet David, that David hastened, and ran toward the army to meet the Philistine. 49 And David put his hand in his bag, and took thence a stone, and slung it, and smote the Philistine in his forehead; and the stone sank into his forehead, and he fell upon his face to the earth.

. . . .

54 And David took the head of the Philistine, and brought it to Jerusalem; but he put his armour in his tent.

55 And when Saul saw David go forth against the Philistine, he said unto Abner, the captain of the host: 'Abner, whose son is this youth?' And Abner said: 'As thy soul liveth, O king, I cannot tell.' 56 And the king said: 'Inquire thou whose son the stripling is.' 57 And as David returned from the slaughter of the Philistine, Abner took him, and brought him before Saul with the head of the Philistine in his hand. 58 And Saul said to him: 'Whose son art thou, thou young man?' And David answered: 'I am the son of thy servant Jesse the Beth-lehemite.'

As Saul had promised, David receives the hand of the royal princess upon his defeat of Goliath, as well as, unexpectedly and to Saul's consternation, the adulation of the people. This sets off another episode of depressive and violent behavior for Saul. The king, however, retains enough slyness to propose David's marriage to Michal, Saul's second daughter who was in love with David, if David would kill several hundred more Philistines. This fairy tale–like reward is prompted by Saul's reasoning that David's likely death in such a fierce battle would obviate the need for Saul personally to get involved in disposing of a growing political threat to his own royal power. In Saul's calculations, he could enjoy the best of both worlds: as king, he could engineer events so that his own power would remain unchallenged, without his being linked to, or held responsible for, David's death.

This bungled machination on the part of Saul eerily foreshadows the more smoothly handled maneuvering engineered by David when he has Uriah placed in the frontlines of battle to conceal the results of his dalliance with Uriah's wife Batsheva. In the latter case, the wrath of God directly descends upon David, resulting in the death of David and Batsheva's first-born baby (David later promises to bequeath his throne to their second-born son, Solomon). For now, it is worth noting that even though Saul's plotting against David is presented in the context of psychological depression, the Hebrew Bible adroitly insists that power always has negative consequences on a leader's spirits, not least upon those who glory in its exercise.

5. David's Adventures in Saul's Court

I Samuel 18

1 And it came to pass, when he had made an end of speaking unto Saul, that the soul of Jonathan was knit with the soul of David, and Jonathan loved him as his own soul. 2 And Saul took him that day, and would let him go no more home to his father's house. 3 Then Jonathan made a covenant with David, because he loved him as his own soul. 4 And Jonathan stripped himself of the robe that was upon him, and gave it to David, and his apparel, even to his sword, and to his bow, and to his girdle. 5 And David went out; whithersoever Saul sent him, he had good success; and Saul set him over the men of war; and it was good in the sight of all the people, and also in the sight of Saul's servants.

6 And it came to pass as they came, when David returned from the slaughter of the Philistine, that the women came out of all the cities of Israel, singing and dancing, to meet king Saul, with timbrels, with joy, and with three-stringed instruments. 7 And the women sang one to another in their play, and said:

Saul hath slain his thousands,

And David his ten thousands.

8 And Saul was very wroth, and this saying displeased him; and he said: 'They have ascribed unto David ten thousands, and to me they have ascribed but thousands; and all he lacketh is the kingdom!' 9 And Saul eyed David from that day and forward.

10 And it came to pass on the morrow, that an evil spirit from God came mightily upon Saul, and he raved in the midst of the

house; and David played with his hand, as he did day by day; and Saul had his spear in his hand. 11 And Saul cast the spear; for he said: 'I will smite David even to the wall.' And David stepped aside out of his presence twice. 12 And Saul was afraid of David, because the LORD was with him, and was departed from Saul. 13 Therefore Saul removed him from him, and made him his captain over a thousand; and he went out and came in before the people. 14 And David had great success in all his ways; and the LORD was with him. 15 And when Saul saw that he had great success, he stood in awe of him. 16 But all Israel and Judah loved David; for he went out and came in before them.

17 And Saul said to David: 'Behold my elder daughter Merab, her will I give thee to wife; only be thou valiant for me, and fight the LORD'S battles.' For Saul said: 'Let not my hand be upon him, but let the hand of the Philistines be upon him.' 18 And David said unto Saul: 'Who am I, and what is my life, or my father's family in Israel, that I should be son-in-law to the king?' 19 But it came to pass at the time when Merab Saul's daughter should have been given to David, that she was given unto Adriel the Meholathite to wife. 20 And Michal Saul's daughter loved David; and they told Saul, and the thing pleased him. 21 And Saul said: 'I will give him her, that she may be a snare to him, and that the hand of the Philistines may be against him.' Wherefore Saul said to David: 'Thou shalt this day be my son-in-law through the one of the twain.' 22 And Saul commanded his servants: 'Speak with David secretly, and say: Behold, the king hath delight in thee, and all his servants love thee; now therefore be the king's son-in-law.' 23 And Saul's servants spoke those words in the ears of David. And David said: 'Seemeth it to you a light thing to be the king's son-in-law, seeing that I am a poor man, and lightly esteemed?' 24 And the servants of Saul told him, saying: 'On this manner spoke David.' 25 And Saul said: 'Thus shall ye say to David: The king desireth not any dowry, but a hundred foreskins of the Philistines, to be avenged of the king's enemies.' For Saul thought to make David fall by the hand of the Philistines. 26 And when his servants told David these words, it pleased David well to be the king's son-in-law. And the days were not expired; 27 and David arose and went, he and his men, and slew of the Philistines two hundred men; and David brought their foreskins, and they gave them in full number to the king, that he might be the king's son-in-law. And Saul gave him

Michal his daughter to wife. 28 And Saul saw and knew that the LORD was with David; and Michal Saul's daughter loved him. 29 And Saul was yet the more afraid of David; and Saul was David's enemy continually.

30 Then the princes of the Philistines went forth; and it came to pass, as often as they went forth, that David prospered more than all the servants of Saul; so that his name was much set by.

For further reading, see I Samuel 21:11 and 29:5.

CHAPTER 5

WOMEN

The world that the Hebrew Bible describes does not valorize women as independent agents. Still, women's voices are evident in its texts, and women's accomplishments are portrayed as crucial for the realization of the Israelites as a nation with a common set of values and goals. The selections here range widely, as indeed do the texts of the Hebrew Bible.

A. A Woman's Fate

In most of the Hebrew biblical texts cited here, the fate of the individual woman is encased within unyielding social structures. This is true of the first two narratives excerpted here (Eve, and Jephtah's nameless daughter). In the third example, however, women do succeed in seeking and achieving justice under their own steam (the prostitutes at King Solomon's court). As in many other narratives of the Hebrew Bible, the treatment of women here is a key to assessing the moral coherence of society at large.

1. Eve's Punishment

God's words to Eve after the disobedience in the Garden of Eden—that she will desire her husband who will dominate her—emphasize the non-voluntary character of Eve's subjection to Adam.[1] The linkage of desire and (lack of) power foreshadows God's words to Cain after he murders Abel; in both cases, the bearer of desire—whether for one's spouse or for a fruitful land to call one's own—is portrayed as ultimately diminished in power.

---

1. The word the Hebrew Bible uses to express Adam's preeminence over his wife Eve is the verb *m'sh'l* (Genesis 3:16). This word is sometimes translated as "to rule" (as it is in the JPS 1917 translation) but really means "to have dominion over" (as I rendered it in Genesis 37:8), or (as I have rendered it in the present context) "to dominate." In Genesis 37:8, it is contrasted with the verb *m'l'kh,* which means "to rule"; whereas *m'l'kh* connotes power exercised under conditions analogous to those we today (following the usage of social contract theorists of the seventeenth and eighteenth centuries) might call "consent," *m'sh'l* connotes power exercised contrary to the will of the subordinate party. For more on this see Malbim's commentary on Genesis 4:6–7.

Similarly, God's advice to Cain (Genesis 4:9–15) mimics the structure of the curse to Eve; Cain's punishment likewise imitates the punishment of Adam. In all these cases, the individual fate of the protagonist has communal implications.

Genesis 3:13–16

13 And the LORD God said unto the woman: 'What is this thou hast done?' And the woman said: 'The serpent beguiled me, and I did eat.' 14 And the LORD God said unto the serpent: 'Because thou hast done this, cursed art thou from among all cattle, and from among all beasts of the field; upon thy belly shalt thou go, and dust shalt thou eat all the days of thy life. 15 And I will put enmity between thee and the woman, and between thy seed and her seed; they shall bruise thy head, and thou shalt bruise their heel.'

16 Unto the woman He said: 'I will greatly multiply thy pain and thy travail; in pain thou shalt bring forth children; and thy desire shall be to thy husband, and he shall dominate[2] thee.'

2. Jephtah's Daughter

The story of the fate of Jephtah's daughter resounds negatively in twenty-first-century ears; it seems to countermand basic Hebrew biblical values supportive of human life and against child sacrifice (Leviticus 18:21) found in the texts of the Hebrew Bible. This point is underlined by the realization that within the Five Books of Moses, there are provisions for annulling unfortunate or non-executable vows.[3] In that context, how could Jephtah assume that his own vow, undertaking to sacrifice whatever should first exit the doors of his house, would obligate him to sacrifice his own daughter?

The fact that, in the text's depiction, the words of Jephtah's vow are improbably taken at face value may point to a related disruption within the structure of Israelite society. Could it be linked to the personal and tribal alienations experienced by Jephtah? (These sources are excerpted in Chapter 4, "Leadership," and are drawn from Judges 11:1–3 and 12:1–4.) Or, as the Midrashic reading has it, are elements of moral dysfunction at the core of

---

2. JPS 1917: "rule over."

3. See the comments in Babylonian Talmud Tractate Chagiga 10a on the biblical episode in the Book of Judges regarding Jephtah, made in the context of the law in Numbers 30 allowing for the nullification of vows in particular circumstances.

this rash vow? (Cf. Bereshit Rabbah 60:3.)[4] This last point finds additional confirmation in the misplaced nature of Jephtah's declaration upon seeing his daughter exit the doors of his house, and his subsequent refusal to mitigate the consequences of his vow: in the manner of many a Greek or traditional fairy-tale protagonist, he seems to accept trading military success for the life of a child, an exchange frowned upon by the Hebrew Bible.

Judges 11:29–40

29 Then the spirit of the LORD came upon Jephthah, and he passed over Gilead and Manasseh, and passed over Mizpeh of Gilead, and from Mizpeh of Gilead he passed over unto the children of Ammon. 30 And Jephthah vowed a vow unto the LORD, and said: 'If Thou wilt indeed deliver the children of Ammon into my hand, 31 then it shall be, that whatsoever cometh forth of the doors of my house to meet me, when I return in peace from the children of Ammon, it shall be the LORD's, and I will offer it up for a burnt-offering.' 32 So Jephthah passed over unto the children of Ammon to fight against them; and the LORD delivered them into his hand. 33 And he smote them from Aroer until thou come to Minnith, even twenty cities, and unto Abel-cheramim, with a very great slaughter. So the children of Ammon were subdued before the children of Israel.

34 And Jephthah came to Mizpah unto his house, and, behold, his daughter came out to meet him with timbrels and with dances; and she was his only child; beside her he had neither son nor daughter. 35 And it came to pass, when he saw her, that he rent his clothes, and said: 'Alas, my daughter! thou hast brought me very low, and thou art become my troubler; for I have opened my mouth unto the LORD, and I cannot go back.' 36 And she said unto him: 'My father, thou hast opened thy mouth unto the LORD; do unto me according to that which hath proceeded out of thy mouth; forasmuch as the LORD hath taken vengeance for thee of thine enemies, even of the children of Ammon.' 37 And she said unto her father: 'Let this thing be done for me: let me alone two months, that I may depart and go down upon the mountains, and bewail my virginity, I and my companions.'

---

4. Bereshit Rabbah 60:3. Bereshit Rabbah is a Midrashic compilation of early Rabbinic commentary on the Five Books of Moses arranged in the order of the volume of the Torah being commented upon. While Midrashic commentary begins with the text of the volume at hand (here, Genesis), its actual subject matter is allusive and ranges widely.

38 And he said: 'Go.' And he sent her away for two months; and she departed, she and her companions, and bewailed her virginity upon the mountains. 39 And it came to pass at the end of two months, that she returned unto her father, who did with her according to his vow which he had vowed; and she had not known man. And it was a custom in Israel, 40 that the daughters of Israel went yearly to lament the daughter of Jephthah the Gileadite four days in a year.

3. Women Seek Justice in King Solomon's Court

Choosing a case featuring litigants from the lowest reaches of society to exemplify the wisdom of its most powerful monarch indicates the Hebrew Bible's rejection of the conventional equation of monarchical status solely with manifestations of power. This particular narrative also reveals insights into the complications of identifying a just verdict.

In this narrative involving women, several questions regarding justice come to the fore. First, can members of the lower—if not, indeed, the most dispossessed—levels of society hope to receive a just hearing in the highest of courts, marked by riches and opulence? Second, can a monarch whose activities seem focused on increasing the glory and renown of his court, both within his own kingdom and in the realm of international power settings, be sensitive to a case involving prostitutes and their contested children? Even if (as the text seems to indicate) these first two questions can be answered positively, a third complication exists: Is it possible to determine a just verdict if the facts of the case are themselves in dispute?

Here, King Solomon reveals his intellectual mastery. The brilliance of Solomon's judgment lies in hearing a case whose only testimony consists of the two conflicting accounts of the two parties in the case, and—despite the unavailability of any outside evidence—still managing to establish the fact of the matter: the identity of the real mother. The truth is revealed in a judgment he asks the parties themselves to make regarding his proposed slicing and sharing of the baby (see below, I Kings 3:16–28). King Solomon's approach shows that all who seek justice in his court, even those from lower social strata, are worthy of close attention—and indeed, why true justice demands nothing less.

I Kings 3:16–28

16 Then came there two women, that were harlots, unto the king, and stood before him. 17 And the one woman said: 'Oh, my

lord, I and this woman dwell in one house; and I was delivered of a child with her in the house. 18 And it came to pass the third day after I was delivered, that this woman was delivered also; and we were together; there was no stranger with us in the house, save we two in the house. 19 And this woman's child died in the night; because she overlay it. 20 And she arose at midnight, and took my son from beside me, while thy handmaid slept, and laid it in her bosom, and laid her dead child in my bosom. 21 And when I rose in the morning to give my child suck, behold, it was dead; but when I had looked well at it in the morning, behold, it was not my son, whom I did bear.' 22 And the other woman said: 'Nay; but the living [child][5] is my son, and the dead is thy son.' And this said: 'No; but the dead is thy son, and the living is my son.' Thus they spoke before the king.

23 Then said the king: 'The one saith: This is my son that liveth, and thy son is the dead; and the other saith: Nay; but thy son is the dead, and my son is the living.' 24 And the king said: 'Fetch me a sword.' And they brought a sword before the king. 25 And the king said: 'Divide the living child in two, and give half to the one, and half to the other.' 26 Then spoke the woman whose the living child was unto the king, for her heart yearned upon her son, and she said: 'Oh, my lord, give her the living child, and in no wise slay it.' But the other said: 'It shall be neither mine nor thine; divide it.' 27 Then the king answered and said: 'Give her the living child, and in no wise slay it: she is the mother thereof.' 28 And all Israel heard of the judgment which the king had judged; and they feared the king; for they saw that the wisdom of God was in him, to do justice.

For further reading see Malbim's modern-era Hebrew biblical commentary on Genesis 4:6–7. See also further selections, in Chapter 7, "Justice."

B. The Communal Position of Women

Women in the Hebrew Bible play prominent roles in the fight to achieve justice and realize redemption. They performatively praise their redemption from Egypt: they are the ones to dance at their delivery from the pursuing Egyptians at the Re[e]d Sea (Exodus 15:20). They claim their right to inherit landholdings in the Promised Land (the Daughters of

---

5. Brackets in the translated text indicate my addition, for clarity of reference.

Zelofchad [Numbers 27:1–11]). Once in the Promised Land, they build cities (Caleb's daughter; see Judges 1:12–15), they fight wars (Deborah in Judges 4:4–23), and they even act on their own to destroy dictators (Judges 9:53–54).

1. Women Recognize the Redemption: Dancing and the Song of Miriam

Exodus 15:20–21

20 And Miriam the prophetess, the sister of Aaron, took a timbrel in her hand; and all the women went out after her with timbrels and with dances. 21 And Miriam sang unto them:

Sing ye to the LORD, for He is highly exalted:
The horse and his rider hath He thrown into the sea.

2. Women Inherit in the Promised Land

The five daughters of Zelophehad are unusual in many ways: they are (several times, in both Numbers 27:1 and 36:11) individually named; they voice their dissatisfaction with what seems to them a lacuna in the law that openly specified only men as heritors, without mentioning the possibility that women might also be heirs to their fathers' landholdings. They take their query straight to the top (Numbers 27:2). The question they ask (Numbers 27:4) is: What justice is there if daughters who are the sole offspring of their families are disallowed from taking their share in landholding? The answer they receive may surprise contemporary readers.

Numbers 27:1–8

1 Then drew near the daughters of Zelophehad, the son of Hepher, the son of Gilead, the son of Machir, the son of Manasseh, of the families of Manasseh the son of Joseph; and these are the names of his daughters: Mahlah, Noah, and Hoglah, and Milcah, and Tirzah. 2 And they stood before Moses, and before Eleazar the priest, and before the princes and all the congregation, at the door of the tent of meeting, saying:

3 'Our father died in the wilderness, and he was not among the company of them that gathered themselves together against the LORD in the company of Korah, but he died in his own sin; and

he had no sons. 4 Why should the name of our father be done away from among his family, because he had no son? Give unto us a possession among the brethren of our father.' 5 And Moses brought their cause before the LORD.

6 And the LORD spoke unto Moses, saying: 7 'The daughters of Zelophehad speak right: thou shalt surely give them a possession of an inheritance among their father's brethren; and thou shalt cause the inheritance of their father to pass unto them. 8 And thou shalt speak unto the children of Israel, saying: If a man die, and have no son, then ye shall cause his inheritance to pass unto his daughter.

For further reading, see Numbers 36:2–12 and Joshua 17:3–6.

3. Women Build Cities

The following selections focus on the central role that women can play in determining the landholding portion among their respective tribes (cf. also Ruth, chapters 3–4). The individual details mentioned in the second selection below, expanding upon the narrative in Joshua, highlight the women's connection to vision, perspicacity, and growth.

Joshua 15:13–19

13 And unto Caleb the son of Jephunneh he gave a portion among the children of Judah, according to the commandment of the LORD to Joshua, even Kiriath-arba, which Arba was the father of Anak—the same is Hebron. 14 And Caleb drove out thence the three sons of Anak, Sheshai, and Ahiman, and Talmai, the children of Anak. 15 And he went up thence against the inhabitants of Debir—now the name of Debir beforetime was Kiriath-sepher. 16 And Caleb said: 'He that smiteth Kiriath-sepher, and taketh it, to him will I give Achsah my daughter to wife.' 17 And Othniel the son of Kenaz, the brother of Caleb, took it; and he gave him Achsah his daughter to wife. 18 And it came to pass, when she came unto him, that she persuaded him to ask of her father a field; and she alighted from off her ass; and Caleb said unto her: 'What wouldest thou?' 19 And she said: 'Give me a blessing; for that thou hast set me in the Southland, give me therefore springs of water.' And he gave her the Upper Springs and the Nether Springs.

For further reading, see Judges 1:8–15.

The next selection from I Chronicles introduces us to the sons of Jacob and their progeny in greater detail than the summary given in Exodus. At the beginning of this selection, Ephraim, Joseph's son and Jacob's grandson, has just finished mourning the death of one of his own sons.

I Chronicles 7:20–24

20 And the sons of Ephraim: Shuthelah—and Bered was his son, and Tahath his son, and Eleadah his son, and Tahath his son, 21 and Zabad his son, and Shuthelah his son—and Ezer, and Elead, whom the men of Gath that were born in the land slew, because they came down to take away their cattle. 22 And Ephraim their father mourned many days, and his brethren came to comfort him. 23 And he went in to his wife, and she conceived, and bore a son, and he called his name Beriah, because it went evil with his house. 24 And his daughter was Sheerah, who built Beth-horon the nether and the upper, and Uzzen-sheerah.

4. Women as Military and Political Leaders

This narrative highlights Deborah, a woman who goes beyond the conventions of the era in assuming remarkable burdens as a leader; she is a judge, and she takes responsibility for organizing the military battle against the Israelites' enemies at that time, the Canaanites.

For her part, Jael on her own devises the plan to eliminate Sisera from ever threatening the Israelites again. Often unnoticed is that by her actions, Yael ("Jael" in the JPS 1917 translation) quietly but decisively ignores the de facto understanding that existed between her community, the Kenites, and the surrounding Canaanites (of whom Sisera was a military leader) in Ancient Israel (Hever, Yael's husband, moves his tent from the Kenites and pitches it next to the Israelite camp [Judges 4:11]).

a. Deborah

Judges 4:1–16

1 And the children of Israel again did that which was evil in the sight of the LORD, when Ehud was dead. 2 And the LORD gave them over into the hand of Jabin king of Canaan, that reigned in Hazor; the captain of whose host[6] was Sisera, who dwelt in Harosheth-goiim. 3 And the children of Israel cried

---

6. JPS 1917: "host."

unto the LORD; for he had nine hundred chariots of iron; and twenty years he mightily oppressed the children of Israel.

4 Now Deborah, a prophetess, the wife of Lappidoth, she judged Israel at that time. 5 And she sat under the palm-tree of Deborah between Ramah and Beth-el in the hill-country of Ephraim; and the children of Israel came up to her for judgment. 6 And she sent and called Barak the son of Abinoam out of Kedesh-naphtali, and said unto him: 'Hath not the LORD, the God of Israel, commanded, saying: Go and draw toward mount Tabor, and take with thee ten thousand men of the children of Naphtali and of the children of Zebulun? 7 And I will draw unto thee to the brook Kishon Sisera, the captain of Jabin's army, with his chariots and his multitude; and I will deliver him into thy hand. 8 And Barak said unto her: 'If thou wilt go with me, then I will go; but if thou wilt not go with me, I will not go.' 9 And she said: 'I will surely go with thee; notwithstanding the journey that thou takest shall not be for thy honour; for the LORD will give Sisera over into the hand of a woman.' And Deborah arose, and went with Barak to Kedesh. 10 And Barak called Zebulun and Naphtali together to Kedesh; and there went up ten thousand men at his feet; and Deborah went up with him.

11 Now Heber the Kenite had severed himself from the Kenites, even from the children of Hobab the father-in-law of Moses, and had pitched his tent as far as Elon-bezaanannim, which is by Kedesh.

12 And they told Sisera that Barak the son of Abinoam was gone up to mount Tabor. 13 And Sisera gathered together all his chariots, even nine hundred chariots of iron, and all the people that were with him, from Harosheth-goiim, unto the brook Kishon. 14 And Deborah said unto Barak: 'Up; for this is the day in which the LORD hath delivered Sisera into thy hand; is not the LORD gone out before thee?' So Barak went down from mount Tabor, and ten thousand men after him. 15 And the LORD discomfited Sisera, and all his chariots, and all his host, with the edge of the sword before Barak; and Sisera alighted from his chariot, and fled away on his feet. 16 But Barak pursued after the chariots, and after the host, unto Harosheth-goiim; and all the host of Sisera fell by the edge of the sword; there was not a man left.

b. Yael

Judges 4:17–24

17 Howbeit Sisera fled away on his feet to the tent of Jael the wife of Heber the Kenite; for there was peace between Jabin the king of Hazor and the house of Heber the Kenite. 18 And Jael went out to meet Sisera, and said unto him: 'Turn in, my lord, turn in to me; fear not.' And he turned in unto her into the tent, and she covered him with a rug. 19 And he said unto her: 'Give me, I pray thee, a little water to drink; for I am thirsty.' And she opened a bottle of milk, and gave him drink, and covered him. 20 And he said unto her: 'Stand in the door of the tent, and it shall be, when any man doth come and inquire of thee, and say: Is there any man here? that thou shalt say: No.'

21 Then Jael Heber's wife took a tent-pin, and took a hammer in her hand, and went softly unto him, and smote the pin into his temples, and it pierced through into the ground; for he was in a deep sleep; so he swooned and died. 22 And, behold, as Barak pursued Sisera, Jael came out to meet him, and said unto him: 'Come, and I will show thee the man whom thou seekest.' And he came unto her; and, behold, Sisera lay dead, and the tent-pin was in his temples. 23 So God subdued on that day Jabin the king of Canaan before the children of Israel. 24 And the hand of the children of Israel prevailed more and more against Jabin the king of Canaan, until they had destroyed Jabin king of Canaan.

Contrary to the self-abnegation traditionally expected of women, Deborah is not shy about recognizing her own centrality in uniting those tribes who successfully fight (and eventually defeat) Sisera. She also gives full credit to Yael, the Kenite woman who quick-wittedly prevents Sisera from living to fight another day.

c. Deborah's Song of Victory

Judges 5:1, 6–18, 24–31

1 Then sang Deborah and Barak the son of Abinoam on that
  day, saying:
. . . .
6 In the days of Shamgar the son of Anath,
In the days of Jael, the highways ceased,
And the travellers walked through byways.

7 The rulers ceased in Israel, they ceased,
Until that thou didst arise, Deborah,
That thou didst arise a mother in Israel.
8 They chose new gods;
Then was war in the gates;
Was there a shield or spear seen
Among forty thousand in Israel?
9 My heart is toward the governors of Israel,
That offered themselves willingly among the people.
Bless ye the LORD.
10 Ye that ride on white asses,
Ye that sit on rich cloths,
And ye that walk by the way, tell of it;
11 Louder than the voice of archers, by the watering-troughs!
There shall they rehearse the righteous acts of the LORD,
Even the righteous acts of His rulers in Israel.
Then the people of the LORD went down to the gates.

12 Awake, awake, Deborah;
Awake, awake, utter a song;
Arise, Barak, and lead thy captivity captive, thou son of
  Abinoam.
13 Then made He a remnant to have dominion over the nobles
  and the people;
The LORD made me have dominion over the mighty.
14 Out of Ephraim came they whose root is in Amalek;
After thee, Benjamin, among thy peoples;
Out of Machir came down governors,
And out of Zebulun they that handle the marshal's staff.
15 And the princes of Issachar were with Deborah;
As was Issachar, so was Barak;
Into the valley they rushed forth at his feet.
Among the divisions of Reuben
There were great resolves of heart.
16 Why sattest thou among the sheep-folds,
To hear the pipings for the flocks?
At the divisions of Reuben
There were great searchings of heart.
17 Gilead abode beyond the Jordan;
And Dan, why doth he sojourn by the ships?
Asher dwelt at the shore of the sea,
And abideth by its bays.

18 Zebulun is a people that jeoparded their lives unto the death,
And Naphtali, upon the high places of the field.

. . . .

24 Blessed above women shall Jael be,
The wife of Heber the Kenite,
Above women in the tent shall she be blessed.
25 Water he asked, milk she gave him;
In a lordly bowl she brought him curd.
26 Her hand she put to the tent-pin,
And her right hand to the workmen's hammer;
And with the hammer she smote Sisera, she smote through his
        head,
Yea, she pierced and struck through his temples.
27 At her feet he sunk, he fell, he lay;
At her feet he sunk, he fell;
Where he sunk, there he fell down dead.
28 Through the window she looked forth, and peered,
The mother of Sisera, through the lattice:
'Why is his chariot so long in coming?
Why tarry the wheels of his chariots?'
29 The wisest of her princesses answer her,
Yea, she returneth answer to herself:
30 'Are they not finding, are they not dividing the spoil?
A damsel, two damsels to every man;
To Sisera a spoil of dyed garments,
A spoil of dyed garments of embroidery,
Two dyed garments of broidery for the neck of every spoiler?'

31 So perish all Thine enemies, O LORD;
But they that love Him be as the sun when he goeth forth in his
        might.
And the land had rest forty years.

d. One Woman Fights the Despot

Deborah and Yael are not the only women who distinguish themselves by combatting dehumanizing dictatorships. Years later, an unnamed woman saves her townspeople and, arguably, the rest of the Israelites from coming under the cruel sway of the would-be despot, Avimelekh[7] (see further Judges 8:7–21).

---

7. JPS 1917: "Abimelekh."

Here is the immediate backstory to this reading: Avimelekh despotically rules over the city of Shekhem, thinking to make it the cornerstone of his planned domination over the entire Israelite land. This point is signaled by the name by which Avimelekh is known, which translates as "my father is king." In other words, Avimelekh's moniker justifies his absolutist position by invoking a supposed dynasty beginning with his father. This contention is duplicitous: Avimelekh's father, Gideon, also known as Yerubaal (Judges 8:35), specifically refuses the throne when the Elders of his tribe offer it to him (see further, Judges 8:22–23, and the selections under "Israelite Deliberation about Monarchy" in Chapter 12).

While not deliberately invoking a cause for the Shekhemites' eventual disenchantment with Avimelekh, the Hebrew biblical text implies that the Shekhemites (maternal relatives of Avimelekh) no longer see any advantage for them in submitting to his dictatorial power. The Hebrew biblical text goes on to describe Avimelekh's utter cruelty in war: he kills all the people in the city of Shekhem by burning them in the tower in which they had sought refuge; he also sows the fields of the city with salt to ensure that the land would be permanently barren as punishment for its inhabitants who had dared to rebel against him. Upon attempting to do the same to the city of Tebetz, however, Avimelekh is caught by a different set of circumstances.

Judges 9:22–23, 26–28, 45–47, 49–55

22 And Abimelech was prince over Israel three years. 23 And God sent an evil spirit between Abimelech and the men of Shechem; and the men of Shechem dealt treacherously with Abimelech;

. . . .

26 And Gaal the son of Ebed came with his brethren, and went on to Shechem; and the men of Shechem put their trust in him. 27 And they went out into the field, and gathered their vineyards, and trod the grapes, and held festival, and went into the house of their god, and did eat and drink, and cursed Abimelech. 28 And Gaal the son of Ebed said: 'Who is Abimelech, and who is Shechem, that we should serve him? is not he the son of Jerubbaal? and Zebul his officer? serve ye the men of Hamor the father of Shechem; but why should we serve him?

. . . .

45 And Abimelech fought against the city all that day; and he took the city, and slew the people that were therein; and he beat down the city, and sowed it with salt.

46 And when all the men of the tower of Shechem heard thereof, they entered into the hold of the house of El-berith. 47 And it was told Abimelech that all the men of the tower of Shechem were gathered together.

. . . .

49 And all the people likewise cut down every man his bough, and followed Abimelech, and put them to the hold, and set the hold on fire upon them; so that all the men of the tower of Shechem died also, about a thousand men and women.

50 Then went Abimelech to Thebez, and encamped against Thebez, and took it. 51 But there was a strong tower within the city, and thither fled all the men and women, even all they of the city, and shut themselves in, and got them up to the roof of the tower. 52 And Abimelech came unto the tower, and fought against it, and went close unto the door of the tower to burn it with fire. 53 And a certain woman cast an upper millstone upon Abimelech's head, and broke his skull. 54 Then he called hastily unto the young man his armour-bearer, and said unto him: 'Draw thy sword, and kill me, that men say not of me: A woman slew him.' And his young man thrust him through, and he died. 55 And when the men of Israel saw that Abimelech was dead, they departed every man unto his place.

After relating Avimelekh's unprecedented cruelty (his brutality towards his countrymen evokes the manner of their enemies, not their compatriots), this episode ends on what seems to be a whimper. Even though the Hebrew biblical text exhibits antimonarchical sentiments through the words of selfless leaders like Yerubaal, also known as Gideon (see above Judges 8:35)—pro-monarchical pronouncements are limited to leaders who prioritize self-aggrandizement above national welfare—there seems as yet to be no awareness on the part of the Israelites that they need to rethink their attitudes towards power and social ethics.

C. Women as Social Barometer

The time-honored status of women as people who customarily remain in the background can make it easy to overlook the structural biases that mask women's voices and the unique contributions that they can make to society. Despite this, women remain aware of the larger implications of the forces that seem to thwart the modest objectives of everyday life.

The readings in this section explore this theme, with stories whose ends might not tie up perfectly, by attending to the complex moral issues explored within the imperfections of daily life. In these selections, women are often portrayed as wiser than their kinsmen and interlocutors: they can understand the political import of angelic messages (Samson's mother) better than their menfolk. Importantly, the women continue to maintain a dialogue with the men in their lives even though (and perhaps, as the conversations of Delilah with the Philistines show, because) these men demonstrably do not comprehend the larger stakes of these discussions. Still, women do not always emerge victorious from these narratives. As a result, these narratives may well leave the contemporary reader less than satisfied.

The final reading in this section, the Concubine in Gibeah narrative, is often characterized as just an example of deadly civil war. We include this text here in this section in order to highlight its importance as a commentary on the injustice of valorizing political power plays over quotidian justice.

1. Veiled Messages: Samson's Birth Is Announced

Judges 13

1 And the children of Israel again did that which was evil in the sight of the LORD; and the LORD delivered them into the hand of the Philistines forty years.

2 And there was a certain man of Zorah, of the family of the Danites, whose name was Manoah; and his wife was barren, and bore not. 3 And the angel of the LORD appeared unto the woman, and said unto her: 'Behold now, thou art barren, and hast not borne; but thou shalt conceive, and bear a son. 4 Now therefore beware, I pray thee, and drink no wine nor strong drink, and eat not any unclean thing. 5 For, lo, thou shalt conceive, and bear a son; and no razor shall come upon his head; for the child shall be a Nazirite unto God from the womb; and he shall begin to save Israel out of the hand of the Philistines.' 6 Then the woman came and told her husband, saying: 'A man of God came unto me, and his countenance was like the countenance of the angel of God, very terrible; and I asked him not whence he was, neither told he me his name; 7 but he said unto me: Behold, thou

shalt conceive, and bear a son; and now drink no wine nor strong drink, and eat not any unclean thing; for the child shall be a Nazirite unto God from the womb to the day of his death.'

8 Then Manoah entreated the LORD, and said: 'Oh, LORD, I pray Thee, let the man of God whom Thou didst send come again unto us, and teach us what we shall do unto the child that shall be born.' 9 And God hearkened to the voice of Manoah; and the angel of God came again unto the woman as she sat in the field; but Manoah her husband was not with her. 10 And the woman made haste, and ran, and told her husband, and said unto him: 'Behold, the man hath appeared unto me, that came unto me that day.' 11 And Manoah arose, and went after his wife, and came to the man, and said unto him: 'Art thou the man that spokest unto the woman?' And he said: 'I am.' 12 And Manoah said: 'Now when thy word cometh to pass, what shall be the rule for the child, and what shall be done with him?'

13 And the angel of the LORD said unto Manoah: 'Of all that I said unto the woman let her beware. 14 She may not eat of any thing that cometh of the grapevine, neither let her drink wine or strong drink, nor eat any unclean thing; all that I commanded her let her observe.' 15 And Manoah said unto the angel of the LORD: 'I pray thee, let us detain thee, that we may make ready a kid for thee.' 16 And the angel of the LORD said unto Manoah: 'Though thou detain me, I will not eat of thy bread; and if thou wilt make ready a burnt-offering, thou must offer it unto the LORD.' For Manoah knew not that he was the angel of the LORD.

17 And Manoah said unto the angel of the LORD: 'What is thy name, that when thy words come to pass we may do thee honour?' 18 And the angel of the LORD said unto him: 'Wherefore askest thou after my name, seeing it is hidden?' 19 So Manoah took the kid with the meal-offering, and offered it upon the rock unto the LORD; and [the angel] did wondrously, and Manoah and his wife looked on. 20 For it came to pass, when the flame went up toward heaven from off the altar, that the angel of the LORD ascended in the flame of the altar; and Manoah and his wife looked on; and they fell on their faces to the ground. 21 But the angel of the LORD did no more appear to Manoah or to his wife. Then Manoah knew that he was the angel of the LORD. 22 And Manoah said unto his wife: 'We shall surely die, because we have seen God.' 23 But his wife said unto him: 'If the LORD were

pleased to kill us, He would not have received a burnt-offering and a meal-offering at our hand, neither would He have shown us all these things, nor would at this time have told such things as these.'

24 And the woman bore a son, and called his name Samson; and the child grew, and the LORD blessed him. 25 And the spirit of the LORD began to move him in Mahaneh-dan, between Zorah and Eshtaol.

2. Comprehension and Machination: Delilah Conquers Samson

In this selection, we witness the complex encounter between two striking personages, Samson and Delilah, neither of whom is easily reducible to a conventional image of, respectively, a "strongman" or a "seductive woman." Not entirely clear, either, are the rationales behind their respective strategies with regard to the Philistines. What is at stake in this confrontation? Who wins? Who loses?

For additional background on these issues, see Chapter 4, "Leadership," in Part I, the section on "The Estranged Leader as a Riddle" (Judges 16).

Judges 16:4–21

4 And it came to pass afterward, that he [Samson] loved a woman in the valley of Sorek, whose name was Delilah. 5 And the lords of the Philistines came up unto her, and said unto her: 'Entice him, and see wherein his great strength lieth, and by what means we may prevail against him, that we may bind him to afflict him; and we will give thee every one of us eleven hundred pieces of silver.' 6 And Delilah said to Samson: 'Tell me, I pray thee, wherein thy great strength lieth, and wherewith thou mightest be bound to afflict thee.' 7 And Samson said unto her: 'If they bind me with seven fresh bowstrings that were never dried, then shall I become weak, and be as any other man.' 8 Then the lords of the Philistines brought up to her seven fresh bowstrings which had not been dried, and she bound him with them. 9 Now she had liers-in-wait abiding in the inner chamber. And she said unto him: 'The Philistines are upon thee, Samson.' And he broke the bowstrings as a string of tow is broken when it toucheth the fire. So his strength was not known. 10 And Delilah said unto Samson: 'Behold, thou hast mocked me, and told me lies; now tell me, I pray thee, wherewith thou mightest be bound.' 11 And

he said unto her: 'If they only bind me with new ropes where-with no work, hath been done, then shall I become weak, and be as any other man.' 12 So Delilah took new ropes, and bound him therewith, and said unto him: 'The Philistines are upon thee, Samson.' And the liers-in-wait were abiding in the inner chamber. And he broke them from off his arms like a thread. 13 And Delilah said unto Samson: 'Hitherto thou hast mocked me, and told me lies; tell me wherewith thou mightest be bound.' And he said unto her: 'If thou weavest the seven locks of my head with the web.' 14 And she fastened it with the pin, and said unto him: 'The Philistines are upon thee, Samson.' And he awoke out of his sleep, and plucked away the pin of the beam, and the web. 15 And she said unto him: 'How canst thou say: I love thee, when thy heart is not with me? thou hast mocked me these three times, and hast not told me wherein thy great strength lieth.' 16 And it came to pass, when she pressed him daily with her words, and urged him, that his soul was vexed unto death. 17 And he told her all his heart, and said unto her: 'There hath not come a razor upon my head; for I have been a Nazirite unto God from my mother's womb; if I be shaven, then my strength will go from me, and I shall become weak, and be like any other man.' 18 And when Delilah saw that he had told her all his heart, she sent and called for the lords of the Philistines, saying: 'Come up this once, for he hath told me all his heart.' Then the lords of the Philistines came up unto her, and brought the money in their hand. 19 And she made him sleep upon her knees; and she called for a man, and had the seven locks of his head shaven off; and she began to afflict him, and his strength went from him. 20 And she said: 'The Philistines are upon thee, Samson.' And he awoke out of his sleep, and said: 'I will go out as at other times, and shake myself.' But he knew not that the LORD was departed from him. 21 And the Philistines laid hold on him, and put out his eyes; and they brought him down to Gaza, and bound him with fetters of brass; and he did grind in the prison-house.

3. The Concubine in Gibeah: Women Mirror a Broken Society

This horrific tale of internecine warfare ending the biblical Book of Judges is conventionally read as advocating for the kind of stability anticipated with the onset of monarchical rule. But in their presentation of the narra-tive, the Hebrew biblical books of Samuel, Kings, and the Later Prophets demonstrate overwhelmingly that injustice often holds central sway in the royal court as well. Consequently, the standard reading of the Hebrew Bible as supporting the Israelite institution of a (centralized) monarchy has comparatively little evidence to support it.

What this narrative does show, in the eerie reprise of the Lot and Sodom story (see Chapter 1, "Cities," particularly the sections on "The City as a Locus of Power" and "City of Evil") is that women—their welfare, and even their lives—are presented here as completely fungible. The concubine epitomizes strangeness: as a concubine, she is bereft of the (limited) legal rights of a full-fledged wife; as an adult woman, she is dominated by her father and then by her common-law husband; as a female, she is thrust into and out of strange places and houses where she is left alone to die. Even in death, she is not accorded a decent burial: her "own" body, by which she pleasured her common-law husband, is utilized by him—cut into pieces—to send a political message to the other Israelites.

The chaos that engulfs the Israelites is not just the civil war that ensues upon the receipt of the Levite's fiery message. More fundamentally, this disorder mirrors the absence of moral compass that characterizes the Israelite nation, in their unethical and antisocial behaviors. The broken body of the Levite's nameless concubine reflects the inhumane nature and structures of Israelite society at that time.

Judges 19

1 And it came to pass in those days, when there was no king in Israel, that there was a certain Levite sojourning on the farther side of the hill-country of Ephraim, who took to him a concubine out of Beth-lehem in Judah. 2 And his concubine turned away from him,[8] and went away from him unto her father's house to Beth-lehem in Judah, and was there the space of four months.

3 And her husband arose, and went after her, to speak kindly unto her, to bring her back, having his servant with him, and a couple of asses; and she brought him into her father's house; and when the father of the damsel saw him, he rejoiced to meet him. 4 And his father-in-law, the damsel's father, retained him; and he abode with him three days; so they did eat and drink, and lodged there. 5 And it came to pass on the fourth day, that they arose early in the morning, and he rose up to depart; and the damsel's father said unto his son-in-law: 'Stay thy heart with a

---

8. JPS 1917: "played the harlot against him."

morsel of bread, and afterward ye shall go your way.' 6 So they
sat down, and did eat and drink, both of them together; and the
damsel's father said unto the man: 'Be content, I pray thee, and
tarry all night, and let thy heart be merry.' 7 And the man rose up
to depart; but his father-in-law urged him, and he lodged there
again. 8 And he arose early in the morning on the fifth day to
depart; and the damsel's father said: 'Stay thy heart, I pray thee,
and tarry ye until the day declineth'; and they did eat, both of
them.

9 And when the man rose up to depart, he, and his concubine,
and his servant, his father-in-law, the damsel's father, said unto
him: 'Behold, now the day draweth toward evening; tarry, I pray
you, all night; behold, the day groweth to an end; lodge here, that
thy heart may be merry; and to-morrow get you early on your
way, that thou mayest go home.' 10 But the man would not tarry
that night, but he rose up and departed, and came over against
Jebus—the same is Jerusalem; and there were with him a couple
of asses saddled; his concubine also was with him. 11 When they
were by Jebus—the day was far spent—the servant said unto his
master: 'Come, I pray thee, and let us turn aside into this city of
the Jebusites, and lodge in it.' 12 And his master said unto him:
'We will not turn aside into the city of a foreigner, that is not of
the children of Israel; but we will pass over to Gibeah.' 13 And he
said unto his servant: 'Come and let us draw near to one of these
places; and we will lodge in Gibeah, or in Ramah.'

14 So they passed on and went their way; and the sun went
down upon them near to Gibeah, which belongeth to Benjamin.
15 And they turned aside thither, to go in to lodge in Gibeah;
and he went in, and sat him down in the broad place of the city;
for there was no man that took them into his house to lodge. 16
And, behold, there came an old man from his work out of the
field at even; now the man was of the hill-country of Ephraim,
and he sojourned in Gibeah; but the men of the place were
Benjamites. 17 And he lifted up his eyes, and saw the wayfaring man in the broad place of the city; and the old man said:
'Whither goest thou? and whence comest thou?' 18 And he said
unto him: 'We are passing from Beth-lehem in Judah unto the
farther side of the hill-country of Ephraim; from thence am
I, and I went to Beth-lehem in Judah, and I am now going to
the house of the LORD; and there is no man that taketh me

into his house. 19 Yet there is both straw and provender for our asses; and there is bread and wine also for me, and for thy handmaid, and for the young man that is with thy servants; there is no want of any thing.' 20 And the old man said: 'Peace be unto thee; howsoever let all thy wants lie upon me; only lodge not in the broad place.' 21 So he brought him into his house, and gave the asses fodder; and they washed their feet, and did eat and drink.

22 As they were making their hearts merry, behold, the men of the city, certain base fellows, beset the house round about, beating at the door; and they spoke to the master of the house, the old man, saying: 'Bring forth the man that came into thy house, that we may know him.' 23 And the man, the master of the house, went out unto them, and said unto them: 'Nay, my brethren, I pray you, do not so wickedly; seeing that this man is come into my house, do not this wanton deed. 24 Behold, here is my daughter a virgin, and his concubine; I will bring them out now, and humble ye them, and do with them what seemeth good unto you; but unto this man do not so wanton a thing.' 25 But the men would not hearken to him; so the man laid hold on his concubine, and brought her forth unto them; and they knew her, and abused her all the night until the morning; and when the day began to spring, they let her go. 26 Then came the woman in the dawning of the day, and fell down at the door of the man's house where her lord was, till it was light. 27 And her lord rose up in the morning, and opened the doors of the house, and went out to go his way; and, behold, the woman his concubine was fallen down at the door of the house, with her hands upon the threshold. 28 And he said unto her. 'Up, and let us be going'; but none answered; then he took her up upon the ass; and the man rose up, and got him unto his place.

29 And when he was come into his house, he took a knife, and laid hold on his concubine, and divided her, limb by limb, into twelve pieces, and sent her throughout all the borders of Israel. 30 And it was so, that all that saw it said: 'Such a thing hath not happened nor been seen from the day that the children of Israel came up out of the land of Egypt unto this day; consider it, take counsel, and speak.'

For further reading, see the section on "Civil War and Violence against Women" in Chapter 11, "Civil War."

D. Women Enable the Davidic Monarchy

In the Hebrew Bible, women may reflect, at times in a passive vein, the moral standards of Israelite society. At the same time, women can serve as effective transmitters of power. As we see in the readings of this section in particular, David ascends to power through his relationships and alliances with women: the fact of his anointment by Samuel is, in and of itself, a necessary but insufficient political condition for securing David's throne. The central position of women in enabling the realization of power represents the Hebrew Bible's unique insight into how power is actually attained and preserved in a world that is, at best, dismissive of women.

1. Women and the Saul-David Rivalry

As the lines between the supporters of Saul and the supporters of David harden, the Hebrew biblical text presents women as embodying each of the two camps. The first texts in this section deal with the reaction to David's triumph over Goliath. In the second presentation (for this volume) of David's triumph over Goliath (I Samuel 18:1–30), it is worth considering these texts in terms of how they reflect Saul's complex political calculations, and his reactions to Michal's defense of David, which must have appeared to Saul as disloyalty of the most acute kind (cf. Lear's response to his children in Shakespeare's *King Lear,* esp. act I, scene 4).

Readers of these texts might think about the multiple ironies in presenting David, a shepherd who is self-confessedly unschooled in the arts of war (but with experience in defending his herd), as victorious over a renowned strongman of the time (Goliath). Readers may also consider Saul's concern about an unknown rival being able to best him politically, without this rival ever expressing even a hidden desire for political power.

On the other hand, there may be reasons for Saul to worry about David as an incipient contender for power. What was at stake for Saul if Goliath had defeated the Israelite troops? What roles do the presence and expressions of the courtier class play in Saul's perception of David as a political rival? What roles do the politics of sex and marriage play in the fraught Saul-David relationship?

I Samuel 18:1–18

1 And it came to pass, when he had made an end of speaking unto Saul, that the soul of Jonathan was knit with the soul of David, and Jonathan loved him as his own soul. 2 And Saul took him that day, and would let him go no more home to his father's house. 3 Then Jonathan made a covenant with David, because he

loved him as his own soul. 4 And Jonathan stripped himself of the robe that was upon him, and gave it to David, and his apparel, even to his sword, and to his bow, and to his girdle. 5 And David went out; whithersoever Saul sent him, he had good success; and Saul set him over the men of war; and it was good in the sight of all the people, and also in the sight of Saul's servants.

6 And it came to pass as they came, when David returned from the slaughter of the Philistine, that the women came out of all the cities of Israel, singing and dancing, to meet king Saul, with timbrels, with joy, and with three-stringed instruments. 7 And the women sang one to another in their play, and said:

Saul hath slain his thousands,

And David his ten thousands.

8 And Saul was very wroth, and this saying displeased him; and he said: 'They have ascribed unto David ten thousands, and to me they have ascribed but thousands; and all he lacketh is the kingdom!' 9 And Saul eyed David from that day and forward.

10 And it came to pass on the morrow, that an evil spirit from God came mightily upon Saul, and he raved in the midst of the house; and David played with his hand, as he did day by day; and Saul had his spear in his hand. 11 And Saul cast the spear; for he said: 'I will smite David even to the wall.' And David stepped aside out of his presence twice. 12 And Saul was afraid of David, because the LORD was with him, and was departed from Saul. 13 Therefore Saul removed him from him, and made him his captain over a thousand; and he went out and came in before the people. 14 And David had great success in all his ways; and the LORD was with him. 15 And when Saul saw that he had great success, he stood in awe of him. 16 But all Israel and Judah loved David; for he went out and came in before them.

17 And Saul said to David: 'Behold my elder daughter Merab, her will I give thee to wife; only be thou valiant for me, and fight the LORD's battles.' For Saul said: 'Let not my hand be upon him, but let the hand of the Philistines be upon him.' 18 And David said unto Saul: 'Who am I, and what is my life, or my father's family in Israel, that I should be son-in-law to the king?'

2. David Marries into the Royal Family

As seen in this selection (and as referenced above in Chapter 4, "Leadership"), Saul offers his eldest daughter, Meirav,[9] to David, as encouragement to continue defending the Israelites from Philistine onslaughts. Saul's gesture is less magnanimous than it seems (I Samuel 18:19, 21, 25, 29); the offer, as well, is short-lived (Meirav is given to someone else in marriage). As it turns out, Saul's youngest daughter, Michal, is in love with David, and they eventually marry. It is worthwhile noting David's realistic assessment of his new fortune, and the skill with which he navigates the shoals of life in the royal court (I Samuel 18: 22–25).

We present this selection again to emphasize the role of women in the politics of the royal court.

I Samuel 18:17–30

17 And Saul said to David: 'Behold my elder daughter Merab, her will I give thee to wife; only be thou valiant for me, and fight the LORD's battles.' For Saul said: 'Let not my hand be upon him, but let the hand of the Philistines be upon him.' 18 And David said unto Saul: 'Who am I, and what is my life, or my father's family in Israel, that I should be son-in-law to the king?' 19 But it came to pass at the time when Merab, Saul's daughter, should have been given to David, that she was given unto Adriel the Meholathite to wife.

20 And Michal Saul's daughter loved David; and they told Saul, and the thing pleased him. 21 And Saul said: 'I will give him her, that she may be a snare to him, and that the hand of the Philistines may be against him.' Wherefore Saul said to David: 'Thou shalt this day be my son-in-law through the one of the twain.' 22 And Saul commanded his servants: 'Speak with David secretly, and say: Behold, the king hath delight in thee, and all his servants love thee; now therefore be the king's son-in-law.' 23 And Saul's servants spoke those words in the ears of David. And David said: 'Seemeth it to you a light thing to be the king's son-in-law, seeing that I am a poor man, and lightly esteemed?' 24 And the servants of Saul told him, saying: 'On this manner spoke David.'

25 And Saul said: 'Thus shall ye say to David: The king desireth not any dowry, but a hundred foreskins of the Philistines, to be

---

9. JPS 1917: "Merab."

avenged of the king's enemies.' For Saul thought to make David
fall by the hand of the Philistines. 26 And when his servants told
David these words, it pleased David well to be the king's son-
in-law. And the days were not expired; 27 and David arose and
went, he and his men, and slew of the Philistines two hundred
men; and David brought their foreskins, and they gave them in
full number to the king, that he might be the king's son-in-law.
And Saul gave him Michal his daughter to wife. 28 And Saul
saw and knew that the LORD was with David; and Michal
Saul's daughter loved him. 29 And Saul was yet the more afraid
of David; and Saul was David's enemy continually.

30 Then the princes of the Philistines went forth; and it came
to pass, as often as they went forth, that David prospered more
than all the servants of Saul; so that his name was much set by.

3. Women and Political Intrigue

Michal's love for David stands him in good stead: she takes David's side in
the power struggle between her husband and her father, King Saul, by lower-
ing David from the window so that he can flee from Saul's wrath. This flight
inaugurates a heightening of the Saul-David rupture, with Saul pursuing
David throughout Israel, involving various towns in the ensuing violence.
An important turning point in David's political fortunes is heralded with
Abigail's support of David and the dedication of her resources to his cause.

Throughout this narrative, David's relations with women—particularly
with his wife Michal—mirror and presage his political position: Saul abro-
gates David's marriage to Michal as a sign of his royal power, displeasure, and
anxiety; but David summons Michal to him when he is officially crowned
king. Ironically—and perhaps, cruelly—David puts Michal aside when she
criticizes his non-royal manner of jubilation upon his accompaniment of
the Holy Ark to the capital city of the monarchy, the newly reconquered
Jerusalem. In the last selection of this section, David puts his own royal
dynasty in jeopardy with his arrogant taking of Batsheva, disregarding the
moral and ethical concerns that arise with his arbitrary exercise of power.

a. Michal Takes David's Side and Saves Him

I Samuel 19:9–22

9 And an evil spirit from the LORD was upon Saul, as he sat
in his house with his spear in his hand; and David was playing

with his hand. 10 And Saul sought to smite David even to the wall with the spear; but he slipped away out of Saul's presence, and he smote the spear into the wall; and David fled, and escaped that night. 11 And Saul sent messengers unto David's house, to watch him, and to slay him in the morning; and Michal David's wife told him, saying: 'If thou save not thy life to-night, to-morrow thou shalt be slain.' 12 So Michal let David down through the window; and he went, and fled, and escaped. 13 And Michal took the teraphim, and laid it in the bed, and put a quilt of goats' hair at the head thereof, and covered it with a cloth. 14 And when Saul sent messengers to take David, she said: 'He is sick.' 15 And Saul sent the messengers to see David, saying: 'Bring him up to me in the bed, that I may slay him.' 16 And when the messengers came in, behold, the teraphim was in the bed, with the quilt of goats' hair at the head thereof. 17 And Saul said unto Michal: 'Why hast thou deceived me thus, and let mine enemy go, that he is escaped?' And Michal answered Saul: 'He said unto me: Let me go; why should I kill thee?'

18 Now David fled, and escaped, and came to Samuel to Ramah, and told him all that Saul had done to him. And he and Samuel went and dwelt in Naioth. 19 And it was told Saul, saying: 'Behold, David is at Naioth in Ramah.' 20 And Saul sent messengers to take David; and when they saw the company of the prophets prophesying, and Samuel standing as head over them, the spirit of God came upon the messengers of Saul, and they also prophesied. 21 And when it was told Saul, he sent other messengers, and they also prophesied. And Saul sent messengers again the third time, and they also prophesied. 22 Then went he also to Ramah, and came to the great cistern that is in Secu; and he asked and said: 'Where are Samuel and David?' And one said: 'Behold, they are at Naioth in Ramah.'

b. Abigail Supports David

I Samuel 25:2–44

2 And there was a man in Maon, whose possessions were in Carmel; and the man was very great, and he had three thousand sheep, and a thousand goats; and he was shearing his sheep in Carmel. 3 Now the name of the man was Nabal; and the name

of his wife Abigail; and the woman was of good understanding, and of a beautiful form; but the man was churlish and evil in his doings; and he was of the house of Caleb. 4 And David heard in the wilderness that Nabal was shearing his sheep. 5 And David sent ten young men, and David said unto the young men: 'Get you up to Carmel, and go to Nabal, and greet him in my name; 6 and thus ye shall say: All hail! and peace be both unto thee, and peace be to thy house, and peace be unto all that thou hast. 7 And now I have heard that thou hast shearers; thy shepherds have now been with us, and we did them no hurt, neither was there aught missing unto them, all the while they were in Carmel. 8 Ask thy young men, and they will tell thee; wherefore let the young men find favour in thine eyes; for we come on a good day; give, I pray thee, whatsoever cometh to thy hand, unto thy servants, and to thy son David.'

9 And when David's young men came, they spoke to Nabal according to all those words in the name of David, and ceased. 10 And Nabal answered David's servants, and said: 'Who is David? and who is the son of Jesse? there are many servants now-a-days that break away every man from his master; 11 shall I then take my bread, and my water, and my flesh that I have killed for my shearers, and give it unto men of whom I know not whence they are?' 12 So David's young men turned on their way, and went back, and came and told him according to all these words. 13 And David said unto his men: 'Gird ye on every man his sword.' And they girded on every man his sword; and David also girded on his sword; and there went up after David about four hundred men; and two hundred abode by the baggage.

14 But one of the young men told Abigail, Nabal's wife, saying: 'Behold, David sent messengers out of the wilderness to salute our master; and he flew upon them. 15 But the men were very good unto us, and we were not hurt, neither missed we any thing, as long as we went with them, when we were in the fields; 16 they were a wall unto us both by night and by day, all the while we were with them keeping the sheep. 17 Now therefore know and consider what thou wilt do; for evil is determined against our master, and against all his house; for he is such a base fellow, that one cannot speak to him.'

18 Then Abigail made haste, and took two hundred loaves, and two bottles of wine, and five sheep ready dressed, and five measures of parched corn, and a hundred clusters of raisins, and two hundred cakes of figs, and laid them on asses. 19 And she said unto her young men: 'Go on before me; behold, I come after you.' But she told not her husband Nabal. 20 And it was so, as she rode on her ass, and came down by the covert of the mountain, that, behold, David and his men came down towards her; and she met them.— 21 Now David had said: 'Surely in vain have I kept all that this fellow hath in the wilderness, so that nothing was missed of all that pertained unto him; and he hath returned me evil for good. 22 God do so unto the enemies of David, and more also, if I leave of all that pertain to him by the morning light so much as one male.'— 23 And when Abigail saw David, she made haste, and alighted from her ass, and fell before David on her face, and bowed down to the ground. 24 And she fell at his feet, and said: 'Upon me, my lord, upon me be the iniquity; and let thy handmaid, I pray thee, speak in thine ears, and hear thou the words of thy handmaid. 25 Let not my lord, I pray thee, regard this base fellow, even Nabal; for as his name is, so is he: Nabal is his name, and churlishness is with him; but I thy handmaid saw not the young men of my lord, whom thou didst send. 26 Now therefore, my lord, as the LORD liveth, and as thy soul liveth, seeing the LORD hath withholden thee from bloodguiltiness, and from finding redress for thyself with thine own hand, now therefore let thine enemies, and them that seek evil to my lord, be as Nabal. 27 And now this present which thy servant hath brought unto my lord, let it be given unto the young men that follow my lord. 28 Forgive, I pray thee, the trespass of thy handmaid; for the LORD will certainly make my lord a sure house, because my lord fighteth the battles of the LORD; and evil is not found in thee all thy days. 29 And though man be risen up to pursue thee, and to seek thy soul, yet the soul of my lord shall be bound in the bundle of life with the LORD thy God; and the souls of thine enemies, them shall he sling out, as from the hollow of a sling. 30 And it shall come to pass, when the LORD shall have done to my lord according to all the good that He hath spoken concerning thee, and shall have appointed thee prince over Israel; 31 that this shall be no stumbling-block unto thee, nor

offence of heart unto my lord, either that thou hast shed blood without cause, or that my lord hath found redress for himself. And when the LORD shall have dealt well with my lord, then remember thy handmaid.'

32 And David said to Abigail: 'Blessed be the LORD, the God of Israel, who sent thee this day to meet me; 33 and blessed be thy discretion, and blessed be thou, that hast kept me this day from bloodguiltiness, and from finding redress for myself with mine own hand. 34 For in very deed, as the LORD, the God of Israel, liveth, who hath withholden me from hurting thee, except thou hadst made haste and come to meet me, surely there had not been left unto Nabal by the morning light so much as one male.' 35 So David received of her hand that which she had brought him; and he said unto her: 'Go up in peace to thy house; see, I have hearkened to thy voice, and have accepted thy person.'

36 And Abigail came to Nabal; and, behold, he held a feast in his house, like the feast of a king; and Nabal's heart was merry within him, for he was very drunken; wherefore she told him nothing, less or more, until the morning light. 37 And it came to pass in the morning, when the wine was gone out of Nabal, that his wife told him these things, and his heart died within him, and he became as a stone. 38 And it came to pass about ten days after, that the LORD smote Nabal, so that he died.

39 And when David heard that Nabal was dead, he said: 'Blessed be the LORD, that hath pleaded the cause of my reproach from the hand of Nabal, and hath kept back His servant from evil; and the evil-doing of Nabal hath the LORD returned upon his own head.' And David sent and spoke concerning Abigail, to take her to him to wife. 40 And when the servants of David were come to Abigail to Carmel, they spoke unto her, saying: 'David hath sent us unto thee, to take thee to him to wife.' 41 And she arose, and bowed down with her face to the earth, and said: 'Behold, thy handmaid is a servant to wash the feet of the servants of my lord.' 42 And Abigail hastened, and arose, and rode upon an ass, with five damsels of hers that followed her; and she went after the messengers of David, and became his wife.

43 David also took Ahinoam of Jezreel; and they became both of them his wives. 44 Now Saul had given Michal his daughter, David's wife, to Palti the son of Laish, who was of Gallim.

c. David Engineers Michal's Return

II Samuel 3:14–16

14 And David sent messengers to Ish-bosheth Saul's son, saying: 'Deliver me my wife Michal, whom I betrothed to me for a hundred foreskins of the Philistines.'

15 And Ish-bosheth sent, and took her from her husband, even from Paltiel the son of Laish.

16 And her husband went with her, weeping as he went, and followed her to Bahurim. Then said Abner unto him: 'Go, return'; and he returned.

d. The Break with Michal

II Samuel 6:15–22

15 So David and all the house of Israel brought up the ark of the LORD with shouting, and with the sound of the horn.

16 And it was so, as the ark of the LORD came into the city of David, that Michal the daughter of Saul looked out at the window, and saw king David leaping and dancing before the LORD; and she despised him in her heart. 17 And they brought in the ark of the LORD, and set it in its place, in the midst of the tent that David had pitched for it; and David offered burnt-offerings and peace-offerings before the LORD. 18 And when David had made an end of offering the burnt-offering and the peace-offerings, he blessed the people in the name of the LORD of hosts. 19 And he dealt among all the people, even among the whole multitude of Israel, both to men and women, to every one a cake of bread, and a cake made in a pan, and a sweet cake. So all the people departed every one to his house.

20 Then David returned to bless his household. And Michal the daughter of Saul came out to meet David, and said: 'How did the king of Israel get him honour to-day, who uncovered himself to-day in the eyes of the handmaids of his servants, as one of the

vain fellows shamelessly uncovereth himself!' 21 And David said unto Michal: 'Before the LORD, who chose me above thy father, and above all his house, to appoint me prince over the people of the LORD, over Israel, before the LORD will I make merry. 22 And I will be yet more vile than thus, and will be base in mine own sight; and with the handmaids whom thou hast spoken of, with them will I get me honour.'

e. The Taking of Batsheva

II Samuel 11

1 And it came to pass, at the return of the year, at the time when kings go out to battle, that David sent Joab, and his servants with him, and all Israel; and they destroyed the children of Ammon, and besieged Rabbah. But David tarried at Jerusalem.

2 And it came to pass at eventide, that David arose from off his bed, and walked upon the roof of the king's house; and from the roof he saw a woman bathing; and the woman was very beautiful to look upon. 3 And David sent and inquired after the woman. And one said: 'Is not this Bath-sheba, the daughter of Eliam, the wife of Uriah the Hittite?' 4 And David sent messengers, and took her; and she came in unto him, and he lay with her; for she was purified from her uncleanness; and she returned unto her house. 5 And the woman conceived; and she sent and told David, and said: 'I am with child.'

6 And David sent to Joab[, saying]: 'Send me Uriah the Hittite.' And Joab sent Uriah to David. 7 And when Uriah was come unto him, David asked of him how Joab did, and how the people fared, and how the war prospered. 8 And David said to Uriah: 'Go down to thy house, and wash thy feet.' And Uriah departed out of the king's house, and there followed him a mess of food from the king. 9 But Uriah slept at the door of the king's house with all the servants of his lord, and went not down to his house. 10 And when they had told David, saying: 'Uriah went not down unto his house', David said unto Uriah: 'Art thou not come from a journey? wherefore didst thou not go down unto thy house?' 11 And Uriah said unto David: 'The ark, and Israel, and Judah, abide in booths; and my lord Joab, and the servants of my lord, are encamped in the open field; shall I then go into my house, to eat and to drink, and to lie with my wife? as thou livest, and as thy

soul liveth, I will not do this thing.' 12 And David said to Uriah: 'Tarry here to-day also, and to-morrow I will let thee depart.' So Uriah abode in Jerusalem that day, and the morrow. 13 And when David had called him, he did eat and drink before him; and he made him drunk; and at even he went out to lie on his bed with the servants of his lord, but went not down to his house.

14 And it came to pass in the morning, that David wrote a letter to Joab, and sent it by the hand of Uriah. 15 And he wrote in the letter, saying: 'Set ye Uriah in the forefront of the hottest battle, and retire ye from him, that he may be smitten, and die.' 16 And it came to pass, when Joab kept watch upon the city, that he assigned Uriah unto the place where he knew that valiant men were. 17 And the men of the city went out, and fought with Joab; and there fell some of the people, even of the servants of David; and Uriah the Hittite died also. 18 Then Joab sent and told David all the things concerning the war; 19 and he charged the messenger, saying: 'When thou hast made an end of telling all the things concerning the war unto the king, 20 it shall be that, if the king's wrath arise, and he say unto thee: Wherefore went ye so nigh unto the city to fight? knew ye not that they would shoot from the wall? 21 who smote Abimelech the son of Jerubbesheth? did not a woman cast an upper millstone upon him from the wall, that he died at Thebez? why went ye so nigh the wall? then shalt thou say: Thy servant Uriah the Hittite is dead also.'

22 So the messenger went, and came and told David all that Joab had sent him for. 23 And the messenger said unto David: 'The men prevailed against us, and came out unto us into the field, and we were upon them even unto the entrance of the gate. 24 And the shooters shot at thy servants from off the wall; and some of the king's servants are dead, and thy servant Uriah the Hittite is dead also.' 25 Then David said unto the messenger: 'Thus shalt thou say unto Joab: Let not this thing displease thee, for the sword devoureth in one manner or another; make thy battle more strong against the city, and overthrow it; and encourage thou him.'

26 And when the wife of Uriah heard that Uriah her husband was dead, she made lamentation for her husband. 27 And when the mourning was past, David sent and took her home to his house, and she became his wife, and bore him a son. But the thing that David had done displeased the LORD.

f. The Parable of the Single Ewe

II Samuel 12:1–24

1 And the LORD sent Nathan unto David. And he came unto him, and said unto him: 'There were two men in one city: the one rich, and the other poor. 2 The rich man had exceeding many flocks and herds; 3 but the poor man had nothing save one little ewe lamb, which he had bought and reared; and it grew up together with him, and with his children; it did eat of his own morsel, and drank of his own cup, and lay in his bosom, and was unto him as a daughter. 4 And there came a traveller unto the rich man, and he spared to take of his own flock and of his own herd, to dress for the wayfaring man that was come unto him, but took the poor man's lamb, and dressed it for the man that was come to him.' 5 And David's anger was greatly kindled against the man; and he said to Nathan: 'As the LORD liveth, the man that hath done this deserveth to die; 6 and he shall restore the lamb fourfold, because he did this thing, and because he had no pity.'

7 And Nathan said to David: 'Thou art the man. Thus saith the LORD, the God of Israel: I anointed thee king over Israel, and I delivered thee out of the hand of Saul; 8 and I gave thee thy master's house, and thy master's wives into thy bosom, and gave thee the house of Israel and of Judah; and if that were too little, then would I add unto thee so much more. 9 Wherefore hast thou despised the word of the LORD, to do that which is evil in My sight? Uriah the Hittite thou hast smitten with the sword, and his wife thou hast taken to be thy wife, and him thou hast slain with the sword of the children of Ammon. 10 Now therefore, the sword shall never depart from thy house; because thou hast despised Me, and hast taken the wife of Uriah the Hittite to be thy wife. 11 Thus saith the LORD: Behold, I will raise up evil against thee out of thine own house, and I will take thy wives before thine eyes, and give them unto thy neighbour, and he shall lie with thy wives in the sight of this sun. 12 For thou didst it secretly; but I will do this thing before all Israel, and before the sun.'

13 And David said unto Nathan: 'I have sinned against the LORD.' And Nathan said unto David: 'The LORD also hath put away thy sin; thou shalt not die. 14 Howbeit, because by this

deed thou hast greatly blasphemed the enemies of the LORD, the child also that is born unto thee shall surely die.' 15 And Nathan departed unto his house. And the LORD struck the child that Uriah's wife bore unto David, and it was very sick. 16 David therefore besought God for the child; and David fasted, and as often as he went in, he lay all night upon the earth. 17 And the elders of his house arose, and stood beside him, to raise him up from the earth; but he would not, neither did he eat bread with them. 18 And it came to pass on the seventh day, that the child died. And the servants of David feared to tell him that the child was dead; for they said: 'Behold, while the child was yet alive, we spoke unto him, and he hearkened not unto our voice; how then shall we tell him that the child is dead, so that he do himself some harm?'

19 But when David saw that his servants whispered together, David perceived that the child was dead; and David said unto his servants: 'Is the child dead?' And they said: 'He is dead.' 20 Then David arose from the earth, and washed, and anointed himself, and changed his apparel; and he came into the house of the LORD, and worshipped; then he came to his own house; and when he required, they set bread before him, and he did eat. 21 Then said his servants unto him: 'What thing is this that thou hast done? thou didst fast and weep for the child, while it was alive; but when the child was dead, thou didst rise and eat bread.' 22 And he said: 'While the child was yet alive, I fasted and wept; for I said: Who knoweth whether the LORD will not be gracious to me, that the child may live? 23 But now he is dead, wherefore should I fast? can I bring him back again? I shall go to him, but he will not return to me.'

24 And David comforted Bath-sheba his wife, and went in unto her, and lay with her; and she bore a son, and called his name Solomon. And the LORD loved him.

CHAPTER 6
TREATIES

A. Treaties Present and Absent

Treaties are an important tool for keeping order in the ancient world. Abraham, an unknown quantity from Mesopotamia, makes treaties with the various leaders he encounters on his travels in and around Canaan (see also Genesis 25:9–10, 49:29–30, and 50:12–13). In these texts, treaties are often abrogated by the stronger party who does not need the treaty (cf. Genesis 26), and the establishment of "peace" is often nothing more than the acknowledgment of an uneasy standoff between the parties. Important purchases (such as burial grounds) are also often confirmed by treaty.

But sometimes treaties fail, or aren't even achieved: some of the nations surrounding the Israelites and their Promised Land—such as Edom—refuse to make treaties with the newly emergent Israelites because they oppose their return to the Promised Land. Also, the newly liberated Israelites are warned against making treaties with the surrounding idol-worshipping Canaanites, lest they turn from their singular monotheism and thus lose Divine protection.

1. Abraham's Treaty with Avimelekh

The treaty between Abraham and Avimelekh harks back to the events of Genesis 20, when Avimelekh narrowly escapes Divine punishment for having unwittingly taken a married woman (Sarah, who was presented as Abraham's sister) into the royal palace. Perhaps fearful of finding himself at a disadvantage, Avimelekh appears with his armed general, as if to say: "I want a true meeting of the minds." Importantly, this treaty takes place after one of Abraham's water wells has been taken over by Avimelekh's Philistines, presaging the situation that obtains with Isaac, whose wells of water are stopped up by the Philistines (Genesis 26).

Genesis 21:22–34

22 And it came to pass at that time, that Abimelech and Phicol the captain of his army[1] spoke unto Abraham, saying: 'God is with thee in all that thou doest. 23 Now therefore swear unto me here by God that thou wilt not deal falsely with me, nor with my son, nor with my son's son; but according to the kindness that I have done unto thee, thou shalt do unto me, and to the land wherein thou hast sojourned.' 24 And Abraham said: 'I will swear.' 25 And Abraham reproved Abimelech because of the well of water, which Abimelech's servants had violently taken away. 26 And Abimelech said: 'I know not who hath done this thing; neither didst thou tell me, neither yet heard I of it, but to-day.'

27 And Abraham took sheep and oxen, and gave them unto Abimelech; and they two made a covenant. 28 And Abraham set seven ewe-lambs of the flock by themselves. 29 And Abimelech said unto Abraham: 'What mean these seven ewe-lambs which thou hast set by themselves?' 30 And he said: 'Verily, these seven ewe-lambs shalt thou take of my hand, that it may be a witness unto me, that I have digged this well.' 31 Wherefore that place was called Beer-sheba; because there they swore both of them. 32 So they made a covenant at Beer-sheba; and Abimelech rose up, and Phicol the captain of his army,[2] and they returned into the land of the Philistines. 33 And Abraham planted a tamarisk-tree in Beer-sheba, and called there on the name of the LORD, the Everlasting God. 34 And Abraham sojourned in the land of the Philistines many days.

2. Isaac's Uneasy Treaty with the Philistines

Readers of this story, which bears many parallels to the story about Abraham's wells cited above, may ask themselves how the relations between Abraham and the Philistines are both similar to, and different from, those recounted in the narrative about Isaac and the Philistines. What do we learn about the permanence of treaties, and the stability of interpretation, from these narratives?

---

1. JPS 1917: "host."

2. JPS 1917: "host."

Genesis 26:12–33

12 And Isaac sowed in that land, and found in the same year a hundred-fold; and the LORD blessed him. 13 And the man waxed great, and grew more and more until he became very great. 14 And he had possessions of flocks, and possessions of herds, and a great household; and the Philistines envied him. 15 Now all the wells which his father's servants had digged in the days of Abraham his father, the Philistines had stopped them, and filled them with earth. 16 And Abimelech said unto Isaac: 'Go from us; for thou art much mightier than we.' 17 And Isaac departed thence, and encamped in the valley of Gerar, and dwelt there. 18 And Isaac digged again the wells of water, which they had digged in the days of Abraham his father; for the Philistines had stopped them after the death of Abraham; and he called their names after the names by which his father had called them.

19 And Isaac's servants digged in the valley, and found there a well of living water. 20 And the herdmen of Gerar strove with Isaac's herdmen, saying: 'The water is ours.' And he called the name of the well Esek; because they contended with him. 21 And they digged another well, and they strove for that also. And he called the name of it Sitnah. 22 And he removed from thence, and digged another well; and for that they strove not. And he called the name of it Rehoboth; and he said: 'For now the LORD hath made room for us, and we shall be fruitful in the land.' 23 And he went up from thence to Beer-sheba. 24 And the LORD appeared unto him the same night, and said: 'I am the God of Abraham thy father. Fear not, for I am with thee, and will bless thee, and multiply thy seed for My servant Abraham's sake.' 25 And he builded an altar there, and called upon the name of the LORD, and pitched his tent there; and there Isaac's servants digged a well.

26 Then Abimelech went to him from Gerar, and Ahuzzath his friend, and Phicol the captain of his army.[3] 27 And Isaac said unto them: 'Wherefore are ye come unto me, seeing ye hate me, and have sent me away from you?' 28 And they said: 'We saw plainly that the LORD was with thee; and we said: Let there now be an oath betwixt us, even betwixt us and thee, and let us make a covenant with thee; 29 that thou wilt do us no hurt, as

---

3. JPS translation: "host."

we have not touched thee, and as we have done unto thee nothing but good, and have sent thee away in peace; thou art now the blessed of the LORD.' 30 And he made them a feast, and they did eat and drink. 31 And they rose up betimes in the morning, and swore one to another; and Isaac sent them away, and they departed from him in peace. 32 And it came to pass the same day, that Isaac's servants came, and told him concerning the well which they had digged, and said unto him: 'We have found water.' 33 And he called it Shibah. Therefore the name of the city is Beer-sheba unto this day.

3. Buying a Burial Ground: Abraham's Treaty with the Hittites

Readers of this section may wonder why Abraham needs to make a treaty with his neighbors in order to purchase a burial place for his wife, Sarah. In what way does the tone of this narrative differ from the tone of the narratives of the previous section? Why?

Genesis 23

1 And the life of Sarah was a hundred and seven and twenty years; these were the years of the life of Sarah.

2 And Sarah died in Kiriatharba—the same is Hebron—in the land of Canaan; and Abraham came to mourn for Sarah, and to weep for her. 3 And Abraham rose up from before his dead, and spoke unto the children of Heth, saying: 4 'I am a stranger and a sojourner with you: give me a possession of a burying-place with you, that I may bury my dead out of my sight.' 5 And the children of Heth answered Abraham, saying unto him: 6 'Hear us, my lord: thou art a mighty prince among us; in the choice of our sepulchres bury thy dead; none of us shall withhold from thee his sepulchre, but that thou mayest bury thy dead.'

7 And Abraham rose up, and bowed down to the people of the land, even to the children of Heth. 8 And he spoke with them, saying: 'If it be your mind that I should bury my dead out of my sight, hear me, and entreat for me to Ephron the son of Zohar, 9 that he may give me the cave of Machpelah, which he hath, which is in the end of his field; for the full price let him give it to me in the midst of you for a possession of a burying-place.'

10 Now Ephron was sitting in the midst of the children of Heth; and Ephron the Hittite answered Abraham in the hearing of the children of Heth, even of all that went in at the gate of his city, saying: 11 'Nay, my lord, hear me: the field give I thee, and the cave that is therein, I give it thee; in the presence of the sons of my people give I it thee; bury thy dead.' 12 And Abraham bowed down before the people of the land.

13 And he spoke unto Ephron in the hearing of the people of the land, saying: 'But if thou wilt, I pray thee, hear me: I will give the price of the field; take it of me, and I will bury my dead there.' 14 And Ephron answered Abraham, saying unto him: 15 'My lord, hearken unto me: a piece of land worth four hundred shekels of silver, what is that betwixt me and thee? bury therefore thy dead.' 16 And Abraham hearkened unto Ephron; and Abraham weighed to Ephron the silver, which he had named in the hearing of the children of Heth, four hundred shekels of silver, current money with the merchant.

17 So the field of Ephron, which was in Machpelah, which was before Mamre, the field, and the cave which was therein, and all the trees that were in the field, that were in all the border thereof round about, were made sure 18 unto Abraham for a possession in the presence of the children of Heth, before all that went in at the gate of his city. 19 And after this, Abraham buried Sarah his wife in the cave of the field of Machpelah before Mamre—the same is Hebron—in the land of Canaan. 20 And the field, and the cave that is therein, were made sure unto Abraham for a possession of a burying-place by the children of Heth.

4. Death and Real Estate

The importance of owning the land to be used for the burial of the dead, and the centrality of this past transaction to the future national self-identification of the Israelites, are both apparent hundreds of years later, when the Israelites enter their Promised Land under the leadership of Joshua. The verse of the selection here refers to the burial of Joseph's bones, resulting from a deathbed promise exacted by Joseph from his brothers (Genesis 50:25). Joseph's bones had been carried out of Egypt by Moses at the time of the Israelite exodus (Exodus 13:19), and were now buried in land that Jacob had previously bought from the Hittites (Genesis 33:19).

Joshua 24:32

32 And the bones of Joseph, which the children of Israel brought up out of Egypt, buried they in Shechem, in the parcel of ground which Jacob bought of the sons of Hamor the father of Shechem for a hundred pieces of money; and they became the inheritance of the children of Joseph.

B. When Not to Make a Treaty

Even though the Patriarchs regularize distinct aspects of their relationships with their Canaanite neighbors through treaties, that practice is specifically disallowed when the Israelites return to their Promised Land after leaving Egypt and wandering in the wilderness for forty years. Why is this the case?

Exodus 34:11–16

11 Observe thou that which I am commanding thee this day; behold, I am driving out before thee the Amorite, and the Canaanite, and the Hittite, and the Perizzite, and the Hivite, and the Jebusite. 12 Take heed to thyself, lest thou make a covenant with the inhabitants of the land whither thou goest, lest they be for a snare in the midst of thee. 13 But ye shall break down their altars, and dash in pieces their pillars, and ye shall cut down their Asherim. 14 For thou shalt bow down to no other god; for the LORD, whose name is Jealous, is a jealous God; 15 lest thou make a covenant with the inhabitants of the land, and they go astray after their gods, and do sacrifice unto their gods, and they call thee, and thou eat of their sacrifice; 16 and thou take of their daughters unto thy sons, and their daughters go astray after their gods, and make thy sons go astray after their gods.

A similar message appears in Deuteronomy 7.

Deuteronomy 7:1–5

1 When the LORD thy God shall bring thee into the land whither thou goest to possess it, and shall cast out many nations before thee, the Hittite, and the Girgashite, and the Amorite, and the Canaanite, and the Perizzite, and the Hivite, and the Jebusite, seven nations greater and mightier than thou; 2 and when the LORD thy God shall deliver them up before thee, and thou shalt smite them; then thou shalt utterly destroy them; thou

shalt make no covenant with them, nor show mercy unto them; 3 neither shalt thou make marriages with them: thy daughter thou shalt not give unto his son, nor his daughter shalt thou take unto thy son. 4 For he will turn away thy son from following Me, that they may serve other gods; so will the anger of the LORD be kindled against you, and He will destroy thee quickly. 5 But thus shall ye deal with them: ye shall break down their altars, and dash in pieces their pillars, and hew down their Asherim, and burn their graven images with fire.

1. A Case Involving Emorites: Sihon, King of Heshbon

The Emorites are one of the Canaanite nations that lived in the environs of the Promised Land. Sihon, King of Heshbon, an Emorite king, refuses to allow the Israelites to pass through his land, or even to sell bread and water to the Israelites on their journey. Sihon attacks the Israelites, and the battle ends in Sihon's destruction. As God had predicted (Deuteronomy 2:31) the Israelites are now able to settle Sihon's land.

Deuteronomy 2:26–34

26 And I sent messengers out of the wilderness of Kedemoth unto Sihon king of Heshbon with words of peace, saying: 27 'Let me pass through thy land; I will go along by the highway, I will neither turn unto the right hand nor to the left. 28 Thou shalt sell me food for money, that I may eat; and give me water for money, that I may drink; only let me pass through on my feet; 29 as the children of Esau that dwell in Seir, and the Moabites that dwell in Ar, did unto me; until I shall pass over the Jordan into the land which the LORD our God giveth us.' 30 But Sihon king of Heshbon would not let us pass by him; for the LORD thy God hardened his spirit, and made his heart obstinate, that He might deliver him into thy hand, as appeareth this day.

31 And the LORD said unto me: 'Behold, I have begun to deliver up Sihon and his land before thee; begin to possess his land.' 32 Then Sihon came out against us, he and all his people, unto battle at Jahaz. 33 And the LORD our God delivered him up before us; and we smote him, and his sons, and all his people. 34 And we took all his cities at that time, and utterly destroyed every city, the men, and the women, and the little ones; we left none remaining.

2. Strange Exceptions: Edom and Moab

Despite the warnings against establishing friendly relations with (some of the) surrounding idolatrous nations, this particular counsel is not a blanket injunction against every overture to other peoples and other nations. The Israelites do try to make a treaty with Edom, and to reach an understanding with Moab, on the way to their Promised Land. Both overtures appear to fail, in the sense that neither nation allows the Israelites to pass through their respective lands, or even to buy food from them.

a. The Case of Edom

Numbers 20:14–21

14 And Moses sent messengers from Kadesh unto the king of Edom: 'Thus saith thy brother Israel: Thou knowest all the travail that hath befallen us; 15 how our fathers went down into Egypt, and we dwelt in Egypt a long time; and the Egyptians dealt ill with us, and our fathers; 16 and when we cried unto the LORD, He heard our voice, and sent an angel, and brought us forth out of Egypt; and, behold, we are in Kadesh, a city in the uttermost of thy border. 17 Let us pass, I pray thee, through thy land; we will not pass through field or through vineyard, neither will we drink of the water of the wells; we will go along the king's highway, we will not turn aside to the right hand nor to the left, until we have passed thy border.' 18 And Edom said unto him: 'Thou shalt not pass through me, lest I come out with the sword against thee.' 19 And the children of Israel said unto him: 'We will go up by the highway; and if we drink of thy water, I and my cattle, then will I give the price thereof; let me only pass through on my feet; there is no hurt.' 20 And he said: 'Thou shalt not pass through.' And Edom came out against him with much people, and with a strong hand. 21 Thus Edom refused to give Israel passage through his border; wherefore Israel turned away from him.

A more nuanced version of these events is given in Deuteronomy 2.

Deuteronomy 2:2–8

2 And the LORD spoke unto me, saying: 3 'Ye have encircled[4] this mountain long enough; turn you northward. 4 And command thou the people, saying: Ye are to pass through the border of your brethren the children of Esau, that dwell in Seir; and they

---

4. JPS 1917: "encompassed."

will be afraid of you; take ye good heed unto yourselves therefore; 5 contend not with them; for I will not give you of their land, no, not so much as for the sole of the foot to tread on; because I have given mount Seir unto Esau for a possession. 6 Ye shall purchase food of them for money, that ye may eat; and ye shall also buy water of them for money, that ye may drink. 7 For the LORD thy God hath blessed thee in all the work of thy hand; He hath known thy walking through this great wilderness; these forty years the LORD thy God hath been with thee; thou hast lacked nothing.' 8 So we passed by from our brethren the children of Esau, that dwell in Seir, from the way of the Arabah, from Elath and from Ezion-geber ...

b. The Case of Moab

Deuteronomy 2:8–9

8 ... And we turned and passed by the way of the wilderness of Moab. 9 And the LORD said unto me: 'Be not at enmity with Moab, neither contend with them in battle; for I will not give thee of his land for a possession; because I have given Ar unto the children of Lot for a possession....'

C. The Case of the Moabites and the Ammonites Contrasted with That of the Edomites and the Egyptians

As in the case of the Edomites (Deuteronomy 2:5), the Israelites are prohibited from waging war against either the Moabites (Deuteronomy 2:9) or the Ammonites (Deuteronomy 1:19), because the land of these nations has been allotted to them by Divine promise. At the same time, a distinction is made between the Edomites and the other two nations: while the Israelites may not despise the Edomite "for he is your brother" (Deuteronomy 23:7), the Ammonites and Moabites are prohibited from ever "entering the congregation of the Lord" (Deuteronomy 23:4; my translation). At first glance, the reason given for this prohibition—"because they met you not with bread and water" (Deuteronomy 23:4)—would seem equally to apply to the Edomites, who are under no such stricture. However, Deuteronomy 23:6 adduces an additional reason for the Israelites to distinguish the case of the Moabites and the Ammonites from that of the Edomites: these two nations had hired Balaam "to curse thee" (Deuteronomy 23:6). In view of what the Hebrew Bible considers to be deep-seated animosity on the part of the Ammonites and the Moabites vis-à-vis the Israelites, the Israelites are commanded not to fight them, but also (prudently?) to keep their distance from them.

By contrast, the Egyptians are not condemned forever even though they once had bitterly oppressed the Israelite nation: after all, before their horrific enslavement of the Israelites, the Egyptians had also allowed Jacob's family, the (proto-) Israelites, to come into their land during a time of famine. That hospitality is recognized by the Hebrew Bible: a people who can be (politically) welcoming, even if they also are slavers, are not totally lost to feelings of human fellowship.

Deuteronomy 23:4–8

4 An Ammonite or a Moabite shall not enter into the assembly of the LORD; even to the tenth generation shall none of them enter into the assembly of the LORD for ever; 5 because they met you not with bread and with water in the way, when ye came forth out of Egypt; and because they hired against thee Balaam the son of Beor from Pethor of Aram-naharaim, to curse thee. 6 Nevertheless the LORD thy God would not hearken unto Balaam; but the LORD thy God turned the curse into a blessing unto thee, because the LORD thy God loved thee. 7 Thou shalt not seek their peace nor their prosperity all thy days for ever.

8 Thou shalt not abhor an Edomite, for he is thy brother; thou shalt not abhor an Egyptian, because thou wast a stranger in his land.

CHAPTER 7

JUSTICE

The Hebrew Bible treats the domain of justice expansively, encompassing relations between people and God, as well as those among people. In neither realm is justice easily assimilable to a model that excludes the possibility of ongoing agency, change, and redemption on the part of those who violate justice. As far in spirit from the ancient Greek notion of tragic inevitability as from the more "modern" type of pessimism at least nominally expressed in Fitzgerald's *The Last Tycoon*,[1] the Hebrew Bible insists that personal, political, and national lives indeed often have second acts. The Hebrew biblical text reminds its readers that people can take advantage of new opportunities if they consciously evaluate their options.

A. Fundamental Justice: Justice of the Earth

This narrative describes what happens when Cain and Abel, sons of Adam, bring offerings to God. God prefers Abel's offering to Cain's, and an episode of jealousy and violence ensues.

Genesis 4:1–16

1 And the man knew Eve his wife; and she conceived and bore Cain, and said: 'I have gotten a man with the help of the LORD.' 2 And again she bore his brother Abel. And Abel was a keeper of sheep, but Cain was a tiller of the ground. 3 And in process of time it came to pass, that Cain brought of the fruit of the ground an offering unto the LORD. 4 And Abel, he also brought of the firstlings of his flock and of the fat thereof. And the LORD had respect unto Abel and to his offering; 5 but unto Cain and to his offering He had not respect. And Cain was very wroth, and his countenance fell. 6 And the LORD said unto Cain: 'Why

---

1. "There are no second acts in American life" (F. Scott Fitzgerald, *The Last Tycoon*, 1941). To be sure, some Fitzgerald scholars insist that this quote is "sort of dashed off in the middle of a bunch of working notes" and thus does not represent Fitzgerald's true opinion about second chances (NPR broadcast May 8, 2013: "Audie Cornish talks to Kirk Curnutt, vice president of the F. Scott Fitzgerald Society.")

art thou wroth? and why is thy countenance fallen? 7 If thou doest well, shall it not be lifted up? and if thou doest not well, sin coucheth at the door; and unto thee is its desire, but thou mayest rule over it.' 8 And Cain spoke unto Abel his brother. And it came to pass, when they were in the field, that Cain rose up against Abel his brother, and slew him.

9 And the LORD said unto Cain: 'Where is Abel thy brother?' And he said: 'I know not; am I my brother's keeper?' 10 And He said: 'What hast thou done? the voice of thy brother's blood crieth unto Me from the ground. 11 And now cursed art thou from the ground, which hath opened her mouth to receive thy brother's blood from thy hand. 12 When thou tillest the ground, it shall not henceforth yield unto thee her strength; a fugitive and a wanderer shalt thou be in the earth.' 13 And Cain said unto the LORD: 'My punishment is greater than I can bear. 14 Behold, Thou hast driven me out this day from the face of the land; and from Thy face shall I be hid; and I shall be a fugitive and a wanderer in the earth; and it will come to pass, that whosoever findeth me will slay me.' 15 And the LORD said unto him: 'Therefore whosoever slayeth Cain, vengeance shall be taken on him sevenfold.' And the LORD set a sign[2] for Cain, lest any finding him should smite him.

16 And Cain went out from the presence of the LORD, and dwelt in the land of Nod,[3] on the east of Eden.

For further reading see also Isaiah 26:21.

B. Justice and the City

For the Hebrew Bible, cities—the consummate social construct of humanity—must also reflect a sense of justice. Without justice, destruction, from within or without, is inevitable.

As we have already seen, this idea finds expression in two stories that focus on justice or its absence. In the case of Sodom, the city that serves as the symbol of injustice, its proposed destruction by God provokes Abraham's own query as to the justice of destroying a city that even in the depths of its depravity might still contain some good people capable of redeeming it. We have also seen the counterweight to the injustice of Sodom expressed

---

2. "*ot*" in Hebrew.

3. [[That is, Wandering.—JPS 1917 eds.]]

in the justice meted out in Solomon's royal court. In both of these cases, the raw expression of power is held to be inimical to the realization of justice: even in Solomon's royal court, as the Hebrew Bible's depiction makes clear (I Kings 3:16–28), Solomon's justice is expressed in his wisdom, not in his exercise of raw power. It is important to note the contrast of this model of justice to the definition of justice put forth by Thrasymachus in Plato's *Republic*.[4]

However, as the next selection points out, the call for justice in and of itself is not enough to prevent Israelite cities from following bad examples of how to achieve it.

Ezekiel 16:48–49

48 As I live, saith the Lord GOD, Sodom thy sister hath not done, she nor her daughters, as thou hast done, thou and thy daughters. 49 Behold, this was the iniquity of thy sister Sodom: pride, fulness of bread, and careless ease was in her and in her daughters; neither did she strengthen the hand of the poor and needy.

C. Social Justice in Concrete Form

Still, the Hebrew Bible is not content with the mere articulation of theoretical generalities about the importance of justice. For the Hebrew Bible, justice must performatively structure all aspects of people's lives. This explains its clarion call for social justice.

For the Hebrew Bible, social justice involves the material way that society is set up and how it institutionalizes its concrete practices. It understands social justice in practical terms: social justice demands that each individual have a stake in a society that works equitably for everyone. In terms of personal responsibility and ethical care, no one is to be marginalized. Humanity is defined in terms of its ability to actualize social justice.

This point is so important that the first set of laws elaborated in the Hebrew Bible, after the dramatic and miraculously presented Theophany on Mount Sinai, highlights the limited nature of servitude. Countering the conventional practices of the ancient Near East (and the ancient world in general), indentured servitude as authorized by the Hebrew Bible is a system that does not emphasize the oppression of the less fortunate. Neither does it fetishize the accumulation of economic wealth by some at the

---

4. This definition is found in ch. 3, pp. 18–19 in Cornford, Plato's *Republic* (New York: Oxford University Press, repr. 1977).

expense of the less fortunate, but rather is presented as the preferred system for working off debts. This point is highlighted by the specific obligations placed upon the master regarding his conduct towards the indentured servant, and the insistence that the master enable the economic independence of the indentured servant after his or her manumission, which must occur after six years.

1. Servitude

Exodus 21:1–4

1 Now these are the ordinances which thou shalt set before them.

2 If thou buy a Hebrew servant, six years he shall serve; and in the seventh he shall go out free for nothing. 3 If he come in by himself, he shall go out by himself; if he be married, then his wife shall go out with him. 4 If his master give him a wife, and she bear him sons or daughters; the wife and her children shall be her master's, and he shall go out by himself.

Deuteronomy 15:12–15, 18

12 If thy brother, a Hebrew man, or a Hebrew woman, be sold unto thee, he shall serve thee six years; and in the seventh year thou shalt let him go free from thee. 13 And when thou lettest him go free from thee, thou shalt not let him go empty; 14 thou shalt furnish him liberally out of thy flock, and out of thy threshing-floor, and out of thy winepress; of that wherewith the LORD thy God hath blessed thee thou shalt give unto him. 15 And thou shalt remember that thou wast a bondman in the land of Egypt, and the LORD thy God redeemed thee; therefore I command thee this thing to-day.

. . . .

18 It shall not seem hard unto thee, when thou lettest him go free from thee; for to the double of the hire of a hireling hath he served thee six years; and the LORD thy God will bless thee in all that thou doest.

To be sure, there are two examples of servitude in which the term of service is described by the Hebrew Bible as lasting "forever": the indentured servant who refuses to leave his (new) master, and the non-Israelite servant

(Leviticus 25:45–46). But as we have already seen in the Introduction to this volume, the seeming finality of what looks like lifetime servitude is not necessarily absolute: the Hebrew Bible insists that humanly determined changes within Israelite society do not last forever. It mandates that personal status and ownership of real estate beyond the traditional landholdings apportioned to the Israelites upon their entry into the Promised Land all revert to their original status and owners with the coming of the Jubilee Year (Leviticus 25:47–54; for more on this topic, see further in this chapter 7, "Economic Implications of Social Justice").

The harsh realities of slavery as it existed in the United States persist in reminding us that immoral systems continue to exact their own price.[5] For the Hebrew Bible, however, the overriding truth of Israelite existence was the duty to remember that their nationhood was born in the inhuman and genocidal Egyptian slavery, a kind of slavery that the Israelites were duty-bound never to perpetrate. Slavery, like the commodification and collection of wives, was an unfortunate fact of the ancient world. Although variations on both practices are found in the Hebrew biblical world, the Hebrew Bible likes neither of them unconditionally, and seeks to regulate them and mitigate their evils.

In the following selection, we read of the requirement to give to others so that nobody becomes, as Marx would later describe the nineteenth-century worker, a slave of their economic circumstances. As we have already seen, this obligation extends even with regard to the departing indentured servant, whom the master must set up economically so as to ensure his/her ability to provide for him/herself.

---

5. Lincoln makes this point poignantly in his Second Inaugural Address: "It may seem strange that any man should dare to ask a just God's assistance in wringing their bread from the sweat of other men's faces; but let us judge not that we be not judged. The prayers of both could not be answered; that of neither has been answered fully. The Almighty has His own purposes. 'Woe unto the world because of offences! for it must needs be that offences come; but woe to that man by whom the offence cometh!' [Matthew 18:7]. If we shall suppose that American Slavery is one of those offences which, in the providence of God, must needs come, but which, having continued through His appointed time, He now wills to remove, and that He gives to both North and South, this terrible war, as the woe due to those by whom the offence came, shall we discern therein any departure from those divine attributes which the believers in a Living God always ascribe to Him? Fondly do we hope—fervently do we pray—that this mighty scourge of war may speedily pass away. Yet, if God wills that it continue, until all the wealth piled by the bond-man's two hundred and fifty years of unrequited toil shall be sunk, and until every drop of blood drawn with the lash, shall be paid by another drawn with the sword, as was said three thousand years ago, so still it must be said 'the judgments of the Lord, are true and righteous altogether'" ([Psalms19:10]).

2. Giving to Others

Deuteronomy 15:7–11

7 If there be among you a needy man, one of thy brethren, within any of thy gates, in thy land which the LORD thy God giveth thee, thou shalt not harden thy heart, nor shut thy hand from thy needy brother; 8 but thou shalt surely open thy hand unto him, and shalt surely lend him sufficient for his need in that which he wanteth.

9 Beware that there be not a base thought in thy heart, saying: 'The seventh year, the year of release, is at hand'; and thine eye be evil against thy needy brother, and thou give him nought; and he cry unto the LORD against thee, and it be sin in thee.

10 Thou shalt surely give him, and thy heart shall not be grieved when thou givest unto him; because that for this thing the LORD thy God will bless thee in all thy work, and in all that thou puttest thy hand unto. 11 For the poor shall never cease out of the land; therefore I command thee, saying: 'Thou shalt surely open thy hand unto thy poor and needy brother, in thy land.'

3. Marginal Positions

Justice is presented as a requirement touching every person in society, including the Levite, the widow, and the orphan: the Hebrew Bible recognizes that social status (e.g., being a Levite, who works in the Holy Temple) is neither a substitute for, nor a guarantee of, having enough to eat. Marginalization of any sort highlights the need for social justice. Emphasizing the importance of this concrete approach, the Hebrew Bible reasserts it in several places.

Deuteronomy 18:1–2

1 The priests the Levites, even all the tribe of Levi, shall have no portion nor inheritance with Israel; they shall eat the offerings of the LORD made by fire, and His inheritance. 2 And they shall have no inheritance among their brethren; the LORD is their inheritance, as He hath spoken unto them.

Deuteronomy 14:27–29

27 And the Levite that is within thy gates, thou shalt not forsake him; for he hath no portion nor inheritance with thee.

28 At the end of every three years, even in the same year, thou shalt bring forth all the tithe of thine increase, and shall lay it up within thy gates. 29 And the Levite, because he hath no portion nor inheritance with thee, and the stranger, and the fatherless, and the widow, that are within thy gates, shall come, and shall eat and be satisfied; that the LORD thy God may bless thee in all the work of thy hand which thou doest.

Deuteronomy 15:7–11

7 If there be among you a needy man, one of thy brethren, within any of thy gates, in thy land which the LORD thy God giveth thee, thou shalt not harden thy heart, nor shut thy hand from thy needy brother; 8 but thou shalt surely open thy hand unto him, and shalt surely lend him sufficient for his need in that which he wanteth. 9 Beware that there be not a base thought in thy heart, saying: 'The seventh year, the year of release, is at hand'; and thine eye be evil against thy needy brother, and thou give him nought; and he cry unto the LORD against thee, and it be sin in thee. 10 Thou shalt surely give him, and thy heart shall not be grieved when thou givest unto him; because that for this thing the LORD thy God will bless thee in all thy work, and in all that thou puttest thy hand unto. 11 For the poor shall never cease out of the land; therefore I command thee, saying: 'Thou shalt surely open thy hand unto thy poor and needy brother, in thy land.'

4. Justice and a Hand Up

For the Hebrew Bible, justice towards the poor is not an exceptional activity, established to gratify pleasant feelings of superiority or self-righteousness, but rather a requirement of everyday life that encompasses even economic productivity. Tellingly, in an agricultural society in which the harvest is the measure of economic accomplishment, the Hebrew Bible establishes limits on what the farmer may appropriate even from his own fields over which he has toiled for many months: no previously harvested field may be gone over, or doubly harvested, to ensure the collection of every last grain. Moreover, the farmer is not to regard his harvest as proof of his moral superiority; instead, it is an opportunity to practice real justice toward those who are in need (readers will note that this is the basis of the Ruth story [Ruth 2:1–23] as it develops in its later chapters).

Deuteronomy 24:19–22

19 When thou reapest thy harvest in thy field, and hast forgot a sheaf in the field, thou shalt not go back to fetch it; it shall be for the stranger, for the fatherless, and for the widow; that the LORD thy God may bless thee in all the work of thy hands.

20 When thou beatest thine olive-tree, thou shalt not go over the boughs again; it shall be for the stranger, for the fatherless, and for the widow. 21 When thou gatherest the grapes of thy vineyard, thou shalt not glean it after thee; it shall be for the stranger, for the fatherless, and for the widow. 22 And thou shalt remember that thou wast a bondman in the land of Egypt; therefore I command thee to do this thing.

5. Justice and Fairness: Honest Weights and Measures

The Hebrew Bible recognizes that justice is not merely an abstract ideal for ensuring the acceptable treatment of those on the margins of society. Rather it is the crucial underpinning of concrete mechanisms for establishing social trust, which is the glue that holds society together. It does so in part by regulating the quantification of commercial exchange: mandating honest weights and measures.

Deuteronomy 25:13–15

13 Thou shalt not have in thy bag diverse weights, a great and a small. 14 Thou shalt not have in thy house diverse measures, a great and a small. 15 A perfect and just weight shalt thou have; a perfect and just measure shalt thou have; that thy days may be long upon the land which the LORD thy God giveth thee.

Leviticus 19:35–37

35 Ye shall do no unrighteousness in judgment, in meteyard, in weight, or in measure. 36 Just balances, just weights, a just ephah, and a just hin, shall ye have: I am the LORD your God, who brought you out of the land of Egypt.

37 And ye shall observe all My statutes, and all Mine ordinances, and do them: I am the LORD.

6. Justice and Equal Shares

The principle of honest weights and measures—and their social corollary of equal shares—is evident in the narrative describing David's practices of equality in the division of the spoils of war. In this selection, David is on the run from King Saul.

I Samuel 30:21–31

21 And David came to the two hundred men, who were so faint that they could not follow David, whom also they had made to abide at the brook Besor; and they went forth to meet David, and to meet the people that were with him; and when David came near to the people, he saluted them. 22 Then answered all the wicked men and base fellows, of those that went with David, and said: 'Because they went not with us, we will not give them aught of the spoil that we have recovered, save to every man his wife and his children, that they may lead them away, and depart.' 23 Then said David: 'Ye shall not do so, my brethren, with that which the LORD hath given unto us, who hath preserved us, and delivered the troop that came against us into our hand. 24 And who will hearken unto you in this matter? for as is the share of him that goeth down to the battle, so shall be the share of him that tarrieth by the baggage; they shall share alike.' 25 And it was so from that day forward, that he made it a statute and an ordinance for Israel unto this day.

26 And when David came to Ziklag, he sent of the spoil unto the elders of Judah, even to his friends, saying: 'Behold a present for you of the spoil of the enemies of the LORD'; 27 to them that were in Beth-el, and to them that were in Ramoth of the South, and to them that were in Jattir; 28 and to them that were in Aroer, and to them that were in Siphmoth, and to them that were in Eshtemoa; 29 and to them that were in Racal, and to them that were in the cities of the Jerahmeelites, and to them that were in the cities of the Kenites; 30 and to them that were in Hormah, and to them that were in Bor-ashan, and to them that were in Athach; 31 and to them that were in Hebron, and to all the places where David himself and his men were wont to haunt.

For further reading, see Hosea 12:7–8.

7. Justice for Those One Dislikes

Putting a finer point on it, the Hebrew Bible insists that even when an individual would rather do things "his" way (the example given is the double share of inheritance that normally accrues to the eldest son), one may not favor the child of the beloved wife over the child of the hated one. Justice trumps human preference.

Deuteronomy 21:15–17

15 If a man have two wives, the one beloved, and the other hated, and they have borne him children, both the beloved and the hated; and if the first-born son be hers that was hated; 16 then it shall be, in the day that he causeth his sons to inherit that which he hath, that he may not make the son of the beloved the first-born before the son of the hated, who is the first-born; 17 but he shall acknowledge the first-born, the son of the hated, by giving him a double portion of all that he hath; for he is the first-fruits of his strength, the right of the first-born is his.

8. Justice and Fairness for One's Enemy

The Hebrew Bible carries this point of fairness much further: justice is to be done even to one's enemy.

Exodus 23:4–5

4 If thou meet thine enemy's ox or his ass going astray, thou shalt surely bring it back to him again.

5 If thou see the ass of him that hateth thee lying under its burden, thou shalt forbear to pass by him; thou shalt surely release it with him.

This point is taken up in greater detail in Deuteronomy 22.

Deuteronomy 22:1–3

1 Thou shalt not see thy brother's ox or his sheep driven away, and hide thyself from them; thou shalt surely bring them back unto thy brother. 2 And if thy brother be not nigh unto thee, and thou know him not, then thou shalt bring it home to thy house, and it shall be with thee until thy brother require it, and

thou shalt restore it to him. 3 And so shalt thou do with his ass; and so shalt thou do with his garment; and so shalt thou do with every lost thing of thy brother's, which he hath lost, and thou hast found; thou mayest not hide thyself.

9. Justice and Equity

In the Hebrew Bible, justice reflects more than a sentimental excess of generosity, or even the recognition of the practical necessity of achieving social stability. It is presented as the ultimate criterion of human relationships in their individual as well as in their communal manifestations. Thus, the Hebrew Bible proclaims directives to establish a judicial system and a system of keeping the social peace.

Traditionally, the double directive to seek and pursue "justice, justice" (Deuteronomy 16:20)[6] is understood to indicate that justice must be pursued in a just manner; thus rejected is the (conventionally understood) Machiavellian rationale that justifies achieving goals by any means possible. This attitude fits in well with the Hebrew Bible's refusal to cater in any absolute manner to any particular social class or economic group in matters of justice (although it can be argued that by the constant repetition of these concerns, the Hebrew Bible is aware that in many cases, these standards may well be honored in the breach).

Deuteronomy 16:18–20

18 Judges and officers shalt thou make thee in all thy gates, which the LORD thy God giveth thee, tribe by tribe; and they shall judge the people with righteous judgment.

19 Thou shalt not wrest judgment; thou shalt not respect persons; neither shalt thou take a gift; for a gift doth blind the eyes of the wise, and pervert the words of the righteous. 20 Justice, justice shalt thou pursue,[7] that thou mayest live, and inherit the land which the LORD thy God giveth thee.

---

6. In *Judaism and Global Survival* (New York: Lantern Books, 2002), Richard J. Schwartz cites Rabbenu Bachya ben Asher, a thirteenth-century Torah commentator, who writes, "Justice whether to your profit or loss, whether in word or action. . . ." Schwartz credits J. H. Hertz for Hertz's own quotation of this passage (in Hertz, *The Pentateuch and Haftorahs* [London: Soncino, 1957], p. 820). Schwartz notes that Rabbi Hertz cites a Chassidic interpretation of this biblical verse: "Do not use unjust means to secure the victory of justice" (ibid., 820).

7. JPS 1917: "follow."

D. Social Justice and Personal Equality

For the socially conscious reader, it may seem strange that the Hebrew Bible accepts unequal distribution of wealth while still insisting that people are equal in their personhood. Rather than seeing this juxtaposition as attempting to bridge contradictory sets of values, it may be useful to reflect that within the ethical system of the Hebrew Bible, wealth is not a marker of moral worth (as Max Weber, in his *Protestant Ethic and the Spirit of Capitalism,* maintains it was for the Puritans).[8] Neither is it, in and of itself, a marker of social value, although some within society may choose to consider it that way. To be sure, the Hebrew Bible does include texts promising good harvests and comfort for obeying the commandments. In the context of the Hebrew Bible, though, these promises do not view wealth as a sign of God's approval, but rather serve to allow people to carry out their lives in a God- and commandment-centered way, as opposed to being obsessed merely with physical survival.

Ancient Israelite society as depicted in the Hebrew Bible was hierarchical: every tribe had its Elders, there was a system of judges, and eventually a royal court. Even so, the Hebrew Bible distinguishes between a person's rank and the respect due that person by virtue of his or her human status. Personhood is not a privilege of the powerful: strangers, orphans, and widows are examples of people who do not have a natural champion for themselves within ancient society, yet who are specifically and repeatedly mentioned in the Hebrew Bible as people who deserve fair and equal treatment.

Within a society and a world where economic and social inequality were often brutal facts of life, the Hebrew Bible insists that personal equality and social responsibility are mandated for everyone. Nobody gets a free pass; and nobody is valued merely as a function of his or her wealth or position.

In the following selections, inferior or subordinate positions are dismissed as reasons for treating others unequally. As for the stranger—the ultimate other, against whom discrimination figures reflexively as a mark of belonging—the Hebrew Bible warns that mistreating the person who is distinctive by virtue of his or her differences represents the ultimate moral incoherence, especially on the part of the Israelites, who had begun their own national existence as strangers and persecuted slaves. Carrying this

---

8. "It is true that the usefulness of a calling, and thus its favor in the sight of God, is measured primarily in moral terms . . . *but the most important criterion is found in private profitableness. . . .*" Max Weber, *The Protestant Ethic and the Spirit of Capitalism,* "Asceticism and The Spirit of Capitalism," tr. Talcott Parsons, ed. Anthony Giddens (New York: Routledge, repr. 2005), p. 108; emphasis mine.

point even further in the book of Leviticus, the Hebrew Bible argues that recognizing the humanity of the other is the key to recognizing the ultimate Other, God.[9] This concept appears in its universalistic implication in the words of Malachi 2:10.

1. Fairness to the Marginalized

Exodus 22:21–26

21 Ye shall not afflict any widow, or fatherless child.

22 If thou afflict them in any wise—for if they cry at all unto Me, I will surely hear their cry—23 My wrath shall wax hot, and I will kill you with the sword; and your wives shall be widows, and your children fatherless.

24 If thou lend money to any of My people, even to the poor with thee, thou shalt not be to him as a creditor; neither shall ye lay upon him interest. 25 If thou at all take thy neighbour's garment to pledge, thou shalt restore it unto him by that the sun goeth down; 26 for that is his only covering, it is his garment for his skin; wherein shall he sleep? and it shall come to pass, when he crieth unto Me, that I will hear; for I am gracious.

Exodus 23:6–8

6 Thou shalt not wrest the judgment of thy poor in his cause. 7 Keep thee far from a false matter; and the innocent and righteous slay thou not; for I will not justify the wicked. 8 And thou shalt take no gift; for a gift blindeth them that have sight, and perverteth the words of the righteous.

---

9. Cf. Levinas, *Totality and Infinity*, tr. Alphonso Lingis (Pittsburgh: Duquesne University Press, 1961, 1969): "The absolute other is the Other. . . . God rises to his supreme and ultimate presence as the contemplative of justice rendered unto men" (pp. 39, 78). Levinas' argument is that the recognition of radical alterity enhances one's own humanity. The interplay between self and other is taken up in eighteenth-century Enlightenment thought, particularly in Rousseau's *Discourse on Inequality*, and remains a central insight in the development of psychological maturation in Lacan's "mirror stage." "The Mirror Stage as Formative of the Function of the I as Revealed in Psychoanalytic Experience" in Jacques Lacan, *Ecrits: A Selection*, tr. Alan Sheridan (New York: Routledge Classics, 2001), pp. 1–9.

2. Don't Treat a Stranger Badly

Exodus 23:9

9 And a stranger shalt thou not oppress; for ye know the heart of a stranger, seeing ye were strangers in the land of Egypt.

Leviticus 19:33–34

33 And if a stranger sojourn with thee in your land, ye shall not do him wrong. 34 The stranger that sojourneth with you shall be unto you as the home-born among you, and thou shalt love him as thyself; for ye were strangers in the land of Egypt: I am the LORD your God.

Deuteronomy 24:17–18

17 Thou shalt not pervert the justice due to the stranger, or to the fatherless; nor take the widow's raiment to pledge.

18 But thou shalt remember that thou wast a bondman in Egypt, and the LORD thy God redeemed thee thence; therefore I command thee to do this thing.

Deuteronomy 10:17–20

17 For the LORD your God, He is God of gods, and Lord of lords, the great God, the mighty, and the awful, who regardeth not persons, nor taketh reward. 18 He doth execute justice for the fatherless and widow, and loveth the stranger, in giving him food and raiment.

19 Love ye therefore the stranger; for ye were strangers in the land of Egypt. 20 Thou shalt fear the LORD thy God; Him shalt thou serve; and to Him shalt thou cleave, and by His name shalt thou swear.

Zechariah 7:8–12

8 And the word of the LORD came unto Zechariah, saying: 9 'Thus hath the LORD of hosts spoken, saying: Execute true judgment, and show mercy and compassion every man to his brother; 10 and oppress not the widow, nor the fatherless, the stranger, nor the poor; and let none of you devise evil against his brother in your heart.

11 But they refused to attend, and turned a stubborn shoulder, and stopped their ears, that they might not hear. 12 Yea, they made their hearts as an adamant stone, lest they should hear the law, and the words which the LORD of hosts had sent by His spirit by the hand of the former prophets; therefore came there great wrath from the LORD of hosts.

Malachi 2:10

10 Have we not all one father?
Hath not one God created us?
Why do we deal treacherously every man against his brother,
Profaning the covenant of our fathers?

3. The Equality of Strangers

According to the Hebrew Bible, strangers are to receive justice like a regular citizen, including the same punishments, if applicable. Importantly, the stranger and convert are considered as "naturally" born Israelites, in terms of both social and religious status: as the selection in Numbers 15:28–29 below shows, all have access to the spiritual services of the priest.

The repeated emphasis on justice for the stranger throughout the texts of the Hebrew Bible highlights its recognition that the liminal status of the stranger has the potential to prevent true justice from being carried out. This emphasis recalls cases of discrimination involving undocumented immigrants, for example, in both historical and twenty-first-century legal proceedings.

Also noteworthy is the connection adduced between the provision of justice to the marginal members of society and the fear of God required of all (Deuteronomy 10:20).

Deuteronomy 24:17–18

17 Thou shalt not pervert the justice due to the stranger, or to the fatherless; nor take the widow's raiment to pledge.

18 But thou shalt remember that thou wast a bondman in Egypt, and the LORD thy God redeemed thee thence; therefore I command thee to do this thing.

Deuteronomy 10:17–20

17 For the LORD your God, He is God of gods, and Lord of lords, the great God, the mighty, and the awful, who regardeth

not persons, nor taketh reward. 18 He doth execute justice for the fatherless and widow, and loveth the stranger, in giving him food and raiment.

19 Love ye therefore the stranger; for ye were strangers in the land of Egypt. 20 Thou shalt fear the LORD thy God; Him shalt thou serve; and to Him shalt thou cleave, and by His name shalt thou swear.

Numbers 15:15–16, 28–29

15 As for the congregation, there shall be one statute both for you, and for the stranger that sojourneth with you, a statute for ever throughout your generations; as ye are, so shall the stranger be before the LORD. 16 One law and one ordinance shall be both for you, and for the stranger that sojourneth with you.

. . . .

28 And the priest shall make atonement for the soul that erreth, when he sinneth through error, before the LORD, to make atonement for him; and he shall be forgiven,

29 both he that is home-born among the children of Israel, and the stranger that sojourneth among them: ye shall have one law for him that doeth aught in error.

4. Does Equality Mean Sameness in the Hebrew Bible?

Importantly, the emphasis on "one rule for all" does not mean that the Hebrew Bible values humanity in its personal, concrete form only to the extent that it is uniform. The Hebrew Bible differentiates between systems of justice, which must be applied with equity for all, and individual difference, which is honored. In fact, it is precisely the requirement that the marginalized members of society be treated with equal justice that underscores the importance of personal difference not being used as an excuse for negative discrimination.

The extent to which the Hebrew Bible honors difference is exemplified by two individuals who are welcomed and valued precisely for the differences that allow them to contribute insights regarding some of the major institutions of Israelite society. These include the establishment of an organized judiciary (Jethro), and the role of the stranger in reorganizing the political institutions of Israelite society (Ruth; see further Chapter 17, "In Foreign Houses and Courts: Exile").

Exodus 18:13–27

13 And it came to pass on the morrow, that Moses sat to judge the people; and the people stood about Moses from the morning unto the evening. 14 And when Moses' father-in-law saw all that he did to the people, he said: 'What is this thing that thou doest to the people? why sittest thou thyself alone, and all the people stand about thee from morning unto even?'

15 And Moses said unto his father-in-law: 'Because the people come unto me to inquire of God; 16 when they have a matter, it cometh unto me; and I judge between a man and his neighbour, and I make them know the statutes of God, and His laws.'

17 And Moses' father-in-law said unto him: 'The thing that thou doest is not good. 18 Thou wilt surely wear away, both thou, and this people that is with thee; for the thing is too heavy for thee; thou art not able to perform it thyself alone. 19 Hearken now unto my voice, I will give thee counsel, and God be with thee: be thou for the people before God, and bring thou the causes unto God. 20 And thou shalt teach them the statutes and the laws, and shalt show them the way wherein they must walk, and the work that they must do.

21 Moreover thou shalt provide out of all the people able men, such as fear God, men of truth, hating unjust gain; and place such over them, to be rulers of thousands, rulers of hundreds, rulers of fifties, and rulers of tens. 22 And let them judge the people at all seasons; and it shall be, that every great matter they shall bring unto thee, but every small matter they shall judge themselves; so shall they make it easier for thee and bear the burden with thee.

23 If thou shalt do this thing, and God command thee so, then thou shalt be able to endure, and all this people also shall go to their place in peace.' 24 So Moses hearkened to the voice of his father-in-law, and did all that he had said. 25 And Moses chose able men out of all Israel, and made them heads over the people, rulers of thousands, rulers of hundreds, rulers of fifties, and rulers of tens. 26 And they judged the people at all seasons: the hard causes they brought unto Moses, but every small matter they judged themselves.

27 And Moses let his father-in-law depart; and he went his way into his own land.

Further details regarding Jethro's departure and the treaty of friendship established between the Israelites and the family of Jethro are given in the following selection from Numbers.

Numbers 10:29–32

29 And Moses said unto Hobab, the son of Reuel the Midianite, Moses' father-in-law: 'We are journeying unto the place of which the LORD said: I will give it you; come thou with us, and we will do thee good; for the LORD hath spoken good concerning Israel.'

30 And he said unto him: 'I will not go; but I will depart to mine own land, and to my kindred.' 31 And he said: 'Leave us not, I pray thee; forasmuch as thou knowest how we are to encamp in the wilderness, and thou shalt be to us instead of eyes. 32 And it shall be, if thou go with us, yea, it shall be, that what good soever the LORD shall do unto us, the same will we do unto thee.'

E. Concrete and Institutional Undertakings to Achieve Social Justice

The Hebrew Bible is not content to remain with generalities. The realization of human equality requires following specific standards of behavior, even when it might threaten the self-conception of the elites. Fairness to the worker, prompt payment of salaries, restoration of textile collateral if that is the debtor's only covering: all these are specified as Hebrew biblical commands to honor the humanity of the socially and economically subordinate.

Deuteronomy 24:10–22

10 When thou dost lend thy neighbour any manner of loan, thou shalt not go into his house to fetch his pledge. 11 Thou shalt stand without, and the man to whom thou dost lend shall bring forth the pledge without unto thee. 12 And if he be a poor man, thou shalt not sleep with his pledge; 13 thou shalt surely restore to him the pledge when the sun goeth down, that he may sleep in his garment, and bless thee; and it shall be righteousness unto thee before the LORD thy God.

14 Thou shalt not oppress a hired servant that is poor and needy, whether he be of thy brethren, or of thy strangers that are in thy

land within thy gates. 15 In the same day thou shalt give him his hire, neither shall the sun go down upon it; for he is poor, and setteth his heart upon it: lest he cry against thee unto the LORD and it be sin in thee.

16 The fathers shall not be put to death for the children, neither shall the children be put to death for the fathers; every man shall be put to death for his own sin.

17 Thou shalt not pervert the justice due to the stranger, or to the fatherless; nor take the widow's raiment to pledge. 18 But thou shalt remember that thou wast a bondman in Egypt, and the LORD thy God redeemed thee thence; therefore I command thee to do this thing.

19 When thou reapest thy harvest in thy field, and hast forgot a sheaf in the field, thou shalt not go back to fetch it; it shall be for the stranger, for the fatherless, and for the widow; that the LORD thy God may bless thee in all the work of thy hands.

At the same time, personal consideration—either for the humanity of the less fortunate or for the class position of the wealthy or influential—may not influence the spirit of justice when it comes to the adjudication of a particular case.

Exodus 23:3–9

3 neither shalt thou favour a poor man in his cause.

4 If thou meet thine enemy's ox or his ass going astray, thou shalt surely bring it back to him again.

5 If thou see the ass of him that hateth thee lying under its burden, thou shalt forbear to pass by him; thou shalt surely release it with him.

6 Thou shalt not wrest the judgment of thy poor in his cause. 7 Keep thee far from a false matter; and the innocent and righteous slay thou not; for I will not justify the wicked. 8 And thou shalt take no gift; for a gift blindeth them that have sight, and perverteth the words of the righteous. 9 And a stranger shalt thou not oppress; for ye know the heart of a stranger, seeing ye were strangers in the land of Egypt.

Similar pronouncements may be found in Leviticus and in Deuteronomy.

Leviticus 19:15

15 Ye shall do no unrighteousness in judgment; thou shalt not respect the person of the poor, nor favour the person of the mighty; but in righteousness shalt thou judge thy neighbour.

Deuteronomy 1:16–17

16 And I charged your judges at that time, saying: 'Hear the causes between your brethren, and judge righteously between a man and his brother, and the stranger that is with him.

17 Ye shall not respect persons in judgment; ye shall hear the small and the great alike; ye shall not be afraid of the face of any man; for the judgment is God's; and the cause that is too hard for you ye shall bring unto me, and I will hear it.'

The following selection in Deuteronomy ensures the authenticity of the judicial system by introducing careful checks against the introduction of false witnesses.

Deuteronomy 19:15–19

15 One witness shall not rise up against a man for any iniquity, or for any sin, in any sin that he sinneth; at the mouth of two witnesses, or at the mouth of three witnesses, shall a matter be establishment.

16 If an unrighteous witness rise up against any man to bear perverted witness against him; 17 then both the men, between whom the controversy is, shall stand before the LORD, before the priests and the judges that shall be in those days.

18 And the judges shall inquire diligently; and, behold, if the witness be a false witness, and hath testified falsely against his brother; 19 then shall ye do unto him, as he had purposed to do unto his brother; so shalt thou put away the evil from the midst of thee.

1. The Social Institutions of Justice

The Hebrew Bible insists that justice cannot be implemented on the basis of emotion or rationality alone.[10] Instead, the Hebrew Bible provides for

---

10. In *Discourse on Inequality*, Jean-Jacques Rousseau makes a similar argument, contrasting the simple woman selling fish in the market who involves herself with her fellows and their quarrels to determine a just outcome, with the cerebral philosopher who studies what is right

social institutions that aim to ensure that justice be practiced coherently and effectively. First among these institutions is the judiciary.

Deuteronomy 17:8–11

8 If there arise a matter too hard for thee in judgment, between blood and blood, between plea and plea, and between stroke and stroke, even matters of controversy within thy gates; then shalt thou arise, and get thee up unto the place which the LORD thy God shall choose. 9 And thou shall come unto the priests the Levites, and unto the judge that shall be in those days; and thou shalt inquire; and they shall declare unto thee the sentence of judgment. 10 And thou shalt do according to the tenor of the sentence, which they shall declare unto thee from that place which the LORD shall choose; and thou shalt observe to do according to all that they shall teach thee. 11 According to the law which they shall teach thee, and according to the judgment which they shall tell thee, thou shalt do; thou shalt not turn aside from the sentence which they shall declare unto thee, to the right hand, nor to the left.

2. Keeping Justice Honest

Establishing a fair judiciary is not a matter of just finding qualified judges and establishing a court system. The people themselves must agree to this system, and must participate in it honestly.

Deuteronomy 19:15–19

15 One witness shall not rise up against a man for any iniquity, or for any sin, in any sin that he sinneth; at the mouth of two witnesses, or at the mouth of three witnesses, shall a matter be establishment. 16 If an unrighteous witness rise up against any man to bear perverted witness against him; 17 then both the men, between whom the controversy is, shall stand before the LORD, before the priests and the judges that shall be in those days. 18 And the judges shall inquire diligently; and, behold, if the witness be a false witness, and hath testified falsely against his brother; 19 then shall ye do unto him, as he had purposed

---

but can't be bothered to do anything about it (trans. G. D. H. Cole. New York: Everyman's Library, reprint edition, 1993, p. 75; Paris: Gallimard, 1959–; OC3: 156).

to do unto his brother; so shalt thou put away the evil from the midst of thee.

F. Economic Implications of Social Justice

The contemporary reader may well be puzzled by the emphasis on justice in so many texts of the Hebrew Bible. Why is this element foregrounded? Why not privilege some other value?

The following selections suggest a practical reason for emphasizing justice for all elements of society. When a society is fair, members of society perceive that they have a stake in keeping the social structure alive. They will therefore work to improve society, thus ensuring its stability and its dynamism. This idea permeates the different Hebrew biblical selections below.

The selection from Leviticus opens with the instruction that individuals' landholdings, described in the text as having been established after Joshua's conquest of the Promised Land (cf. the Book of Joshua), may not be sold in perpetuity. Every fifty years, the "Jubilee" that was proclaimed required that traditional landholdings return to their erstwhile landholders (or their inheritors).[11] The anticipated result (historically, this system was imperfectly sustained) was the prevention of an overwhelming concentration of land (the primary indicator of wealth at that time as presented by the Hebrew biblical text) in the hands of a select landowning class.

But the corollary is equally important: every individual, no matter how bad she or he deems her or his luck to be, has the sense that the cards are not irretrievably stacked against her or him: there is still a chance to get things "right." The added details and exceptions—regarding a house in a walled city, an economic entity viewed as fundamentally different from a field in an agricultural society, or the personal status of long-term servants—emphasizes

---

11. Careful readers of this selection will note the term "redeemer/redemption" of the land. Essentially, the Hebrew Bible introduces several ways to ensure that the landholding of any individual will not be sold in perpetuity. One is the general reconsolidation of traditional landholdings at the proclamation of the Jubilee Year. The second is a bit more complicated: the Hebrew Bible allows that the erstwhile seller of his or her traditional landholding may have a reversal of fortune and may want to buy that landholding back (there is a complicated valuation to establish a fair price, which is a function of the years left to the Jubilee, in which case the landholding would be automatically returned; see Leviticus 25:25–27). Because of the different (financial) status of an urban house (in a walled city), far less time is allowed for repurchase of that house once it is sold, and the "liberation" laws of the Jubilee do not apply to it. Since the Levites have such a minute amount of land apportioned to them (just forty-eight cities, with surrounding fields), their fields may not be sold, although their houses may and can be repurchased at any time, without the one-year limitations normally applied to other urban houses (within a walled city).

the society-wide application of these ideas. Even in the personal context, the Hebrew Bible rejects the building of empires.[12]

Leviticus 25:23–43

23 And the land shall not be sold in perpetuity; for the land is Mine; for ye are strangers and settlers with Me. 24 And in all the land of your possession ye shall grant a redemption for the land.

25 If thy brother be waxen poor, and sell some of his possession, then shall his kinsman that is next unto him come, and shall redeem that which his brother hath sold. 26 And if a man have no one to redeem it, and he be waxen rich and find sufficient means to redeem it; 27 then let him count the years of the sale thereof, and restore the overplus unto the man to whom he sold it; and he shall return unto his possession. 28 But if he have not sufficient means to get it back for himself, then that which he hath sold shall remain in the hand of him that hath bought it until the year of jubilee; and in the jubilee it shall go out, and he shall return unto his possession.

29 And if a man sell a dwelling-house in a walled city, then he may redeem it within a whole year after it is sold; for a full year shall he have the right of redemption. 30 And if it be not redeemed within the space of a full year, then the house that is in the walled city shall be made sure in perpetuity to him that bought it, throughout his generations; it shall not go out in the jubilee. 31 But the houses of the villages which have no wall round about them shall be reckoned with the fields of the country; they may be redeemed, and they shall go out in the jubilee. 32 But as for the cities of the Levites, the houses of the cities of their possession, the Levites shall have a perpetual right of redemption. 33 And if a man purchase of the Levites, then the house that was sold in the city of his possession, shall go out in the jubilee; for the houses of the cities of the Levites are their possession among the children of Israel. 34 But the fields of the open land about their cities may not be sold; for that is their perpetual possession.

35 And if thy brother be waxen poor, and his means fail with thee; then thou shalt uphold him: as a stranger and a settler shall

---

12. See Jonathan Sacks' *The Politics of Hope* (London: Vintage, 2000).

he live with thee. 36 Take thou no interest of him or increase; but fear thy God; that thy brother may live with thee. 37 Thou shalt not give him thy money upon interest, nor give him thy victuals for increase. 38 I am the LORD your God, who brought you forth out of the land of Egypt, to give you the land of Canaan, to be your God.

39 And if thy brother be waxen poor with thee, and sell himself unto thee, thou shalt not make him to serve as a bondservant. 40 As a hired servant, and as a settler, he shall be with thee; he shall serve with thee unto the year of jubilee. 41 Then shall he go out from thee, he and his children with him, and shall return unto his own family, and unto the possession of his fathers shall he return. 42 For they are My servants, whom I brought forth out of the land of Egypt; they shall not be sold as bondmen. 43 Thou shalt not rule over him with rigour; but shalt fear thy God.

G. The Philosophy and Poetry of Justice: Using Justice to Evaluate Moral Coherence

For the Hebrew Bible, a just society enables people to conduct not just a dialogue about God, but also a dialogue with God (cf. Abraham's argument about Sodom above, in Genesis 18:20–32). The Hebrew Bible thus promotes justice as an essential part of creating the moral coherence and meaning that allows society to flourish. Without justice, neither the community nor the individual can be said to exist in a way that makes sense, or that allows for the establishment of meaning beyond the immediacy of one's own desires.

Justice is such a central value for the Hebrew Bible that it imputes the lack of justice as the primary reason for the exile that would beset the Israelites if they continued in their pernicious ways, as the following selections show.

1. Amos 2:6

6 Thus saith the LORD:
For three transgressions of Israel,
Yea, for four, I will not reverse it:
Because they sell the righteous for silver,
And the needy for a pair of shoes;

2. The Parable of the Vineyard

In Isaiah's parable of the vineyard, God presents exile as a punishment for the lack of justice in Israelite society. In Isaiah's terms, exile means that innocent people suffer along with the guilty. How does one read this text? Does the Israelite lack of justice mean that God has also given up on justice? Is God punishing the Israelites just for being disobedient? Is God's anger a sign of lashing out? Or does God, by removing His protection, allow Israelites to see how the world operates when overwhelming strength is viewed as the only necessary justification for any action?

Isaiah 5:1–7, 13–17

1 Let me sing of my well-beloved,
A song of my beloved touching his vineyard.
My well-beloved had a vineyard
In a very fruitful hill;
2 And he digged it, and cleared it of stones,
And planted it with the choicest vine,
And built a tower in the midst of it,
And also hewed out a vat therein;
And he looked that it should bring forth grapes,
And it brought forth wild grapes.
3 And now, O inhabitants of Jerusalem and men of Judah,
Judge, I pray you, betwixt me and my vineyard.
4 What could have been done more to my vineyard,
That I have not done in it?
Wherefore, when I looked that it should bring forth grapes,
Brought it forth wild grapes?

5 And now come, I will tell you
What I will do to my vineyard:
I will take away the hedge thereof,
And it shall be eaten up;
I will break down the fence thereof,
And it shall be trodden down;
6 And I will lay it waste:
It shall not be pruned nor hoed,
But there shall come up briers and thorns;
I will also command the clouds
That they rain no rain upon it.

7 For the vineyard of the LORD of hosts is the house of Israel,
And the men of Judah the plant of His delight;

And He looked for justice, but behold violence;
For righteousness, but behold a cry.

. . . .

13 Therefore My people are gone into captivity,
For want of knowledge;
And their honourable men are famished,
And their multitude are parched with thirst.
14 Therefore the nether-world hath enlarged her desire,
And opened her mouth without measure;
And down goeth their glory, and their tumult, and their uproar,
And he that rejoiceth among them.
15 And man is bowed down,
And man is humbled,
And the eyes of the lofty are humbled;
16 But the LORD of hosts is exalted through justice,
And God the Holy One is sanctified through righteousness.
17 Then shall the lambs feed as in their pasture,
And the waste places of the fat ones shall wanderers eat.

3. Immoral Actions, Philosophical Incoherence, and Meaninglessness

For Isaiah, the ultimate destruction that occurs as a result of moral corruption is not just the punishment that has been prophesied (national exile), but also the self-destructive futility of life that lacks a moral center. Readers may consider how Isaiah's condemnation of those "that call evil good" takes issue with Thrasymachus' equation of moral meaning ("justice") with (political) power.[13] The following passage occurs towards the end of Isaiah's parable of the vineyard.

Isaiah 5:20–24

20 Woe unto them that call evil good,
And good evil;
That change darkness into light,
And light into darkness;
That change bitter into sweet,
And sweet into bitter!

---

13. See ch. 3, pp. 18–20, in Cornford, Plato's *Republic* (New York: Oxford University Press, repr. 1977).

21 Woe unto them that are wise in their own eyes,
And prudent in their own sight!

22 Woe unto them that are mighty to drink wine,
And men of strength to mingle strong drink;
23 That justify the wicked for a reward,
And take away the righteousness of the righteous from him!
24 Therefore as the tongue of fire devoureth the stubble,
And as the chaff is consumed in the flame,
So their root shall be as rottenness,
And their blossom shall go up as dust;
Because they have rejected the law of the LORD of hosts,
And contemned the word of the Holy One of Israel.

For further reading, see Isaiah 10:13–15.

4. Arguments for Justice

In Isaiah 45:9, the prophet underlines the logical incoherence of challenging the true order of morality and justice. Similar themes are found in Isaiah 29 (the Allegory of the Sealed Book, Isaiah 29:11–16) where the prophet chastises the people with pretending to believe in God while acting immorally, just like a person who pretends to read a book that, because of this individual's illiteracy, remains sealed. Isaiah's comments on the foreign politics of the period assume a similar tone (Isaiah 30:1–3, 5)—as does the depiction of the ultimate salvation (Isaiah 32:3–5).

Ezekiel 14:1–4 utilizes the equation between moral corruption and philosophical incoherence in like manner.

a. Isaiah 45:9

9 Woe unto him that striveth with his Maker,
As a potsherd with the potsherds of the earth!
Shall the clay say to him that fashioned it: 'What makest thou?'
Or: 'Thy work, it hath no hands'?

For further reading see also Isaiah 43:9–10 and Isaiah 44, which selections describe politics as a justified Divine trial.

b. Allegory of the Sealed Book

Isaiah 29:11–16

11 And the vision of all this is become unto you as the words of
a writing that is sealed, which men deliver to one that is learned,

saying: 'Read this, I pray thee'; and he saith: 'I cannot, for it is sealed'; 12 and the writing is delivered to him that is not learned, saying: 'Read this, I pray thee'; and he saith: 'I am not learned.'

13 And the Lord said:
Forasmuch as this people draw near,
And with their mouth and with their lips do honour Me,
But have removed their heart far from Me,
And their fear of Me is a commandment of men learned by rote;
14 Therefore, behold, I will again do a marvellous work among this people,
Even a marvellous work and a wonder;
And the wisdom of their wise men shall perish,
And the prudence of their prudent men shall be hid.

15 Woe unto them that seek deep to hide their counsel from the LORD,
And their works are in the dark,
And they say: 'Who seeth us? and who knoweth us?'
16 O your perversity! Shall the potter be esteemed as clay;
That the thing made should say of him that made it: 'He made me not';
Or the thing framed say of him that framed it: 'He hath no understanding?'

For further reading, see Ezekiel 14:1–4.

5. Interrogating Justice: Does Justice Have Meaning?

a. Job: The Trial of Theodicy; the Moral Coherence of Life Questioned

Job turns the world of the prophets on its head. By presenting us with a good man who suffers just because of a heavenly bet, the narrative forces the reader to question whether life has meaning beyond the momentary satisfaction of human needs and passions. Questions that come to mind for the twenty-first-century reader include: Why is this story presented as a trial? Does that deepen the moral questions at its center? Is there a better way to interrogate these issues?

Job 1

1 THERE was a man in the land of Uz, whose name was Job; and that man was whole-hearted and upright, and one that feared God, and shunned evil. 2 And there were born unto him seven

sons and three daughters. 3 His possessions also were seven thousand sheep, and three thousand camels, and five hundred yoke of oxen, and five hundred she-asses, and a very great household; so that this man was the greatest of all the children of the east. 4 And his sons used to go and hold a feast in the house of each one upon his day; and they would send and invite their three sisters to eat and to drink with them. 5 And it was so, when the days of their feasting were gone about, that Job sent and sanctified them, and rose up early in the morning, and offered burnt-offerings according to the number of them all; for Job said: 'It may be that my sons have sinned, and blasphemed God in their hearts.' Thus did Job continually.

6 Now it fell upon a day, that the sons of God came to present themselves before the LORD, and Satan[14] came also among them. 7 And the LORD said unto Satan: 'Whence comest thou?' Then Satan answered the LORD, and said: 'From going to and fro in the earth, and from walking up and down in it.' 8 And the LORD said unto Satan: 'Hast thou considered My servant Job, that there is none like him in the earth, a whole-hearted and an upright man, one that feareth God, and shunneth evil?' 9 Then Satan answered the LORD, and said: 'Doth Job fear God for nought? 10 Hast not Thou made a hedge about him, and about his house, and about all that he hath, on every side? Thou hast blessed the work of his hands, and his possessions are increased in the land. 11 But put forth Thy hand now, and touch all that he hath, surely he will blaspheme Thee to Thy face.' 12 And the LORD said unto Satan: 'Behold, all that he hath is in thy power; only upon himself put not forth thy hand.' So Satan went forth from the presence of the LORD.

13 And it fell on a day when his sons and his daughters were eating and drinking wine in their eldest brother's house, 14 that there came a messenger unto Job, and said: 'The oxen were plowing, and the asses feeding beside them; 15 and the Sabeans made a raid, and took them away; yea, they have slain the servants with the edge of the sword; and I only am escaped alone to tell thee.' 16 While he was yet speaking, there came also another, and said: 'A fire of God is fallen from heaven, and hath burned up the sheep, and the servants, and consumed them; and I only am escaped alone to tell thee.' 17 While he was yet speaking, there

---

14. [That is, the Adversary.—JPS 1917 eds.]

came also another, and said: 'The Chaldeans set themselves in three bands, and fell upon the camels, and have taken them away, yea, and slain the servants with the edge of the sword; and I only am escaped alone to tell thee.' 18 While he was yet speaking, there came also another, and said: 'Thy sons and thy daughters were eating and drinking wine in their eldest brother's house; 19 And, behold, there came a great wind from across the wilderness, and smote the four corners of the house, and it fell upon the young people, and they are dead; and I only am escaped alone to tell thee.'

20 Then Job arose, and rent his mantle, and shaved his head, and fell down upon the ground, and worshipped; 21 And he said;

Naked came I out of my mother's womb,
And naked shall I return thither;
The LORD gave, and the LORD hath taken away;
Blessed be the name of the LORD.
22 For all this Job sinned not, nor ascribed aught unseemly to
    God.

b. David and the Gibeonites: Can Justice Always Be Achieved?

The following narrative presents an often overlooked episode in the saga of David's accession to the Israelite monarchy. Perhaps this is because its evocation of the complex and convoluted Saul-David rivalry comes at a point where David has clearly acceded to the throne, and thus seems less relevant. Perhaps, too, because its intertextual references and allusions to past events seem haphazard and not easily understood. To navigate the text more easily, we will first locate the events in their narratological context.

In this episode, David is approached by the Gibeonites. Their identity at first seems mysterious: they are not an Israelite group, and they don't seem to be part of the local enemies that have surrounded the Israelites and have caused them trouble ever since they have settled in their Promised Land. A previous Hebrew biblical text provides a clue to their identity: in Joshua 9, the Gibeonites are described as a group native to the Canaanite area that the Israelites were settling as part of their Promised Land, and are there identified with another such group, the Hivvites (or Hivites) (Joshua 9:7). But unlike the nations in or around the Promised Land that decide to battle the Israelites to the death, the Gibeonites in Joshua 9 seek to ensure their own survival by tricking the Israelites: they dress up in tattered clothes and carry with them rotting food to give credibility to their story of coming from a land far away from Canaan. They then sue for peace, alluding to the wondrous victories achieved by the Israelites in their attempts to resettle their Promised Land. Joshua is taken in by their story and grants them their wish, promising to let them live. When the Gibeonites' deceptive story is uncovered, the Israelites are faced with a dilemma: on the one hand, they have been commanded by God to battle all nations in their Promised Land who do not welcome them (which includes the Gibeonites inasmuch as their idol-worship is itself viewed as creating an unfriendly atmosphere for the Israelites, whom the Hebrew Bible recognizes as ever-ready to succumb to idol-worship and its relatively amoral lifestyle). On the other hand, the Israelites are required, by the same Code of Law that mandates fealty to their God, to abide by the terms of their sworn oath. What to do?

Attentive readers will recall a similar dilemma posed in the insalubrious story of the Concubine in Gibeah narrative (Judges 21:1–25): there, too, the issue is posed in terms of breaking a vow versus allowing an untenable state of affairs to continue. There, as here, a compromise is reached: in the case of the Gibeonites, they are allowed to live, and are relegated as "hewers of wood and drawers of water" (Joshua 9:27) for the Israelites. Importantly, the Gibeonites do not become slaves: while they are not full-fledged citizens, they are entrusted with the important task of chopping wood for the altar of the Tabernacle, a job bearing considerable prestige, which also helps explain the details of the following narrative.

The Gibeonites are mentioned again in II Samuel 21. There they are identified as belonging to the survivors of the Emorites (or Amorites).[15] How many groups may have counted as Emorites is unclear (in Joshua 10, fives kings of the Emorites wage war on the Gibeonites for having made peace with the Israelites), but Emorites had already been identified in Joshua 9:1–3 as one of the seven major nations that had been living in or around the Promised Land. In passages in Deuteronomy, one Emorite king, Sihon, King of Heshbon, not only refuses to let the Israelites pass through his land or sell food to them, but also goes out to battle them. He and his army are vanquished, killed in battle, by the Israelites (Deuteronomy 2:32–33). A similar narrative describes the actions of a neighboring Emorite king, Og, King of Bashan: he also instigates a war with the Israelites, and he is also killed, along with his army, in battle (Deuteronomy 3:1–5). In both cases, the Israelites destroy the inhabitants of the cities of these kings (Deuteronomy 2:34, 3:6) and conquer their territories for themselves.

---

15. Some commentators suggest that the puzzle of the Hebrew Bible's identification of the Gibeonites with the Hivvite nation (Joshua 9:7), and, later, with the Emorite nation (II Samuel 21:2) may be solved by assuming that the Hivvites and the Emorites in effect joined with each other; Genesis 10:17 lists the Hivvites and the Emorites as two separate Canaanite groupings, but subsequent amalgamation would explain the double affiliation of the Gibeonites. This theory is consistent with the notation in II Samuel that the Gibeonites derive from what was left of the Emorites [II Samuel 21:2]).

II Samuel 21, however, informs readers that a remnant of the Emorites, the Gibeonites, suffered a loss (one not sanctioned by God) even after they had made peace with the Israelites—this time, at the hands of Saul. Although the text does not specify precisely which episode it is referring to, it seems plausible that during Saul's murderous rampage against the priestly city of Nob, in which Saul was so angry that the priests of Nob had given David some food that he killed the whole city in revenge (I Samuel 22), some Gibeonites were also killed.[16] The Gibeonites now come to David seeking restitution (II Samuel 21).

In the narrative in II Samuel, the lack of rainfall for three years running clues David in to the fact that the Gibeonites have a moral claim that needs to be addressed—and if David has any doubts on that score, the direct communication from God (II Samuel 21:1) lays them to rest. Crucially, the Gibeonites do not want to be bought off: monetary reparations will not assuage their moral claims. Instead, they seek the deaths of the sons of the man who had killed their Gibeonite compatriots: they ask for the remaining seven sons of Saul to be given to them for the administration of death sentences. Because of David's own oath to Jonathan (Saul's son who had died with him on Mount Gilboa while fighting the Philistines), promising that Jonathan's sons would not be harmed by David (I Samuel 20:16–17), David spares Jonathan's son Mefibosheth but does hand over seven of Saul's sons who are killed by the Gibeonites. Their hanging carcasses are left to rot in the fields, in contravention of Israelite law (Deuteronomy 21:23).

In a way—symbolic, and perhaps even fundamental—justice (in the sense of the "balancing of scales") may be said to be restored: the Gibeonites were unjustifiably killed; now, so too are the sons of Saul, the force behind the rampage at Nob. But twenty-first-century sensibilities do not take kindly to this simplistic notion of justice. Indeed, the story in II Samuel 21 appears to contravene Hebrew biblical concepts of justice (see the earlier selections in this chapter), which emphasize fairness in both theory and practice, and which specifically do not define justice as a question of human retribution (Deuteronomy 1:17), instead viewing justice as a matter of moral coherence. How can killing the sons of a dead king bring about justice for murdered Gibeonites? Does feeding the spiral of retribution bring about justice? The complexity of the events leading up to a bloody finish clues the reader in that this is not just a saga of justice defined as "tit-for-tat." Rather, this narrative asks its readers to interrogate the nature of justice itself, as well as to consider how—and to what extent—past injustices can be rectified in the present day.

---

16. Babylonian Talmud Bava Kama 119a.

Even apart from the issue of whether justice is achieved in this narrative, its denouement seems unsatisfactory to modern ears. God does send rain, the harvest is saved, and life goes on, but things don't go "back to normal" until the strange intervention of Rizpah the daughter of Aiah, whose children are among those handed over to the Gibeonites: in a manner similar to Sophocles' Antigone,[17] it is she who prevents the desecration of the dead bodies by wild birds and beasts—in this case, by guarding the bodies by day and by night. More to the point for this Hebrew biblical narrative, it is the actions of Rizpah that remind David of what he needs to do to finally close the chapter on the violent deaths of Saul and Jonathan: it is now that David finally retrieves their bones, together with the bones of those sons of Saul hung by the Gibeonites. It is debatable whether justice in this narrative is actually achieved; to the extent that the narrative comes to closure, its catalyst is the vigilance of a woman.

II Samuel 21:1–14

1 And there was a famine in the days of David three years, year after year; and David sought the face of the Lord. And the Lord said: 'It is for Saul, and for his bloody house, because he put to death the Gibeonites.' 2 And the king called the Gibeonites, and said unto them—now the Gibeonites were not of the children of Israel, but of the remnant of the Amorites; and the children of Israel had sworn unto them; and Saul sought to slay them in his zeal for the children of Israel and Judah— 3 and David said unto the Gibeonites: 'What shall I do for you? and wherewith shall I make atonement, that ye may bless the inheritance of the Lord?' 4 And the Gibeonites said unto him: 'It is no matter of silver or gold between us and Saul, or his house; neither is it for us to put any man to death in Israel.' And he said: 'What say ye that I should do for you?' 5 And they said unto the king: 'The man that consumed us, and that devised against us, so that we have been destroyed from remaining in any of the borders of Israel, 6 let seven men of his sons be delivered unto us, and we will hang them up unto the Lord in Gibeah of Saul, the chosen of the Lord.' And the king said: 'I will deliver them.'

---

17. In Sophocles' *Antigone*, the eponymous protagonist rejects the decree of King Creon forbidding the burial of her brother Polyneices (and thus leaving his corpse exposed to vultures) in favor of the higher law of the gods mandating burial of the dead; she buries her brother and is consequently put to death by Creon. In the biblical story, no royal decree forbidding burial is noted (and Hebrew biblical law mandates the swift burial of the dead [Deuteronomy 21:23]).

7 But the king spared Mephibosheth, the son of Jonathan the son of Saul, because of the Lord's oath that was between them, between David and Jonathan the son of Saul. 8 But the king took the two sons of Rizpah the daughter of Aiah, whom she bore unto Saul, Armoni and Mephibosheth; and the five sons of Michal the daughter of Saul, whom she bore to Adriel the son of Barzillai the Meholathite; 9 and he delivered them into the hands of the Gibeonites, and they hanged them in the mountain before the Lord, and they fell all seven together; and they were put to death in the days of harvest, in the first days, at the beginning of barley harvest.

10 And Rizpah the daughter of Aiah took sackcloth, and spread it for her upon the rock, from the beginning of harvest until water was poured upon them from heaven; and she suffered neither the birds of the air to rest on them by day, nor the beasts of the field by night. 11 And it was told David what Rizpah the daughter of Aiah, the concubine of Saul, had done. 12 And David went and took the bones of Saul and the bones of Jonathan his son from the men of Jabesh-gilead, who had stolen them from the broad place of Beth-shan, where the Philistines had hanged them, in the day that the Philistines slew Saul in Gilboa; 13 and he brought up from thence the bones of Saul and the bones of Jonathan his son; and they gathered the bones of them that were hanged. 14 And they buried the bones of Saul and Jonathan his son in the country of Benjamin in Zela, in the sepulchre of Kish his father; and they performed all that the king commanded. And after that God was entreated for the land.

CHAPTER 8
SOCIAL ORDER

A. Judicial Appointments

What makes for a workable social order? Which values should be championed to facilitate its creation? What sorts of public officials need to be appointed to realize its aims?

One group that appears in almost all of the Hebrew biblical texts that deal with social order is the Elders. This group, whose composition changes over time, seems to have an advisory as well as a judicial character, operating on both local and national levels. Its members, tribally appointed, also periodically make their opinions felt on the national level. The Hebrew Bible, laconic about administrative matters, presents a few tantalizing texts for the reader to ponder.

In the texts of the Hebrew Bible, social order begins with the establishment of institutions that safeguard social trust, and which make certain that the marginalized and the weak are not taken advantage of by people who can afford to disregard the law. This is the background to the practical directive to establish courts, particularly at the local level (poor people are less likely to afford expensive trips to argue their cases at a distant, central location). As we have noted, justice in the Hebrew Bible is more than a theoretical idea; it is an empirical mandate.

Deuteronomy 16:18–19

18 Judges and officers shalt thou make thee in all thy gates, which the LORD thy God giveth thee, tribe by tribe; and they shall judge the people with righteous judgment.

19 Thou shalt not wrest judgment; thou shalt not respect persons; neither shalt thou take a gift; for a gift doth blind the eyes of the wise, and pervert the words of the righteous.

B. Elders

1. Authorizing Leaders and Kings

The establishment of social order depends on more than just the presence of official organizations. Human beings populate these organizations, and as individuals, exhibit different reactions to the situations that they face. Even when officially institutionalized, the role of advisors shifts with the perceptions of the officials who run these groups. As we know from our experiences in studying politics and living with its real-life consequences, this personal quality, which is not subject to precise measurement, can often mean the difference between political success and failure.

The story of Jephtah, which we have already read (see Judges 11, in Chapter 5, "Women"), highlights the advisory process amongst the Elders of Gilead by which Jephtah is chosen (as the banished son of a prostitute, Jephtah had already run away from his family and lived in a foreign land). The role of the Elders is similarly decisive in the next political stage of Israelite development: the recognition of David as king over the united Israelite tribes.

II Samuel 5:1–5

1 Then came all the tribes of Israel to David unto Hebron, and spoke, saying: 'Behold, we are thy bone and thy flesh. 2 In times past, when Saul was king over us, it was thou that didst lead out and bring in Israel; and the LORD said to thee: Thou shalt feed My people Israel, and thou shalt be prince over Israel.' 3 So all the elders of Israel came to the king to Hebron; and king David made a covenant with them in Hebron before the LORD; and they anointed David king over Israel.

4 David was thirty years old when he began to reign, and he reigned forty years. 5 In Hebron he reigned over Judah seven years and six months; and in Jerusalem he reigned thirty and three years over all Israel and Judah.

2. Advising Kings

By the time we read of the exploits of Ahab, king of the Northern Kingdom (the Israelite monarchy is divided after the death of Solomon), hearing the Elders' advice appears to be a natural part of the monarch's deliberative process in arriving at a conclusion regarding projected actions.

I Kings 20:1–13

1 And Ben-hadad the king of Aram gathered all his host together; and there were thirty and two kings with him, and horses and chariots; and he went up and besieged Samaria, and fought against it. 2 And he sent messengers to Ahab king of Israel, into the city, 3 and said unto him: 'Thus saith Ben-hadad: Thy silver and thy gold is mine; thy wives also and thy children, even the goodliest, are mine.' 4 And the king of Israel answered and said: 'It is according to thy saying, my lord, O king: I am thine, and all that I have.' 5 And the messengers came again, and said: 'Thus speaketh Ben-hadad, saying: I sent indeed unto thee, saying: Thou shalt deliver me thy silver, and thy gold, and thy wives, and thy children; 6 but I will send my servants unto thee tomorrow about this time, and they shall search thy house, and the houses of thy servants; and it shall be, that whatsoever is pleasant in thine eyes, they shall put it in their hand, and take it away.'

7 Then the king of Israel called all the elders of the land, and said: 'Mark, I pray you, and see how this man seeketh mischief; for he sent unto me for my wives, and for my children, and for my silver, and for my gold; and I denied him not.' 8 And all the elders and all the people said unto him: 'Hearken thou not, neither consent.' 9 Wherefore he said unto the messengers of Ben-hadad: 'Tell my lord the king: All that thou didst send for to thy servant at the first I will do; but this thing I may not do.' And the messengers departed, and brought him back word. 10 And Ben-hadad sent unto him, and said: 'The gods do so unto me, and more also, if the dust of Samaria shall suffice for handfuls for all the people that follow me.' 11 And the king of Israel answered and said: 'Tell him: Let not him that girdeth on his armour boast himself as he that putteth it off.' 12 And it came to pass, when [Ben-hadad] heard this message, as he was drinking, he and the kings, in the booths, that he said unto his servants: 'Set yourselves in array.' And they set themselves in array against the city.

13 And, behold, a prophet came near unto Ahab king of Israel, and said: 'Thus saith the LORD: Hast thou seen all this great multitude? behold, I will deliver it into thy hand this day; and thou shalt know that I am the LORD.'

CHAPTER 9

ISRAELITE NATIONAL IDENTITY

In the pages of the Hebrew Bible, Israelite national identity is not a fixed concept; rather, it evolves through time. First self-consciously expressed as a union of individuals and tribes (Jacob's Final Blessing; in Genesis 49:1–28), the Israelites' national sense of who they are changes with their own perceived needs and wishes: How will they be ruled? (See Chapter 12, "Monarchy.") What do they expect from their leaders? (See Chapter 4, "Leadership.") Is tribal or national identification primary? What does it mean to be "chosen"? What role do values play in constructing a national identity? (See Chapter 7, "Social Justice and Personal Equality.")

A. Communal Identity Bestowed

Expressed as a poetic mixture of fatherly concern and parental guidance, Jacob's final blessing to his sons also envisions them as an embryonic nation. With individual sons and tribes imagined as undertaking the specific tasks that together constitute the makings of a national whole, Jacob allocates various assignments among the future members of this nation. In his blessings, Jacob pictures the unity that will come of this diversity: he imagines that some will judge the nation, some will farm the land, some will engage in trade, and some will rule.

To be sure, areas of strife are indicated, some of which are realized in the pages of the Hebrew biblical text. The prodigious blessing to Jacob's preferred son, Joseph, can be seen as a potential challenge to the political dominion that is given to Judah; indeed, the divided Israelite kingdom breaks exactly along those lines: the Northern Kingdom is colloquially called "Ephraim" after one of Joseph's sons; the Southern Kingdom, known as "the Kingdom of Judah," is centered around Jerusalem and includes the territory of the tribe of Judah (see also I Chronicles 5:1–2).

1. The Blessings of Jacob

Genesis 49:1–28

1 And Jacob called unto his sons, and said: 'Gather yourselves together, that I may tell you that which shall befall you in the end of days.

2 Assemble yourselves, and hear, ye sons of Jacob;
And hearken unto Israel your father.

3 Reuben, thou art my first-born,
My might, and the first-fruits of my strength;
The excellency of dignity, and the excellency of power.

4 Unstable as water, have not thou the excellency;
Because thou wentest up to thy father's bed;
Then defiledst thou it—he went up to my couch.

5 Simeon and Levi are brethren;
Weapons of violence their kinship.

6 Let my soul not come into their council;
Unto their assembly let my glory not be not united;
For in their anger they slew men,
And in their self-will they houghed oxen.

7 Cursed be their anger, for it was fierce,
And their wrath, for it was cruel;
I will divide them in Jacob,
And scatter them in Israel.

8 Judah, thee shall thy brethren praise;
Thy hand shall be on the neck of thine enemies;
Thy father's sons shall bow down before thee.

9 Judah is a lion's whelp;
From the prey, my son, thou art gone up.
He stooped down, he couched as a lion,
And as a lioness; who shall rouse him up?

10 The sceptre shall not depart from Judah,
Nor the ruler's staff from between his feet,
As long as men come to Shiloh;
And unto him shall the obedience of the peoples be.

11 Binding his foal unto the vine,
And his ass's colt unto the choice vine;
He washeth his garments in wine,
And his vesture in the blood of grapes;

12 His eyes shall be red with wine,

And his teeth white with milk.
13 Zebulun shall dwell at the shore of the sea,
And he shall be a shore for ships,
And his flank shall be upon Zidon.

14 Issachar is a large-boned ass,
Couching down between the sheep-folds.
15 For he saw a resting-place that it was good,
And the land that it was pleasant;
And he bowed his shoulder to bear,
And became a servant under task-work.

16 Dan shall judge his people,
As one of the tribes of Israel.
17 Dan shall be a serpent in the way,
A horned snake in the path,
That biteth the horse's heels,
So that his rider falleth backward.
18 I wait for Thy salvation, O Lord.

19 Gad, a troop shall troop upon him;
But he shall troop upon their heel.
20 As for Asher, his bread shall be fat,
And he shall yield royal dainties.

21 Naphtali is a hind let loose:
He giveth goodly words.

22 Joseph is a fruitful vine,
A fruitful vine by a fountain;
Its branches run over the wall.
23 The archers have dealt bitterly with him,
And shot at him, and hated him;
24 But his bow abode firm,
And the arms of his hands were made supple,
By the hands of the Mighty One of Jacob,
From thence, from the Shepherd, the Stone of Israel,
25 Even by the God of thy father, who shall help thee,
And by the Almighty, who shall bless thee,
With blessings of heaven above,
Blessings of the deep that coucheth beneath,
Blessings of the breasts, and of the womb.
26 The blessings of thy father
Are mighty beyond the blessings of my progenitors

Unto the utmost bound of the everlasting hills;
They shall be on the head of Joseph,
And on the crown of the head of the prince among his brethren.

27 Benjamin is a wolf that raveneth;
In the morning he devoureth the prey,
And at even he divideth the spoil.'

28 All these are the twelve tribes of Israel, and this is it that their
father spoke unto them and blessed them; every one according
to his blessing he blessed them.

2. The Blessings of Moses

By the time Moses blesses the Israelites before his death, the family group
over which Jacob presided has grown into a nation that is about to enter its
Promised Land. Unlike Jacob, whose blessings oscillate between his own
comments upon some of his sons' past actions and his vision of their future
existence in their Promised Land, Moses in his benediction relates to the
Israelites entirely as members of a fully energized nation. The individually
directed blessings to each tribe stress the unique and diverse qualities that
each tribe brings to the national life and spirit.

Moses views his legacy to the Israelites, whom he has nurtured through
their liberation from Egypt and their sojourn in the wildnerness, as a common life directed by the prescriptives of the Torah that he had transmitted
to them; he envisions a dynamic national life for his beloved people.

Deuteronomy 33

וזאת הברכה[1]

1 And this is the blessing wherewith Moses the man of God
blessed the children of Israel before his death.
2 And he said:
The LORD came from Sinai,
And rose from Seir unto them;
He shined forth from mount Paran,
And He came from the myriads holy,
At His right hand was a fiery law unto them.
3 Yea, He loveth the peoples,
All His holy ones—they are in Thy hand;

---

1. Following the traditional approach of the JPS 1917 translation, the name of this section of
the Torah headlining Moses' final words and blessings to the Israelites are given in Hebrew
as well; the words translate as "and this is the blessing."

And they sit down at Thy feet,
Receiving of Thy words.
4 Moses commanded us a law,
An inheritance of the congregation of
Jacob.
5 And there was a king in Jeshurun,
When the heads of the people were gathered,
All the tribes of Israel together.

6 Let Reuben live, and not die
In that his men become few.

7 And this for Judah, and he said:
Hear, LORD, the voice of Judah,
And bring him in unto his people;
His hands shall contend for him,
And Thou shalt be a help against his adversaries.

8 And of Levi he said:
Thy Thummim and Thy Urim be with Thy holy one,
Whom Thou didst prove at Massah,
With whom Thou didst strive at the waters of Meribah;
9 Who said of his father, and of his mother: 'I have not seen him';
Neither did he acknowledge his brethren,
Nor knew he his own children;
For they have observed Thy word,
And keep Thy covenant.
10 They shall teach Jacob Thine ordinances,
And Israel Thy law;
They shall put incense before Thee,
And whole burnt-offering upon Thine altar.
11 Bless, LORD, his substance,
And accept the work of his hands;
Smite through the loins of them that rise up against him,
And of them that hate him, that they rise not again.

12 Of Benjamin he said:
The beloved of the LORD shall dwell in safety by Him;
He covereth him all the day,
And He dwelleth between his shoulders.

13 And of Joseph he said:
Blessed of the LORD be his land;
For the precious things of heaven, for the dew,

And for the deep that coucheth beneath,
14 And for the precious things of the fruits of the sun,
And for the precious things of the yield of the moons,
15 And for the tops of the ancient mountains,
And for the precious things of the everlasting hills,
16 And for the precious things of the earth and the fulness
  thereof,
And the good will of Him that dwelt in the bush;
Let the blessing come upon the head of Joseph,
And upon the crown of the head of him that is prince among his
  brethren.
17 His firstling bullock, majesty is his;
And his horns are the horns of the wild-ox;
With them he shall gore the peoples all of them, even the ends
  of the earth;
And they are the ten thousands of Ephraim,
And they are the thousands of Manasseh.

18 And of Zebulun he said:
Rejoice, Zebulun, in thy going out,
And, Issachar, in thy tents.
19 They shall call peoples unto the mountain;
There shall they offer sacrifices of righteousness;
For they shall suck the abundance of the seas,
And the hidden treasures of the sand.

20 And of Gad he said:
Blessed be He that enlargeth Gad;
He dwelleth as a lioness,
And teareth the arm, yea, the crown of the head.
21 And he chose a first part for himself,
For there a portion of a ruler was reserved;
And there came the heads of the people,
He executed the righteousness of the LORD,
And His ordinances with Israel.

22 And of Dan he said:
Dan is a lion's whelp,
That leapeth forth from Bashan.

23 And of Naphtali he said:
O Naphtali, satisfied with favour,
And full with the blessing of the LORD:

Possess thou the sea and the south.

24 And of Asher he said:
Blessed be Asher above sons;
Let him be the favoured of his brethren,
And let him dip his foot in oil.
25 Iron and brass shall be thy bars;
And as thy days, so shall thy strength be.

26 There is none like unto God, O Jeshurun,
Who rideth upon the heaven as thy help,
And in His excellency on the skies.
27 The eternal God is a dwelling-place,
And underneath are the everlasting arms;
And He thrust out the enemy from before thee,
And said: 'Destroy.'
28 And Israel dwelleth in safety,
The fountain of Jacob alone,
In a land of corn and wine;
Yea, his heavens drop down dew.
29 Happy art thou, O Israel, who is like unto thee?
A people saved by the LORD,
The shield of thy help,
And that is the sword of thy excellency!
And thine enemies shall dwindle away before thee;
And thou shalt tread upon their high places.

B. Israelite Self-Identity

1. Shared Ethic and Experience

One of the first things that God imparts to the Israelites—indeed, the very premise of their liberation from slavery in Egypt—is the declaration of their chosenness. This chosenness is manifested in the Hebrew Bible as the gift of land promised to their forefathers, as well as in an epiphany, the Theophany at Mount Sinai. As the Israelites come to understand, being "chosen" involves heavy responsibilities and is not necessarily, or even at all, a matter of privilege. "Holiness" in this context does not mean social elevation; rather, it is a matter of focus, of dedication to special tasks. The first selection describes the preparation for receiving the Torah on Mount Sinai.

Exodus 19:3–6

3 And Moses went up unto God, and the LORD called unto him out of the mountain, saying: 'Thus shalt thou say to the house of Jacob, and tell the children of Israel: 4 Ye have seen what I did unto the Egyptians, and how I bore you on eagles' wings, and brought you unto Myself. 5 Now therefore, if ye will hearken unto My voice indeed, and keep My covenant, then ye shall be Mine own treasure from among all peoples; for all the earth is Mine; 6 and ye shall be unto Me a kingdom of priests, and a holy nation. These are the words which thou shalt speak unto the children of Israel.'

The narrative in Deuteronomy emphasizes the Israelites' monotheistic belief as their unique quality, as highlighted in the following selections.

Deuteronomy 4:5–16, 20–21, 31–35

5 Behold, I have taught you statutes and ordinances, even as the LORD my God commanded me, that ye should do so in the midst of the land whither ye go in to possess it. 6 Observe therefore and do them; for this is your wisdom and your understanding in the sight of the peoples, that, when they hear all these statutes, shall say: 'Surely this great nation is a wise and understanding people.' 7 For what great nation is there, that hath God so nigh unto them, as the LORD our God is whensoever we call upon Him? 8 And what great nation is there, that hath statutes and ordinances so righteous as all this law, which I set before you this day?

9 Only take heed to thyself, and keep thy soul diligently, lest thou forget the things which thine eyes saw, and lest they depart from thy heart all the days of thy life; but make them known unto thy children and thy children's children; 10 the day that thou stoodest before the LORD thy God in Horeb, when the LORD said unto me: 'Assemble Me the people, and I will make them hear My words that they may learn to fear Me all the days that they live upon the earth, and that they may teach their children.' 11 And ye came near and stood under the mountain; and the mountain burned with fire unto the heart of heaven, with darkness, cloud, and thick darkness. 12 And the LORD spoke unto you out of the midst of the fire; ye heard the voice of words, but ye saw no form; only a voice. 13 And He declared unto you His covenant, which He commanded you to perform, even the ten words; and He wrote them upon two tables of stone. 14 And

the LORD commanded me at that time to teach you statutes and ordinances, that ye might do them in the land whither ye go over to possess it. 15 Take ye therefore good heed unto yourselves—for ye saw no manner of form on the day that the LORD spoke unto you in Horeb out of the midst of the fire— 16 lest ye deal corruptly, and make you a graven image, even the form of any figure, the likeness of male or female.

. . . .

20 But you hath the LORD taken and brought forth out of the iron furnace, out of Egypt, to be unto Him a people of inheritance, as ye are this day.

21 Now the LORD was angered with me for your sakes, and swore that I should not go over the Jordan, and that I should not go in unto that good land, which the LORD thy God giveth thee for an inheritance;

. . . .

31 for the LORD thy God is a merciful God; He will not fail thee, neither destroy thee, nor forget the covenant of thy fathers which He swore unto them. 32 For ask now of the days past, which were before thee, since the day that God created man upon the earth, and from the one end of heaven unto the other, whether there hath been any such thing as this great thing is, or hath been heard like it? 33 Did ever a people hear the voice of God speaking out of the midst of the fire, as thou hast heard, and live? 34 Or hath God assayed to go and take Him a nation from the midst of another nation, by trials, by signs, and by wonders, and by war, and by a mighty hand, and by an outstretched arm, and by great terrors, according to all that the LORD your God did for you in Egypt before thine eyes? 35 Unto thee it was shown, that thou mightiest know that the LORD, He is God; there is none else beside Him.

Deuteronomy 7:6–9

6 For thou art a holy people unto the LORD thy God: the LORD thy God hath chosen thee to be His own treasure, out of all peoples that are upon the face of the earth. 7 The LORD did not set His love upon you, nor choose you, because ye were more in number than any people—for ye were the fewest of all peoples— 8 but because the LORD loved you, and because He

would keep the oath which He swore unto your fathers, hath the LORD brought you out with a mighty hand, and redeemed you out of the house of bondage, from the hand of Pharaoh king of Egypt. 9 Know therefore that the LORD thy God, He is God; the faithful God, who keepeth covenant and mercy with them that love Him and keep His commandments to a thousand generations;

In the writings of the prophets, "chosenness" takes on a moral quality of fulfilling ongoing ethical duties. Particularly potent examples are presented in the words of Amos.

Amos 3:1–2, 11

1 Hear this word that the LORD hath spoken against you, O children of Israel, against the whole family which I brought up out of the land of Egypt, saying:
2 You only have I known of all the families of the earth;
Therefore I will visit upon you all your iniquities.
. . . .
11 Therefore thus saith the Lord GOD:
An adversary, even round about the land!
And he shall bring down thy strength from thee,
And thy palaces shall be spoiled.

Amos 5:7–8, 11–15, 21–24

7 Ye who turn judgment to wormwood,
And cast righteousness to the ground;
8 Him that maketh the Pleiades and Orion,
And bringeth on the shadow of death in the morning,
And darkeneth the day into night;
That calleth for the waters of the sea,
And poureth them out upon the face of the earth;
The LORD is His name;
. . . .
11 Therefore, because ye trample upon the poor,
And take from him exactions of wheat;
Ye have built houses of hewn stone,
But ye shall not dwell in them,
Ye have planted pleasant vineyards,
But ye shall not drink wine thereof.
12 For I know how manifold are your transgressions,
And how mighty are your sins;

Ye that afflict the just, that take a ransom,
And that turn aside the needy in the gate.
13 Therefore the prudent doth keep silence in such a time;
For it is an evil time.

14 Seek good, and not evil, that ye may live;
And so the LORD, the God of hosts, will be with you, as ye say.
15 Hate the evil, and love the good,
And establish justice in the gate;
It may be that the LORD, the God of hosts,
Will be gracious unto the remnant of Joseph.
. . . .
21 I hate, I despise your feasts,
And I will take no delight in your solemn assemblies.
22 Yea, though ye offer me burnt-offerings and your meal-
offerings,
I will not accept them;
Neither will I regard the peace-offerings of your fat beasts.
23 Take thou away from Me the noise of thy songs;
And let Me not hear the melody of thy psalteries.
24 But let justice well up as waters,
And righteousness as a mighty stream.

2. Geographic Identity?

But national identity is not only a matter of shared ethical ideas and practices in specific cases. Strains in Israelite national identity are already apparent by the time the Israelites are ready to enter their Promised Land: the
richness of the first part of the land that they see may persuade some of the
tribes to settle down before securing the full extent of the Promised Land
for all of their fellows. In the following sections, the Israelites work out their
national identity as a matter of recognizing concrete responsibilities toward
one another.

Numbers 32:1–32

1 Now the children of Reuben and the children of Gad had
a very great multitude of cattle; and when they saw the land of
Jazer, and the land of Gilead, that, behold, the place was a place
for cattle, 2 the children of Gad and the children of Reuben came
and spoke unto Moses, and to Eleazar the priest, and unto the
princes of the congregation, saying: 3 'Ataroth, and Dibon, and
Jazer, and Nimrah, and Heshbon, and Elealeh, and Sebam, and

Nebo, and Beon, 4 the land which the LORD smote before the congregation of Israel, is a land for cattle, and thy servants have cattle.' 5 And they said: 'If we have found favour in thy sight, let this land be given unto thy servants for a possession; bring us not over the Jordan.'

6 And Moses said unto the children of Gad and to the children of Reuben: 'Shall your brethren go to the war, and shall ye sit here? 7 And wherefore will ye turn away the heart of the children of Israel from going over into the land which the LORD hath given them?

. . . .

14 And, behold, ye are risen up in your fathers' stead, a brood of sinful men, to augment yet the fierce anger of the LORD toward Israel. 15 For if ye turn away from after Him, He will yet again leave them in the wilderness; and so ye will destroy all this people.'

16 And they came near unto him, and said: 'We will build sheepfolds here for our cattle, and cities for our little ones; 17 but we ourselves will be ready armed to go before the children of Israel, until we have brought them unto their place; and our little ones shall dwell in the fortified cities because of the inhabitants of the land. 18 We will not return unto our houses, until the children of Israel have inherited every man his inheritance. 19 For we will not inherit with them on the other side of the Jordan, and forward, because our inheritance is fallen to us on this side of the Jordan eastward.'

20 And Moses said unto them: 'If ye will do this thing: if ye will arm yourselves to go before the LORD to the war, 21 and every armed man of you will pass over the Jordan before the LORD, until He hath driven out His enemies from before Him, 22 and the land be subdued before the LORD, and ye return afterward; then ye shall be clear before the LORD, and before Israel, and this land shall be unto you for a possession before the LORD. 23 But if ye will not do so, behold, ye have sinned against the LORD; and know ye your sin which will find you. 24 Build you cities for your little ones, and folds for your sheep; and do that which hath proceeded out of your mouth.'

25 And the children of Gad and the children of Reuben spoke unto Moses, saying: 'Thy servants will do as my lord commandeth.

26 Our little ones, our wives, our flocks, and all our cattle, shall be there in the cities of Gilead; 27 but thy servants will pass over, every man that is armed for war, before the LORD to battle, as my lord saith.'

28 So Moses gave charge concerning them to Eleazar the priest, and to Joshua the son of Nun, and to the heads of the fathers' houses of the tribes of the children of Israel. 29 And Moses said unto them: 'If the children of Gad and the children of Reuben will pass with you over the Jordan, every man that is armed to battle, before the LORD, and the land shall be subdued before you, then ye shall give them the land of Gilead for a possession; 30 but if they will not pass over with you armed, they shall have possessions among you in the land of Canaan.' 31 And the children of Gad and the children of Reuben answered, saying: 'As the LORD hath said unto thy servants, so will we do. 32 We will pass over armed before the LORD into the land of Canaan, and the possession of our inheritance shall remain with us beyond the Jordan.'

For further reading see Deuteronomy 3:18–20, and Joshua 1:12–17 and 22:1–9.

3. Diversity or National Implosion?

In accordance with their promise to Moses, the tribal members of Reuben and Gad (and part of the tribe of Manasseh) do participate in the fight for the rest of the Promised Land on the other side of the Jordan River before settling back into their rich pasture land on the eastern banks of the Jordan River. When the time comes for all the tribes to possess their landholdings, the tribes settling in the Promised Land on the western side of the Jordan River object to the tribes of Reuben, Gad, and part of the tribe of Manasseh, settling at a distance from the majority of the nation. This resulting physical distance might, they fear, impede a sense of common destiny and national identity that should unify all the tribes of the Israelite nation. The trans-Jordan tribes reply that they will remain faithful to the monotheistic beliefs of the Israelites that have united them at least since the Theophany on Mount Sinai. More specifically, they pledge to adhere to the central locale of prayer and sacrifice that was planned for the religious community of Israelites, and undertake not to create diverse religious traditions and practices of their own.

Joshua 22:10–34

10 And when they came unto the region about the Jordan, that is in the land of Canaan, the children of Reuben and the children of Gad and the half-tribe of Manasseh built there an altar by the Jordan, a great altar to look upon. 11 And the children of Israel heard say: 'Behold, the children of Reuben and the children of Gad and the half-tribe of Manasseh have built an altar in the forefront of the land of Canaan, in the region about the Jordan, on the side that pertaineth to the children of Israel.' 12 And when the children of Israel heard of it, the whole congregation of the children of Israel gathered themselves together at Shiloh, to go up against them to war.

13 And the children of Israel sent unto the children of Reuben, and to the children of Gad, and to the half-tribe of Manasseh, into the land of Gilead, Phinehas the son of Eleazar the priest; 14 and with him ten princes, one prince of a fathers' house for each of the tribes of Israel; and they were every one of them head of their fathers' houses among the thousands of Israel. 15 And they came unto the children of Reuben, and to the children of Gad, and to the half-tribe of Manasseh, unto the land of Gilead, and they spoke with them, saying: 16 'Thus saith the whole congregation of the LORD: What treachery is this that ye have committed against the God of Israel, to turn away this day from following the LORD, in that ye have builded you an altar, to rebel this day against the LORD? 17 Is the iniquity of Peor too little for us, from which we have not cleansed ourselves unto this day, although there came a plague upon the congregation of the LORD, 18 that ye must turn away this day from following the LORD? and it will be, seeing ye rebel to-day against the LORD, that to-morrow He will be wroth with the whole congregation of Israel. 19 Howbeit, if the land of your possession be unclean, then pass ye over unto the land of the possession of the LORD, wherein the LORD'S tabernacle dwelleth, and take possession among us; but rebel not against the LORD, nor rebel against us, in building you an altar besides the altar of the LORD our God. 20 Did not Achan the son of Zerah commit a trespass concerning the devoted thing, and wrath fell upon all the congregation of Israel? and that man perished not alone in his iniquity.'

21 Then the children of Reuben and the children of Gad and the half-tribe of Manasseh answered, and spoke unto the heads

of the thousands of Israel: 22 'God, God, the LORD, God, God, the LORD, He knoweth, and Israel he shall know; if it be in rebellion, or if in treachery against the LORD—save Thou us not this day— 23 that we have built us an altar to turn away from following the LORD; or if to offer thereon burnt-offering or meal-offering, or if to offer sacrifices of peace-offerings thereon, let the LORD Himself require it; 24 and if we have not rather out of anxiety about a matter done this, saying: In time to come your children might speak unto our children, saying: What have ye to do with the LORD, the God of Israel? 25 for the LORD hath made the Jordan a border between us and you, ye children of Reuben and children of Gad; ye have no portion in the LORD; so might your children make our children cease from fearing the LORD. 26 Therefore we said: Let us now prepare to build us an altar, not for burnt-offering, nor for sacrifice; 27 but it shall be a witness between us and you, and between our generations after us, that we may do the service of the LORD before Him with our burnt-offerings, and with our sacrifices, and with our peace-offerings; that your children may not say to our children in time to come: Ye have no portion in the LORD. 28 Therefore said we: It shall be, when they so say to us or to our generations in time to come, that we shall say: Behold the pattern of the altar of the LORD, which our fathers made, not for burnt-offering, nor for sacrifice; but it is a witness between us and you. 29 Far be it from us that we should rebel against the LORD, and turn away this day from following the LORD, to build an altar for burnt-offering, for meal-offering, or for sacrifice, besides the altar of the LORD our God that is before His tabernacle.'

30 And when Phinehas the priest, and the princes of the congregation, even the heads of the thousands of Israel that were with him, heard the words that the children of Reuben and the children of Gad and the children of Manasseh spoke, it pleased them well. 31 And Phinehas the son of Eleazar the priest said unto the children of Reuben, and to the children of Gad, and to the children of Manasseh: 'This day we know that the LORD is in the midst of us, because ye have not committed this treachery against the LORD; now have ye delivered the children of Israel out of the hand of the LORD.' 32 And Phinehas the son of Eleazar the priest, and the princes, returned from the children of Reuben, and from the children of Gad, out of the land of Gilead, unto the land of Canaan, to the children of Israel, and brought

them back word. 33 And the thing pleased the children of Israel; and the children of Israel blessed God, and spoke no more of going up against them to war, to destroy the land wherein the children of Reuben and the children of Gad dwelt. 34 And the children of Reuben and the children of Gad called the altar—: 'for it is a witness between us that the LORD is God.

Beyond these assurances, Joshua requests a greater oath of fealty from the Israelite community as a whole regarding the maintenance of Israelite distinctiveness—specifically in terms of their fealty to the commandments of the Torah—before his death.

Joshua 24:20–28

20 If ye forsake the LORD, and serve strange gods, then He will turn and do you evil, and consume you, after that He hath done you good.'

21 And the people said unto Joshua: 'Nay; but we will serve the LORD.' 22 And Joshua said unto the people: 'Ye are witnesses against yourselves that ye have chosen you the LORD, to serve Him.—And they said: 'We are witnesses.'— 23 Now therefore put away the strange gods which are among you, and incline your heart unto the LORD, the God of Israel.' 24 And the people said unto Joshua: 'The LORD our God will we serve, and unto His voice will we hearken.'

25 So Joshua made a covenant with the people that day, and set them a statute and an ordinance in Shechem. 26 And Joshua wrote these words in the book of the law of God; and he took a great stone, and set it up there under the oak that was by the sanctuary of the LORD. 27 And Joshua said unto all the people: 'Behold, this stone shall be a witness against us; for it hath heard all the words of the LORD which He spoke unto us; it shall be therefore a witness against you, lest ye deny your God.' 28 So Joshua sent the people away, every man unto his inheritance.

CHAPTER 10

VIOLENCE

Plato's *Republic* famously presents the model political state as autarkic and, ideally, self-perpetuating under the leadership of the wise Guardians (to be sure, the end of the *Republic* also describes the messy and often violent degeneration of the ideal state). Later depictions of model states, like Thomas More's *Utopia*, also present a world in which violence is depicted as characteristic of lesser, imperfect regimes.

The political reality of the Israelites presented in the Hebrew Bible is not depicted as taking place in a world that can even remotely be construed as ideal. Even in their beginnings as a small tribal clan, Jacob and his wives and children are conscious of being surrounded by unfriendly neighbors (Genesis 34:30). Later on, as the Israelites camp and travel through foreign lands, they are harassed, enslaved, cursed, and subjected to hostilities from nations that travel far from their own homelands to eradicate what must have seemed to them to be a small band of erstwhile downtrodden slaves (Exodus 17:8). During their sojourn in the wilderness on their way to the Promised Land, the Israelites are additionally riven with feuds, plagues, and violence that threaten to end their national existence. Even reaching their goal is no panacea: their ancestral land, when they finally arrive at its borders, is inhabited by warlike nations that refuse to make peace with the Israelites, and whose lifestyle is anathema to this (isolated) monotheistic nation.

Among the questions raised as we read selected narratives from the Hebrew Bible's multifaceted treatment of the theme of violence are these: Is violence an endemic part of Israelite (or any national) existence? How can we account for the depictions of, and exhortations to practice, violence in the very texts of the Hebrew Bible that also passionately proclaim the need for peace, justice, and equity?[1]

---

1. The tendency to confuse texts depicting violence in the Hebrew Bible with violent actions committed in the name of religion is evident in Karen Armstrong's *Fields of Blood: Religion and the History of Violence* (New York: Knopf, 2014). Aside from a muddled treatment of the consequences of the encounter with modernity on the expression of religious violence (e.g., pp. 566, 587–98), Armstrong's failure to fully explore the differences between "faith" and "religion" (as Hobbes notably does in *Leviathan*) severely crimps her presentation of modern responses. As a result, her presentation devolves into a series of arbitrarily chosen political heroes and rogues (e.g., pp. 658–63). Similarly, her failure to distinguish between different

A. The Rape of Dinah and Violence

The negative appraisals of Simeon's and Levi's violence against the city and family of Shekhem[2] (Genesis 34:1–2) place less emphasis on the event that elicits their extreme behavior: the rape and kidnapping of their sister Dinah. While contemporary dwellers in sheltered venues may not (always) be able to relate to this horrifying set of circumstances, the Hebrew biblical narrative makes it clear that the "marriage negotiations" for Dinah take place under highly charged circumstances: Dinah remains a prisoner in the household of the person who had repeatedly raped her. How true do the rapist's professions of love ring in the reader's ears, when even today, many contemporary legal systems in "advanced" democracies still fail to sufficiently distinguish between an act of rape and a "demonstration of love"?[3]

Readers who view superficially the proposals of Hamor (Shekhem's father and the ruler of the eponymous city in which they live) may believe that his ideas of uniting his city with Jacob's clan are sincerely meant. But when viewed against the background of circumstances and events as they are depicted—rape and kidnapping—Hamor's suggestions of uniting the two groups through marriage (Genesis 34:9–10) are more easily seen as a cover for the eventual planned colonization of the smaller family (Jacob's clan) by the larger and wealthier city-state (Hamor's city of Shekhem). This point becomes obvious when neither an apology nor a statement of contrition regarding the violence done to Dinah is forthcoming from any of the protagonists. Indeed, the resounding silence of Shekhem and his city indicates that for them, the violent treatment and shaming of Dinah is quite routine in their way of "doing business."[4] Shekhem compounds this moral insensitivity by treating his projected marriage with Dinah as merely a transactional matter of convenience: "Let me find favor in your eyes, and whatever you say to me I will give" (Genesis 34:11); as if Dinah and her

---

interpretations of biblical texts informs the flat rendition of her selected Hebrew biblical presentations, which neglect the nuances of the bonds that can unite text, faith, and differing styles of democratic governance.

2. JPS 1917: "Shechem."

3. A particularly trenchant discussion built on this distinction is offered by Catharine MacKinnon's *Toward a Feminist Theory of the State* (Cambridge, MA: Harvard University Press, 1989; esp. pp. 155–84;184–95).

4. The indifference displayed by the city of Shekhem is particularly obvious when contrasted to the portrayed reaction of another city in the ancient Mediterranean world to a moral outrage that takes place in its midst: Thebe's horror at the punishment meted out by Creon in *Antigone*, when Haemon protests that "*the city mourns for the girl*" (Sophocles, *Antigone*, ed. David Franklin and John Harrison [New York: Cambridge University Press, 2003; l. 645]; emphasis mine).

feelings about what had happened to her are fungible, with everything being made "right" by the correct "bride price."

Given a culture that acts in ways which disregard individual boundaries in favor of allowing the strongest to get their way, it is no wonder that Simeon and Levi must approach their target with "guile": how else would a small band of brothers rescue their sister from an unfriendly city? In many ways, Simeon's and Levi's feelings of rage (as distinct from the violence that they perpetrate) seem to be reactions against this cold-blooded commodification of Dinah and her sense of self. It is this objectification that is the ultimate "defiling of Dinah," as we will see further on.

Readers who wish to see in the ensuing maelstrom of violence a vindication of family honor to the exclusion of all other considerations, including the honor and well-being of the rape victim herself, fail to take seriously the evidence of the text. Despite their trickery and the disproportionate scale of the retribution they imprudently exact on the city of Shekhem, Simeon and Levi correctly recognize the injury suffered by their sister at the hands of Shekhem as involving more than family honor; had that been the case, marriage on the terms (deceptively) proposed by the sons of Jacob might possibly have, post-facto, "erased" the problem. Moreover, unlike some adherents of cultures that, even in modern times, react to unwanted couplings with "honor killings" of the women involved (the horrific "logical" outcome in many systems that evaluate women solely in terms of their sexual "purity" is to eradicate all evidence of a reality that flies in the face of such narrow classifications), Simeon and Levi do not abandon their sister, and they certainly do not kill her. They take Dinah home (34:26). The Midrash submits that she resides in Simeon's house, under his protection, for the rest of her life.[5]

Genesis 34

And Dinah the daughter of Leah, whom she had borne unto Jacob, went out to see the daughters of the land. 2 And Shechem the son of Hamor the Hivite, the prince of the land, saw her; and he took her, and lay with her, and humbled her. 3 And his soul did cleave unto Dinah the daughter of Jacob, and he loved the damsel, and spoke comfortingly unto the damsel. 4 And Shechem spoke unto his father Hamor, saying: 'Get me this damsel to wife.'

5. Bereshit Rabbah 80:11. Bereshit Rabbah is a Midrashic reading of the Hebrew Bible (Bereshit Rabbah concentrates on Bereshit, or Genesis, the first volume of the Five Books of Moses). Midrashic commentary is (largely) a product of the post–Second Temple era; compilation dates for Bereshit Rabbah range from the third to the fifth centuries C.E.

5 Now Jacob heard that he had defiled Dinah his daughter; and his sons were with his cattle in the field; and Jacob held his peace until they came. 6 And Hamor the father of Shechem went out unto Jacob to speak with him. 7 And the sons of Jacob came in from the field when they heard it; and the men were grieved, and they were very wroth, because he had wrought a vile deed in Israel in lying with Jacob's daughter; which thing ought not to be done.

8 And Hamor spoke with them, saying 'The soul of my son Shechem longeth for your daughter. I pray you give her unto him to wife. 9 And make ye marriages with us; give your daughters unto us, and take our daughters unto you. 10 And ye shall dwell with us; and the land shall be before you; dwell and trade ye therein, and get you possessions therein.' 11 And Shechem said unto her father and unto her brethren: 'Let me find favour in your eyes, and what ye shall say unto me I will give. 12 Ask me never so much dowry and gift, and I will give according as ye shall say unto me; but give me the damsel to wife.'

13 And the sons of Jacob answered Shechem and Hamor his father with guile, and spoke, because he had defiled Dinah their sister, 14 and said unto them: 'We cannot do this thing, to give our sister to one that is uncircumcised; for that were a reproach unto us. 15 Only on this condition will we consent unto you: if ye will be as we are, that every male of you be circumcised; 16 then will we give our daughters unto you, and we will take your daughters to us, and we will dwell with you, and we will become one people. 17 But if ye will not hearken unto us, to be circumcised; then will we take our daughter, and we will be gone.'

18 And their words pleased Hamor, and Shechem Hamor's son. 19 And the young man deferred not to do the thing, because he had delight in Jacob's daughter. And he was honoured above all the house of his father. 20 And Hamor and Shechem his son came unto the gate of their city, and spoke with the men of their city, saying: 21 'These men are peaceable with us; therefore let them dwell in the land, and trade therein; for, behold, the land is large enough for them; let us take their daughters to us for wives, and let us give them our daughters. 22 Only on this condition will the men consent unto us to dwell with us, to become one people, if every male among us be circumcised, as they are circumcised. 23 Shall not their cattle and their substance and all

their beasts be ours? only let us consent unto them, and they will dwell with us.' 24 And unto Hamor and unto Shechem his son hearkened all that went out of the gate of his city; and every male was circumcised, all that went out of the gate of his city.

25 And it came to pass on the third day, when they were in pain, that two of the sons of Jacob, Simeon and Levi, Dinah's brethren, took each man his sword, and came upon the city unawares, and slew all the males. 26 And they slew Hamor and Shechem his son with the edge of the sword, and took Dinah out of Shechem's house, and went forth. 27 The sons of Jacob came upon the slain, and spoiled the city, because they had defiled their sister. 28 They took their flocks and their herds and their asses, and that which was in the city and that which was in the field; 29 and all their wealth, and all their little ones and their wives, took they captive and spoiled, even all that was in the house.

30 And Jacob said to Simeon and Levi: 'Ye have troubled me, to make me odious unto the inhabitants of the land, even unto the Canaanites and the Perizzites; and, I being few in number, they will gather themselves together against me and smite me; and I shall be destroyed, I and my house.' 31 And they said: 'Should one deal with our sister as with a harlot?'

B. Jacob's Reckoning with Simeon and Levi

Upon his deathbed, Jacob's words to this violent duo are harsh: he blames them for their propensity towards violence, charging them with mishandling the reaction to the rape of Dinah, and for the aggression with which that they later treated their brother, Joseph. In the end, Jacob dissociates himself from them—"let my soul not come into their council . . . be not joined to their company" (Genesis 49:5–7)—and bars them from any contiguous landholding in the Promised Land (both tribes of Simeon and Levi were restricted to scattered cities throughout Ancient Israel). In a world where property is a sign of manhood, and where violence is often exercised as an excuse for "masculinity," Jacob effectively "unmans" them.

Genesis 49:5–7

5 Simeon and Levi are brethren;
Weapons of violence their kinship.
6 Let my soul not come into their council;
Unto their assembly let my glory not be not united;

For in their anger they slew men, And in their self-will they
   houghed oxen.
7 Cursed be their anger, for it was fierce,
And their wrath, for it was cruel;
I will divide them in Jacob,
And scatter them in Israel

C. Violence and Slavery

In the following selection, the slavery endured by the Israelites in Egypt
is presented not just as a morally wrong-headed way to avoid payment for
services rendered (for example, the building of store-cities for the Egyptians
by the enslaved Israelites), but rather as an act of genocidal hatred.
Contemporary readers may want to consider how slavery has functioned in
the political consolidation of modern national identity; examples, unfortu-
nately, abound.

For readers of the twenty-first century, it is worth noting how the Hebrew
Bible presents the methods of persuasion—not to say propaganda—that the
Pharaoh in ancient Egypt (the "Exodus" Pharaoh) uses to persuade his people of the need to oppress a (relatively) new minority amongst them. To be
sure, the tendency of ancient Egyptian culture has already been presented as
one involving separation from any culture perceived as foreign to their own:
hence the previous notations in the Hebrew Bible of the Egyptian repug-
nance towards eating with the Hebrews (Genesis 43:32); likewise, of the
Egyptian disgust towards the traditional Israelite livelihood, shepherding
(Genesis 46:34). The larger point here, however, is that the "new" Pharaoh
in this text inverts the relative situation of power and powerlessness between
the Egyptians and the Israelites (a minority ensconced in a particular neigh-
borhood—Goshen—doing work that the Egyptians despised), thereby creating a justification for his plan to persecute and annihilate the Israelites.

The Joseph that the Pharaoh of Egypt "knew not" refers to the Israelite
Joseph, son of Jacob, who several decades before had been instrumental
in saving Egypt and its inhabitants from perishing during the years-long
famine through a combination of food storage and economic centralization
(Genesis 41:17–57, 43:13–26).

Exodus 1:8–22

8 Now there arose a new king over Egypt, who knew not
Joseph. 9 And he said unto his people: 'Behold, the people of the
children of Israel are too many and too mighty for us; 10 come,
let us deal wisely with them, lest they multiply, and it come to

pass, that, when there befalleth us any war, they also join them-selves unto our enemies, and fight against us, and get them up out of the land.' 11 Therefore they did set over them tax-masters[6] to afflict them with their burdens. And they built for Pharaoh store-cities, Pithom and Raamses. 12 But the more they afflicted them, the more they multiplied and the more they spread abroad. And they were adread because of the children of Israel. 13 And the Egyptians made the children of Israel to serve with rigour. 14 And they made their lives bitter with hard service, in mortar and in brick, and in all manner of service in the field; in all their service, wherein they made them serve with rigour.

15 And the king of Egypt spoke to the Hebrew[7] midwives, of whom the name of the one was Shiphrah, and the name of the other Puah; 16 and he said: 'When ye do the office of a midwife to the Hebrew women, ye shall look upon the birthstool: if it be a son, then ye shall kill him; but if it be a daughter, then she shall live.' 17 But the midwives feared God, and did not as the king of Egypt commanded them, but saved the men-children alive. 18 And the king of Egypt called for the midwives, and said unto them: 'Why have ye done this thing, and have saved the men-children alive?' 19 And the midwives said unto Pharaoh: 'Because the Hebrew women are not as the Egyptian women; for they are lively, and are delivered ere the midwife come unto them.' 20 And God dealt well with the midwives; and the people multiplied, and waxed very mighty. 21 And it came to pass, because the midwives feared God, that He made them houses. 22 And Pharaoh charged all his people, saying: 'Every son that is born ye shall cast into the river, and every daughter ye shall save alive.'

---

6. The JPS 1917 translation of the Hebrew term *sarei misim* is "taskmasters." Interestingly, the biblical word *misim* actualy means "tax," which may suggest that Israelite servitude in Egypt begins first with their being deprived of their equal status as citizens, by being forced to pay a particular "tax" to the regime. My thanks to Leslie and Mitch Morrison for their helpful comments on this point.

7. The adjectival structure of the descriptive "Hebrew midwives" is ambiguous in the Hebrew biblical text: it is not clear if these were Israelite midwives (in which case the term "Hebrew" would designate their national identity), or Egyptian midwives assigned to assist the Israelite women in the process of giving birth (in which case the term "Hebrew" would designate the function of these midwives, i.e., they were midwives assigned to the Hebrews). Particularly in the latter case, the civilly disobedient refusal of these midwives to murder Israelite baby boys born after the Pharaoh's decree indicates their enormous moral courage.

The Hebrew Bible records that when Moses, on behalf of the oppressed Israelites, requests leave from the Egyptian Pharaoh to practice their religious rites in the wilderness (a three-day journey away), the Pharaoh reacts not to the fact of the slavery but to the temerity of the request itself: an enslaved people is not supposed to have any identity left over from their servitude to their masters that would allow them to imagine fulfilling religious rituals of their own. Consequently, the slavery becomes even harsher, and the Israelites suffer further violence at the hands of their taskmasters.

Exodus 5:1–21

1 And afterward Moses and Aaron came, and said unto Pharaoh: 'Thus saith the LORD, the God of Israel: Let My people go, that they may hold a feast unto Me in the wilderness.' 2 And Pharaoh said: 'Who is the LORD, that I should hearken unto His voice to let Israel go? I know not the LORD, and moreover I will not let Israel go.' 3 And they said: 'The God of the Hebrews hath met with us. Let us go, we pray thee, three days' journey into the wilderness, and sacrifice unto the LORD our God; lest He fall upon us with pestilence, or with the sword.'

4 And the king of Egypt said unto them: 'Wherefore do ye, Moses and Aaron, cause the people to break loose from their work? get you unto your burdens.' 5 And Pharaoh said: 'Behold, the people of the land are now many, and will ye make them rest from their burdens?' 6 And the same day Pharaoh commanded the taskmasters[8] of the people, and their officers, saying: 7 'Ye shall no more give the people straw to make brick, as heretofore. Let them go and gather straw for themselves. 8 And the tale of the bricks, which they did make heretofore, ye shall lay upon them; ye shall not diminish aught thereof; for they are idle; therefore they cry, saying: Let us go and sacrifice to our God. 9 Let heavier work be laid upon the men, that they may labour therein; and let them not regard lying words.'

---

8. The Hebrew biblical term is *nogsim*, which JPS 1917 accurately translates as "taskmasters" (cf. note 6 in this chapter for a discussion of the term *sarei misim*, which JPS 1917 also, though less literally, translates as "taskmasters"). The *nogsim* are the Egyptian taskmasters who supervise the Israelite police officers (*shotrim*), who are personally responsible that the work quotas of the Israelite slaves be fulfilled. It might be logical to assume that the *shotrim* might beat the Israelite slaves who cannot fulfill their work quotas. Instead, it is the *shotrim* who are beaten by the *nogsim* when the work quotas fall short (cf. Rashi s.v. Exodus 5:14). I thank Mitch and Leslie Morrison for their insights into this topic.

10 And the taskmasters over[9] the people went out, and their officers, and they spoke to the people, saying: 'Thus saith Pharaoh: I will not give you straw. 11 Go yourselves, get you straw where ye can find it; for nought of your work shall be diminished.' 12 So the people were scattered abroad throughout all the land of Egypt to gather stubble for straw. 13 And the taskmasters were urgent, saying: 'Fulfil your work, your daily task, as when there was straw.' 14 And the officers of the children of Israel, whom Pharaoh's taskmasters had set over them, were beaten, saying: 'Wherefore have ye not fulfilled your appointed task in making brick both yesterday and today as heretofore?'

15 Then the officers of the children of Israel came and cried unto Pharaoh, saying: 'Wherefore dealest thou thus with thy servants? 16 There is no straw given unto thy servants, and they say to us: Make brick; and, behold, thy servants are beaten, but the fault is in thine own people.' 17 But he said: 'Ye are idle, ye are idle; therefore ye say: Let us go and sacrifice to the LORD. 18 Go therefore now, and work; for there shall no straw be given you, yet shall ye deliver the tale of bricks.' 19 And the officers of the children of Israel did see that they were set on mischief, when they said: 'Ye shall not diminish aught from your bricks, your daily task.' 20 And they met Moses and Aaron, who stood in the way, as they came forth from Pharaoh; 21 and they said unto them: 'The LORD look upon you, and judge; because ye have made our savour to be abhorred in the eyes of Pharaoh, and in the eyes of his servants, to put a sword in their hand to slay us.'

D. Verbal Violence: Cursing Them Out

Even after their liberation from genocidal Egyptian slavery, the Israelites are subject to destructive campaigns at the hands of other nations in the ancient Near East. These nations' usage of a soothsayer to weaken a (purported) enemy by cursing them out may strike the contemporary reader as something of a bad joke. Nevertheless, in the ancient world, placing curses on one's enemies was an important psychological weapon.

The pervasiveness of this practice indicates the depths of hatred that the monotheistic Israelites evoked in this context: their (would-be) cursers

---

9. JPS 1917: "of."

come from the peoples of Moab and Midian, nations that themselves were not within the borders of the Promised Land, and who consequently did not need to fear that the Israelites would want to conquer their territory. This raises an interesting question: Of what were the Moabites afraid? Can the emotion of fear (on the part of a people) be stimulated (by its leadership, for example), and utilized as a political strategy to solidify the extent of a nation's power?

Numbers 22:1–7

1 And the children of Israel journeyed, and pitched in the plains of Moab beyond the Jordan at Jericho.

בלק[10]

2 And Balak the son of Zippor saw all that Israel had done to the Amorites.

3 And Moab was sore afraid of the people, because they were many; and Moab was overcome with dread because of the children of Israel. 4 And Moab said unto the elders of Midian: 'Now will this multitude lick up all that is round about us, as the ox licketh up the grass of the field.'—And Balak the son of Zippor was king of Moab at that time.— 5 And he sent messengers unto Balaam the son of Beor, to Pethor, which is by the River, to the land of the children of his people, to call him, saying: 'Behold, there is a people come out from Egypt; behold, they cover the face of the earth, and they abide over against me. 6 Come now therefore, I pray thee, curse me this people; for they are too mighty for me; peradventure I shall prevail, that we may smite them, and that I may drive them out of the land; for I know that he whom thou blessest is blessed, and he whom thou cursest is cursed.' 7 And the elders of Moab and the elders of Midian departed with the rewards of divination in their hand; and they came unto Balaam, and spoke unto him the words of Balak.

---

10. In deference to the traditional awareness of the Jewish Publication Society 1917 translation of the Hebrew Bible, we have kept its traditional *parasha* designations, which highlight the traditional readings of the portion of the Hebrew Bible read each week during synagogue services on the Sabbath. Each *parasha* has its own name; the portion here, given in its original Hebrew as per the JPS 1917 translation, is called "Balak," the name of the Midianite king who hires the Moabite soothsayer Balaam to curse the Israelites (how broad-minded is it to name an important division of the Torah after an enemy of one's own people!).

E. Killing Each Other

The Hebrew Bible treats violence between people as something to be avoided, as evidence (except in cases of self-defense or defense of the weak) of bad moral values. How then to explain what looks like a wholesale promotion of violence by the Levites against those who worshipped the Golden Calf? Many different readings have been proposed to answer this question. One reading argues that this shows a deplorable propensity towards violence on the part of the Levites, which sits uneasily with twentieth- and twenty-first-century witnesses to ethnic cleansing, or to the even more horrific state-sponsored annihilation of the Holocaust. Another reading contends that this approach does not take account of the many other texts of the Hebrew Bible that deprecate violence, even in places where one might feel more inclined to turn a blind eye to its enactment (see the provisions made for the City of Refuge in Chapter 1, "Cities," among others).

In the narratives of the Hebrew Bible, the Israelites are subject not just to violence emanating from the outside, but also to violence from within, the violence of Israelite against Israelite. The next selection focuses on Moses' descent from Mount Sinai with the Tablets of the Ten Commandments, and his indignant reaction to the idolatry he finds practiced in his absence by great numbers of the Israelites, who are killed. At the same time, Moses refuses to accept God's condemnation of the entire nation: he actively prays for national forgiveness; should God refuse to grant this, Moses asks that God remove him from "Thy book which Thou hast written"—arguably the Torah, whose Ten Commandments Moses had just transmitted to the Israelites. Importantly, Moses does not value his position of leader above the survival of his people: Moses understands that no leader is greater than his mission.

Exodus 32:19–28, 30–32

19 And it came to pass, as soon as he came nigh unto the camp, that he saw the calf and the dancing; and Moses' anger waxed hot, and he cast the tables out of his hands, and broke them beneath the mount. 20 And he took the calf which they had made, and burnt it with fire, and ground it to powder, and strewed it upon the water, and made the children of Israel drink of it. 21 And Moses said unto Aaron: 'What did this people unto thee, that thou hast brought a great sin upon them?' 22 And Aaron said: 'Let not the anger of my lord wax hot; thou knowest the people, that they are set on evil. 23 So they said unto me: Make us a god, which shall go before us; for as for this Moses, the man that brought us up out of the land of Egypt, we know not what is

become of him. 24 And I said unto them: Whosoever hath any gold, let them break it off; so they gave it me; and I cast it into the fire, and there came out this calf.' 25 And when Moses saw that the people were broken loose—for Aaron had let them loose for a derision among their enemies— 26 then Moses stood in the gate of the camp, and said: 'Whoso is on the LORD's side, let him come unto me.' And all the sons of Levi gathered themselves together unto him. 27 And he said unto them: 'Thus saith the LORD, the God of Israel: Put ye every man his sword upon his thigh, and go to and fro from gate to gate throughout the camp, and slay every man his brother, and every man his companion, and every man his neighbour.' 28 And the sons of Levi did according to the word of Moses; and there fell of the people that day about three thousand men.

. . . .

30 And it came to pass on the morrow, that Moses said unto the people: 'Ye have sinned a great sin; and now I will go up unto the LORD, peradventure I shall make atonement for your sin.' 31 And Moses returned unto the LORD, and said: 'Oh, this people have sinned a great sin, and have made them a god of gold. 32 Yet now, if Thou wilt forgive their sin—; and if not, blot me, I pray Thee, out of Thy book which Thou hast written.'

F. Violence and Eradication

The introduction to this volume already notes—in contrast to the value system of the ancient Greeks in particular—the lack of enthusiasm in Israelite consciousness and practice for the practice of warfare. The Israelites do fight wars against other nations (mainly, as portrayed in the Hebrew Bible, in self-defense, or on God's direct command), but they do not fetishize the act of war, and they do not view military prowess as central either to the expression of leadership, or to their identity as a people. Still, an argument supporting the warlike nature of the Israelites has been made with reference to the commandment for total war against the nation of Amalek—which itself was embarked on annihilating the Israelites who had straggled out of Egypt (Exodus 17:8–9, and Deuteronomy 25:17–19).[11]

Emphasizing the restricted nature of war as characterized in the Hebrew Bible, the rules of warfare begin, amazingly enough, with the list of

---

11. Walzer's *In God's Shadow* makes a similar argument.

people who are not to be drafted. The seemingly inapposite middle verses of this selection (Deuteronomy 20:12–18) are more fully explicated in the next section.

Deuteronomy 20

1 When thou goest forth to battle against thine enemies, and seest horses, and chariots, and a people more than thou, thou shalt not be afraid of them; for the LORD thy God is with thee, who brought thee up out of the land of Egypt. 2 And it shall be, when ye draw nigh unto the battle, that the priest shall approach and speak unto the people, 3 and shall say unto them: 'Hear, O Israel, ye draw nigh this day unto battle against your enemies; let not your heart faint; fear not, nor be alarmed, neither be ye affrighted at them; 4 for the LORD your God is He that goeth with you, to fight for you against your enemies, to save you.'

5 And the officers shall speak unto the people, saying: 'What man is there that hath built a new house, and hath not dedicated it? let him go and return to his house, lest he die in the battle, and another man dedicate it. 6 And what man is there that hath planted a vineyard, and hath not used the fruit thereof? let him go and return unto his house, lest he die in the battle, and another man use the fruit thereof. 7 And what man is there that hath betrothed a wife, and hath not taken her? let him go and return unto his house, lest he die in the battle, and another man take her.' 8 And the officers shall speak further unto the people, and they shall say: 'What man is there that is fearful and faint-hearted? let him go and return unto his house, lest his brethren's heart melt as his heart.'

. . . .

10 When thou drawest nigh unto a city to fight against it, then proclaim peace unto it. 11 And it shall be, if it make thee answer of peace, and open unto thee, then it shall be, that all the people that are found therein shall become tributary unto thee, and shall serve thee. 12 And if it will make no peace with thee, but will make war against thee, then thou shalt besiege it. 13 And when the LORD thy God delivereth it into thy hand, thou shalt smite every male thereof with the edge of the sword; 14 but the women, and the little ones, and the cattle, and all that is in the city, even all the spoil thereof, shalt thou take for a prey unto thyself; and thou shalt eat the spoil of thine enemies, which the

LORD thy God hath given thee. 15 Thus shalt thou do unto all the cities which are very far off from thee, which are not of the cities of these nations.

16 Howbeit of the cities of these peoples, that the LORD thy God giveth thee for an inheritance, thou shalt save alive nothing that breatheth, 17 but thou shalt utterly destroy them: the Hittite, and the Amorite, the Canaanite, and the Perizzite, the Hivite, and the Jebusite; as the LORD thy God hath commanded thee; 18 that they teach you not to do after all their abominations, which they have done unto their gods, and so ye sin against the LORD your God.

19 When thou shalt besiege a city a long time, in making war against it to take it, thou shalt not destroy the trees thereof by wielding an axe against them; for thou mayest eat of them, but thou shalt not cut them down; for is the tree of the field man, that it should be besieged of thee? 20 Only the trees of which thou knowest that they are not trees for food, them thou mayest destroy and cut down, that thou mayest build bulwarks against the city that maketh war with thee, until it fall.

G. National Violence

This section deals with the instances in the texts of the Hebrew Bible that appear to advocate violence against other nations that are not like the Israelites. These passages evoke discomfort among some contemporary readers of the Hebrew Bible because they seem to run counter to the Hebrew Bible's overriding emphasis on peace and welcome towards the stranger, understood as people who are precisely unlike the expected "average person." The larger philosophical implications of these issues are dealt with more extensively in the Introduction to this volume.

In an even more complicated move, the violence described in these passages—particularly in Deuteronomy 20, highlighting nations that do not agree to Israelite terms of peace, and, more specifically, the violence recommended towards the Canaanite nations living in the ancestral land that has been repeatedly pledged to the Israelites by Divine promise—seems oddly placed within a chapter focusing on the limitations of how war is to be waged (starting with a limited draft, and ending with the prohibition of destroying trees even within the battlefield). Arguably, this apparently misguided juxtaposition is itself the message of the section. The Hebrew Bible does not valorize violence, but it does recognize that war is sometimes a political and military necessity that, if it needs to be waged, had best be won. Unlike what would be expected of a manifesto advocating total destruction of the enemy, the text in Deuteronomy 20, mandating destruction of the seven Canaanite nations, is crucially placed within a larger section insisting upon overtures of peace before commencing battle, thus belying the simplistic reading of this verse as an imperative to "total war."

Another narrative that dismays some modern readers of the Hebrew Bible, by virtue of what they construe as troubling support for bloodthirstiness in its texts, focuses on the narrative at the end of the Book of Esther. But the actual account in the Book of Esther reveals that portraying this war of survival as a no-holds-barred massacre completely disregards the context of the narrative. This is crucial for understanding the actual text: the account of the battle waged by the Persian Jews for their survival against the legally sanctioned hostilities of their enemies within the Persian Empire takes place against the background of the decree that Haman had influenced King Ahaseurus to sign (Esther 3:9–15). In the narrative of the text, Persian law at that time is described as mandating that edicts signed by the king be non-rescindable (Esther 8:8). Consequently, the Persian Jews are obliged to fight if they want to survive (Esther 8:3–14).

In this context, the recitation of the results of the war at the end of the Book of Esther is not, as has erroneously been argued, a glorification of war and its outcomes.[12] This last point is manifestly demonstrated in the text by its insistence on the claim that while the Persian Jews fight for their lives, they refuse to take advantage of the most obvious gratuity of war (at that time): in direct opposition to what Haman had prospectively allowed to their genocidal neighbors, the Persian Jews deliberately refrain from touching any of the spoils of war.[13] Notably, they choose to commemorate their salvation not by martial demonstrations, but by dynamic reenactments of community: sending food to each other, and giving gifts to the needy (Esther 9:18–19, 19:22).

Esther 3:8–15

8 And Haman said unto king Ahasuerus: 'There is a certain people scattered abroad and dispersed among the peoples in all the provinces of thy kingdom; and their laws are diverse from

---

12. Eliot Horowitz's *Reckless Rites* (Princeton, NJ: Princeton University Press, 2006) is an example of this misguided approach. As I have already argued in my *Conceiving a Nation* (pp. 164–94), Horowitz overlooks the context of this narrative, which is a defensive battle that the Persian Jews must fight for their lives against their enemies, who had already been primed to fight against all the Jews in the Persian Empire with the purpose of annihilating them.

13. The Book of Esther notes this twice, at 9:10 and 9:15.

those of every people; neither keep they the king's laws; therefore it profiteth not the king to suffer them. 9 If it please the king, let it be written that they be destroyed; and I will pay ten thousand talents of silver into the hands of those that have the charge of the king's business, to bring it into the king's treasuries.'

10 And the king took his ring from his hand, and gave it unto Haman the son of Hammedatha the Agagite, the Jews' enemy. 11 And the king said unto Haman: 'The silver is given to thee, the people also, to do with them as it seemeth good to thee.'

12 Then were the king's scribes called in the first month, on the thirteenth day thereof, and there was written, according to all that Haman commanded, unto the king's satraps, and to the governors that were over every province, and to the princes of every people; to every province according to the writing thereof, and to every people after their language; in the name of king Ahasuerus was it written, and it was sealed with the king's ring.

13 And letters were sent by posts into all the king's provinces, to destroy, to slay, and to cause to perish, all Jews, both young and old, little children and women, in one day, even upon the thirteenth day of the twelfth month, which is the month Adar, and to take the spoil of them for a prey. 14 The copy of the writing, to be given out for a decree in every province, was to be published unto all peoples, that they should be ready against that day. 15 The posts went forth in haste by the king's commandment, and the decree was given out in Shushan the castle; and the king and Haman sat down to drink; but the city of Shushan was perplexed.

Esther 8:3–14

3 And Esther spoke yet again before the king, and fell down at his feet, and besought him with tears to put away the mischief of Haman the Agagite, and his device that he had devised against the Jews. 4 Then the king held out to Esther the golden sceptre. So Esther arose, and stood before the king. 5 And she said: 'If it please the king, and if I have found favour in his sight, and the thing seem right before the king, and I be pleasing in his eyes, let it be written to reverse the letters devised by Haman the son of Hammedatha the Agagite, which he wrote to destroy the Jews that are in all the king's provinces; 6 for how can I endure to see

the evil that shall come unto my people? or how can I endure to see the destruction of my kindred?'

7 Then the king Ahasuerus said unto Esther the queen and to Mordecai the Jew: 'Behold, I have given Esther the house of Haman, and him they have hanged upon the gallows, because he laid his hand upon the Jews. 8 Write ye also concerning the Jews, as it liketh you, in the king's name, and seal it with the king's ring; for the writing which is written in the king's name, and sealed with the king's ring, may no man reverse.' 9 Then were the king's scribes called at that time, in the third month, which is the month Sivan, on the three and twentieth day thereof; and it was written according to all that Mordecai commanded concerning the Jews, even to the satraps, and the governors and princes of the provinces which are from India unto Ethiopia, a hundred twenty and seven provinces, unto every province according to the writing thereof, and unto every people after their language, and to the Jews according to their writing, and according to their language. 10 And they wrote in the name of king Ahasuerus, and sealed it with the king's ring, and sent letters by posts on horseback, riding on swift steeds that were used in the king's service, bred of the stud; 11 that the king had granted the Jews that were in every city to gather themselves together, and to stand for their life, to destroy, and to slay, and to cause to perish, all the forces of the people and province that would assault them, their little ones and women, and to take the spoil of them for a prey, 12 upon one day in all the provinces of king Ahasuerus, namely, upon the thirteenth day of the twelfth month, which is the month Adar. 13 The copy of the writing, to be given out for a decree in every province, was to be published unto all the peoples, and that the Jews should be ready against that day to avenge themselves on their enemies. 14 So the posts that rode upon swift steeds that were used in the king's service went out, being hastened and pressed on by the king's commandment; and the decree was given out in Shushan the castle.

Esther 9:18–22

18 But the Jews that were in Shushan assembled together on the thirteenth day thereof, and on the fourteenth thereof; and on the fifteenth day of the same they rested, and made it a day of feasting and gladness. 19 Therefore do the Jews of the villages,

that dwell in the unwalled towns, make the fourteenth day of the month Adar a day of gladness and feasting, and a good day, and of sending portions one to another.

20 And Mordecai wrote these things, and sent letters unto all the Jews that were in all the provinces of the king Ahasuerus, both nigh and far, 21 to enjoin them that they should keep the fourteenth day of the month Adar, and the fifteenth day of the same, yearly, 22 the days wherein the Jews had rest from their enemies, and the month which was turned unto them from sorrow to gladness, and from mourning into a good day; that they should make them days of feasting and gladness, and of sending portions one to another, and gifts to the poor.

CHAPTER 11
CIVIL WAR

Civil War is among the most elemental dangers a nation can face because it potentially can destroy the nation entangled within it.[1] The Israelites are subjected to so much internecine warfare in the pages of the Hebrew Bible that redemption is portrayed as the absence of this internal plague.

A. An Uneasy "Peace"

The Hebrew Bible portrays intermittent civil war as splitting the Israelite community both before and after it sets up a monarchy. Even during the period of the Judges, when there is no centralized government, the Israelite tribes fight a civil war of such ferocity that it threatens to wipe out one entire tribe. Significantly, this war is set off (and only misleadingly "settled") by violence against women.

As we will see later, civil war besets monarchical government as well: Saul's reign is riven by the civil war between Saul and David. Even David's monarchy does not rest easy: his son, Absalom, revolts against him, an episode that ends with a bereaved father, and a kingdom divided by loyalties whose rifts are (bloodily) resolved only after Solomon takes the throne. The following selections describe and interrogate the political repercussions of civil war within a society that is more often at odds than at peace even within itself.

Contemporary readers of the Hebrew Bible might question whether politics—understood here as ordered systems of power—is portrayed in its pages as the source of, or perhaps the solution to, internecine warfare.

B. Civil War and Violence against Women

Judges 19–21

As we have already read (see Judges 19–21 in Chapter 5, "Women"), a seemingly trivial domestic contretemps—the Levite must extract his concubine

---

1. In his *Leviathan*, Thomas Hobbes famously compares civil war in the polity to the physical death of an individual (*Leviathan* Introduction, p. 271, ed. C. B. Macpherson [New York: Penguin, repr. 1986]).

from her father's house in Beth-Lehem/Yehudah, where she has returned—
flares into a full-scale moral fiasco, when an apparently innocuous overnight
stay in the village of Gibeah leads to the rape and murder of this concubine
(Judges 19). Despite the identity of the Gibeahites as full-fledged members of the Benjaminite tribe, this turn of events is considered by the other
tribes to be distinctly antithetical to the beliefs and practices that traditionally unite the diverse tribes into a distinct Israelite nation (see readings in
Chapter 9, "Israelite National Identity").

In Judges 20, we read of the civil war amongst the Israelite tribes,
united against the tribe of Benjamin, who had refused to hand over the
miscreant Gibeahite townspeople for judgment according to traditional
Israelite practices, and who were consequently viewed as extending de facto
approval of the violent turn of events at Gibeah together with their horrific
aftermath.

Judges 20

1 Then all the children of Israel went out, and the congregation was assembled as one man, from Dan even to Beer-sheba,
with the land of Gilead, unto the LORD at Mizpah. 2 And the
chiefs of all the people, even of all the tribes of Israel, presented
themselves in the assembly of the people of God, four hundred
thousand footmen that drew sword.— 3 Now the children of
Benjamin heard that the children of Israel were gone up to
Mizpah.—And the children of Israel said: 'Tell us, how was this
wickedness brought to pass?'

4 And the Levite, the husband of the woman that was murdered, answered and said: 'I came into Gibeah that belongeth
to Benjamin, I and my concubine, to lodge. 5 And the men of
Gibeah rose against me, and beset the house round about upon
me by night; me they thought to have slain, and my concubine
they forced, and she is dead. 6 And I took my concubine, and
cut her in pieces, and sent her throughout all the country of the
inheritance of Israel; for they have committed lewdness and
wantonness in Israel. 7 Behold, ye are all here, children of Israel,
give here your advice and counsel.' 8 And all the people arose as
one man, saying: 'We will not any of us go to his tent, neither will
we any of us turn unto his house.

9 But now this is the thing which we will do to Gibeah: we will
go up against it by lot; 10 and we will take ten men of a hundred
throughout all the tribes of Israel, and a hundred of a thousand,

and a thousand out of ten thousand, to fetch victuals for the people, that they may do, when they come to a Gibeah of Benjamin, according to all the wantonness that they have wrought in Israel.' 11 So all the men of Israel were gathered against the city, knit together as one man.

12 And the tribes of Israel sent men through all the tribe of Benjamin, saying: 'What wickedness is this that is come to pass among you? 13 Now therefore deliver up the men, the base fellows that are in Gibeah, that we may put them to death, and put away evil from Israel.' But the children of Benjamin would not hearken to the voice of their brethren the children of Israel. 14 And the children of Benjamin gathered themselves together out of their cities unto Gibeah, to go out to battle against the children of Israel. 15 And the children of Benjamin numbered on that day out of the cities twenty and six thousand men that drew sword, besides the inhabitants of Gibeah, who numbered seven hundred chosen men. 16 All this people, even seven hundred chosen men, were left-handed; every one could sling stones at a hair-breadth, and not miss.

17 And the men of Israel, beside Benjamin, numbered four hundred thousand men that drew sword; all these were men of war. 18 And the children of Israel arose, and went up to Beth-el, and asked counsel of God; and they said: 'Who shall go up for us first to battle against the children of Benjamin?' And the LORD said: 'Judah first.' 19 And the children of Israel rose up in the morning, and encamped against Gibeah. 20 And the men of Israel went out to battle against Benjamin; and the men of Israel set the battle in array against them at Gibeah. 21 And the children of Benjamin came forth out of Gibeah, and destroyed down to the ground of the Israelites on that day twenty and two thousand men. 22 And the people, the men of Israel, encouraged themselves, and set the battle again in array in the place where they set themselves in array the first day. 23 And the children of Israel went up and wept before the LORD until even; and they asked of the LORD, saying: 'Shall I again draw nigh to battle against the children of Benjamin my brother?' And the LORD said: 'Go up against him.'

24 And the children of Israel came near against the children of Benjamin the second day. 25 And Benjamin went forth against them out of Gibeah the second day, and destroyed down to the

ground of the children of Israel again eighteen thousand men; all these drew the sword. 26 Then all the children of Israel, and all the people, went up, and came unto Beth-el, and wept, and sat there before the LORD, and fasted that day until even; and they offered burnt-offerings and peace-offerings before the LORD. 27 And the children of Israel asked of the LORD—for the ark of the covenant of God was there in those days, 28 and Phinehas, the son of Eleazar, the son of Aaron, stood before it in those days—saying: 'Shall I yet again go out to battle against the children of Benjamin my brother, or shall I cease?' And the LORD said: 'Go up; for tomorrow I will deliver him into thy hand.' 29 And Israel set liers-in-wait against Gibeah round about.

30 And the children of Israel went up against the children of Benjamin on the third day, and set themselves in array against Gibeah, as at other times. 31 And the children of Benjamin went out against the people, and were drawn away from the city; and they began to smite and kill of the people, as at other times, in the field, in the highways, of which one goeth up to Beth-el, and the other to Gibeah, about thirty men of Israel. 32 And the children of Benjamin said: 'They are smitten down before us, as at the first.' But the children of Israel said: 'Let us flee, and draw them away from the city unto the highways.' 33 And all the men of Israel rose up out of their place, and set themselves in array at Baaltamar; and the liers-in-wait of Israel broke forth out of their place, even out of Maareh-geba. 34 And there came over against Gibeah ten thousand chosen men out of all Israel, and the battle was sore; but they knew not that evil was close upon them. 35 And the LORD smote Benjamin before Israel; and the children of Israel destroyed of Benjamin that day twenty and five thousand and a hundred men; all these drew the sword.

36 So the children of Benjamin saw that they were smitten. And the men of Israel gave place to Benjamin, because they trusted unto the liers-in-wait whom they had set against Gibeah.— 37 And the liers-in-wait hastened, and rushed upon Gibeah; and the liers-in-wait drew forth, and smote all the city with the edge of the sword. 38 Now there was an appointed sign between the men of Israel and the liers-in-wait, that they should make a great beacon of smoke rise up out of the city.— 39 And the

men of Israel turned in the battle, and Benjamin began to smite and kill of the men of Israel about thirty persons; for they said: 'Surely they are smitten down before us, as in the first battle.' 40 But when the beacon began to arise up out of the city in a pillar of smoke, the Benjamites looked behind them, and, behold, the whole of the city went up in smoke to heaven. 41 And the men of Israel turned, and the men of Benjamin were amazed; for they saw that evil was come upon them. 42 Therefore they turned their backs before the men of Israel unto the way of the wilderness; but the battle followed hard after them; and they that came out of the city destroyed them in the midst of the men of Israel. 43 They inclosed the Benjamites round about, and chased them, and overtook them at their resting-place, as far as over against Gibeah toward the sunrising. 44 And there fell of Benjamin eighteen thousand men; all these were men of valour. 45 And they turned and fled toward the wilderness unto the rock of Rimmon; and they gleaned of them in the highways five thousand men; and followed hard after them unto Gidom, and smote of them two thousand men. 46 So that all who fell that day of Benjamin were twenty and five thousand men that drew the sword; all these were men of valour. 47 But six hundred men turned and fled toward the wilderness unto the rock of Rimmon, and abode in the rock of Rimmon four months. 48 And the men of Israel turned back upon the children of Benjamin, and smote them with the edge of the sword, both the entire city, and the cattle, and all that they found; moreover all the cities which they found they set on fire.

When the United Israelite tribes defeat the Benjaminites after a series of bloody battles, a general oath is taken among the United Israelite tribes to refuse to give any of their daughters in marriage to the remaining Benjaminites. The consequence of this resolution, the Israelites soon realize, is to irretrievably change the nature of the Israelite nation, because one tribe (the Benjaminites) would eventually die out. But the Israelites feel stuck: they are bound by the terms of their vow, and yet, keeping that vow would result in a vital change in the makeup of the Israelite nation, which itself would be morally problematic.

What to do? The people come up with a "solution": they figure out that members of one town, Jabesh-Gilead, had not heeded the previous call to arms against the erring Benjaminites; consequently, they kill out the members of that town and hand over the remaining four hundred virgins to the Benjaminite men. But there are still Benjaminite men left without wives. The Elders then suggest that at the festival in Shiloh, these remaining Benjaminites grab the unmarried girls who customarily dance in the fields. That "solution" ends the narrative.

Contemporary readers may question the apparently straightforward conclusion at the end of the Book of Judges, which seems to impute the social and moral chaos in Israelite society at this time to the lack of a king. As we will see in subsequent selections, the monarchy does not do away with moral chaos; arguably, the presence of monarchy increases the instances of moral disorder. More generally, the clash between the seeming self-satisfaction of the last verse of the Book of Judges, and the obvious counterexamples furnished by the books of Samuel and of Kings, raises the possibility that the tone of the Hebrew biblical text may veer from the simply expository and verge into sarcasm at certain key points in its narrative. The text of the Hebrew Bible may be more self-aware than the modern reader is prepared to admit.

Judges 21

1 Now the men of Israel had sworn in Mizpah, saying: 'There shall not any of us give his daughter unto Benjamin to wife.' 2 And the people came to Beth-el, and sat there till even before God, and lifted up their voices, and wept sore. 3 And they said: 'O LORD, the God of Israel, why is this come to pass in Israel, that there should be to-day one tribe lacking in Israel?' 4 And it came to pass on the morrow that the people rose early, and built there an altar, and offered burnt-offerings and peace-offerings. 5 And the children of Israel said: 'Who is there among all the tribes of Israel that came not up in the assembly unto the LORD?' For they had made a great oath concerning him that came not up unto the LORD to Mizpah, saying: 'He shall surely be put to death.'

6 And the children of Israel repented them for Benjamin their brother, and said: 'There is one tribe cut off from Israel this day. 7 How shall we do for wives for them that remain, seeing we have sworn by the LORD that we will not give them of our daughters to wives?' 8 And they said: 'What one is there of the tribes of Israel that came not up unto the LORD to Mizpah?' And, behold, there came none to the camp from Jabesh-gilead to the assembly. 9 For when the people were numbered, behold, there were none of the inhabitants of Jabesh-gilead there. 10 And the congregation sent thither twelve thousand men of the valiantest,

and commanded them, saying: 'Go and smite the inhabitants of Jabesh-gilead with the edge of the sword, with the women and the little ones. 11 And this is the thing that ye shall do: ye shall utterly destroy every male, and every woman that hath lain by man.' 12 And they found among the inhabitants of Jabesh-gilead four hundred young virgins, that had not known man by lying with him; and they brought them unto the camp to Shiloh, which is in the land of Canaan.

13 And the whole congregation sent and spoke to the children of Benjamin that were in the rock of Rimmon, and proclaimed peace unto them. 14 And Benjamin returned at that time; and they gave them the women whom they had saved alive of the women of Jabesh-gilead; and yet so they sufficed them not. 15 And the people repented them for Benjamin, because that the LORD had made a breach in the tribes of Israel.

16 Then the elders of the congregation said: 'How shall we do for wives for them that remain, seeing the women are destroyed out of Benjamin?' 17 And they said: 'They that are escaped must be as an inheritance for Benjamin, that a tribe be not blotted out from Israel. 18 Howbeit we may not give them wives of our daughters.' For the children of Israel had sworn, saying: 'Cursed be he that giveth a wife to Benjamin.' 19 And they said: 'Behold, there is the feast of the LORD from year to year in Shiloh, which is on the north of Beth-el, on the east side of the highway that goeth up from Beth-el to Shechem, and on the south of Lebonah.' 20 And they commanded the children of Benjamin, saying: 'Go and lie in wait in the vineyards; 21 and see, and, behold, if the daughters of Shiloh come out to dance in the dances, then come ye out of the vineyards, and catch you every man his wife of the daughters of Shiloh, and go to the land of Benjamin. 22 And it shall be, when their fathers or their brethren come to strive with us, that we will say unto them: Grant them graciously unto us; because we took not for each man of them his wife in battle; neither did ye give them unto them, that ye should now be guilty.' 23 And the children of Benjamin did so, and took them wives, according to their number, of them that danced, whom they carried off; and they went and returned unto their inheritance, and built the cities, and dwelt in them. 24 And the children of Israel departed thence at that time, every man to his tribe and to his family, and they

went out from thence every man to his inheritance. 25 In those days there was no king in Israel; every man did that which was right in his own eyes.

C. Political Civil War

1. The Saul-David Rivalry

The Hebrew Bible portrays the onset of monarchy with division among the people, starting with those who were not impressed with the choice of Saul to begin with (see I Samuel 10:24–27). This point contains much irony: the request for a monarch had seemed to unite the people, but its realization actually does quite the opposite, as seen in the following selections.

I Samuel 19:1–10

1 And Saul spoke to Jonathan his son, and to all his servants, that they should slay David; but Jonathan Saul's son delighted much in David. 2 And Jonathan told David, saying: 'Saul my father seeketh to slay thee; now therefore, I pray thee, take heed to thyself in the morning, and abide in a secret place, and hide thyself. 3 And I will go out and stand beside my father in the field where thou art, and I will speak with my father of thee; and if I see aught, I will tell thee.'

4 And Jonathan spoke good of David unto Saul his father, and said unto him: 'Let not the king sin against his servant, against David; because he hath not sinned against thee, and because his work hath been very good towards thee; 5 for he put his life in his hand, and smote the Philistine, and the LORD wrought a great victory for all Israel; thou sawest it, and didst rejoice; wherefore then wilt thou sin against innocent blood, to slay David without a cause?' 6 And Saul hearkened unto the voice of Jonathan; and Saul swore: 'As the LORD liveth, he shall not be put to death.' 7 And Jonathan called David, and Jonathan told him all those things. And Jonathan brought David to Saul, and he was in his presence, as beforetime.

8 And there was war again; and David went out, and fought with the Philistines, and slew them with a great slaughter; and they fled before him. 9 And an evil spirit from the LORD was upon Saul, as he sat in his house with his spear in his hand; and

David was playing with his hand. 10 And Saul sought to smite David even to the wall with the spear; but he slipped away out of Saul's presence, and he smote the spear into the wall; and David fled, and escaped that night.

I Samuel 20:30–34

30 Then Saul's anger was kindled against Jonathan, and he said unto him: 'Thou son of perverse rebellion, do not I know that thou hast chosen the son of Jesse to thine own shame, and unto the shame of thy mother's nakedness? 31 For as long as the son of Jesse liveth upon the earth, thou shalt not be established, nor thy kingdom. Wherefore now send and fetch him unto me, for he deserveth to die.' 32 And Jonathan answered Saul his father, and said unto him: 'Wherefore should he be put to death? what hath he done?' 33 And Saul cast his spear at him to smite him; whereby Jonathan knew that it was determined of his father to put David to death. 34 So Jonathan arose from the table in fierce anger, and did eat no food the second day of the month; for he was grieved for David, and because his father had put him to shame.

For further reading see I Samuel 20:1–17 (Jonathan's friendship treaty with David); I Samuel 21, 22, and 23:15–25; I Samuel 24 (episodes of Saul's violence against David); I Samuel 27:3–12 and 8–17 (David's exile with the Philistines); II Samuel 2:25–32; II Samuel 3:1, 6–13, and 20–33; and II Samuel 4:1–12 (civil war between supporters of Saul and David).

2. Absalom's Rebellion against David: Protracted Resolution/s

The rebellion of Absalom against his father, King David, may be seen as over-determined, with reasons ranging from an overwhelming desire for power on Absalom's part, to Absalom's anger about his sister Tamar's rape by her half-brother, Amnon. This rape had gone largely unpunished by King David until Absalom took matters into his own hands (II Samuel 13); this led to Absalom's subsequent exile from the king's court.

II Samuel 14:25–26

25 Now in all Israel there was none to be so much praised as Absalom for his beauty; from the sole of his foot even to the crown of his head there was no blemish in him. 26 And when he polled his head—now it was at every year's end that he polled

it; because the hair was heavy on him, therefore he polled it—he weighed the hair of his head at two hundred shekels, after the king's weight.

II Samuel 15:1–17

1 And it came to pass after this, that Absalom prepared him a chariot and horses, and fifty men to run before him. 2 And Absalom used to rise up early, and stand beside the way of the gate; and it was so, that when any man had a suit which should come to the king for judgment, then Absalom called unto him, and said: 'Of what city art thou?' And he said: 'Thy servant is of one of the tribes of Israel.' 3 And Absalom said unto him: 'See, thy matters are good and right; but there is no man deputed of the king to hear thee.' 4 Absalom said moreover: 'Oh that I were made judge in the land, that every man who hath any suit or cause might come unto me, and I would do him justice!' 5 And it was so, that when any man came nigh to prostrate himself before him, he put forth his hand, and took hold of him, and kissed him. 6 And on this manner did Absalom to all Israel that came to the king for judgment; so Absalom stole the hearts of the men of Israel.

7 And it came to pass at the end of forty years, that Absalom said unto the king: 'I pray thee, let me go and pay my vow, which I have vowed unto the LORD, in Hebron. 8 For thy servant vowed a vow while I abode at Geshur in Aram, saying: If the LORD shall indeed bring me back to Jerusalem, then I will serve the LORD.' 9 And the king said unto him: 'Go in peace.' So he arose, and went to Hebron. 10 But Absalom sent spies throughout all the tribes of Israel, saying: 'As soon as ye hear the sound of the horn, then ye shall say: Absalom is king in Hebron.' 11 And with Absalom went two hundred men out of Jerusalem, that were invited, and went in their simplicity; and they knew not any thing. 12 And Absalom sent for Ahithophel the Gilonite, David's counsellor, from his city, even from Giloh, while he offered the sacrifices. And the conspiracy was strong; for the people increased continually with Absalom.

13 And there came a messenger to David, saying: 'The hearts of the men of Israel are after Absalom.' 14 And David said unto all his servants that were with him at Jerusalem: 'Arise, and let us flee; for else none of us shall escape from Absalom; make speed

to depart, lest he overtake us quickly, and bring down evil upon us, and smite the city with the edge of the sword.' 15 And the king's servants said unto the king: 'Behold, thy servants are ready to do whatsoever my lord the king shall choose.' 16 And the king went forth, and all his household after him. And the king left ten women, that were concubines, to keep the house. 17 And the king went forth, and all the people after him; and they waited in Beth-merhak.

It is interesting, but perhaps not unexpected, that Absalom's rebellion against King David reactivates the Saul-David divide, which itself recalls the matriarchal rivalry (Genesis 30:1) between Rachel (Saul is a descendant of Benjamin, Rachel's youngest child) and Leah (David comes from the tribe of Judah, Leah's fourth child, and is himself identified in Jacob's final blessing as the tribe who will be the political ruler over the Israelites).

II Samuel 16:5–15, 20–23

5 And when king David came to Bahurim, behold, there came out thence a man of the family of the house of Saul, whose name was Shimei, the son of Gera; he came out, and kept on cursing as he came. 6 And he cast stones at David, and at all the servants of king David; and all the people and all the mighty men were on his right hand and on his left. 7 And thus said Shimei when he cursed: 'Begone, begone, thou man of blood, and base fellow; 8 the LORD hath returned upon thee all the blood of the house of Saul, in whose stead thou hast reigned; and the LORD hath delivered the kingdom into the hand of Absalom thy son; and, behold, thou art taken in thine own mischief, because thou art a man of blood.'

9 Then said Abishai the son of Zeruiah unto the king: 'Why should this dead dog curse my lord the king? let me go over, I pray thee, and take off his head.' 10 And the king said: 'What have I to do with you, ye sons of Zeruiah? So let him curse, because the LORD hath said unto him: Curse David; who then shall say: Wherefore hast thou done so?' 11 And David said to Abishai, and to all his servants: 'Behold, my son, who came forth of my body, seeketh my life; how much more this Benjamite now? let him alone, and let him curse; for the LORD hath bidden him. 12 It may be that the LORD will look on mine eye, and that the LORD will requite me good for his cursing of me this day.' 13 So David and his men went by the way; and Shimei went along on

the hill-side over against him, and cursed as he went, and threw stones at him, and cast dust. 14 And the king, and all the people that were with him, came weary; and he refreshed himself there.

15 And Absalom, and all the people, the men of Israel, came to Jerusalem, and Ahithophel with him.

. . . .

20 Then said Absalom to Ahithophel: 'Give your counsel what we shall do.' 21 And Ahithophel said unto Absalom: 'Go in unto thy father's concubines, that he hath left to keep the house; and all Israel will hear that thou art abhorred of thy father; then will the hands of all that are with thee be strong.' 22 So they spread Absalom a tent upon the top of the house; and Absalom went in unto his father's concubines in the sight of all Israel.— 23 Now the counsel of Ahithophel, which he counselled in those days, was as if a man inquired of the word of God; so was all the counsel of Ahithophel both with David and with Absalom.

3. More Civil War to Oust David

II Samuel 20:1–22

1 Now there happened to be there a base fellow, whose name was Sheba, the son of Bichri, a Benjamite; and he blew the horn, and said: 'We have no portion in David, neither have we inheritance in the son of Jesse; every man to his tents, O Israel.' 2 So all the men of Israel went up from following David, and followed Sheba the son of Bichri; but the men of Judah did cleave unto their king, from the Jordan even to Jerusalem.

3 And David came to his house at Jerusalem; and the king took the ten women his concubines, whom he had left to keep the house, and put them in ward, and provided them with sustenance, but went not in unto them. So they were shut up unto the day of their death, in widowhood, with their husband alive.

4 Then said the king to Amasa: 'Call me the men of Judah together within three days, and be thou here present.' 5 So Amasa went to call the men of Judah together; but he tarried longer than the set time which he had appointed him. 6 And David said to Abishai: 'Now will Sheba the son of Bichri do us

more harm than did Absalom; take thou thy lord's servants, and pursue after him, lest he get him fortified cities, and escape out of our sight.' 7 And there went out after him Joab's men, and the Cherethites and the Pelethites, and all the mighty men; and they went out of Jerusalem, to pursue after Sheba the son of Bichri. 8 When they were at the great stone which is in Gibeon, Amasa came to meet them. And Joab was girded with his apparel of war that he had put on, and thereon was a girdle with a sword fastened upon his loins in the sheath thereof; and as he went forth it fell out. 9 And Joab said to Amasa: 'Is it well with thee, my brother?' And Joab took Amasa by the beard with his right hand to kiss him.

10 But Amasa took no heed to the sword that was in Joab's hand; so he smote him therewith in the groin, and shed out his bowels to the ground, and struck him not again; and he died.

And Joab and Abishai his brother pursued after Sheba the son of Bichri. 11 And there stood by him one of Joab's young men, and said: 'He that favoureth Joab, and he that is for David let him follow Joab.' 12 And Amasa lay wallowing in his blood in the midst of the highway. And when the man saw that all the people stood still, he carried Amasa out of the highway into the field, and cast a garment over him, when he saw that every one that came by him stood still. 13 When he was removed out of the highway, all the people went on after Joab, to pursue after Sheba the son of Bichri.

14 And he went through all the tribes of Israel unto Abel, and to Beth-maacah, and all the Berites; and they were gathered together, and went in also after him. 15 And they came and besieged him in Abel of Beth-maacah, and they cast up a mound against the city, and it stood in the moat; and all the people that were with Joab battered the wall, to throw it down.

16 Then cried a wise woman out of the city: 'Hear, hear; say, I pray you, unto Joab: Come near hither, that I may speak with thee.' 17 And he came near unto her; and the woman said: 'Art thou Joab?' And he answered: 'I am.' Then she said unto him: 'Hear the words of thy handmaid.' And he answered: 'I do hear.' 18 Then she spoke, saying: 'They were wont to speak in old time, saying: They shall surely ask counsel at Abel; and so they ended the matter. 19 We are of them that are peaceable and faithful in Israel; seekest thou to destroy a city and a mother in Israel? why

wilt thou swallow up the inheritance of the LORD?' 20 And
Joab answered and said: 'Far be it, far be it from me, that I should
swallow up or destroy. 21 The matter is not so; but a man of the
hill-country of Ephraim, Sheba the son of Bichri by name, hath
lifted up his hand against the king, even against David; deliver
him only, and I will depart from the city.' And the woman said
unto Joab: 'Behold, his head shall be thrown to thee over the
wall.' 22 Then the woman went unto all the people in her wisdom. And they cut off the head of Sheba the son of Bichri, and
threw it out to Joab. And he blew the horn, and they were dispersed from the city, every man to his tent. And Joab returned to
Jerusalem unto the king.

4. Palace Revolts

Even after this final (Saulide) rebellion against King David is put down and
David is returned to his throne, things are not quite secure. This is revealed
after David's death: one mark of a stable political system, including a monarchy, is that the identity of the new ruler is unquestioned. This is not the
case after David's death: there are numerous contenders for the throne, and
Solomon is acknowledged as king only after a protracted palace struggle.
Chief among the pretenders to King David's throne is Adoniya, who tries
to establish his royal identity by requesting marriage with Avishag, King
David's bed-warmer in his old age. In this excerpt, we see Solomon's realization that his hold on power is not yet solidified, a process that takes up the
rest of the chapter.

As a matter of careful reading into the intricacies of court intrigue,
the contemporary reader should ponder: Why does Solomon's mother,
Bathsheva, forward Adoniya's claim to her son?

I Kings 2:10–22

10 And David slept with his fathers, and was buried in the city
of David. 11 And the days that David reigned over Israel were
forty years: seven years reigned he in Hebron, and thirty and
three years reigned he in Jerusalem. 12 And Solomon sat upon
the throne of David his father; and his kingdom was established
firmly.

13 Then Adonijah the son of Haggith came to Bath-sheba the
mother of Solomon. And she said: 'Comest thou peaceably?' And
he said: 'Peaceably.' 14 He said moreover: 'I have somewhat to say

unto thee.' And she said: 'Say on.' 15 And he said: 'Thou knowest that the kingdom was mine, and that all Israel set their faces on me, that I should reign; howbeit the kingdom is turned about, and is become my brother's; for it was his from the LORD. 16 And now I ask one petition of thee, deny me not.' And she said unto him: 'Say on.' 17 And he said: 'Speak, I pray thee, unto Solomon the king—for he will not say thee nay—that he give me Abishag the Shunammite to wife.' 18 And Bath-sheba said: 'Well; I will speak for thee unto the king.'

19 Bath-sheba therefore went unto king Solomon, to speak unto him for Adonijah. And the king rose up to meet her, and bowed down unto her, and sat down on his throne, and caused a throne to be set for the king's mother; and she sat on his right hand. 20 Then she said: 'I ask one small petition of thee; deny me not.' And the king said unto her: 'Ask on, my mother; for I will not deny thee.' 21 And she said: 'Let Abishag the Shunammite be given to Adonijah thy brother to wife.' 22 And king Solomon answered and said unto his mother: 'And why dost thou ask Abishag the Shunammite for Adonijah? ask for him the kingdom also; for he is mine elder brother; even for him, and for Abiathar the priest, and for Joab the son of Zeruiah.'

5. The Final Divide: The Israelite Kingdom Is Split

The Israelite Kingdom remains split for more years than it stays together. As we have already noticed regarding the rebellions against King David (see above), the fault lines in the Israelite monarchy resolve themselves according to the ancient matriarchal division between Rachel and Leah. In the pages of the Hebrew Bible, time alone does not heal this ancient divide.

Ironically, even Solomon, the most powerful king of the Israelites, whose power and wisdom is unquestioned and who achieves international renown, is not able to stabilize the transmission of power (which, oddly enough, his father King David, whose power was constantly challenged, was, after a fashion, able to do). In Solomon's case, it is not the identity of the next ruler that is at stake (everyone agrees that the crown devolves to Rehoboam), but rather the identity and extent of the kingdom itself. In a certain sense, what comes into question, after Solomon's reconceptualization of the nature and extent of Israelite sovereignty, is the role of the people themselves in the constitution of monarchy.

It is important to note that traditionally, for the Israelites, the role of the people had always been central to the establishment of monarchy, including the acquiescence to specific monarchs: the monarchy itself is established in response to the people's request (I Samuel 8), and Saul's actual power is established by the renewal of his monarchy (by acclamation) at Gilgal (I Samuel 11:15). Similarly, the people's acknowledgment of David as kin enables him to establish political control over all of the Israelite tribes (see selections in Chapter 11, "Civil War").

After Solomon's death, a seemingly trivial but, in view of Israelite political experience at that time, extremely crucial request of Solomon's son, Rehoboam, leads to the kingdom's irretrievable division. Contemporary readers might speculate: Why are two sides of the debate presented in terms of young (inexperienced) and old (mature) advisors?

I Kings 12:1–14, 16–20

1 And Rehoboam went to Shechem; for all Israel were come to Shechem to make him king. 2 And it came to pass, when Jeroboam the son of Nebat heard of it—for he was yet in Egypt, whither he had fled from the presence of king Solomon, and Jeroboam dwelt in Egypt, 3 and they sent and called him—that Jeroboam and all the congregation of Israel came, and spoke unto Rehoboam, saying: 4 'Thy father made our yoke grievous; now therefore make thou the grievous service of thy father, and his heavy yoke which he put upon us, lighter, and we will serve thee.' 5 And he said unto them: 'Depart yet for three days, then come again to me.' And the people departed.

6 And king Rehoboam took counsel with the old men, that had stood before Solomon his father while he yet lived, saying: 'What counsel give ye me to return answer to this people?' 7 And they spoke unto him, saying: 'If thou wilt be a servant unto this people this day, and wilt serve them, and answer them, and speak good words to them, then they will be thy servants for ever.' 8 But he forsook the counsel of the old men which they had given him, and took counsel with the young men that were grown up with him, that stood before him. 9 And he said unto them: 'What counsel give ye, that we may return answer to this people, who have spoken to me, saying: Make the yoke that thy father did put upon us lighter?' 10 And the young men that were grown up with him spoke unto him, saying: 'Thus shalt thou say unto this people that spoke unto thee, saying: Thy father made our yoke heavy, but

make thou it lighter unto us; thus shalt thou speak unto them: My little finger is thicker than my father's loins. 11 And now whereas my father did burden you with a heavy yoke, I will add to your yoke; my father chastised you with whips, but I will chastise you with scorpions.'

12 So Jeroboam and all the people came to Rehoboam the third day, as the king bade, saying: 'Come to me again the third day.' 13 And the king answered the people roughly, and forsook the counsel of the old men which they had given him; 14 and spoke to them after the counsel of the young men, saying: 'My father made your yoke heavy, but I will add to your yoke; my father chastised you with whips, but I will chastise you with scorpions.'

. . . .

16 And when all Israel saw that the king hearkened not unto them, the people answered the king, saying: 'What portion have we in David? neither have we inheritance in the son of Jesse; to your tents, O Israel; now see to thine own house, David.' So Israel departed unto their tents. 17 But as for the children of Israel that dwelt in the cities of Judah, Rehoboam reigned over them. 18 Then king Rehoboam sent Adoram, who was over the levy; and all Israel stoned him with stones, so that he died. And king Rehoboam made speed to get him up to his chariot, to flee to Jerusalem. 19 So Israel rebelled against the house of David, unto this day. 20 And it came to pass, when all Israel heard that Jeroboam was returned, that they sent and called him unto the congregation, and made him king over all Israel; there was none that followed the house of David, but the tribe of Judah only.

6. Consequences of a Divided Kingdom

In the next reading of this section, we see how Jeroboam (the new king of the Northern Kingdom) manipulates religious symbols and practices to prevent peaceful coexistence and cooperation between the two kingdoms. Ironically, Jeroboam institutes precisely the religious division that the Israelites had sworn to avoid with the settling of two tribes on the other side of the Jordan (see Chapter 9, "Israelite National Identity"). With that, Jeroboam introduces officially approved idolatry into the political sphere, which places the uniqueness of the Israelite national identity into jeopardy.

I Kings 12:25–33

25 Then Jeroboam built Shechem in the hill-country of Ephraim, and dwelt therein; and he went out from thence, and built Penuel. 26 And Jeroboam said in his heart: 'Now will the kingdom return to the house of David. 27 If this people go up to offer sacrifices in the house of the LORD at Jerusalem, then will the heart of this people turn back unto their lord, even unto Rehoboam king of Judah; and they will kill me, and return to Rehoboam king of Judah.' 28 Whereupon the king took counsel, and made two calves of gold; and he said unto them: 'Ye have gone up long enough to Jerusalem; behold thy gods, O Israel, which brought thee up out of the land of Egypt.' 29 And he set the one in Beth-el, and the other put he in Dan. 30 And this thing became a sin; for the people went to worship before the one, even unto Dan. 31 And he made houses of high places, and made priests from among all the people, that were not of the sons of Levi. 32 And Jeroboam ordained a feast in the eighth month, on the fifteenth day of the month, like unto the feast that is in Judah, and he went up unto the altar; so did he in Beth-el, to sacrifice unto the calves that he had made; and he placed in Beth-el the priests of the high places that he had made. 33 And he went up unto the altar which he had made in Beth-el on the fifteenth day in the eighth month, even in the month which he had devised of his own heart; and he ordained a feast for the children of Israel, and went up unto the altar, to offer.

The split of the Solomonic Kingdom into Northern and Southern kingdoms wreaks havoc on the history of the Southern Kingdom as well. Although the Southern Kingdom of Judah is centered around the Holy Temple, built by Solomon for the monotheistic worship of God, the Kingdom of Judah also falls into idol worship.

The next selection deals with the murder of all those in line for the throne of the Kingdom of Judah by the wicked Queen Athaliah. But the youngest member of the royal line, Joash, is secreted by the Judahite Princess Jehosheba and is crowned king. Subsequently, a covenant is established between the King, the People, and God.

Contemporary readers may want to consider this tripartite connection between the Divine, the monarch, and the people: What is the role of each side in this complex relationship? Is the Hebrew Bible here recommending the establishment of a polity together with an official religion that holds political sway? Are clergy embedded within this sort of government?

(See "State and Religion" in the Introduction to this volume; and further, in Chapter 16, "Human Rights and Secularism in the Hebrew Bible" for further treatment of these issues).

II Kings 11:1–17

1 Now when Athaliah the mother of Ahaziah saw that her son was dead, she arose and destroyed all the seed royal. 2 But Jehosheba, the daughter of king Joram, sister of Ahaziah, took Joash the son of Ahaziah, and stole him away from among the king's sons that were slain, even him and his nurse, and put them in the bed-chamber; and they hid him from Athaliah, so that he was not slain. 3 And he was with her hid in the house of the LORD six years; and Athaliah reigned over the land.

4 And in the seventh year Jehoiada sent and fetched the captains over hundreds, of the Carites and of the guard, and brought them to him into the house of the LORD; and he made a covenant with them, and took an oath of them in the house of the LORD, and showed them the king's son. 5 And he commanded them, saying: 'This is the thing that ye shall do: a third part of you, that come in on the sabbath, and that keep the watch of the king's house— 6 now another third part was at the gate Sur, and another third part at the gate behind the guard—shall keep the watch of the house, and be a barrier. 7 And the other two parts of you, even all that go forth on the sabbath, shall keep the watch of the house of the LORD about the king. 8 And ye shall compass the king round about, every man with his weapons in his hand; and he that cometh within the ranks, let him be slain; and be ye with the king when he goeth out, and when he cometh in.'

9 And the captains over hundreds did according to all that Jehoiada the priest commanded; and they took every man his men, those that were to come in on the sabbath, with those that were to go out on the sabbath, and came to Jehoiada the priest. 10 And the priest delivered to the captains over hundreds the spear and shields that had been king David's, which were in the house of the LORD. 11 And the guard stood, every man with his weapons in his hand, from the right side of the house to the left side of the house, along by the altar and the house, by the king round about. 12 Then he brought out the king's son, and put upon him the crown and the insignia; and they made him king,

and anointed him; and they clapped their hands, and said: 'Long live the king.'

13 And when Athaliah heard the noise of the guard and of the people, she came to the people into the house of the LORD. 14 And she looked, and, behold, the king stood on the platform, as the manner was, and the captains and the trumpets by the king; and all the people of the land rejoiced, and blew with trumpets. Then Athaliah rent her clothes, and cried: 'Treason, treason.' 15 And Jehoiada the priest commanded the captains of hundreds, the officers of the host, and said unto them: 'Have her forth between the ranks; and him that followeth her slay with the sword'; for the priest said: 'Let her not be slain in the house of the LORD.' 16 So they made way for her; and she went by the way of the horses' entry to the king's house; and there was she slain.

17 And Jehoiada made a covenant between the LORD and the king and the people, that they should be the LORD'S people; between the king also and the people.

See also II Kings 23:1–2.

7. The Redemptive Implication

In its political sense, civil war is seen as a failure of national cohesion. Isaiah proposes a theological understanding of the phenomenon. Civil war does not just reflect and presage sin; it also mirrors and foretells political and moral disaster.

Isaiah 9:15–20

15 For they that lead this people cause them to err;
And they that are led of them are destroyed.
16 Therefore the Lord shall have no joy in their young men,
Neither shall He have compassion on their fatherless and widows;
For every one is ungodly and an evil-doer,
And every mouth speaketh wantonness. For all this His anger is
      not turned away,
But His hand is stretched out still.

17 For wickedness burneth as the fire;
It devoureth the briers and thorns;
Yea, it kindleth in the thickets of the forest,

And they roll upward in thick clouds of smoke.
18 Through the wrath of the LORD of hosts is the land burnt up;
The people also are as the fuel of fire;
No man spareth his brother.
19 And one snatcheth on the right hand, and is hungry;
And he eateth on the left hand, and is not satisfied;
They eat every man the flesh of his own arm:
20 Manasseh, Ephraim; and Ephraim, Manasseh;
And they together are against Judah.
For all this His anger is not turned away,
But His hand is stretched out still.

By contrast, redemption is presented as embodying political (and, by implication, moral) wholeness: in the ideal world, both politics and spirituality can express moral coherence.

Isaiah 11:12–13

12 And He will set up an ensign for the nations,
And will assemble the dispersed of Israel,
And gather together the scattered of Judah
From the four corners of the earth.
13 The envy also of Ephraim shall depart,
And they that harass Judah shall be cut off;
Ephraim shall not envy Judah,
And Judah shall not vex Ephraim.

8. Jeremiah and Ezekiel: Prophecies of Civil and Political Peace

Jeremiah and Ezekiel prophesy similar messages of civil and political peace.

Jeremiah 3:18

18 'In those days the house of Judah shall walk with the house of Israel, and they shall come together out of the land of the north to the land that I have given for an inheritance unto your fathers.'

Ezekiel 37:15–27

15 And the word of the LORD came unto me, saying: 16 'And thou, son of man, take thee one stick, and write upon it: For Judah, and for the children of Israel his companions; then take

another stick, and write upon it: For Joseph, the stick of Ephraim, and of all the house of Israel his companions; 17 and join them for thee one to another into one stick, that they may become one in thy hand. 18 And when the children of thy people shall speak unto thee, saying: Wilt thou not tell us what thou meanest by these? 19 say into them: Thus saith the Lord GOD: Behold, I will take the stick of Joseph, which is in the hand of Ephraim, and the tribes of Israel his companions; and I will put them unto him together with the stick of Judah, and make them one stick, and they shall be one in My hand. 20 And the sticks whereon thou writest shall be in thy hand before their eyes.

21 And say unto them: Thus saith the Lord GOD: Behold, I will take the children of Israel from among the nations, whither they are gone, and will gather them on every side, and bring them into their own land; 22 and I will make them one nation in the land, upon the mountains of Israel, and one king shall be king to them all; and they shall be no more two nations, neither shall they be divided into two kingdoms any more at all; 23 neither shall they defile themselves any more with their idols, nor with their detestable things, nor with any of their transgressions; but I will save them out of all their dwelling-places, wherein they have sinned, and will cleanse them; so shall they be My people, and I will be their God. 24 And My servant David shall be king over them, and they all shall have one shepherd; they shall also walk in Mine ordinances, and observe My statutes, and do them. 25 And they shall dwell in the land that I have given unto Jacob My servant, wherein your fathers dwelt; and they shall dwell therein, they, and their children, and their children's children, for ever; and David My servant shall be their prince for ever. 26 Moreover I will make a covenant of peace with them—it shall be an everlasting covenant with them; and I will establish them, and multiply them, and will set My sanctuary in the midst of them for ever. 27 My dwelling-place also shall be over them; and I will be their God, and they shall be My people.

CHAPTER 12
MONARCHY

One of the most fraught questions in the Hebrew Bible is the issue of national governance. How should the Israelites be ruled? Is monarchy a good option for them? For any nation? (Compare the eighteenth-century discussions of monarchy that surround the American Revolution.) In both its narrative and legalistic texts, the Hebrew Bible presents a nuanced and complex exposition of this issue.

A. Historical Presentation

As we have seen (see Genesis 10:1–7 in Chapter 1, "The City as a Locus of Power"), the first monarch mentioned in the Hebrew Bible is Nimrod. He is highlighted not just for being the first (recorded) king in the Bible, but also for the extent of his empire and the establishment of multiple cities. For further reading see Genesis 36:31–43 and I Chronicles 1:43–54 (the Edomite kings "that reigned . . . before there was a king in Israel").

B. Rules Governing the Israelite Monarchy

The Hebrew Bible speaks about the possibility—even, given the context of the era, the probability—of monarchy in the Promised Land (Deuteronomy 17:14–20). Importantly, there are several key constraints imposed by its conception of monarchy. These are particularly notable in this era of empire, which existed among many of the Israelite neighbors. In contrast to the monarchical examples of the surrounding neighbors, the Israelite king was not allowed to be too rich, or too laden with the signs of a permissive or luxurious lifestyle (he is enjoined from having too many wives or horses). The Israelite king had to remember his roots both politically and philosophically: he is not above his brothers when it comes to the absolute fealty to God demanded of him—which is likewise demanded of them, his putative subjects. To this end, he must keep with himself and read from a scroll of the Torah, which defines the national uniqueness and tasks of all of the Israelites.

Deuteronomy 17:14–20

14 When thou art come unto the land which the LORD thy God giveth thee, and shalt possess it, and shalt dwell therein; and shalt say: 'I will set a king over me, like all the nations that are round about me'; 15 thou shalt in any wise set him king over thee, whom the LORD thy God shall choose; one from among thy brethren shalt thou set king over thee; thou mayest not put a foreigner over thee, who is not thy brother. 16 Only he shall not multiply horses to himself, nor cause the people to return to Egypt, to the end that he should multiply horses; forasmuch as the LORD hath said unto you: 'Ye shall henceforth return no more that way.' 17 Neither shall he multiply wives to himself, that his heart turn not away; neither shall he greatly multiply to himself silver and gold. 18 And it shall be, when he sitteth upon the throne of his kingdom, that he shall write him a copy of this law in a book, out of that which is before the priests the Levites. 19 And it shall be with him, and he shall read therein all the days of his life; that he may learn to fear the LORD his God, to keep all the words of this law and these statutes, to do them; 20 that his heart be not lifted up above his brethren, and that he turn not aside from the commandment, to the right hand, or to the left; to the end that he may prolong his days in his kingdom, he and his children, in the midst of Israel.

C. Ranging Israelite Deliberations about Monarchy

But the Israelites, living among nations that are secure militarily and that are also monarchies and empires, quickly identify political security with a certain type of government: centralized monarchy. Already in the times of the Judges, the Israelites seek to establish monarchy among themselves. In this selection, they ask Gideon, who finally succeeds in vanquishing the Midianites—whose increasingly violent raids imperiled the safety of the Israelites within their own borders—to be their king.

Judges 8:22–23

22 Then the men of Israel said unto Gideon: 'Rule thou over us, both thou, and thy son, and thy son's son also; for thou hast saved us out of the hand of Midian.' 23 And Gideon said unto them: 'I will not rule over you, neither shall my son rule over you; the LORD shall rule over you.'

But not every leader is as uninterested in political power as Gideon. After Gideon's death, one of his sons, Avimelekh (whose name translates as "my father is king"—as if Avimelekh wants to claim for himself the dynastic right to rule) banks on his family connections (his father, Yerubaal/Gideon, had saved the Israelites from a troublesome enemy, while his mother was herself a Shekhemite) to justify his efforts, directed first towards the Shekhemites, to be accepted as king.

The following selections reveal how self-regarding desires for power end in chaos rather than order. In the end, even the Shekhemites' selfish reasons for supporting Avimelekh result in utter destruction.

Judges 8:30–31, 34–35

30 And Gideon had threescore and ten sons of his body begotten; for he had many wives. 31 And his concubine that was in Shechem, she also bore him a son, and he called his name Abimelech.

. . . .

34 And the children of Israel remembered not the LORD their God, who had delivered them out of the hand of all their enemies on every side; 35 neither showed they kindness to the house of Jerubbaal, namely Gideon, according to all the goodness which he had shown unto Israel.

Judges 9:1–6

1 And Abimelech the son of Jerubbaal went to Shechem unto his mother's brethren, and spoke with them, and with all the family of the house of his mother's father, saying: 2 'Speak, I pray you, in the ears of all the men of Shechem: Which is better for you, that all the sons of Jerubbaal, who are threescore and ten persons, rule over you, or that one rule over you? remember also that I am your bone and your flesh.' 3 And his mother's brethren spoke of him in the ears of all the men of Shechem all these words; and their hearts inclined to follow Abimelech; for they said: 'He is our brother.' 4 And they gave him threescore and ten pieces of silver out of the house of Baal-berith, wherewith Abimelech hired vain and light fellows, who followed him. 5 And he went unto his father's house at Ophrah, and slew his brethren the sons of Jerubbaal, being threescore and ten persons, upon one stone; but Jotham the youngest son of Jerubbaal was left; for he hid himself.

6 And all the men of Shechem assembled themselves together, and all Beth-millo, and went and made Abimelech king, by the terebinth of the pillar that was in Shechem.

The one son of Gideon whom Avimelekh does not manage to murder (he is small and easily hidden) has the courage to speak out against Avimelekh's brand of absolute monarchy. Importantly, he chooses to speak this parable against the backdrop of Mount Gerizim, where the Israelites are reminded of the blessings and curses that would befall them depending on whether they heeded or, alternatively, ignored the Divine Commandments as taught to them in the Torah, given to them by Moses.

Contemporary readers might want to consider why Jotham chooses to speak in parabolic terms, and why specific trees are used to personify political groupings.

D. The Parable of the Trees

Judges 9:7–21

7 And when they told it to Jotham, he went and stood in the top of mount Gerizim, and lifted up his voice, and cried, and said unto them: 'Hearken unto me, ye men of Shechem, that God may hearken unto you.

8 The trees went forth on a time to anoint a king over them; and they said unto the olive-tree: Reign thou over us.

9 But the olive-tree said unto them: Should I leave my fatness, seeing that by me they honour God and man, and go to hold sway over the trees?

10 And the trees said to the fig-tree: Come thou, and reign over us.

11 But the fig-tree said unto them: Should I leave my sweetness, and my good fruitage, and go to hold sway over the trees?

12 And the trees said unto the vine: Come thou, and reign over us.

13 And the vine said unto them: Should I leave my wine, which cheereth God and man, and go to hold sway over the trees?

14 Then said all the trees unto the bramble: Come thou, and reign over us. 15 And the bramble said unto the trees: If in truth

ye anoint me king over you, then come and take refuge in my shadow; and if not, let fire come out of the bramble, and devour the cedars of Lebanon.

16 Now therefore, if ye have dealt truly and uprightly, in that ye have made Abimelech king, and if ye have dealt well with Jerubbaal and his house, and have done unto him according to the deserving of his hands—17 for my father fought for you, and adventured his life, and delivered you out of the hand of Midian; 18 and ye are risen up against my father's house this day, and have slain his sons, threescore and ten persons, upon one stone, and have made Abimelech, the son of his maid-servant, king over the men of Shechem, because he is your brother—19 if ye then have dealt truly and uprightly with Jerubbaal and with his house this day, then rejoice ye in Abimelech, and let him also rejoice in you. 20 But if not, let fire come out from Abimelech, and devour the men of Shechem, and Beth-millo; and let fire come out from the men of Shechem, and from Beth-millo, and devour Abimelech.'

21 And Jotham ran away, and fled, and went to Beer, and dwelt there, for fear of Abimelech his brother.

E. Israelite Monarchical Rule

Lacking the experience of institutionalized centralized leadership, it seems strange that the Israelites would request a centralized monarchy as a system of rule. As depicted in the Book of Judges, leaders had up to this point functioned on an ad hoc basis to take care of persistent problems (the military raids of Sisera, for example), which were often more local than national in nature.

To be sure, there are some leaders whose singular function focuses national attention on them: the role of Eli, the High Priest, is one such example in the Book of Samuel. Also, Samuel is presented as a judge who conscientiously "rides circuit" to ensure that justice reaches all parts of the Israelite community (I Samuel 7:15–17), and who is scrupulously honest: unlike his sons, Samuel does not take bribes.

Despite these discrete instances of honest (and proto-national) leadership, however, the Israelites insist on demanding a king. Viewing the nations around them who constantly prey on their borders, the Israelites equate these nations' military abilities with their centralized form of monarchy under an all-powerful ruler. The Israelites are tired of being victims. Anticipating the formulation of Dostoevsky's Grand Inquisitor in his novel *The Brothers Karamazov*, the Israelites are ready to trade their (localized) freedoms for the certainty of political and economic stability.

Even the possibility of their children being forcibly drafted to royal service does not hold them back: the Israelites focus on the glitter of the royal court, with the economic wealth that comes in its train, rather than on their probable loss of autonomy. As to the theological issue—preferring vassalage to a king rather than directing their energies towards serving God—that subject does not even rise to the attention of the Israelites. The Israelites define their difficulties in terms of politics and defense; their very neglect of how this political change could (and, in the depiction of the Hebrew Bible, did) affect their relationship with God is, as voiced by the text in the Hebrew Bible, the essence of the problem (cf. I Samuel 8:1–22 above).

The prophet Samuel is commanded to anoint Saul, a Benjaminite, who is wary of taking on the public role of monarch. Saul's reception is rocky: he is anointed privately, then publicly, but is not fully accepted by the people as king until his second public coronation at Gilgal. But, despite some important military victories that establish Saul in the eyes of the people as a leader who can organize them in battle and deliver decisive military defeats to their enemies, Saul winds up losing the monarchy.

Contemporary readers of the text may wonder whether Saul loses the monarchy because he fails to demonstrate leadership qualities: Saul is remarkably quiet, even when anointed, when people disparage him (cf. I Samuel 10:27 below). Or readers may ask whether the Hebrew Bible faults him solely for his lack of fealty to the Divine word (I Samuel 15:28). If so, how does one explain David's hold on power even when disobeying important Divine imperatives? (See "The Taking of Batsheva" in Chapter 5, "Women.")

Additionally, Saul's maladies challenge the contemporary reader to assess the psychological stresses of leadership on its possessors, and to explore the possibilities of preventing the worst effects of these pressures from destroying the individual political actor involved in the realities of acquiring and maintaining power.

1. Saul Is Annointed

I Samuel 10:1–9, 17–27

1 Then Samuel took the vial of oil, and poured it upon his head, and kissed him, and said: 'Is it not that the LORD hath

anointed thee to be prince over His inheritance? 2 When thou art departed from me to-day, then thou shalt find two men by the tomb of Rachel, in the border of Benjamin at Zelzah; and they will say unto thee: The asses which thou wentest to seek are found; and, lo, thy father hath left off caring for the asses, and is anxious concerning you, saying: What shall I do for my son? 3 Then shalt thou go on forward from thence, and thou shalt come to the terebinth of Tabor, and there shall meet thee there three men going up to God to Beth-el, one carrying three kids, and another carrying three loaves of bread, and another carrying a bottle of wine. 4 And they will salute thee, and give thee two cakes of bread; which thou shalt receive of their hand. 5 After that thou shalt come to the hill of God, where is the garrison of the Philistines; and it shall come to pass, when thou art come thither to the city, that thou shalt meet a band of prophets coming down from the high place with a psaltery, and a timbrel, and a pipe, and a harp, before them; and they will be prophesying. 6 And the spirit of the LORD will come mightily upon thee, and thou shalt prophesy with them, and shalt be turned into another man.

7 And let it be, when these signs are come unto thee, that thou do as thy hand shall find; for God is with thee. 8 And thou shalt go down before me to Gilgal; and, behold, I will come down unto thee, to offer burnt-offerings, and to sacrifice sacrifices of peace-offerings; seven days shalt thou tarry, till I come unto thee, and tell thee what thou shalt do.'

9 And it was so, that when he had turned his back to go from Samuel, God gave him another heart; and all those signs came to pass that day.

. . . .

17 And Samuel called the people together unto the LORD to Mizpah. 18 And he said unto the children of Israel: 'Thus saith the LORD, the God of Israel: I brought up Israel out of Egypt, and I delivered you out of the hand of the Egyptians, and out of the hand of all the kingdoms that oppressed you.

19 But ye have this day rejected your God, who Himself saveth you out of all your calamities and your distresses; and ye have said unto Him: Nay, but set a king over us. Now therefore present yourselves before the LORD by your tribes, and by your

thousands.' 20 So Samuel brought all the tribes of Israel near, and the tribe of Benjamin was taken. 21 And he brought the tribe of Benjamin near by their families, and the family of the Matrites was taken; and Saul the son of Kish was taken; but when they sought him, he could not be found. 22 Therefore they asked of the LORD further: 'Is there yet a man come hither?' And the LORD answered: 'Behold, he hath hid himself among the baggage.'

23 And they ran and fetched him thence; and when he stood among the people, he was higher than any of the people from his shoulders and upward. 24 And Samuel said to all the people: 'See ye him whom the LORD hath chosen, that there is none like him among all the people?' And all the people shouted, and said: 'Long live the king.'

25 Then Samuel told the people the manner of the kingdom, and wrote it in a book, and laid it up before the LORD. And Samuel sent all the people away, every man to his house. 26 And Saul also went to his house to Gibeah; and there went with him the men of valour, whose hearts God had touched. 27 But certain base fellows said: 'How shall this man save us?' And they despised him, and brought him no present. But he was as one that held his peace.

2. Saul's Victory and the Second Coronation

I Samuel 11:1–7, 11–15

1 Then Nahash the Ammonite came up, and encamped against Jabesh-gilead; and all the men of Jabesh said unto Nahash: 'Make a covenant with us, and we will serve thee.' 2 And Nahash the Ammonite said unto them: 'On this condition will I make it with you, that all your right eyes be put out; and I will lay it for a reproach upon all Israel.' 3 And the elders of Jabesh said unto him: 'Give us seven days' respite, that we may send messengers unto all the borders of Israel; and then, if there be none to deliver us, we will come out to thee.' 4 Then came the messengers to Gibeath-shaul, and spoke these words in the ears of the people; and all the people lifted up their voice, and wept.

5 And, behold, Saul came following the oxen out of the field; and Saul said: 'What aileth the people that they weep?' And they told him the words of the men of Jabesh. 6 And the spirit of God came mightily upon Saul when he heard those words, and his anger was kindled greatly. 7 And he took a yoke of oxen, and cut them in pieces, and sent them throughout all the borders of Israel by the hand of messengers, saying: 'Whosoever cometh not forth after Saul and after Samuel, so shall it be done unto his oxen.' And the dread of the LORD fell on the people, and they came out as one man.

. . . .

11 And it was so on the morrow, that Saul put the people in three companies; and they came into the midst of the camp in the morning watch, and smote the Ammonites until the heat of the day; and it came to pass, that they that remained were scattered, so that two of them were not left together. 12 And the people said unto Samuel: 'Who is he that said: Shall Saul reign over us? bring the men, that we may put them to death.' 13 And Saul said: 'There shall not a man be put to death this day; for to-day the LORD hath wrought deliverance in Israel.'

14 Then said Samuel to the people: 'Come and let us go to Gilgal, and renew the kingdom there.' 15 And all the people went to Gilgal; and there they made Saul king before the LORD in Gilgal; and there they sacrificed sacrifices of peace-offerings before the LORD; and there Saul and all the men of Israel rejoiced greatly.

With this military victory and second coronation, it seems the Saul's kingdom is securely established. But, as we already know, Saul winds up losing his kingdom (I Samuel 15), and his successor, David, is crowned even in his lifetime.

3. Establishment of the Davidic Kingdom

Despite Samuel's prophetic status, even he does not immediately recognize David's ability to rule. Samuel's failure of vision underlines the lesson that God wants him to internalize: even with Divine aid, accurate human interpretation is needed if good outcomes are to prevail.

It turns out that Samuel doesn't perceive David's fitness for leadership because David lacks what is normally perceived as the "signs" of leadership.

Unlike Saul, David does not look like a king: he is short, and has red hair. But he does have fine eyes.

Perhaps ironically, David's tenure as king does not look like a model for holding onto power and establishing his dynasty: his reign sees many more wars than Saul's rule, and David commits many sins, arguably more and of greater severity than his predecessor. But David remains true to God, and in the end, correctly orders his priorities. Unlike Saul, David freely admits his wrongdoings (at least to God). Modern readers may ask: Are the differences between Saul and David as presented by the Hebrew Bible enough to account for the differing levels of success that they enjoy as leaders?

a. David Is Anointed

I Samuel 16

1 And the LORD said unto Samuel: 'How long wilt thou mourn for Saul, seeing I have rejected him from being king over Israel? fill thy horn with oil, and go, I will send thee to Jesse the Beth-lehemite; for I have provided Me a king among his sons.' 2 And Samuel said: 'How can I go? if Saul hear it, he will kill me.' And the LORD said: 'Take a heifer with thee, and say: I am come to sacrifice to the LORD. 3 And call Jesse to the sacrifice, and I will tell thee what thou shalt do; and thou shalt anoint unto Me him whom I name unto thee.' 4 And Samuel did that which the LORD spoke, and came to Beth-lehem. And the elders of the city came to meet him trembling, and said: 'Comest thou peaceably?' 5 And he said: 'Peaceably; I am come to sacrifice unto the LORD; sanctify yourselves and come with me to the sacrifice.' And he sanctified Jesse and his sons, and called them to the sacrifice.

6 And it came to pass, when they were come, that he beheld Eliab, and said: 'Surely the LORD's anointed is before Him.' 7 But the LORD said unto Samuel: 'Look not on his countenance, or on the height of his stature; because I have rejected him; for it is not as man seeth: for man looketh on the outward appearance, but the LORD looketh on the heart.' 8 Then Jesse called Abinadab, and made him pass before Samuel. And he said: 'Neither hath the LORD chosen this.' 9 Then Jesse made Shammah to pass by. And he said: 'Neither hath the LORD chosen this.' 10 And Jesse made seven of his sons to pass before Samuel. And Samuel said unto Jesse: 'The LORD hath not chosen these.'

11 And Samuel said unto Jesse: 'Are here all thy children?' And he said: 'There remaineth yet the youngest, and, behold, he keepeth the sheep.' And Samuel said unto Jesse: 'Send and fetch him; for we will not sit down till he come hither.' 12 And he sent, and brought him in. Now he was ruddy, and withal of beautiful eyes, and goodly to look upon. And the LORD said: 'Arise, anoint him; for this is he.' 13 Then Samuel took the horn of oil, and anointed him in the midst of his brethren; and the spirit of the LORD came mightily upon David from that day forward. So Samuel rose up, and went to Ramah.

14 Now the spirit of the LORD had departed from Saul, and an evil spirit from the LORD terrified him. 15 And Saul's servants said unto him: 'Behold now, an evil spirit from God terrifieth thee. 16 Let our lord now command thy servants, that are before thee, to seek out a man who is a skilful player on the harp; and it shall be, when the evil spirit from God cometh upon thee, that he shall play with his hand, and thou shalt be well.' 17 And Saul said unto his servants: 'Provide me now a man that can play well, and bring him to me.' 18 Then answered one of the young men, and said: 'Behold, I have seen a son of Jesse the Beth-lehemite, that is skilful in playing, and a mighty man of valour, and a man of war, and prudent in affairs, and a comely person, and the LORD is with him.' 19 Wherefore Saul sent messengers unto Jesse, and said: 'Send me David thy son, who is with the sheep.' 20 And Jesse took an ass laden with bread, and a bottle of wine, and a kid, and sent them by David his son unto Saul. 21 And David came to Saul, and stood before him; and he loved him greatly; and he became his armour-bearer. 22 And Saul sent to Jesse, saying: 'Let David, I pray thee, stand before me; for he hath found favour in my sight.' 23 And it came to pass, when the [evil] spirit from God was upon Saul, that David took the harp, and played with his hand; so Saul found relief, and it was well with him, and the evil spirit departed from him.

b. David Is Acclaimed as King

After the death of Saul, the first chapters of II Samuel focus on the battles that David fights with the Israelite tribes that do not want to recognize him as king of the entire Israelite nation, and who prefer to follow Saul's son, Ishbosheth. It is not until chapter 5 of the Second Book of Samuel that David is recognized as king, not just in Hebron over the tribe of Judah but over all the Israelite tribes. Note the role of the Elders in affirming this new power structure.

II Samuel 5:6–10

The earlier part of this passage (II Samuel 5:1–5) is cited above in the section "David Is Anointed." But that earlier presentation emphasizes the role of the Elders and the people as a whole in authorizing David's rule. The inclusion of the passage here notes David's conquest of Jerusalem, the establishment of his capital city there, and the founding of the Davidic kingdom, all important developments in David's consolidation of power as king of the United Israelite tribes.

> 6 And the king and his men went to Jerusalem against the Jebusites, the inhabitants of the land, who spoke unto David, saying: 'Except thou take away the blind and the lame, thou shalt not come in hither'; thinking: 'David cannot come in hither.' 7 Nevertheless David took the stronghold of Zion; the same is the city of David. 8 And David said on that day: 'Whosoever smiteth the Jebusites, and getteth up to the gutter, and [taketh away] the lame and the blind, that are hated of David's soul—.' Wherefore they say: 'There are the blind and the lame; he cannot come into the house.' 9 And David dwelt in the stronghold, and called it the city of David. And David built round about from Millo and inward. 10 And David waxed greater and greater; for the LORD, the God of hosts, was with him.

Of all of David's wives, Bathsheva is the only one who actively ensures her son's position as heir to David's throne. As Queen-Mother, she is painfully aware of the often deadly maneuverings at the royal court, and she does not hesitate to drop well-placed hints that would help Solomon's situation (see Chapter 11, "Civil War," regarding the matter with Adoniya [I Kings 2]).

I Kings 1:5–30

> 5 Now Adonijah the son of Haggith exalted himself, saying: 'I will be king'; and he prepared him chariots and horsemen, and fifty men to run before him. 6 And his father had not grieved him all his life in saying: 'Why hast thou done so?' and he was also a very goodly man; and he was born after Absalom. 7 And he conferred with Joab the son of Zeruiah, and with Abiathar the priest; and they following Adonijah helped him. 8 But Zadok the priest, and Benaiah the son of Jehoiada, and Nathan the prophet, and Shimei, and Rei, and the mighty men that belonged

to David, were not with Adonijah. 9 And Adonijah slew sheep and oxen and fatlings by the stone of Zoheleth, which is beside En-rogel; and he called all his brethren the king's sons, and all the men of Judah the king's servants; 10 but Nathan the prophet, and Benaiah, and the mighty men, and Solomon his brother, he called not.

11 Then Nathan spoke unto Bath-sheba the mother of Solomon, saying: 'Hast thou not heard that Adonijah the son of Haggith doth reign, and David our lord knoweth it not? 12 Now therefore come, let me, I pray thee, give thee counsel, that thou mayest save thine own life, and the life of thy son Solomon. 13 Go and get thee in unto king David, and say unto him: Didst not thou, my lord, O king, swear unto thy handmaid, saying: Assuredly Solomon thy son shall reign after me, and he shall sit upon my throne? why then doth Adonijah reign? 14 Behold, while thou yet talkest there with the king, I also will come in after thee, and confirm thy words.'

15 And Bath-sheba went in unto the king into the chamber.— Now the king was very old; and Abishag the Shunammite min- istered unto the king.— 16 And Bath-sheba bowed, and pros- trated herself unto the king. And the king said: 'What wouldest thou?' 17 And she said unto him: 'My lord, thou didst swear by the LORD thy God unto thy handmaid: Assuredly Solomon thy son shall reign after me, and he shall sit upon my throne. 18 And now, behold, Adonijah reigneth; and thou, my lord the king, knowest it not. 19 And he hath slain oxen and fatlings and sheep in abundance, and hath called all the sons of the king, and Abiathar, the priest, and Joab the captain of the host; but Solomon thy servant hath he not called. 20 And thou, my lord the king, the eyes of all Israel are upon thee, that thou shouldest tell them who shall sit on the throne of my lord the king after him. 21 Otherwise it will come to pass, when my lord the king shall sleep with his fathers, that I and my son Solomon shall be counted offenders.'

22 And, lo, while she yet talked with the king, Nathan the prophet came in. 23 And they told the king, saying: 'Behold Nathan the prophet.' And when he was come in before the king, he bowed down before the king with his face to the ground. 24 And Nathan said: 'My lord, O king, hast thou said: Adonijah shall reign after me, and he shall sit upon my throne? 25 For he

is gone down this day, and hath slain oxen and fatlings and sheep in abundance, and hath called all the king's sons, and the captains of the host, and Abiathar the priest; and, behold, they eat and drink before him, and say: Long live king Adonijah. 26 But me, even me thy servant, and Zadok the priest, and Benaiah the son of Jehoiada, and thy servant Solomon hath he not called. 27 Is this thing done by my lord the king, and thou hast not declared unto thy servant who should sit on the throne of my lord the king after him?'

28 Then king David answered and said: 'Call Bath-sheva to me.'[1] And she came into the king's presence, and stood before the king. 29 And the king swore and said: 'As the LORD liveth, who hath redeemed my soul out of all adversity, 30 verily as I swore unto thee by the LORD, the God of Israel, saying: Assuredly Solomon thy son shall reign after me, and he shall sit upon my throne in my stead; verily so will I do this day.'

4. Solomon: The Opulent Monarchy

Why does a monarch choose to live opulently? What political messages are sent by a wealthy court? What snares lie in waiting within its intricacies? Does Solomon's court compare to the opulence of France's Louis XIV? Or are they fundamentally different in tone and character?

I Kings 5:1–8[2]

1 And Solomon ruled over all the kingdoms from the River unto the land of the Philistines, and unto the border of Egypt; they brought presents, and served Solomon all the days of his life.

2 And Solomon's provision for one day was thirty measures of fine flour, and threescore measures of meal; 3 ten fat oxen, and twenty oxen out of the pastures, and a hundred sheep, beside harts, and gazelles, and roebucks, and fatted fowl. 4 For he had

---

1. My translation. The JPS version is 'Call me Bath-sheba' which, in modern usage, would make it appear that King David is asking to be called by another name (not his own), which is clearly not the intent of the passage here.

2. In the JPS 1917 translation, verse 1 as cited here is presented as the last verse of I Kings 4. In the Mechon Mamre translation, however, this verse is presented as the first verse of I Kings 5. The logical fit of the subject matter of verse 1 as here cited is to I Kings 5 and not to I Kings 4. I have therefore elected to follow the lead of the Mechon Mamre translation of the Hebrew Bible in this case.

dominion over all the region on this side the River, from Tiphsah even to Gaza, over all the kings on this side the River; and he had peace on all sides round about him. 5 And Judah and Israel dwelt safely, every man under his vine and under his fig-tree, from Dan even to Beer-sheba, all the days of Solomon.

6 And Solomon had forty thousand stalls of horses for his chariots, and twelve thousand horsemen. 7 And those officers provided victual for king Solomon, and for all that came unto king Solomon's table, every man in his month; they let nothing be lacking. 8 Barley also and straw for the horses and swift steeds brought they unto the place where it should be, every man according to his charge.

A particularly famous example of Solomon's wide-ranging alliances is his association with the Queen of Sheba. This reading describes in greater detail the grandeur of Solomon's royal court.

I Kings 10:4–10, 13–29

4 And when the queen of Sheba had seen all the wisdom of Solomon, and the house that he had built, 5 and the food of his table, and the sitting of his servants, and the attendance of his ministers, and their apparel, and his cupbearers, and his burnt-offering which he offered in the house of the LORD, there was no more spirit in her. 6 And she said to the king: 'It was a true report that I heard in mine own land of thine acts, and of thy wisdom. 7 Howbeit I believed not the words, until I came, and mine eyes had seen it; and, behold, the half was not told me; thou hast wisdom and prosperity exceeding the fame which I heard. 8 Happy are thy men, happy are these thy servants, that stand continually before thee, and that hear thy wisdom. 9 Blessed be the LORD thy God, who delighted in thee, to set thee on the throne of Israel; because the LORD loved Israel for ever, therefore made He thee king, to do justice and righteousness.' 10 And she gave the king a hundred and twenty talents of gold, and of spices very great store, and precious stones; there came no more such abundance of spices as these which the queen of Sheba gave to king Solomon.

. . . .

13 And king Solomon gave to the queen of Sheba all her desire, whatsoever she asked, beside that which Solomon gave her of his

royal bounty. So she turned, and went to her own land, she and her servants.

14 Now the weight of gold that came to Solomon in one year was six hundred threescore and six talents of gold, 15 beside that which came of the merchants, and of the traffic of the traders, and of all the kings of the mingled people and of the governors of the country. 16 And king Solomon made two hundred targets of beaten gold: six hundred shekels of gold went to one target. 17 And he made three hundred shields of beaten gold: three pounds of gold went to one shield; and the king put them in the house of the forest of Lebanon.

18 Moreover the king made a great throne of ivory, and overlaid it with the finest gold. 19 There were six steps to the throne, and the top of the throne was round behind; and there were arms on either side by the place of the seat, and two lions standing beside the arms. 20 And twelve lions stood there on the one side and on the other upon the six steps; there was not the like made in any kingdom.

21 And all king Solomon's drinking-vessels were of gold, and all the vessels of the house of the forest of Lebanon were of pure gold; none were of silver; it was nothing accounted of in the days of Solomon. 22 For the king had at sea a navy of Tarshish with the navy of Hiram; once every three years came the navy of Tarshish, bringing gold, and silver, ivory, and apes, and peacocks.

23 So king Solomon exceeded all the kings of the earth in riches and in wisdom. 24 And all the earth sought the presence of Solomon, to hear his wisdom, which God had put in his heart. 25 And they brought every man his present, vessels of silver, and vessels of gold, and raiment, and armour, and spices, horses, and mules, a rate year by year.

26 And Solomon gathered together chariots and horsemen; and he had a thousand and four hundred chariots, and twelve thousand horsemen, that he bestowed in the chariot cities, and with the king at Jerusalem. 27 And the king made silver to be in Jerusalem as stones, and cedars made he to be as the sycamore-trees that are in the Lowland, for abundance. 28 And the horses which Solomon had were brought out of Egypt; also out of Keveh, the king's merchants buying them of the men of Keveh at a price. 29 And a chariot came up and went out of Egypt for six

hundred shekels of silver, and a horse for a hundred and fifty; and so for all the kings of the Hittites, and for the kings of Aram, did they bring them out by their means.

Notably, Solomon does not invest in all this opulence just for his own personal glory. His most intricate enterprise is the construction of the Temple in Jerusalem, devoted to the worship of the monotheistic God of the Israelites, and open to all peoples of the world. Solomon organizes complex partnerships with his allies to scout for the finest materials, and organizes immense influxes of labor to find the best craftspeople to build what the Hebrew Bible describes as one of the finest structures of the ancient world.

I Kings 5:15–32

15 And Hiram king of Tyre sent his servants unto Solomon; for he had heard that they had anointed him king in the room of his father; for Hiram was ever a lover of David. 16 And Solomon sent to Hiram, saying: 17 'Thou knowest how that David my father could not build a house for the name of the LORD his God for the wars which were about him on every side, until the LORD put them under the soles of my feet. 18 But now the LORD my God hath given me rest on every side; there is neither adversary, nor evil occurrence. 19 And, behold, I purpose to build a house for the name of the LORD my God, as the LORD spoke unto David my father, saying: Thy son, whom I will set upon thy throne in thy room, he shall build the house for My name. 20 Now therefore command thou that they hew me cedar-trees out of Lebanon; and my servants shall be with thy servants; and I will give thee hire for thy servants according to all that thou shalt say; for thou knowest that there is not among us any that hath skill to hew timber like unto the Zidonians.'

21 And it came to pass, when Hiram heard the words of Solomon, that he rejoiced greatly, and said: 'Blessed be the LORD this day, who hath given unto David a wise son over this great people.' 22 And Hiram sent to Solomon, saying: 'I have heard that which thou hast sent unto me; I will do all thy desire concerning timber of cedar, and concerning timber of cypress. 23 My servants shall bring them down from Lebanon unto the sea; and I will make them into rafts to go by sea unto the place that thou shalt appoint me, and will cause them to be broken up

there, and thou shalt receive them; and thou shalt accomplish my desire, in giving food for my household.'

24 So Hiram gave Solomon timber of cedar and timber of cypress according to all his desire. 25 And Solomon gave Hiram twenty thousand measures of wheat for food to his household, and twenty measures of beaten oil; thus gave Solomon to Hiram year by year. 26 And the LORD gave Solomon wisdom, as He promised him; and there was peace between Hiram and Solomon; and they two made a league together.

27 And king Solomon raised a levy out of all Israel; and the levy was thirty thousand men. 28 And he sent them to Lebanon, ten thousand a month by courses: a month they were in Lebanon, and two months at home; and Adoniram was over the levy. 29 And Solomon had threescore and ten thousand that bore burdens, and fourscore thousand that were hewers in the mountains; 30 besides Solomon's chief officers that were over the work, three thousand and three hundred, who bore rule over the people that wrought in the work. 31 And the king commanded, and they quarried great stones, costly stones, to lay the foundation of the house with hewn stone. 32 And Solomon's builders and Hiram's builders and the Gebalites did fashion them, and prepared the timber and the stones to build the house.

Solomon acts multilaterally, both internationally and domestically. As noted above, he welcomes aid and trade from neighboring countries in gathering materials to build the Temple, and utilizes complex population shifts to organize skilled craftsworkers for his agenda. The Hebrew Bible notes that Solomon raises immense taxes to fund his enterprises. Later, as we will see, these immense expenditures will fuel resentment.

For now, however, Solomon understands the importance of uniting all Israelite population groups under his banner—especially when it involves the touchstone act, transferring the Holy Ark into the precincts of the Temple. Careful readers may want to compare Solomon's careful handling of this phase with his father's looser approach, accompanied by dancing, together with the reproaches that ensued (see Chapter 5, "Women"; "The Break with Michal" [II Samuel 6]). One important difference between the two ceremonies involved in bringing the Holy Ark to the Temple (in David's case, to the Tabernacle) lies in Solomon's highlighting of the universal aspect of the Temple that is open to all peoples of the world for the worship of God.

I Kings 8:1–5

1 Then Solomon assembled the elders of Israel, and all the heads of the tribes, the princes of the fathers' houses of the children of Israel, unto king Solomon in Jerusalem, to bring up the ark of the covenant of the LORD out of the city of David, which is Zion. 2 And all the men of Israel assembled themselves unto king Solomon at the feast, in the month Ethanim, which is the seventh month.

3 And all the elders of Israel came, and the priests took up the ark. 4 And they brought up the ark of the LORD, and the tent of meeting, and all the holy vessels that were in the Tent; even these did the priests and the Levites bring up. 5 And king Solomon and all the congregation of Israel, that were assembled unto him, were with him before the ark, sacrificing sheep and oxen, that could not be told nor numbered for multitude.

Despite the opulence that he purposefully introduces into the building of the Temple, Solomon understands that the Temple is built as a God-focused enterprise, not a monarch-centered structure. Significantly, he views the Temple as a place of unity and peace for all of humanity, not just for his own nation. Solomon's prayer upon the Temple's completion is lengthy, and offers an important glimpse into his mindset.

I Kings 8:26–36, 41–43

26 Now therefore, O God of Israel, let Thy word, I pray Thee, be verified, which Thou didst speak unto Thy servant David my father.

27 But will God in very truth dwell on the earth? behold, heaven and the heaven of heavens cannot contain Thee; how much less this house that I have builded! 28 Yet have Thou respect unto the prayer of Thy servant, and to his supplication, O LORD my God, to hearken unto the cry and to the prayer which Thy servant prayeth before Thee this day; 29 that Thine eyes may be open toward this house night and day, even toward the place whereof Thou hast said: My name shall be there; to hearken unto the prayer which Thy servant shall pray toward this place. 30 And hearken Thou to the supplication of Thy servant, and of Thy people Israel, when they shall pray toward this place; yea, hear Thou in heaven Thy dwelling-place; and when Thou hearest, forgive.

31 If a man sin against his neighbour, and an oath be exacted of him to cause him to swear, and he come and swear before Thine altar in this house; 32 then hear Thou in heaven, and do, and judge Thy servants, condemning the wicked, to bring his way upon his own head; and justifying the righteous, to give him according to his righteousness.

33 When Thy people Israel are smitten down before the enemy, when they do sin against Thee, if they turn again to Thee, and confess Thy name, and pray and make supplication unto Thee in this house; 34 then hear Thou in heaven, and forgive the sin of Thy people Israel, and bring them back unto the land which Thou gavest unto their fathers.

35 When heaven is shut up, and there is no rain, when they do sin against Thee; if they pray toward this place, and confess Thy name, and turn from their sin, when Thou dost afflict them; 36 then hear Thou in heaven, and forgive the sin of Thy servants, and of Thy people Israel, when Thou teachest them the good way wherein they should walk; and send rain upon Thy land, which Thou hast given to Thy people for an inheritance.

. . . .

41 Moreover concerning the stranger that is not of Thy people Israel, when he shall come out of a far country for Thy name's sake— 42 for they shall hear of Thy great name, and of Thy mighty hand, and of Thine outstretched arm—when he shall come and pray toward this house; 43 hear Thou in heaven Thy dwelling-place, and do according to all that the stranger calleth to Thee for; that all the peoples of the earth may know Thy name, to fear Thee, as doth Thy people Israel, and that they may know that Thy name is called upon this house which I have built.

A similar message regarding universal prayer is found in the following selection from Micah 4.

Micah 4:2–4

2 And many nations shall go and say:
'Come ye, and let us go up to the mountain of the LORD,
And to the house of the God of Jacob;
And He will teach us of His ways,
And we will walk in His paths';
For out of Zion shall go forth the law,

And the word of the LORD from Jerusalem.
3 And He shall judge between many peoples,
And shall decide concerning mighty nations afar off;
And they shall beat their swords into plowshares,
And their spears into pruninghooks;
Nation shall not lift up sword against nation,
Neither shall they learn war any more.
4 But they shall sit every man under his vine and under his
    fig-tree;
And none shall make them afraid;
For the mouth of the Lord of hosts hath spoken.

CHAPTER 13

FOREIGN AFFAIRS

Although the Hebrew Bible utilizes an historical arc to present the organization and social components of Israelite society, it devotes relatively little space to the maneuverings behind, or even the visible conduct of, the foreign affairs represented within its texts. Perhaps this is due to their nature: with the Hebrew Bible's emphasis on the moral imperatives of social arrangements and human relationships, issues regarding manifestations of power abroad hold relatively little interest. Indeed, its stress on the moral integrity of the individual human being regardless of social status is one of the reasons the Hebrew Bible may be seen as constituting one of the earliest arguments against the power-based justification of empire. For the Hebrew Bible, the dominion of empire could never justify its juggernaut against individual rights and existence.

When the Hebrew Bible does depict the conduct of foreign affairs, it appears to be more interested in the implications of these external occurrences for the moral coherence of Israelite society back home. This theme links the Hebrew Bible's cautions against close relations with the Israelites' polytheistic Canaanite neighbors, its critique of Solomon's expansion of his own empire, and the thundering warnings of the Prophets regarding the exile that would befall the Israelites if they did not mend their ways. For the Hebrew Bible, God is an active, if largely unseen, player in the conduct of foreign affairs, whose reactions are ignored at the perils of the human functionaries—notably, kings and their advisors—who more openly operate in them.

A. Sending Spies

Whether sending spies to check out the Promised Land before actually entering it is Moses' idea, a concession to the Israelites' request (Deuteronomy 1:22–23), or a suggestion from God (Numbers 13:1–3), it does not work out well for the Israelites. The Israelites are persuaded by the glum report of ten of the spies that they would not be able to take over their Promised Land. The Israelite cries through the night are the reason adduced in the Hebrew Bible for God's punishment: only those Israelite males younger than twenty (with certain exceptions, like Joshua and Caleb, who gave positive reports about the Israelites' ability to enter into the Promised Land) would enter it; the rest of the (male) Israelites would die in the wilderness.

Notwithstanding this reaction, some enterprising Israelites attempt to battle their way into the Promised Land; they all perish.

1. God Tells the Israelites to Send Spies

Numbers 13:1–3, 17–33

1 And the LORD spoke unto Moses, saying:

2 'Send thou men, that they may spy out the land of Canaan, which I give unto the children of Israel; of every tribe of their fathers shall ye send a man, every one a prince among them.'

3 And Moses sent them from the wilderness of Paran according to the commandment of the LORD; all of them men who were heads of the children of Israel.

. . . .

17 And Moses sent them to spy out the land of Canaan, and said unto them: 'Get you up here into the South, and go up into the mountains; 18 and see the land, what it is; and the people that dwelleth therein, whether they are strong or weak, whether they are few or many; 19 and what the land is that they dwell in, whether it is good or bad; and what cities they are that they dwell in, whether in camps, or in strongholds; 20 and what the land is, whether it is fat or lean, whether there is wood therein, or not. And be ye of good courage, and bring of the fruit of the land.'—Now the time was the time of the first-ripe grapes.—

21 So they went up, and spied out the land from the wilderness of Zin unto Rehob, at the entrance to Hamath. 22 And they went up into the South, and came unto Hebron; and Ahiman, Sheshai, and Talmai, the children of Anak, were there.—Now Hebron was built seven years before Zoan in Egypt.— 23 And they came unto the valley of Eshcol, and cut down from thence a branch with one cluster of grapes, and they bore it upon a pole between two; they took also of the pomegranates, and of the figs.—24 That place was called the valley of Eshcol,[1] because of the cluster which the children of Israel cut down from thence.—

---

1. [That is, a cluster.—JPS 1917 eds.]

25 And they returned from spying out the land at the end of forty days. 26 And they went and came to Moses, and to Aaron, and to all the congregation of the children of Israel, unto the wilderness of Paran, to Kadesh; and brought back word unto them, and unto all the congregation, and showed them the fruit of the land.

27 And they told him, and said: 'We came unto the land whither thou sentest us, and surely it floweth with milk and honey; and this is the fruit of it. 28 Howbeit the people that dwell in the land are fierce, and the cities are fortified, and very great; and moreover we saw the children of Anak there. 29 Amalek dwelleth in the land of the South; and the Hittite, and the Jebusite, and the Amorite, dwell in the mountains; and the Canaanite dwelleth by the sea, and along by the side of the Jordan.' 30 And Caleb stilled the people toward Moses, and said: 'We should go up at once, and possess it; for we are well able to overcome it.'

31 But the men that went up with him said: 'We are not able to go up against the people; for they are stronger than we.' 32 And they spread an evil report of the land which they had spied out unto the children of Israel, saying: 'The land, through which we have passed to spy it out, is a land that eateth up the inhabitants thereof; and all the people that we saw in it are men of great stature. 33 And there we saw the Nephilim, the sons of Anak, who come of the Nephilim; and we were in our own sight as grasshoppers, and so we were in their sight.'

2. The Israelites React to the Negative Report

Numbers 14:1–10, 28–34, 39–45

1 And all the congregation lifted up their voice, and cried; and the people wept that night.

2 And all the children of Israel murmured against Moses and against Aaron; and the whole congregation said unto them: 'Would that we had died in the land of Egypt! or would we had died in this wilderness! 3 And wherefore doth the LORD bring us unto this land, to fall by the sword? Our wives and our little ones will be a prey; were it not better for us to return into Egypt?'

4 And they said one to another: 'Let us make a captain, and let us return into Egypt.'

5 Then Moses and Aaron fell on their faces before all the assembly of the congregation of the children of Israel. 6 And Joshua the son of Nun and Caleb the son of Jephunneh, who were of them that spied out the land, rent their clothes. 7 And they spoke unto all the congregation of the children of Israel, saying: 'The land, which we passed through to spy it out, is an exceeding good land. 8 If the LORD delight in us, then He will bring us into this land, and give it unto us—a land which floweth with milk and honey. 9 Only rebel not against the LORD, neither fear ye the people of the land; for they are bread for us; their defence is removed from over them, and the LORD is with us; fear them not.'

10 But all the congregation sought to[2] stone them with stones, when the glory of the LORD appeared in the tent of meeting unto all the children of Israel.

. . . .

28 Say unto them: As I live, saith the LORD, surely as ye have spoken in Mine ears, so will I do to you: 29 your carcasses shall fall in this wilderness, and all that were numbered of you, according to your whole number, from twenty years old and upward, ye that have murmured against Me; 30 surely ye shall not come into the land, concerning which I lifted up My hand that I would make you dwell therein, save Caleb the son of Jephunneh, and Joshua the son of Nun. 31 But your little ones, that ye said would be a prey, them will I bring in, and they shall know the land which ye have rejected. 32 But as for you, your carcasses shall fall in this wilderness. 33 And your children shall be wanderers in the wilderness forty years, and shall bear your strayings, until your carcasses be consumed in the wilderness. 34 After the number of the days in which ye spied out the land, even forty days, for every day a year, shall ye bear your iniquities, even forty years, and ye shall know My displeasure.

. . . .

39 And Moses told these words unto all the children of Israel; and the people mourned greatly.

---

2. JPS 1917: "bade."

40 And they rose up early in the morning, and got them up to the top of the mountain, saying: 'Lo, we are here, and will go up unto the place which the LORD hath promised; for we have sinned.'

41 And Moses said: 'Wherefore now do ye transgress the commandment of the LORD, seeing it shall not prosper? 42 Go not up, for the LORD is not among you; that ye be not smitten down before your enemies. 43 For there the Amalekite and the Canaanite are before you, and ye shall fall by the sword; forasmuch as ye are turned back from following the LORD, and the LORD will not be with you.'

44 But they presumed to go up to the top of the mountain; nevertheless the ark of the covenant of the LORD, and Moses, departed not out of the camp. 45 Then the Amalekite and the Canaanite, who dwelt in that hill-country, came down, and smote them and beat them down, even unto Hormah.

3. The Israelites Ask to Send Spies

Deuteronomy 1:22–30, 41–46

22 And ye came near unto me every one of you, and said: 'Let us send men before us, that they may search the land for us, and bring us back word of the way by which we must go up, and the cities unto which we shall come.' 23 And the thing pleased me well; and I took twelve men of you, one man for every tribe; 24 and they turned and went up into the mountains, and came unto the valley of Eshcol, and spied it out. 25 And they took of the fruit of the land in their hands, and brought it down unto us, and brought us back word, and said: 'Good is the land which the LORD our God giveth unto us.'

26 Yet ye would not go up, but rebelled against the commandment of the LORD your God; 27 and ye murmured in your tents, and said: 'Because the LORD hated us, He hath brought us forth out of the land of Egypt, to deliver us into the hand of the Amorites, to destroy us. 28 Whither are we going up? our brethren have made our heart to melt, saying: The people is greater and taller than we; the cities are great and fortified up to heaven; and moreover we have seen the sons of the Anakim

there.' 29 Then I said unto you: 'Dread not, neither be afraid of them. 30 The LORD your God who goeth before you, He shall fight for you, according to all that He did for you in Egypt before your eyes;

. . . .

41 Then ye answered and said unto me: 'We have sinned against the LORD, we will go up and fight, according to all that the LORD our God commanded us.' And ye girded on every man his weapons of war, and deemed it a light thing to go up into the hill-country.

42 And the LORD said unto me: 'Say unto them: Go not up, neither fight; for I am not among you; lest ye be smitten before your enemies.' 43 So I spoke unto you, and ye hearkened not; but ye rebelled against the commandment of the LORD, and were presumptuous, and went up into the hill-country. 44 And the Amorites, that dwell in that hill-country, came out against you, and chased you, as bees do, and beat you down in Seir, even unto Hormah. 45 And ye returned and wept before the LORD; but the LORD hearkened not to your voice, nor gave ear unto you. 46 So ye abode in Kadesh many days, according unto the days that ye abode there.

B. Advisory Role of the Elders in Foreign Affairs

In domestic affairs, Elders are consulted in the matter of authorizing a king (David, Saul), and assembled by Solomon to accompany him in placing the Holy Ark in the newly constructed Temple (I Kings 8:1). But they also play an important role in foreign affairs. In the following selection (presented here again in light of its military significance—see Chapter 8, "Advising Kings," for the appearance of part of this text in a different context), Ahab asks for guidance from the Elders when neighboring Syria seems ready to go to war. Tensions quickly escalate, and Ahab's army routs the enemy.

I Kings 20:1–21

1 And Ben-hadad the king of Aram gathered all his host together; and there were thirty and two kings with him, and horses and chariots; and he went up and besieged Samaria, and fought against it. 2 And he sent messengers to Ahab king of Israel, into the city, 3 and said unto him: 'Thus saith Ben-hadad:

Thy silver and thy gold is mine; thy wives also and thy children, even the goodliest, are mine.' 4 And the king of Israel answered and said: 'It is according to thy saying, my lord, O king: I am thine, and all that I have.' 5 And the messengers came again, and said: 'Thus speaketh Ben-hadad, saying: I sent indeed unto thee, saying: Thou shalt deliver me thy silver, and thy gold, and thy wives, and thy children; 6 but I will send my servants unto thee tomorrow about this time, and they shall search thy house, and the houses of thy servants; and it shall be, that whatsoever is pleasant in thine eyes, they shall put it in their hand, and take it away.'

7 Then the king of Israel called all the elders of the land, and said: 'Mark, I pray you, and see how this man seeketh mischief; for he sent unto me for my wives, and for my children, and for my silver, and for my gold; and I denied him not.' 8 And all the elders and all the people said unto him: 'Hearken thou not, neither consent.' 9 Wherefore he said unto the messengers of Ben-hadad: 'Tell my lord the king: All that thou didst send for to thy servant at the first I will do; but this thing I may not do.' And the messengers departed, and brought him back word.

10 And Ben-hadad sent unto him, and said: 'The gods do so unto me, and more also, if the dust of Samaria shall suffice for handfuls for all the people that follow me.' 11 And the king of Israel answered and said: 'Tell him: Let not him that girdeth on his armour boast himself as he that putteth it off.' 12 And it came to pass, when [Ben-hadad] heard this message, as he was drinking, he and the kings, in the booths, that he said unto his servants: 'Set yourselves in array.' And they set themselves in array against the city.

13 And, behold, a prophet came near unto Ahab king of Israel, and said: 'Thus saith the LORD: Hast thou seen all this great multitude? behold, I will deliver it into thy hand this day; and thou shalt know that I am the LORD.' 14 And Ahab said: 'By whom?' And he said: 'Thus saith the LORD: By the young men of the princes of the provinces.' Then he said: 'Who shall begin the battle?' And he answered: 'Thou.' 15 Then he numbered the young men of the princes of the provinces, and they were two hundred and thirty-two; and after them he numbered all the people, even all the children of Israel, being seven thousand.

16 And they went out at noon. But Ben-hadad was drinking himself drunk in the booths, he and the kings, the thirty and two kings that helped him. 17 And the young men of the princes of the provinces went out first; and Ben-hadad sent out, and they told him, saying: 'There are men come out from Samaria.' 18 And he said: 'Whether they are come out for peace, take them alive; or whether they are come out for war, take them alive.' 19 So these went out of the city, the young men of the princes of the provinces, and the army which followed them. 20 And they slew every one his man; and the Arameans fled, and Israel pursued them; and Ben-hadad the king of Aram escaped on a horse with horsemen. 21 And the king of Israel went out, and smote the horses and chariots, and slew the Arameans with a great slaughter.

C. Judean Kings as Vassals

But not all neighbors are so easily defeated. In the next selection, the Judean kings are virtual vassals to the Egyptian Empire, which has King Josiah killed and crowns as puppet ruler whoever seems the most likely passive member of the royal family. As we know, the Kingdom of Judah that is subjected to the Egyptian Empire in this passage would shortly be destroyed by the Babylonians.

II Kings 23:31–37

31 Jehoahaz was twenty and three years old when he began to reign; and he reigned three months in Jerusalem; and his mother's name was Hamutal the daughter of Jeremiah of Libnah. 32 And he did that which was evil in the sight of the LORD, according to all that his fathers had done. 33 And Pharaoh-necoh put him in bands at Riblah in the land of Hamath, that he might not reign in Jerusalem; and put the land to a fine of a hundred talents of silver, and a talent of gold.

34 And Pharaoh-necoh made Eliakim the son of Josiah king in the room of Josiah his father, and changed his name to Jehoiakim; but he took Jehoahaz away; and he came to Egypt, and died there. 35 And Jehoiakim gave the silver and the gold to Pharaoh; but he taxed the land to give the money according to the commandment of Pharaoh; he exacted the silver and the gold of the people of the land, of every one according to his taxation, to give it unto Pharaoh-necoh.

36 Jehoiakim was twenty and five years old when he began to reign; and he reigned eleven years in Jerusalem; and his mother's name was Zebudah the daughter of Pedaiah of Rumah. 37 And he did that which was evil in the sight of the LORD, according to all that his fathers had done.

D. Prophets and Foreign Affairs

In the opinion of the Prophet, foreign affairs is just one more arena in which God works His will, despite human machinations that attempt to sway people and events their way.

Isaiah 10:5–11

5 O Assyria,[3] the rod of Mine anger,
In whose hand as a staff is Mine indignation!
6 I do send him against an ungodly nation,
And against the people of My wrath do I give him a charge,
To take the spoil, and to take the prey,
And to tread them down like the mire of the streets.
7 Howbeit he meaneth not so,
Neither doth his heart think so;
But it is in his heart to destroy,
And to cut off nations not a few.
8 For he saith: 'Are not my princes all of them kings?
9 Is not Calno as Carchemish?
Is not Hamath as Arpad?
Is not Samaria as Damascus?
10 As my hand hath reached the kingdoms of the idols,
Whose graven images did exceed them of Jerusalem and of
    Samaria;
11 Shall I not, as I have done unto Samaria and her idols,
So do to Jerusalem and her idols?'

---

3. JPS 1917: "Asshur."

Chapter 14

Political Corruption of Monarchs, Priests, and People

What happens to the governance of a people if corruption overtakes its leaders? its clergy? the people themselves? The Hebrew Bible does not shy away from these issues, as evidenced by the following selections.

A. Solomon Loses the Kingdom

If even the beloved and nurtured Solomon, builder of the Holy Temple, can lose his moral bearings and have his kingdom consequently taken from him, the contemporary reader may wonder whether the texts of the Hebrew Bible leave any room for imperfection.

Still, even though the Hebrew Bible depicts God as using language reminiscent of the words with which Samuel had berated Saul, God does not completely tear away the kingdom from Solomon. Rather, the divided Israelite kingdoms are each made smaller and weaker, as if to combat the kind of Empire to which Solomon seemed to be aspiring. From the time of Nimrod, the Hebrew Bible views empire-builders dubiously—as self-interested leaders who can easily overlook the essence of their job, which is to establish justice and a fair social structure for all inhabitants—but who concentrate instead on developing their own personal and imperial "brand."

I Kings 11:1–4, 9–13, 26–40, 43

These texts are presented here again because of the larger implications of Solomon's imperial ways: Not only are his actions tolerating idolatry not pleasing to God, but they also call into question his larger political goals, together with the actions on which he had prided building his expanded Israelite kingdom—his large network of foreign alliances.

> 1 Now king Solomon loved many foreign women, besides the daughter of Pharaoh, women of the Moabites, Ammonites, Edomites, Zidonians, and Hittites; 2 of the nations concerning which the LORD said unto the children of Israel: 'Ye shall not

go among them, neither shall they come among you; for surely they will turn away your heart after their gods'; Solomon did cleave unto these in love. 3 And he had seven hundred wives, princesses, and three hundred concubines; and his wives turned away his heart.

4 For it came to pass, when Solomon was old, that his wives turned away his heart after other gods; and his heart was not whole with the LORD his God, as was the heart of David his father.

. . . .

9 And the LORD was angry with Solomon, because his heart was turned away from the LORD, the God of Israel, who had appeared unto him twice, 10 and had commanded him concerning this thing, that he should not go after other gods; but he kept not that which the LORD commanded. 11 Wherefore the LORD said unto Solomon: 'Forasmuch as this hath been in thy mind, and thou hast not kept My covenant and My statutes, which I have commanded thee, I will surely rend the kingdom from thee, and will give it to thy servant. 12 Notwithstanding in thy days I will not do it, for David thy father's sake; but I will rend it out of the hand of thy son. 13 Howbeit I will not rend away all the kingdom; but I will give one tribe to thy son; for David My servant's sake, and for Jerusalem's sake which I have chosen.'

. . . .

26 And Jeroboam the son of Nebat, an Ephraimite of Zeredah, a servant of Solomon, whose mother's name was Zeruah, a widow, he also lifted up his hand against the king. 27 And this was the cause that he lifted up his hand against the king: Solomon built Millo, and repaired the breach of the city of David his father. 28 And the man Jeroboam was a mighty man of valour; and Solomon saw the young man that he was industrious, and he gave him charge over all the labour of the house of Joseph.

29 And it came to pass at that time, when Jeroboam went out of Jerusalem, that the prophet Ahijah the Shilonite found him in the way; now Ahijah had clad himself with a new garment; and they two were alone in the field. 30 And Ahijah laid hold of the new garment that was on him, and rent it in twelve pieces. 31 And he said to Jeroboam: 'Take thee ten pieces; for thus saith

the LORD, the God of Israel: Behold, I will rend the kingdom out of the hand of Solomon, and will give ten tribes to thee— 32 but he shall have one tribe, for My servant David's sake, and for Jerusalem's sake, the city which I have chosen out of all the tribes of Israel— 33 because that they have forsaken Me, and have worshipped Ashtoreth the goddess of the Zidonians, Chemosh the god of Moab, and Milcom the god of the children of Ammon; and they have not walked in My ways, to do that which is right in Mine eyes, and to keep My statutes and Mine ordinances, as did David his father. 34 Howbeit I will not take the whole kingdom out of his hand; but I will make him prince all the days of his life, for David My servant's sake, whom I chose, because he kept My commandments and My statutes; 35 but I will take the kingdom out of his son's hand, and will give it unto thee, even ten tribes. 36 And unto his son will I give one tribe, that David My servant may have a lamp alway before Me in Jerusalem, the city which I have chosen Me to put My name there. 37 And I will take thee, and thou shalt reign over all that thy soul desireth, and shalt be king over Israel. 38 And it shall be, if thou wilt hearken unto all that I command thee, and wilt walk in My ways, and do that which is right in Mine eyes, to keep My statutes and My commandments, as David My servant did, that I will be with thee, and will build thee a sure house, as I built for David, and will give Israel unto thee. 39 And I will for this afflict the seed of David, but not for ever.'

40 Solomon sought therefore to kill Jeroboam; but Jeroboam arose, and fled into Egypt, unto Shishak king of Egypt, and was in Egypt until the death of Solomon.

. . . .

43 And Solomon slept with his fathers, and was buried in the city of David his father; and Rehoboam his son reigned in his stead.

B. Naboth's Vineyard

The story of Naboth's Vineyard portrays a depth of corruption that has become more than just a metaphor of spiritual malfunction. It shows rather the lethal results of a degraded exercise of power that takes whatever it wants. Individual human life doesn't stand a chance when measured against the entitlement of a king's desires.

I Kings 21

1 And it came to pass after these things, that Naboth the Jezreelite had a vineyard, which was in Jezreel, hard by the palace of Ahab, king of Samaria. 2 And Ahab spoke unto Naboth, saying: 'Give me thy vineyard, that I may have it for a garden of herbs, because it is near unto my house; and I will give thee for it a better vineyard than it; or, if it seem good to thee, I will give thee the worth of it in money.' 3 And Naboth said to Ahab: 'The LORD forbid it me, that I should give the inheritance of my fathers unto thee.' 4 And Ahab came into his house sullen and displeased because of the word which Naboth the Jezreelite had spoken to him; for he had said: 'I will not give thee the inheritance of my fathers.' And he laid him down upon his bed, and turned away his face, and would eat no bread.

5 But Jezebel his wife came to him, and said unto him: 'Why is thy spirit so sullen, that thou eatest no bread?' 6 And he said unto her: 'Because I spoke unto Naboth the Jezreelite, and said unto him: Give me thy vineyard for money; or else, if it please thee, I will give thee another vineyard for it; and he answered: I will not give thee my vineyard.' 7 And Jezebel his wife said unto him: 'Dost thou now govern the kingdom of Israel? arise, and eat bread, and let thy heart be merry; I will give thee the vineyard of Naboth the Jezreelite.' 8 So she wrote letters in Ahab's name, and sealed them with his seal, and sent the letters unto the elders and to the nobles that were in his city, and that dwelt with Naboth. 9 And she wrote in the letters, saying: 'Proclaim a fast, and set Naboth at the head of the people; 10 and set two men, base fellows, before him, and let them bear witness against him, saying: Thou didst curse God and the king. And then carry him out, and stone him, that he die.'

11 And the men of his city, even the elders and the nobles who dwelt in his city, did as Jezebel had sent unto them, according as it was written in the letters which she had sent unto them. 12 They proclaimed a fast, and set Naboth at the head of the people. 13 And the two men, the base fellows, came in and sat before him; and the base fellows bore witness against him, even against Naboth, in the presence of the people, saying: 'Naboth did curse God and the king.' Then they carried him forth out of the city, and stoned him with stones, that he died. 14 Then they sent to Jezebel, saying: 'Naboth is stoned, and is dead.' 15 And it

came to pass, when Jezebel heard that Naboth was stoned, and was dead, that Jezebel said to Ahab: 'Arise, take possession of the vineyard of Naboth the Jezreelite, which he refused to give thee for money; for Naboth is not alive, but dead.' 16 And it came to pass, when Ahab heard that Naboth was dead, that Ahab rose up to go down to the vineyard of Naboth the Jezreelite, to take possession of it.

17 And the word of the LORD came to Elijah the Tishbite, saying: 18 'Arise, go down to meet Ahab king of Israel, who dwelleth in Samaria; behold, he is in the vineyard of Naboth, whither he is gone down to take possession of it. 19 And thou shalt speak unto him, saying: Thus saith the LORD: Hast thou murdered[1] and also inherited?[2] and thou shalt speak unto him, saying: Thus saith the LORD: In the place where dogs licked the blood of Naboth shall dogs lick thy blood, even thine.'

20 And Ahab said to Elijah: 'Hast thou found me, O mine enemy?' And he answered: 'I have found thee; because thou hast given thyself over to do that which is evil in the sight of the LORD. 21 Behold, I will bring evil upon thee, and will utterly sweep thee away, and will cut off from Ahab every man-child, and him that is shut up and him that is left at large in Israel. 22 And I will make thy house like the house of Jeroboam the son of Nebat, and like the house of Baasa the son of Ahijah, for the provocation wherewith thou hast provoked Me, and hast made Israel to sin. 23 And of Jezebel also spoke the LORD, saying: The dogs shall eat Jezebel in the moat of Jezreel. 24 Him that dieth of Ahab in the city the dogs shall eat; and him that dieth in the field shall the fowls of the air eat.' 25 But there was none like unto Ahab, who did give himself over to do that which was evil in the sight of the LORD, whom Jezebel his wife stirred up. 26 And he did very abominably in following idols, according to all that the Amorites did, whom the LORD cast out before the children of Israel.

27 And it came to pass, when Ahab heard those words, that he rent his clothes, and put sackcloth upon his flesh, and fasted, and lay in sackcloth, and went softly. 28 And the word of the LORD came to Elijah the Tishbite, saying: 29 'Seest thou how

---

1. JPS 1917: "killed."

2. JPS 1917: "taken possession."

Ahab humbleth himself before Me? because he humbleth himself before Me, I will not bring the evil in his days; but in his son's
days will I bring the evil upon his house.'

C. Royal Corruption and Corruption of the People

Like Samuel, the later prophets also warn about choosing monarchs who do
not fulfill their missions properly due to their own inadequate moral priorities. In this case, the corruption is present not just in the monarchs, but also
in the people who support them.

Hosea 8:3–4, 7

3 Israel hath cast off that which is good;
The enemy shall pursue him.
4 They have set up kings, but not from Me,
They have made princes, and I knew it not;
Of their silver and their gold have they made them idols,
That they may be cut off.
. . . . .
7 For they sow the wind, and they shall reap the whirlwind;
It hath no stalk, the bud that shall yield no meal;
If so be it yield, strangers shall swallow it up.

In the midst of corruption, the job of speaking truth to power is not an
enviable one. Like Elijah at the time of King Ahab, Jeremiah is hated by the
King; unlike Elijah, Jeremiah is actually imprisoned for speaking his piece.

Jeremiah 37

1 And Zedekiah the son of Josiah reigned as king, instead of
Coniah the son of Jehoiakim, whom Nebuchadrezzar king of
Babylon made king in the land of Judah. 2 But neither he, nor
his servants, nor the people of the land, did hearken unto the
words of the LORD, which He spoke by the prophet Jeremiah.

3 And Zedekiah the king sent Jehucal the son of Shelemiah,
and Zephaniah the son of Maaseiah the priest, to the prophet
Jeremiah, saying: 'Pray now unto the LORD our God for us.'
4 Now Jeremiah came in and went out among the people; for
they had not put him into prison. 5 And Pharaoh's army was
come forth out of Egypt; and when the Chaldeans that besieged
Jerusalem heard tidings of them, they broke up from Jerusalem.

6 Then came the word of the LORD unto the prophet Jeremiah, saying: 7 'Thus saith the LORD, the God of Israel: Thus shall ye say to the king of Judah, that sent you unto Me to inquire of Me: Behold, Pharaoh's army, which is come forth to help you, shall return to Egypt into their own land. 8 And the Chaldeans shall return, and fight against this city; and they shall take it, and burn it with fire. 9 Thus saith the LORD: Deceive not yourselves, saying: The Chaldeans shall surely depart from us; for they shall not depart. 10 For though ye had smitten the whole army of the Chaldeans that fight against you, and there remained but wounded men among them, yet would they rise up every man in his tent, and burn this city with fire.'

11 And it came to pass, that when the army of the Chaldeans was broken up from Jerusalem for fear of Pharaoh's army, 12 then Jeremiah went forth out of Jerusalem to go into the land of Benjamin, to receive his portion there, in the midst of the people. 13 And when he was in the gate of Benjamin, a captain of the ward was there, whose name was Irijah, the son of Shelemiah, the son of Hananiah; and he laid hold on Jeremiah the prophet, saying: 'Thou fallest away to the Chaldeans.' 14 Then said Jeremiah: 'It is false; I fall not away to the Chaldeans'; but he hearkened not to him; so Irijah laid hold on Jeremiah, and brought him to the princes. 15 And the princes were wroth with Jeremiah, and smote him, and put him in prison in the house of Jonathan the scribe; for they had made that the prison.

16 When Jeremiah was come into the dungeon-house, and into the cells, and Jeremiah had remained there many days; 17 then Zedekiah the king sent, and fetched him; and the king asked him secretly in his house, and said: 'Is there any word from the LORD?' And Jeremiah said: 'There is.' He said also: 'Thou shalt be delivered into the hand of the king of Babylon.' 18 Moreover Jeremiah said unto king Zedekiah: 'Wherein have I sinned against thee, or against thy servants, or against this people, that ye have put me in prison? 19 Where now are your prophets that prophesied unto you, saying: The king of Babylon shall not come against you, nor against this land? 20 And now hear, I pray thee, O my lord the king: let my supplication, I pray thee, be presented before thee; that thou cause me not to return to the house of Jonathan the scribe, lest I die there.' 21 Then Zedekiah the king commanded, and they committed Jeremiah into the court of the

guard, and they gave him daily a loaf of bread out of the bakers' street, until all the bread in the city was spent. Thus Jeremiah remained in the court of the guard.

For all his political bravery, Jeremiah is not a favorite of the people, either.

Jeremiah 26

1 In the beginning of the reign of Jehoiakim the son of Josiah, king of Judah, came this word from the LORD, saying: 2 'Thus saith the LORD: Stand in the court of the LORD'S house, and speak unto all the cities of Judah, which come to worship in the LORD's house, all the words that I command thee to speak unto them; diminish not a word. 3 It may be they will hearken, and turn every man from his evil way; that I may repent Me of the evil, which I purpose to do unto them because of the evil of their doings. 4 And thou shalt say unto them: Thus saith the LORD: If ye will not hearken to Me, to walk in My law, which I have set before you, 5 to hearken to the words of My servants the prophets, whom I send unto you, even sending them betimes and often, but ye have not hearkened; 6 then will I make this house like Shiloh, and will make this city a curse to all the nations of the earth.'

7 So the priests and the prophets and all the people heard Jeremiah speaking these words in the house of the LORD. 8 Now it came to pass, when Jeremiah had made an end of speaking all that the LORD had commanded him to speak unto all the people, that the priests and the prophets and all the people laid hold on him, saying: 'Thou shalt surely die. 9 Why hast thou prophesied in the name of the LORD, saying: This house shall be like Shiloh, and this city shall be desolate, without an inhabitant?' And all the people were gathered against Jeremiah in the house of the LORD.

10 When the princes of Judah heard these things, they came up from the king's house unto the house of the LORD; and they sat in the entry of the new gate of the LORD's house. 11 Then spoke the priests and the prophets unto the princes and to all the people, saying: 'This man is worthy of death; for he hath prophesied against this city, as ye have heard with your ears.' 12 Then spoke Jeremiah unto all the princes and to all the people, saying: 'The LORD sent me to prophesy against this house and against this city all the words that ye have heard. 13

Therefore now amend your ways and your doings, and hearken to the voice of the LORD your God; and the LORD will repent Him of the evil that He hath pronounced against you. 14 But as for me, behold, I am in your hand; do with me as is good and right in your eyes. 15 Only know ye for certain that, if ye put me to death, ye will bring innocent blood upon yourselves, and upon this city, and upon the inhabitants thereof; for of a truth the LORD hath sent me unto you to speak all these words in your ears.'

16 Then said the princes and all the people unto the priests and to the prophets: 'This man is not worthy of death; for he hath spoken to us in the name of the LORD our God.' 17 Then rose up certain of the elders of the land, and spoke to all the assembly of the people, saying: 18 'Micah the Morashtite prophesied in the days of Hezekiah king of Judah; and he spoke to all the people of Judah, saying: Thus saith the LORD of hosts:

Zion shall be plowed as a field,
And Jerusalem shall become heaps,
And the mountain of the house as the high places of a forest.

19 Did Hezekiah king of Judah and all Judah put him at all to death? did he not fear the LORD, and entreat the favour of the LORD, and the LORD repented Him of the evil which He had pronounced against them? Thus might we procure great evil against our own souls.'

20 And there was also a man that prophesied in the name of the LORD, Uriah the son of Shemaiah of Kiriath-jearim; and he prophesied against this city and against this land according to all the words of Jeremiah; 21 and when Jehoiakim the king, with all his mighty men, and all the princes, heard his words, the king sought to put him to death; but when Uriah heard it, he was afraid, and fled, and went into Egypt; 22 and Jehoiakim the king sent men into Egypt, Elnathan the son of Achbor, and certain men with him, into Egypt;

23 and they fetched forth Uriah out of Egypt, and brought him unto Jehoiakim the king; who slew him with the sword, and cast his dead body into the graves of the children of the people. 24 Nevertheless the hand of Ahikam the son of Shaphan was with Jeremiah, that they should not give him into the hand of the people to put him to death.

D. Priestly Corruption

The Hebrew Bible traces the existence of corruption arising from unethical power plays even to pre-monarchical times. In the following selection, it points out the corruption of those individuals who are supposed to help the people serve God, but who instead use their positions to increase their own wealth and sense of self-importance.

I Samuel 2:12–17, 22–36

12 Now the sons of Eli were base men; they knew not the LORD. 13 And the custom of the priests with the people was, that, when any man offered sacrifice, the priest's servant came, while the flesh was in seething, with a flesh-hook of three teeth in his band; 14 and he struck it into the pan, or kettle, or caldron, or pot; all that the flesh-hook brought up the priest took therewith. So they did unto all the Israelites that came thither in Shiloh.

15 Yea, before the fat was made to smoke, the priest's servant came, and said to the man that sacrificed: 'Give flesh to roast for the priest; for he will not have sodden flesh of thee, but raw.' 16 And if the man said unto him: 'Let the fat be made to smoke first of all, and then take as much as thy soul desireth'; then he would say: 'Nay, but thou shalt give it me now; and if not, I will take it by force.'

17 And the sin of the young men was very great before the LORD; for the men dealt contemptuously with the offering of the LORD.

. . . .

22 Now Eli was very old; and he heard all that his sons did unto all Israel, and how that they lay with the women that did service at the door of the tent of meeting. 23 And he said unto them: 'Why do ye such things? for I hear evil reports concerning you from all this people. 24 Nay, my sons; for it is no good report which I hear the LORD's people do spread abroad. 25 If one man sin against another, God shall judge him; but if a man sin against the LORD, who shall entreat for him?' But they hearkened not unto the voice of their father, because the LORD would slay them. 26 And the child Samuel grew on, and increased in favour both with the LORD, and also with men.

27 And there came a man of God unto Eli, and said unto him: 'Thus saith the LORD: Did I reveal Myself unto the house of thy father, when they were in Egypt in bondage to Pharaoh's house? 28 And did I choose him out of all the tribes of Israel to be My priest, to go up unto Mine altar, to burn incense, to wear an ephod before Me? and did I give unto the house of thy father all the offerings of the children of Israel made by fire? 29 Wherefore kick ye at My sacrifice and at Mine offering, which I have commanded in My habitation; and honourest thy sons above Me, to make yourselves fat with the chiefest of all the offerings of Israel My people?

30 Therefore the LORD, the God of Israel, saith: I said indeed that thy house, and the house of thy father, should walk before Me for ever; but now the LORD saith: Be it far from Me: for them that honour Me I will honour, and they that despise Me shall be lightly esteemed. 31 Behold, the days come, that I will cut off thine arm, and the arm of thy father's house, that there shall not be an old man in thy house. 32 And thou shalt behold a rival in My habitation, in all the good which shall be done to Israel; and there shall not be an old man in thy house for ever. 33 Yet will I not cut off every man of thine from Mine altar, to make thine eyes to fail, and thy heart to languish; and all the increase of thy house shall die young men.

34 And this shall be the sign unto thee, that which shall come upon thy two sons, on Hophni and Phinehas: in one day they shall die both of them. 35 And I will raise Me up a faithful priest, that shall do according to that which is in My heart and in My mind; and I will build him a sure house; and he shall walk before Mine anointed for ever. 36 And it shall come to pass, that every one that is left in thy house shall come and bow down to him for a piece of silver and a loaf of bread, and shall say: Put me, I pray thee, into one of the priests' offices, that I may eat a morsel of bread.'

I Samuel 3:11–14

11 And the LORD said to Samuel: 'Behold, I will do a thing in Israel, at which both the ears of every one that heareth it shall tingle. 12 In that day I will perform against Eli all that I have spoken concerning his house, from the beginning even unto the end.

13 For I have told him that I will judge his house for ever, for the iniquity, in that he knew that his sons did bring a curse upon themselves, and he rebuked them not. 14 And therefore I have sworn unto the house of Eli, that the iniquity of Eli's house shall not be expiated with sacrifice nor offering for ever.'

E. Corruption of Prophets

In addition to dealing with the animosity of the royal court, and of the ordinary people who do not want to hear his prophecies of doom, Jeremiah inveighs against the more reassuring messages of the false prophets. The contemporary reader is sensitive to the horror that shines through Jeremiah's words: the false prophets are people who knew better than to spread false hope, but who choose to lie to their communities in order to keep their positions of comfort and honor. The image of the false shepherd is key to Jeremiah's various analyses of political corruption, and inversely calls to mind King David, the faithful guardian of his family's sheep at the time of his anointing as king.

Jeremiah 23:1–6, 11–40

1 Woe unto the shepherds that destroy and scatter

The sheep of My pasture! saith the LORD.

2 Therefore thus saith the LORD, the God of Israel, against the shepherds that feed My people: Ye have scattered My flock, and driven them away, and have not taken care of them; behold, I will visit upon you the evil of your doings, saith the LORD. 3 And I will gather the remnant of My flock out of all the countries whither I have driven them, and will bring them back to their folds; and they shall be fruitful and multiply. 4 And I will set up shepherds over them, who shall feed them; and they shall fear no more, nor be dismayed, neither shall any be lacking, saith the LORD.

5 Behold, the days come, saith the LORD, that I will raise unto David a righteous shoot, and he shall reign as king and prosper, and shall execute justice and righteousness in the land.

6 In his days Judah shall be saved, and Israel shall dwell safely; and this is his name whereby he shall be called, The LORD is our righteousness.

. . . .

11 For both prophet and priest are ungodly;
Yea, in My house have I found their wickedness,
Saith the LORD.
12 Wherefore their way shall be unto them as slippery places in
the darkness,
They shall be thrust, and fall therein;
For I will bring evil upon them,
Even the year of their visitation,
Saith the LORD.
13 And I have seen unseemliness in the prophets of Samaria:
They prophesied by Baal,
And caused My people Israel to err.
14 But in the prophets of Jerusalem I have seen a horrible thing:
They commit adultery, and walk in lies,
And they strengthen the hands of evil-doers,
That none doth return from his wickedness;
They are all of them become unto Me as Sodom,
And the inhabitants thereof as Gomorrah.
15 Therefore thus saith the LORD of hosts concerning the
prophets:
Behold, I will feed them with wormwood,
And make them drink the water of gall;
For from the prophets of Jerusalem
Is ungodliness gone forth into all the land.
16 Thus saith the LORD of hosts:
Hearken not unto the words of the prophets that prophesy unto
you,
They lead you unto vanity;
They speak a vision of their own heart,
And not out of the mouth of the LORD.
17 They say continually unto them that despise Me:
'The LORD hath said: Ye shall have peace';
And unto every one that walketh in the stubbornness of his own
heart they say:
'No evil shall come upon you';
18 For who hath stood in the council of the LORD,
That he should perceive and hear His word?
Who hath attended to His word, and heard it?
19 Behold, a storm of the LORD is gone forth in fury,
Yea, a whirling storm;

It shall whirl upon the head of the wicked.
20 The anger of the LORD shall not return,
Until He have executed, and till He have performed the purposes
    of His heart;
In the end of days ye shall consider it perfectly.
21 I have not sent these prophets, yet they ran;
I have not spoken to them, yet they prophesied.
22 But if they have stood in My council,
Then let them cause My people to hear My words, And turn
    them from their evil way,
And from the evil of their doings.
23 Am I a God near at hand, saith the LORD,
And not a God afar off?
24 Can any hide himself in secret places
That I shall not see him? saith the LORD.
Do not I fill heaven and earth?
Saith the LORD.
25 I have heard what the prophets have said,
That prophesy lies in My name, saying:
'I have dreamed, I have dreamed.'
26 How long shall this be?
Is it in the heart of the prophets that prophesy lies,
And the prophets of the deceit of their own heart?
27 That think to cause My people to forget My name
By their dreams which they tell every man to his neighbour,
As their fathers forgot My name for Baal.
28 The prophet that hath a dream, let him tell a dream;
And he that hath My word; let him speak My word faithfully.
What hath the straw to do with the wheat?
Saith the LORD.
29 Is not My word like as fire?
Saith the LORD;
And like a hammer that breaketh the rock in pieces?

30 Therefore, behold, I am against the prophets, saith the
LORD, that steal My words every one from his neighbour. 31
Behold, I am against the prophets, saith the LORD, that use
their tongues and say: 'He saith.' 32 Behold, I am against them
that prophesy lying dreams, saith the LORD, and do tell them,
and cause My people to err by their lies, and by their wantonness; yet I sent them not, nor commanded them; neither can they
profit this people at all, saith the LORD.

33 And when this people, or the prophet, or a priest, shall ask thee, saying: 'What is the burden of the LORD?' then shalt thou say unto them: 'What burden! I will cast you off, saith the LORD.' 34 And as for the prophet, and the priest, and the people, that shall say: 'The burden of the LORD', I will even punish that man and his house. 35 Thus shall ye say every one to his neighbour, and every one to his brother: 'What hath the LORD answered?' and: 'What hath the LORD spoken?' 36 And the burden of the LORD shall ye mention no more; for every man's own word shall be his burden; and would ye pervert the words of the living God, of the LORD of hosts our God? 37 Thus shalt thou say to the prophet: 'What hath the LORD answered thee?' and: 'What hath the LORD spoken?' 38 But if ye say: 'The burden of the LORD'; therefore thus saith the LORD: Because ye say this word: 'The burden of the LORD', and I have sent unto you, saying: 'Ye shall not say: The burden of the LORD'; 39 therefore, behold, I will utterly tear you out, and I will cast you off, and the city that I gave unto you and to your fathers, away from My presence; 40 and I will bring an everlasting reproach upon you, and a perpetual shame, which shall not be forgotten.

The prophecy of Ezekiel describes the final liberation in which God will wipe out the obscurity of falsehood that masquerades as truth, and when the word of God will be clear to all listeners.

Ezekiel 13:3–12

3 Thus saith the Lord GOD: Woe unto the vile prophets, that follow their own spirit, and things which they have not seen! 4 O Israel, thy prophets have been like foxes in ruins. 5 Ye have not gone up into the breaches, neither made up the hedge for the house of Israel, to stand in the battle in the day of the LORD. 6 They have seen vanity and lying divination, that say: The LORD saith; and the LORD hath not sent them, yet they hope that the word would be confirmed! 7 Have ye not seen a vain vision, and have ye not spoken a lying divination, whereas ye say: The LORD saith; albeit I have not spoken?

8 Therefore thus saith the Lord GOD: Because ye have spoken vanity, and seen lies, therefore, behold, I am against you, saith the Lord GOD. 9 And My hand shall be against the prophets that see vanity, and that divine lies; they shall not be in the council of My people, neither shall they be written in the register

of the house of Israel, neither shall they enter into the land of Israel; and ye shall know that I am the Lord GOD. 10 Because, even because they have led My people astray, saying: Peace, and there is no peace; and when it buildeth up a slight wall, behold, they daub it with whited plaster; 11 say unto them that daub it with whited plaster, that it shall fall; there shall be an overflowing shower, and ye, O great hailstones, shall fall, and a stormy wind shall break forth, 12 and, lo, when the wall is fallen, shall it not be said unto you: Where is the daubing wherewith ye have daubed it?

CHAPTER 15

STANDING UP FOR THE ISRAELITES

For the Hebrew Bible, leadership does not mean what was commonly assumed by its bearers in the ancient world—that is, the appropriation of privilege. On the contrary, the good leader stands up for his people, even if it means prophesying against the monarch, or arguing with God. God values this aspect of true leadership, to the point that God is portrayed as removing the prophetic leadership from Elijah and directing him to deliver it to Elisha for just that reason (I Kings 19:13–16).

This aspect of faithful leadership is apparent from the very inception of Israelite nationhood. Shortly after the Theophany on Mount Sinai, the Israelites (not knowing the whereabouts of their leader, Moses) create an idol (the Golden Calf) and begin to worship it. God responds by telling Moses that He will destroy the backsliders and build a new nation from Moses. If a leader sees himself as crucial to a people's existence, God's solution makes eminent sense: on a purely functional level, creating a nation out of "good" material is infinitely more rational than continuing to work with "the crooked timber of humanity."[1] Moses, however, declines to argue with God on the grounds of efficiency. He simply responds with prayer, and also a rejoinder.

A. The Cases of Moses and Elijah

In the following selection, Moses makes it clear that he sees for himself no destiny as a leader apart from his association with the Israelites as they are, not as they might be.

Exodus 32:9–14, 31–32

9 And the LORD said unto Moses: 'I have seen this people, and, behold, it is a stiffnecked people. 10 Now therefore let Me

---

1. Kant writes, "Out of the crooked timber of humanity, no straight thing was ever made" ("Idea for a Universal History with a Cosmopolitan Intent"; Prop. 6). Taken to its ultimate conclusion, this would preclude the achievement of moral perfection on the human level. This is indeed the point: human beings may not achieve perfection, but they do inspire change and improvement. For Kant, ultimately, this is where the achievements of the Enlightenment rest ("What Is Enlightenment?").

alone, that My wrath may wax hot against them, and that I may consume them; and I will make of thee a great nation.'

11 And Moses besought the LORD his God, and said: 'LORD, why doth Thy wrath wax hot against Thy people, that Thou hast brought forth out of the land of Egypt with great power and with a mighty hand? 12 Wherefore should the Egyptians speak, saying: For evil did He bring them forth, to slay them in the mountains, and to consume them from the face of the earth? Turn from Thy fierce wrath, and repent of this evil against Thy people. 13 Remember Abraham, Isaac, and Israel, Thy servants, to whom Thou didst swear by Thine own self, and saidst unto them: I will multiply your seed as the stars of heaven, and all this land that I have spoken of will I give unto your seed, and they shall inherit it for ever.'

14 And the LORD repented of the evil which He said He would do unto His people.

. . . .

31 And Moses returned unto the LORD, and said: 'Oh, this people have sinned a great sin, and have made them a god of gold. 32 Yet now, if Thou wilt forgive their sin—; and if not, blot me, I pray Thee, out of Thy book which Thou hast written.'

The following selection takes place after the Israelites, disappointed with the majority report of the spies after their quick excursion to the Promised Land, want to appoint a new leader and return to the land they already know: Egypt.

Numbers 14:11–20

11 And the LORD said unto Moses: 'How long will this people despise Me? and how long will they not believe in Me, for all the signs which I have wrought among them? 12 I will smite them with the pestilence, and destroy them, and will make of thee a nation greater and mightier than they.'

13 And Moses said unto the LORD: 'When the Egyptians shall hear—for Thou broughtest up this people in Thy might from among them— 14 they will say to the inhabitants of this land, who have heard that Thou LORD art in the midst of this people; inasmuch as Thou LORD art seen face to face, and Thy cloud standeth over them, and Thou goest before them, in a pillar of cloud by day, and in a pillar of fire by night; 15 now if Thou

shalt kill this people as one man, then the nations which have heard the fame of Thee will speak, saying: 16 Because the LORD was not able to bring this people into the land which He swore unto them, therefore He hath slain them in the wilderness.

17 And now, I pray Thee, let the power of the Lord be great, according as Thou hast spoken, saying: 18 The LORD is slow to anger, and plenteous in lovingkindness, forgiving iniquity and transgression, and that will by no means clear the guilty; visiting the iniquity of the fathers upon the children, upon the third and upon the fourth generation.19 Pardon, I pray Thee, the iniquity of this people according unto the greatness of Thy lovingkindness, and according as Thou hast forgiven this people, from Egypt even until now.'

20 And the LORD said: 'I have pardoned according to thy word.'

Unlike Moses, the prophet Elijah, faced with idolatrous Israelites in the Northern Kingdom many years later, does not combine this recognition of moral wrongdoing on the part of the people with a desire to protect them. As a result, Elijah is required to hand over to Elisha the mantle of leadership as a national prophet.

I Kings 19:9–16

9 And he[2] came thither unto a cave, and lodged there; and, behold, the word of the LORD came to him, and He said unto him: 'What doest thou here, Elijah?' 10 And he said: 'I have been very jealous for the LORD, the God of hosts; for the children of Israel have forsaken Thy covenant, thrown down Thine altars, and slain Thy prophets with the sword; and I, even I only, am left; and they seek my life, to take it away.'

11 And He said: 'Go forth, and stand upon the mount before the LORD.' And, behold, the LORD passed by, and a great and strong wind rent the mountains, and broke in pieces the rocks before the LORD; but the LORD was not in the wind; and after the wind an earthquake; but the LORD was not in the earthquake; 12 and after the earthquake a fire; but the LORD was not in the fire; and after the fire a still small voice.

13 And it was so, when Elijah heard it, that he wrapped his face in his mantle, and went out, and stood in the entrance of the

---

2. Elijah.

cave. And, behold, there came a voice unto him, and said: 'What doest thou here, Elijah?' 14 And he said: 'I have been very jealous for the LORD, the God of hosts; for the children of Israel have forsaken Thy covenant, thrown down Thine altars, and slain Thy prophets with the sword; and I, even I only, am left; and they seek my life, to take it away.'

15 And the LORD said unto him: 'Go, return on thy way to the wilderness of Damascus; and when thou comest, thou shalt anoint Hazael to be king over Aram; 16 and Jehu the son of Nimshi shalt thou anoint to be king over Israel; and Elisha the son of Shaphat of Abel-meholah shalt thou anoint to be prophet in your place.[3]

B. The Plea of Amos

In its presentation of the troubled relationship between idolatrous Israelites and an angry, or disappointed, God who desires their fealty, the Hebrew Bible seems at times to hold out little hope for a workable solution that might avoid the punishment of exile and the concomitant threat of national oblivion. Interestingly, the prophet Amos holds forth another possibility for God: to act primarily not as a vengeful or angry God, but as a God concerned about His people, even if they do sin. Amos argues: If God mows down the people even if that is what "justice" demands, how will the Israelites survive? For they are small. And God agrees.

Amos 7:1–6

1 Thus the Lord GOD showed me; and, behold, He formed locusts in the beginning of the shooting up of the latter growth; and, lo, it was the latter growth after the king's mowings. 2 And if it had come to pass, that when they had made an end of eating the grass of the land—so I said:

O Lord GOD, forgive, I beseech Thee;
How shall Jacob stand? for he is small.

3 The LORD repented concerning this; 'It shall not be', saith the LORD.

4 Thus the Lord GOD showed me; and, behold, the Lord GOD called to contend by fire; and it devoured the great deep, and would have eaten up the land. 5 Then said I:

---

3. JPS 1917: "your room."

O Lord GOD, cease, I beseech Thee;
How shall Jacob stand? for he is small.

6 The LORD repented concerning this; 'This also shall not be',
saith the Lord GOD.

But prophesizing doom carries with it its own politically negative repercussions. And so Amos is advised to keep quiet: he receives the prophecy, but he does not publicize it, itself a source of tension.

Amos 7:7–16

7 Thus He showed me; and, behold, the Lord stood beside a
wall made by a plumbline, with a plumbline in His hand. 8 And
the LORD said unto me: 'Amos, what seest thou?' And I said: 'A
plumbline.' Then said the Lord:

Behold, I will set a plumbline in the midst of My people Israel;
I will not again pardon them any more;
9 And the high places of Isaac shall be desolate,
And the sanctuaries of Israel shall be laid waste;
And I will rise against the house of Jeroboam with the sword.

10 Then Amaziah the priest of Beth-el sent to Jeroboam king
of Israel, saying: 'Amos hath conspired against thee in the midst
of the house of Israel; the land is not able to bear all his words.
11 For thus Amos saith:

Jeroboam[4] shall die by the sword,
And Israel shall surely be led away captive out of his land.'

12 Also Amaziah said unto Amos: 'O thou seer, go, flee thee
away into the land of Judah, and there eat bread, and prophesy
there; 13 but prophesy not again any more at Beth-el, for it is the
king's sanctuary, and it is a royal house.'

14 Then answered Amos, and said to Amaziah: 'I was no
prophet, neither was I a prophet's son; but I was a herdman, and
a dresser of sycamore-trees; 15 and the LORD took me from
following the flock, and the LORD said unto me: Go, prophesy
unto My people Israel. 16 Now therefore hear thou the word of
the LORD:

Thou sayest: Prophesy not against Israel,
And preach not against the house of Isaac;

---

4. Jeroboam II of the Northern Kingdom.

CHAPTER 16

HUMAN RIGHTS AND SECULARISM IN THE HEBREW BIBLE

The selections in this chapter build on the Hebrew Bible's recognition that justice must exist in society for it to function well. Moreover, biblical justice demands what we have come to envision as human rights—namely, the ability of each human being to make claims regarding equity between rich and poor, citizen and stranger, enemy and friend, etc. (Chapter 7)—even if the Hebrew Bible does not explicitly refer to them either as "rights" or as inherent in the individual; functionally, as we have seen, they generally operate both as rights and as inherent within the individual. Contrary to what might be negatively viewed as the absence of the institutionalization of human-rights enforcement, the Hebrew Bible insists that linking human rights to a particular set of institutional or organizational requirements would weaken the moral centrality of human rights in the lives of each individual (cf. the parallel argument regarding systematization in the Introduction to this volume, "Freedom without Systematization" pp. lxi–lxiii). Human rights, as understood by the Hebrew Bible, depend on the moral autonomy of each individual, which itself implies that each person must recognize the social implications of actions—even those which might, at least in twenty-first–century understandings, seem to be wholly personal in nature. In its evaluation of the moral complexities of individual and society interaction, the Hebrew Bible is cognizant of the multiple contexts of human activity.

The Hebrew Bible insists on squarely facing the complications of real life, including the need to reconcile what often appear to be competing values, when engaging in the kind of practical judgment needed to lead a fully realized moral life. This insistence is also evident in its consideration of what are often seen, particularly in the modern world, as the contrasting values of religious piety and moral humanism (conventionally identified with secularism). The Hebrew Bible refuses such moral dualism: on the contrary, it insists that outward piety alone, without true consideration for other human beings as the creations of God, is both impious and anti-humanistic ("For they proceed from evil to evil, / And Me they know not, / Saith the LORD." [Jeremiah 9:2]).

As already seen in the Introduction to this volume, the notion of secularism in the Hebrew Bible does not follow the conventional dualistic understanding of this concept. Rather, secularism as construed by the Hebrew Bible insists on both social and moral connectivity as well as an awareness of the Divine (which necessarily imposes limitations on human self-willed activity). Levinas' linkage of the "other" of human solidarity and the Divine Other that elicits human awe mirrors this complex position of the Hebrew Bible: its rejection of the arbitrariness of power, whether individual, social, ritualistic, or political. In that sense, the Hebrew Bible valorizes secularism not (as in more contemporary understandings of this term) as excising the Divine from public life, but rather as refusing to use religion and religious posturing to determine matters of political import. In what can be seen as a paradoxical statement, secularism in the Hebrew Bible implies not an estrangement from God, but an intimate acknowledgment of the Divine. This is what allows dignity to be attributed to all people, transcending the boundaries of socio-economic status and social recognition, and encompassing even the finality of death (Deuteronomy 21:1–9).

The first selection in this chapter expands upon the moral autonomy inherent in each individual, regardless of family status.

A. Personal Responsibility, Moral Autonomy, and Social Context

1. Personal Responsibility

A stereotype regarding the Hebrew Bible is that its moral directives unequivocally subordinate personal responsibility to collective and generational responsibility, be it that of the Israelites as a whole, a particular tribe, or a family within that nation. In contemporary popular culture, "the sins of the fathers are visited on their sons" (a paraphrastic allusion to Exodus 20:5, Deuteronomy 5:9, and Exodus 34:6–7) is often cited proverbially to evoke a sense of collective and even inherited responsibility for past misdeeds. Yet, as shown in the selections below, the Hebrew Bible includes verses with a countervailing message as well. Whatever the concrete effects of one's sin on subsequent generations, it is clear that personal responsibility before God is a major biblical leitmotif.

Deuteronomy 24:16

16 The fathers shall not be put to death for the children, neither shall the children be put to death for the fathers; every man shall be put to death for his own sin.

The following selection from the prophecy of Ezekiel reveals a more complex dialogue, in which the interlocutor wants to know why the interconnected nature of social structures—the family, for example—does not influence the accounting of moral responsibility. In that context, the question of time comes up: What happens when the iniquitous person begins to act in a moral fashion? Is he still caught within the traces of his past immorality? To these questions, the Hebrew biblical text answers that social connectedness is not, of itself, a justification for punishment; neither does history cast a pall over all future actions (a moral approach different from the ancient Greek understanding of the inexorable pull of fate). In all cases, the principle of individual moral responsibility prevails.

Ezekiel 18:21–23

21 But if the wicked turn from all his sins that he hath committed, and keep all My statutes, and do that which is lawful and right, he shall surely live, he shall not die.

22 None of his transgressions that he hath committed shall be remembered against him; for his righteousness that he hath done he shall live.

23 Have I any pleasure at all that the wicked should die? saith the Lord GOD; and not rather that he should return from his ways, and live?

2. Social Responsibility

Still, the Hebrew Bible does not confuse individual moral responsibility and autonomy with moral isolation. The Israelites are united in destiny, and cannot exempt themselves from the less comfortable aspects of what it means to be part of a nation and community. In the (slightly emended) words of John Donne, no human being is an island.

Deuteronomy 29:9–10, 13–20

9 Ye are standing this day all of you before the LORD your God: your heads, your tribes, your elders, and your officers, even all the men of Israel,

10 your little ones, your wives, and thy stranger that is in the midst of thy camp, from the hewer of thy wood unto the drawer of thy water; 11 that thou shouldest enter into the covenant of the LORD thy God—and into His oath—which the LORD thy God maketh with thee this day;

. . . .

13 Neither with you only do I make this covenant and this oath;
14 but with him that standeth here with us this day before the

LORD our God, and also with him that is not here with us this day—15 for ye know how we dwelt in the land of Egypt; and how we came through the midst of the nations through which ye passed; 16 and ye have seen their detestable things, and their idols, wood and stone, silver and gold, which were with them—

17 lest there should be among you man, or woman, or family, or tribe, whose heart turneth away this day from the LORD our God, to go to serve the gods of those nations; lest there should be among you a root that beareth gall and wormwood;

18 and it come to pass, when he heareth the words of this curse, that he bless himself in his heart, saying: 'I shall have peace, though I walk in the stubbornness of my heart—that the watered be swept away with the dry';

19 the LORD will not be willing to pardon him, but then the anger of the LORD and His jealousy shall be kindled against that man, and all the curse that is written in this book shall lie upon him, and the LORD shall blot out his name from under heaven;

20 and the LORD shall separate him unto evil out of all the tribes of Israel, according to all the curses of the covenant that is written in this book of the law.

a. Responsibility towards Strangers

The verses in a selection below (Exodus 22:1–8) focus on the ability to depend on the honesty and accountability of one's fellow citizens: that they not steal your animals or crops when you are not looking, that they not set fire to your field (however unintentionally), and so on.

In addition, there is another level of social responsibility highlighted in the texts of the Hebrew Bible. What does one owe to a stranger in need of help? What if that person is already dead? Can a social debt be said to exist merely by virtue of one's placement within a society? Contemporary readers may wonder: Why is there an implication of social guilt in the discovery of the corpse of a slain man who is anonymous and perhaps even unidentifiable (Deuteronomy 21: 7–9)?

Deuteronomy 21:1–9

1 If one be found slain in the land which the LORD thy God giveth thee to possess it, lying in the field, and it be not known who hath smitten him; 2 then thy elders and thy judges shall

come forth, and they shall measure unto the cities which are round about him that is slain.

3 And it shall be, that the city which is nearest unto the slain man, even the elders of that city shall take a heifer of the herd, which hath not been wrought with, and which hath not drawn in the yoke. 4 And the elders of that city shall bring down the heifer unto a rough valley, which may neither be plowed nor sown, and shall break the heifer's neck there in the valley.

5 And the priests the sons of Levi shall come near—for them the LORD thy God hath chosen to minister unto Him, and to bless in the name of the LORD; and according to their word shall every controversy and every stroke be. 6 And all the elders of that city, who are nearest unto the slain man, shall wash their hands over the heifer whose neck was broken in the valley. 7 And they shall speak and say: 'Our hands have not shed this blood, neither have our eyes seen it. 8 Forgive, O LORD, Thy people Israel, whom Thou hast redeemed, and suffer not innocent blood to remain in the midst of Thy people Israel.' And the blood shall be forgiven them.

9 So shalt thou put away the innocent blood from the midst of thee, when thou shalt do that which is right in the eyes of the LORD.

3. Moral Context

What does community identity and responsibility mean? The Hebrew Bible gives concrete meaning to those abstract terms.

Exodus 22:1–8

1 If a thief be found breaking in, and be smitten so that he dieth, there shall be no bloodguiltiness for him. 2 If the sun be risen upon him, there shall be bloodguiltiness for him—he shall make restitution; if he have nothing, then he shall be sold for his theft. 3 If the theft be found in his hand alive, whether it be ox, or ass, or sheep, he shall pay double.

4 If a man cause a field or vineyard to be eaten, and shall let his beast loose, and it feed in another man's field; of the best of his own field, and of the best of his own vineyard, shall he make restitution.

5 If fire break out, and catch in thorns, so that the shocks of corn, or the standing corn, or the field are consumed; he that kindled the fire shall surely make restitution.

6 If a man deliver unto his neighbour money or stuff to keep, and it be stolen out of the man's house; if the thief be found, he shall pay double. 7 If the thief be not found, then the master of the house shall come near unto God,[1] to see whether he have not put his hand unto his neighbour's goods. 8 For every matter of trespass, whether it be for ox, for ass, for sheep, for raiment, or for any manner of lost thing, whereof one saith: 'This is it,' the cause of both parties shall come before God; he whom God shall condemn shall pay double unto his neighbour.

In the following selection, Jeremiah portrays the obverse of social responsibility: he wishes to live in the actual wilderness rather than dwell in the wasteland of lies that destroys social comity. Contemporary readers may wonder about the logical connections presented in this text, linking the excess of selfishness, the destruction of society, and the perceived distance from God.

Jeremiah 9:1–8

1 Oh that I were in the wilderness,
In a lodging-place of wayfaring men,
That I might leave my people,
And go from them!
For they are all adulterers,
An assembly of treacherous men.
2 And they bend their tongue, their bow of falsehood;
And they are grown mighty in the land, but not for truth;
For they proceed from evil to evil,
And Me they know not,
Saith the LORD.
3 Take ye heed every one of his neighbour,
And trust ye not in any brother;
For every brother acteth subtly,
And every neighbour goeth about with slanders.
4 And they deceive every one his neighbour,
And truth they speak not;
They have taught their tongue to speak lies,
They weary themselves to commit iniquity.

---

1. [[That is, the judges.—JPS 1917 eds.]]

5 Thy habitation is in the midst of deceit;
Through deceit they refuse to know Me,
Saith the LORD.
6 Therefore thus saith the LORD of hosts:
Behold, I will smelt them, and try them;
For how else should I do,
Because of the daughter of My people?
7 Their tongue is a sharpened arrow,
It speaketh deceit;
One speaketh peaceably to his neighbour with his mouth,
But in his heart he layeth wait for him.
8 Shall I not punish them for these things?
Saith the LORD;
Shall not My soul be avenged
On such a nation as this?

The Hebrew Bible's implicit recognition of human rights as an outgrowth of human identity as opposed to religious piety is rooted in its characterization of all of humanity from its inception as created in the image of God (Genesis 1:27). It also underlies the Later Prophets' call for social justice as an inextricable part of what it means to adhere to God's plan for humanity in general, and for the Israelites in particular.

The Later Prophets' juxtaposition of the Israelites' punctilious observance of religious law with their flagrant dehumanization of their fellows has led some readers to conclude that the Hebrew Bible itself promotes human rights above religious adherence. This attitude has inspired its own defenders but neglects important nuances of the Hebrew biblical text. The Later Prophets' call for decency as a matrix for treating all human beings (cf. Jeremiah 9:2) specifically links "man's inhumanity to man" with a dearth of true belief in God. The Hebrew biblical prophets knew well that it is much easier to flaunt observance of religious minutiae, claiming that to be a sign of true righteousness, than to treat all human beings with the dignity that they deserve. Treating other human beings with dignity because it is the right thing to do is much harder on a long-term basis than "doing good" out of a desire for a reputation of self-ennobling distinction.[2] For the Hebrew Bible, just behavior towards all human beings, as well as practicing a life of religious fealty, are both crucial to the service of God and necessary for full moral expression as a human being.

---

2. Socrates has Glaucon make a similar point in his *Republic* (ed. Cornford, New York: Oxford University Press, pp. 43–47).

B. Does the Hebrew Bible Promote Justice above Religious Fealty?

Although the Hebrew Bible is most often classified as a parochial text, it emphasizes moral teachings that apply across the board to all human beings, and does not privilege a fellowship of religion above the human kindness that is owed to all human beings equally. Similarly, the Hebrew Bible does not endorse using religion as an automatic marker of moral probity (attendance at prayers or rituals is not a "get out of jail free" card; see Jeremiah 7:2–4). Decency and difference (see Jethro [Exodus 18:13–27] and Ruth [chap. 1–4]) are welcomed together.

For contemporary readers of the Hebrew Bible, the words of Amos, rejecting religious ritual that is empty of moral content, is often confused with understanding the prophet as rejecting religious ritual as such. Rather, Amos is making an important logical and moral argument: injustice cannot coexist with true faith, even if the outward details of ritual are obsessively pursued. Amos tells the Israelites that God is not as easily confused as themselves or as their neighbors, in front of whom they posture.

Amos 5:15, 21–24

15 Hate the evil, and love the good,
And establish justice in the gate;
It may be that the LORD, the God of hosts,
Will be gracious unto the remnant of Joseph.

. . . .

21 I hate, I despise your feasts,
And I will take no delight in your solemn assemblies.
22 Yea, though ye offer me burnt-offerings and your meal-
offerings,
I will not accept them;
Neither will I regard the peace-offerings of your fat beasts.
23 Take thou away from Me the noise of thy songs;
And let Me not hear the melody of thy psalteries.
24 But let justice well up as waters,
And righteousness as a mighty stream.

A similar message is expressed in the following selection from Hosea.

Hosea 6:6–7

6 For I desire mercy, and not sacrifice,
And the knowledge of God rather than burnt-offerings.

7 But they like men have transgressed the covenant;
There have they dealt treacherously against Me.

Micah's message is similar. In this selection, Micah recalls how enemies in the past—like Balak and Bil'am, who wanted to curse the Israelites—utilized the trappings of religious ritual for nefarious purposes. This is the context in which Micah compares the soulless rituals of the Israelites in this text. His message is that true belief requires humble action rooted in faith, not in social posturing before others.

Micah 6:5–8

5 O My people, remember now what Balak king of Moab devised,
And what Balaam the son of Beor answered him;
From Shittim unto Gilgal,
That ye may know the righteous acts of the LORD.
6 'Wherewith shall I come before the LORD,
And bow myself before God on high?
Shall I come before Him with burnt-offerings,
With calves of a year old?
7 Will the LORD be pleased with thousands of rams,
With ten thousands of rivers of oil?
Shall I give my first-born for my transgression,
The fruit of my body for the sin of my soul?'
8 It hath been told thee, O man, what is good,
And what the LORD doth require of thee:
Only to do justly, and to love mercy, and to walk humbly with
   thy God.

Malachi portrays God as being tired of this hypocrisy: What religious or moral value is there in the man who can abandon the wife of his youth for selfish companionship? Scholastic argumentation—"proving" that evil is good (verse 17 below)—is not confused by God for real service of the Divine. For the Hebrew Bible, immorality in one's own actions results in injustice that affects all of society.

Malachi 2:13–17

13 And this further ye do:
Ye cover the altar of the LORD with tears,
With weeping, and with sighing,
Insomuch that He regardeth not the offering any more,
Neither receiveth it with good will at your hand.
14 Yet ye say: 'Wherefore?'

Because the LORD hath been witness
Between thee and the wife of thy youth,
Against whom thou hast dealt treacherously,
Though she is thy companion,
And the wife of thy covenant.
15 And not one hath done so
Who had exuberance of spirit!
For what seeketh the one?
A seed given of God.
Therefore take heed to your spirit,
And let none deal treacherously against the wife of his youth.
16 For I hate putting away,
Saith the LORD, the God of Israel,
And him that covereth his garment with violence,
Saith the LORD of hosts;
Therefore take heed to your spirit,
That ye deal not treacherously.
17 Ye have wearied the LORD with your words.
Yet ye say: 'Wherein have we wearied Him?'
In that ye say: 'Every one that doeth evil
Is good in the sight of the LORD,
And He delighteth in them;
Or where is the God of justice?'

Likewise, the words of the prophet Jeremiah warn that God is not deceived by hypocritical words of outward religiosity and clinging to ritual. Rather, says Jeremiah, be just to each other (verse 5 below) and treat the marginalized members of society fairly (verse 6), if you want to continue living in the Promised Land. Otherwise, cautions the prophet to his interlocutors, be aware that God is not fooled by religious and moral hypocrisy: the fetishized object (the Temple) will not save the sinning Israelites and will itself be destroyed.

Jeremiah 7:1–5

1 The word that came to Jeremiah from the LORD, saying: 2 Stand in the gate of the LORD'S house, and proclaim there this word, and say: Hear the word of the LORD, all ye of Judah, that enter in at these gates to worship the LORD.

3 Thus saith the LORD of hosts, the God of Israel:

Amend your ways and your doings, and I will cause you to dwell in this place. 4 Trust ye not in lying words, saying: 'The temple of the LORD, the temple of the LORD, the temple of the LORD, are these.'

5 Nay, but if ye thoroughly amend your ways and your doings; if ye thoroughly execute justice between a man and his neighbour; 6 if ye oppress not the stranger, the fatherless, and the widow, and shed not innocent blood in this place, neither walk after other gods to your hurt; 7 then will I cause you to dwell in this place, in the land that I gave to your fathers, for ever and ever.

8 Behold, ye trust in lying words, that cannot profit. 9 Will ye steal, murder, and commit adultery, and swear falsely, and offer unto Baal, and walk after other gods whom ye have not known, 10 and come and stand before Me in this house, whereupon My name is called, and say: 'We are delivered', that ye may do all these abominations?

11 Is this house, whereupon My name is called, become a den of robbers in your eyes? Behold, I, even I, have seen it, saith the LORD. 12 For go ye now unto My place which was in Shiloh, where I caused My name to dwell at the first, and see what I did to it for the wickedness of My people Israel.

13 And now, because ye have done all these works, saith the LORD, and I spoke unto you, speaking betimes and often, but ye heard not, and I called you, but ye answered not; 14 therefore will I do unto the house, whereupon My name is called, wherein ye trust, and unto the place which I gave to you and to your fathers, as I have done to Shiloh. 15 And I will cast you out of My sight, as I have cast out all your brethren, even the whole seed of Ephraim.

Isaiah proclaims a similar message in the following selection.

Isaiah 58:1–8

1 Cry aloud, spare not,
Lift up thy voice like a horn,
And declare unto My people their transgression,
And to the house of Jacob their sins.
2 Yet they seek Me daily,
And delight to know My ways;
As a nation that did righteousness,
And forsook not the ordinance of their God,
They ask of Me righteous ordinances,

They delight to draw near unto God.

3 'Wherefore have we fasted, and Thou seest not?

Wherefore have we afflicted our soul, and Thou takest no knowledge?'—

Behold, in the day of your fast ye pursue your business,

And exact all your labours.

4 Behold, ye fast for strife and contention,

And to smite with the fist of wickedness;

Ye fast not this day

So as to make your voice to be heard on high.

5 Is such the fast that I have chosen?

The day for a man to afflict his soul?

Is it to bow down his head as a bulrush,

And to spread sackcloth and ashes under him?

Wilt thou call this a fast,

And an acceptable day to the LORD?

6 Is not this the fast that I have chosen?

To loose the fetters of wickedness,

To undo the bands of the yoke,

And to let the oppressed go free,

And that ye break every yoke?

7 Is it not to deal thy bread to the hungry,

And that thou bring the poor that are cast out to thy house?

When thou seest the naked, that thou cover him,

And that thou hide not thyself from thine own flesh?

8 Then shall thy light break forth as the morning,

And thy healing shall spring forth speedily;

And thy righteousness shall go before thee,

The glory of the LORD shall be thy rearward.

C. Cataclysmic Consequences of a Society without Justice

In wonderfully compressed form, Amos delivers this message of intertwined misery and hope. The falsity of measures, the injustice that passes for the normal state of affairs, will themselves cause the inversion of all that is expected of nature and in society: noon will turn into darkness, festivals will become sites of mourning. At the same time, the famine—the dearth of food—that is prophesied to come if the Israelites do not mend their ways will itself set up a hunger of a new kind: for the spirituality that has been lost; for the God that has been ignored.

Amos 8:4–11

4 Hear this, O ye that would swallow the needy,
And destroy the poor of the land,
5 Saying: 'When will the new moon be gone, that we may sell grain?
And the sabbath, that we may set forth corn?
Making the ephah small, and the shekel great,
And falsifying the balances of deceit;
6 That we may buy the poor for silver,
And the needy for a pair of shoes,
And sell the refuse of the corn?'
7 The LORD hath sworn by the pride of Jacob:
Surely I will never forget any of their works.
8 Shall not the land tremble for this,
And every one mourn that dwelleth therein?
Yea, it shall rise up wholly like the River;
And it shall be troubled and sink again, like the River of Egypt.
9 And it shall come to pass in that day,
Saith the Lord GOD,
That I will cause the sun to go down at noon,
And I will darken the earth in the clear day.
10 And I will turn your feasts into mourning,
And all your songs into lamentation;
And I will bring up sackcloth upon all loins,
And baldness upon every head;
And I will make it as the mourning for an only son,
And the end thereof as a bitter day.
11 Behold, the days come, saith the Lord GOD,
That I will send a famine in the land,
Not a famine of bread, nor a thirst for water,
But of hearing the words of the LORD.

Ezekiel delivers his message in full form, with the bloody implications of suffering already evident. Importantly, it is less the failure to follow religious ritual that is cited as the cause of this punishment than the lack of justice, the widening of oppression, and the failure to treat one another as human beings with moral rights.

Ezekiel 22:2–31

2 'Now, thou, son of man, wilt thou judge, wilt thou judge the bloody city? then cause her to know all her abominations.

3 And thou shalt say: Thus saith the Lord GOD: O city that sheddest blood in the midst of thee, that thy time may come, and that makest idols unto thyself to defile thee; 4 thou art become guilty in thy blood that thou hast shed, and art defiled in thine idols which thou hast made; and thou hast caused thy days to draw near, and art come even unto thy years; therefore have I made thee a reproach unto the nations, and a mocking to all the countries! 5 Those that are near, and those that are far from thee, shall mock thee, thou defiled of name and full of tumult.

6 Behold, the princes of Israel, every one according to his might, have been in thee to shed blood. 7 In thee have they made light of father and mother; in the midst of thee have they dealt by oppression with the stranger; in thee have they wronged the fatherless and the widow.

8 Thou hast despised My holy things, and hast profaned My sabbaths. 9 In thee have been talebearers to shed blood; and in thee they have eaten upon the mountains; in the midst of thee they have committed lewdness. 10 In thee have they uncovered their fathers' nakedness; in thee have they humbled her that was unclean in her impurity. 11 And each hath committed abomination with his neighbour's wife; and each hath lewdly defiled his daughter-in-law; and each in thee hath humbled his sister, his father's daughter. 12 In thee have they taken gifts to shed blood; thou hast taken interest and increase, and thou hast greedily gained of thy neighbours by oppression, and hast forgotten Me, saith the Lord GOD.

13 Behold, therefore, I have smitten My hand at thy dishonest gain which thou hast made, and at thy blood which hath been in the midst of thee. 14 Can thy heart endure, or can thy hands be strong, in the days that I shall deal with thee? I the LORD have spoken it, and will do it.

15 And I will scatter thee among the nations, and disperse thee through the countries; and I will consume thy filthiness out of thee. 16 And thou shalt be profaned in thyself, in the sight of the nations; and thou shalt know that I am the LORD.'

17 And the word of the LORD came unto me, saying: 18 'Son of man, the house of Israel is become dross unto Me; all of them are brass and tin and iron and lead, in the midst of the

furnace; they are the dross of silver. 19 Therefore thus saith the Lord GOD: Because ye are all become dross, therefore, behold, I will gather you into the midst of Jerusalem. 20 As they gather silver and brass and iron and lead and tin into the midst of the furnace, to blow the fire upon it, to melt it; so will I gather you in Mine anger and in My fury, and I will cast you in, and melt you.

21 Yea, I will gather you, and blow upon you with the fire of My wrath, and ye shall be melted in the midst thereof. 22 As silver is melted in the midst of the furnace, so shall ye be melted in the midst thereof; and ye shall know that I the LORD have poured out My fury upon you.'

23 And the word of the LORD came unto me, saying: 24 'Son of man, say unto her: Thou art a land that is not cleansed, nor rained upon in the day of indignation. 25 There is a conspiracy of her prophets in the midst thereof, like a roaring lion ravening the prey; they have devoured souls, they take treasure and precious things, they have made her widows many in the midst thereof. 26 Her priests have done violence to My law, and have profaned My holy things; they have put no difference between the holy and the common, neither have they taught difference between the unclean and the clean, and have hid their eyes from My sabbaths, and I am profaned among them. 27 Her princes in the midst thereof are like wolves ravening the prey: to shed blood, and to destroy souls, so as to get dishonest gain. 28 And her prophets have daubed for them with whited plaster, seeing falsehood, and divining lies unto them, saying: Thus saith the Lord GOD, when the LORD hath not spoken.

29 The people of the land have used oppression, and exercised robbery, and have wronged the poor and needy, and have oppressed the stranger unlawfully. 30 And I sought for a man among them, that should make up the hedge, and stand in the breach before Me for the land, that I should not destroy it; but I found none. 31 Therefore have I poured out Mine indignation upon them; I have consumed them with the fire of My wrath; their own way have I brought upon their heads, saith the Lord GOD.'

For further reading see Isaiah 59:12–15.

D. (Social) Justice and (Divine) Redemption

The similarity of the underlying values of both religious faith and humanistic activities are emphasized in the Hebrew Bible by its linkage of social redemption and a renewed reverence for God.

In the selection here, Isaiah, like Amos, intertwines messages of reproof and hope. The strength of Isaiah's words is that he, like Amos, can see the common roots of both sin and redemption.

Isaiah 1:11–27

11 To what purpose is the multitude of your sacrifices unto Me?
Saith the LORD;
I am full of the burnt-offerings of rams,
And the fat of fed beasts; And I delight not in the blood
Of bullocks, or of lambs, or of he-goats.
12 When ye come to appear before Me,
Who hath required this at your hand,
To trample My courts?
13 Bring no more vain oblations;
It is an offering of abomination unto Me;
New moon and sabbath, the holding of convocations—
I cannot endure iniquity along with the solemn assembly.
14 Your new moons and your appointed seasons
My soul hateth;
They are a burden unto Me;
I am weary to bear them.
15 And when ye spread forth your hands,
I will hide Mine eyes from you;
Yea, when ye make many prayers,
I will not hear;
Your hands are full of blood.
16 Wash you, make you clean,
Put away the evil of your doings
From before Mine eyes,
Cease to do evil;
17 Learn to do well;
Seek justice, relieve the oppressed,
Judge the fatherless, plead for the widow.
18 Come now, and let us reason together,
Saith the LORD;

Though your sins be as scarlet,
They shall be as white as snow;
Though they be red like crimson,
They shall be as wool.
19 If ye be willing and obedient,
Ye shall eat the good of the land;
20 But if ye refuse and rebel,
Ye shall be devoured with the sword;
For the mouth of the LORD hath spoken.
21 How is the faithful city
Become a harlot!
She that was full of justice,
Righteousness lodged in her,
But now murderers.
22 Thy silver is become dross,
Thy wine mixed with water.
23 Thy princes are rebellious,
And companions of thieves;
Every one loveth bribes,
And followeth after rewards;
They judge not the fatherless,
Neither doth the cause of the widow come unto them.
24 Therefore saith the Lord, the LORD of hosts,
The Mighty One of Israel:
Ah, I will ease Me of Mine adversaries,
And avenge Me of Mine enemies;
25 And I will turn My hand upon thee,
And purge away thy dross as with lye,
And will take away all thine alloy;
26 And I will restore thy judges as at the first, And thy counsel-
     lors as at the beginning;
Afterward thou shalt be called The city of righteousness,
The faithful city.
27 Zion shall be redeemed with justice,
And they that return of her with righteousness.

For further reading see Ezekiel 18:5–20 and Jeremiah 7: 2–4 (above).

CHAPTER 17

IN FOREIGN HOUSES AND COURTS: EXILE

Like civil war, exile often portends the end of a people, at least in terms of its autonomous existence and self-conception. Not so in the Hebrew Bible. In fact, with its origins in the slavery of an Egyptian exile, Israelite communal history can be depicted as beginning in exile (as, indeed, does the onset of human history, after expulsion from the Garden of Eden). Some consequences of this paradox are evident in the following selections.

A. Joseph, the Dreamer's Son

Like his father Jacob, who dreamed of God's protection for his safekeeping while on the run from his brother Esau (Genesis 28:12–22), Joseph also dreams through his brothers' bitter resentment (see Chapter 2, "Dreams"). Portrayed as a passive character throughout the process of being sold as a slave, Joseph comes into his own and begins to function as a political player even while he is a slave, and later, as an interpreter of dreams, in Egypt.

In this selection, Joseph's experience as a slave, itself a tenuous position lacking any claims or rights of its own, reaches its lowest point when he becomes the object of his mistress' desires. The sexual harassment of Joseph is heightened, in ways that contemporary readers identify with modern challenges to human rights, by the ability of the dominant actor in this misbegotten sexualization of power, Potiphar's wife, to twist the evidence in order to claim that Joseph, not she, was the sexual aggressor. In the context of the brutal reality of Egyptian society and empire, Joseph is "lucky" to be "only" imprisoned, and not summarily executed (think of the miscarriage of justice in the multiple trials involving the Scottsboro boys [1931–1937]).[1]

---

1. These cases involved African American youth who were accused of raping a white woman in Alabama in 1931, and who were subsequently denied even the semblance of fair hearings or fair trials: lynch mobs, frame-ups, and rushed trials were just some of the elements of the miscarriage of justice visited upon the defendants.

1. Joseph as a Slave in Egypt

Genesis 39:1–20

1 And Joseph was brought down to Egypt; and Potiphar, an officer of Pharaoh's, the captain of the guard, an Egyptian, bought him of the hand of the Ishmaelites, that had brought him down thither. 2 And the LORD was with Joseph, and he was a prosperous man; and he was in the house of his master the Egyptian.

3 And his master saw that the LORD was with him, and that the LORD made all that he did to prosper in his hand. 4 And Joseph found favour in his sight, and he ministered unto him. And he appointed him overseer over his house, and all that he had he put into his hand.

5 And it came to pass from the time that he appointed him overseer in his house, and over all that he had, that the LORD blessed the Egyptian's house for Joseph's sake; and the blessing of the LORD was upon all that he had, in the house and in the field. 6 And he left all that he had in Joseph's hand; and, having him, he knew not aught save the bread which he did eat. And Joseph was of beautiful form, and fair to look upon.

7 And it came to pass after these things, that his master's wife cast her eyes upon Joseph; and she said: 'Lie with me.' 8 But he refused, and said unto his master's wife: 'Behold, my master, having me, knoweth not what is in the house, and he hath put all that he hath into my hand; 9 he is not greater in this house than I; neither hath he kept back any thing from me but thee, because thou art his wife. How then can I do this great wickedness, and sin against God?'

10 And it came to pass, as she spoke to Joseph day by day, that he hearkened not unto her, to lie by her, or to be with her. 11 And it came to pass on a certain day, when he went into the house to do his work, and there was none of the men of the house there within, 12 that she caught him by his garment, saying: 'Lie with me.' And he left his garment in her hand, and fled, and got him out.

13 And it came to pass, when she saw that he had left his garment in her hand, and was fled forth, 14 that she called unto the men of her house, and spoke unto them, saying: 'See, he hath

brought in a Hebrew unto us to mock us; he came in unto me to lie with me, and I cried with a loud voice. 15 And it came to pass, when he heard that I lifted up my voice and cried, that he left his garment by me, and fled, and got him out.' 16 And she laid up his garment by her, until his master came home. 17 And she spoke unto him according to these words, saying: 'The Hebrew servant, whom thou hast brought unto us, came in unto me to mock me. 18 And it came to pass, as I lifted up my voice and cried, that he left his garment by me, and fled out.'

19 And it came to pass, when his master heard the words of his wife, which she spoke unto him, saying: 'After this manner did thy servant to me'; that his wrath was kindled. 20 And Joseph's master took him, and put him into the prison, the place where the king's prisoners were bound; and he was there in the prison.

Joseph's experiences in jail eerily reprise those in Potiphar's house: his combination of intellect and honesty makes him indispensable to those in power; in both circumstances, he ends up running the location of his imprisonment. But the notice taken of him during his imprisonment here eventually leads, although slowly, to his audience with the Pharaoh, and his eventual freedom.

Genesis 39:21–23

21 But the LORD was with Joseph, and showed kindness unto him, and gave him favour in the sight of the keeper of the prison.

22 And the keeper of the prison committed to Joseph's hand all the prisoners that were in the prison; and whatsoever they did there, he was the doer of it. 23 The keeper of the prison looked not to any thing that was under his hand, because the LORD was with him; and that which he did, the LORD made it to prosper.

See also Genesis 40:1–13 in Chapter 2, "Dreams."

2. *Joseph Interprets Dreams*

Joseph accedes to power upon his successful interpretation of the Pharaoh's dreams. The success of his interpretation can be attributed not only to his plausible elucidation of the elements of the dream, but also to his proposal of solutions to problems that the Pharaoh was not even yet consciously aware of facing: the coming years of famine. Unlike Joseph's prior experiences with his brothers, and as manifested already by his conversations with the chief butler and the chief baker in prison, he is now sensitive to the hidden messages of his interlocutors, and can respond to them in a way that opens up the possibilities of further solutions. In Joseph's life, dreams had gotten him into trouble with his brothers. But dreams also serve as Joseph's proving grounds: the dream-interpreter is ready to lead (see Genesis 41:37–46 in Chapter 2, "Dreams").

Genesis 41:37–49

37 And the thing was good in the eyes of Pharaoh, and in the eyes of all his servants.

38 And Pharaoh said unto his servants: 'Can we find such a one as this, a man in whom the spirit of God is?' 39 And Pharaoh said unto Joseph: 'Forasmuch as God hath shown thee all this, there is none so discreet and wise as thou. 40 Thou shalt be over my house, and according unto thy word shall all my people be ruled; only in the throne will I be greater than thou.' 41 And Pharaoh said unto Joseph: 'See, I have set thee over all the land of Egypt.'

42 And Pharaoh took off his signet ring from his hand, and put it upon Joseph's hand, and arrayed him in vestures of fine linen, and put a gold chain about his neck. 43 And he made him to ride in the second chariot which he had; and they cried before him: 'Abrech'; and he set him over all the land of Egypt. 44 And Pharaoh said unto Joseph: 'I am Pharaoh, and without thee shall no man lift up his hand or his foot in all the land of Egypt.' 45 And Pharaoh called Joseph's name Zaphenath-paneah; and he gave him to wife Asenath the daughter of Poti-phera priest of On. And Joseph went out over the land of Egypt.—

46 And Joseph was thirty years old when he stood before Pharaoh king of Egypt.—

And Joseph went out from the presence of Pharaoh, and went throughout all the land of Egypt. 47 And in the seven years of plenty the earth brought forth in heaps. 48 And he gathered up all the food of the seven years which were in the land of Egypt, and laid up the food in the cities; the food of the field, which was round about every city, laid he up in the same. 49 And Joseph laid up corn as the sand of the sea, very much, until they left off numbering; for it was without number.

As with Joseph's prior interpretations of dreams, his readings of the dreams at the royal court prove prophetic. Arguably, however, Joseph's solutions have an unforeseen double-edge: the centralization of economic power under the Pharaoh has been viewed as laying the institutional foundation for the eventual slavery of the Israelites in Egypt, implemented by another Pharaoh in the Book of Exodus. Readers of the twenty-first century might ponder a current takeaway of an ancient text: centralization, while promoting efficiency, is not always an unmitigated good.

Readers may further wonder: Why was this possibility not anticipated, particularly by a nuanced interpreter like Joseph? Perhaps the answer lies in the text's rapid conflation of events, both political and personal, in Joseph's life. In texts as in life, problems and solutions are often obscured by the swift experiences of passing events, whose future implications are not always obvious.

3. Political Changes and the Famine in Egypt

Genesis 47:13–26

13 And there was no bread in all the land; for the famine was very sore, so that the land of Egypt and the land of Canaan languished by reason of the famine. 14 And Joseph gathered up all the money that was found in the land of Egypt, and in the land of Canaan, for the corn which they bought; and Joseph brought the money into Pharaoh's house.

15 And when the money was all spent in the land of Egypt, and in the land of Canaan, all the Egyptians came unto Joseph, and said: 'Give us bread; for why should we die in thy presence? for our money faileth.' 16 And Joseph said: 'Give your cattle, and I will give you [bread] for your cattle, if money fail.' 17 And they brought their cattle unto Joseph. And Joseph gave them bread in exchange for the horses, and for the flocks, and for the herds, and for the asses; and he fed them with bread in exchange for all their cattle for that year.

18 And when that year was ended, they came unto him the second year, and said unto him: 'We will not hide from my lord, how that our money is all spent; and the herds of cattle are my lord's; there is nought left in the sight of my lord, but our bodies, and our lands. 19 Wherefore should we die before thine eyes, both we and our land? buy us and our land for bread, and we and our land

will be bondmen unto Pharaoh; and give us seed, that we may live, and not die, and that the land be not desolate.'

20 So Joseph bought all the land of Egypt for Pharaoh; for the Egyptians sold every man his field, because the famine was sore upon them; and the land became Pharaoh's. 21 And as for the people, he removed them city by city, from one end of the border of Egypt even to the other end thereof. 22 Only the land of the priests bought he not, for the priests had a portion from Pharaoh, and did eat their portion which Pharaoh gave them; wherefore they sold not their land.

23 Then Joseph said unto the people: 'Behold, I have bought you this day and your land for Pharaoh. Lo, here is seed for you, and ye shall sow the land. 24 And it shall come to pass at the ingatherings, that ye shall give a fifth unto Pharaoh, and four parts shall be your own, for seed of the field, and for your food, and for them of your households, and for food for your little ones.' 25 And they said: 'Thou hast saved our lives. Let us find favour in the sight of my lord, and we will be Pharaoh's bondmen.' 26 And Joseph made it a statute concerning the land of Egypt unto this day, that Pharaoh should have the fifth; only the land of the priests alone became not Pharaoh's.

4. Joseph's Revelation: Reinterpreting History and Preparing for National Existence

Viewing the Joseph narrative just as a literary romance emphasizes its "fairy-tale" quality and ending: the youth who was the butt of his elder brothers' animosity winds up, after many picaresque adventures and twists of fate, holding his family's livelihood and survival in the palm of his hand. But the actual details of Joseph's speech to his brothers upon his revelation to them reveal a more complicated understanding: Joseph is charting the development of his family from a band of conflicting brothers to the seeds of a nation. See "The Blessings of Jacob" (Genesis 49) in Chapter 9, "Israelite National Identity."

Genesis 45:1–11

1 Then Joseph could not refrain himself before all them that stood by him; and he cried: 'Cause every man to go out from me.' And there stood no man with him, while Joseph made

himself known unto his brethren. 2 And he wept aloud; and the Egyptians heard, and the house of Pharaoh heard.

3 And Joseph said unto his brethren: 'I am Joseph; doth my father yet live?' And his brethren could not answer him; for they were affrighted at his presence. 4 And Joseph said unto his brethren: 'Come near to me, I pray you.' And they came near. And he said: 'I am Joseph your brother, whom ye sold into Egypt.

5 And now be not grieved, nor angry with yourselves, that ye sold me hither; for God did send me before you to preserve life. 6 For these two years hath the famine been in the land; and there are yet five years, in which there shall be neither plowing nor harvest. 7 And God sent me before you to give you a remnant on the earth, and to save you alive for a great deliverance. 8 So now it was not you that sent me hither, but God; and He hath made me a father to Pharaoh, and lord of all his house, and ruler over all the land of Egypt.

9 Hasten ye, and go up to my father, and say unto him: Thus saith thy son Joseph: God hath made me lord of all Egypt; come down unto me, tarry not. 10 And thou shalt dwell in the land of Goshen, and thou shalt be near unto me, thou, and thy children, and thy children's children, and thy flocks, and thy herds, and all that thou hast; 11 and there will I sustain thee; for there are yet five years of famine; lest thou come to poverty, thou, and thy household, and all that thou hast.

B. Women and Youth in Exile

Women face special challenges in exile: more vulnerable physically, they also are easily used as bait to extract concessions from their defeated people or even to hasten assimilation and thus accelerate the destruction of their people. As liminal members of their own societies, women's survival in foreign courts is not a matter of course. In the texts of the Hebrew Bible, their ability to transform (and, to an extent, safeguard) the continued existence of their people is nothing short of amazing.

As stated above, the Hebrew Bible presents human history as a consequence of exile: starting from Adam and Eve's banishment from the Garden of Eden (Genesis 3:24), continuing in Cain's finding refuge in urban places (Genesis 4:17), and encompassing the migration to the plains of Shinnar (Genesis 11:2). Different reasons are given for all of these instances of exile or migration, but none of them are linked to the nationhood, ethnicity, or identity of a distinctive family unit until the experiences of Joseph, who is consistently identified in Egypt as a "Hebrew" or as a "Hebrew slave." When Joseph is elevated by the Pharaoh to vizier, he gets a new Egyptian name; Joseph's ethnic and family heritage is then revealed anew when he identifies himself with his brothers as the son of Jacob of Canaan.

The Book of Esther is placed centuries later in the Persian Empire. In this text, the Israelites are identified as a people in exile and are named for the first time as Jews: "Yehudim," in the parlance of the Book of Esther, not "Israelites," as in the rest of the Hebrew Bible. In the context of the narrative, Esther is triply displaced; that is to say, she is the protagonist of three sorts of "exiles": as a Jew, she has been forcibly removed to a foreign land; as an orphan, she has been dislocated from her family of origin; as a woman, she is forced to take part in a pageant at the royal Persian court when Ahasuerus searches for a new queen; and as the "winner" of that contest, she must now negotiate her life in perpetual displacement. The stresses on Esther increase when she must act to save her people in the context of her completely anonymous identity (nobody at court knows that she is Jewish), dealing with an adversary who has singlehandedly changed the corridors of power at a royal court ruled by the arbitrary whims of a despot.

1. The Book of Esther (Chapters 1–7)

As with the narrative of Joseph, the book of Esther is often seriously misunderstood as nothing more than a fairy tale in Hebrew biblical guise. While the selection here focuses on Esther's displacement as a product of (triple) exile, the more complicated (and often misread) last chapters of the book focus on the reconstitution of a nation through the reinterpretation of texts, the realization of the multidimensionality of text, and the institution of new practices within which to reinscribe a nation that can continue to flourish, even in exile.

Esther 1

1 NOW IT came to pass in the days of Ahasuerus—this is Ahasuerus who reigned, from India even unto Ethiopia, over a hundred and seven and twenty provinces— 2 that in those days, when the king Ahasuerus sat on the throne of his kingdom, which was in Shushan the castle,

3 in the third year of his reign, he made a feast unto all his princes and his servants; the army of Persia and Media, the nobles and princes of the provinces, being before him; 4 when he

showed the riches of his glorious kingdom and the honour of his excellent majesty, many days, even a hundred and fourscore days.

5 And when these days were fulfilled, the king made a feast unto all the people that were present in Shushan the castle, both great and small, seven days, in the court of the garden of the king's palace; 6 there were hangings of white, fine cotton, and blue, bordered with cords of fine linen and purple, upon silver rods and pillars of marble; the couches were of gold and silver, upon a pavement of green, and white, and shell, and onyx marble. 7 And they gave them drink in vessels of gold—the vessels being diverse one from another—and royal wine in abundance, according to the bounty of the king. 8 And the drinking was according to the law; none did compel; for so the king had appointed to all the officers of his house, that they should do according to every man's pleasure.

9 Also Vashti the queen made a feast for the women in the royal house which belonged to king Ahasuerus. 10 On the seventh day, when the heart of the king was merry with wine, he commanded Mehuman, Bizzetha, Harbona, Bigtha, and Abagtha, Zethar, and Carcas, the seven chamberlains that ministered in the presence of Ahasuerus the king, 11 to bring Vashti the queen before the king with the crown royal, to show the peoples and the princes her beauty; for she was fair to look on. 12 But the queen Vashti refused to come at the king's commandment by the chamberlains; therefore was the king very wroth, and his anger burned in him.

13 Then the king said to the wise men, who knew the times— for so was the king's manner toward all that knew law and judgment; 14 and the next unto him was Carshena, Shethar, Admatha, Tarshish, Meres, Marsena, and Memucan, the seven princes of Persia and Media, who saw the king's face, and sat the first in the kingdom: 15 'What shall we do unto the queen Vashti according to law, forasmuch as she hath not done the bidding of the king Ahasuerus by the chamberlains?'

16 And Memucan answered before the king and the princes: 'Vashti the queen hath not done wrong to the king only, but also to all the princes, and to all the peoples, that are in all the provinces of the king Ahasuerus. 17 For this deed of the queen will come abroad unto all women, to make their husbands contemptible in their eyes, when it will be said: The king Ahasuerus

commanded Vashti the queen to be brought in before him, but she came not. 18 And this day will the princesses of Persia and Media who have heard of the deed of the queen say the like unto all the king's princes. So will there arise enough contempt and wrath.

19 If it please the king, let there go forth a royal commandment from him, and let it be written among the laws of the Persians and the Medes, that it be not altered, that Vashti come no more before king Ahasuerus, and that the king give her royal estate unto another that is better than she. 20 And when the king's decree which he shall make shall be published throughout all his kingdom, great though it be, all the wives will give to their husbands honour, both to great and small.'

21 And the word pleased the king and the princes; and the king did according to the word of Memucan; 22 for he sent letters into all the king's provinces, into every province according to the writing thereof, and to every people after their language, that every man should bear rule in his own house, and speak according to the language of his people.

Esther 2

1 After these things, when the wrath of king Ahasuerus was assuaged, he remembered Vashti, and what she had done, and what was decreed against her. 2 Then said the king's servants that ministered unto him: 'Let there be sought for the king young virgins fair to look on; 3 and let the king appoint officers in all the provinces of his kingdom, that they may gather together all the fair young virgins unto Shushan the castle, to the house of the women, unto the custody of Hegai the king's chamberlain, keeper of the women; and let their ointments be given them; 4 and let the maiden that pleaseth the king be queen instead of Vashti.' And the thing pleased the king; and he did so.

5 There was a certain Jew in Shushan the castle, whose name was Mordecai the son of Jair the son of Shimei the son of Kish, a Benjamite, 6 who had been carried away from Jerusalem with the captives that had been carried away with Jeconiah king of Judah, whom Nebuchadnezzar the king of Babylon had carried away. 7 And he brought up Hadassah, that is, Esther, his uncle's daughter; for she had neither father nor mother, and the maiden

was of beautiful form and fair to look on; and when her father and mother were dead, Mordecai took her for his own daughter.

8 So it came to pass, when the king's commandment and his decree was published, and when many maidens were gathered together unto Shushan the castle, to the custody of Hegai, that Esther was taken into the king's house, to the custody of Hegai, keeper of the women. 9 And the maiden pleased him, and she obtained kindness of him; and he speedily gave her her ointments, with her portions, and the seven maidens, who were meet to be given her out of the king's house; and he advanced her and her maidens to the best place in the house of the women. 10 Esther had not made known her people nor her kindred; for Mordecai had charged her that she should not tell it. 11 And Mordecai walked every day before the court of the women's house, to know how Esther did, and what would become of her.

12 Now when the turn of every maiden was come to go in to king Ahasuerus, after that it had been done to her according to the law for the women, twelve months—for so were the days of their anointing accomplished, to wit, six months with oil of myrrh, and six month with sweet odours, and with other ointments of the women— 13 when then the maiden came unto the king, whatsoever she desired was given her to go with her out of the house of the women unto the king's house. 14 In the evening she went, and on the morrow she returned into the second house of the women, to the custody of Shaashgaz, the king's chamberlain, who kept the concubines; she came in unto the king no more, except the king delighted in her, and she were called by name.

15 Now when the turn of Esther, the daughter of Abihail the uncle of Mordecai, who had taken her for his daughter, was come to go in unto the king, she required nothing but what Hegai the king's chamberlain, the keeper of the women, appointed. And Esther obtained favour in the sight of all them that looked upon her. 16 So Esther was taken unto king Ahasuerus into his house royal in the tenth month, which is the month Tebeth, in the seventh year of his reign. 17 And the king loved Esther above all the women, and she obtained grace and favour in his sight more than all the virgins; so that he set the royal crown upon her head, and made her queen instead of Vashti. 18 Then the king made a great feast unto all his princes and his servants, even Esther's feast; and

he made a release to the provinces, and gave gifts, according to the bounty of the king.

19 And when the virgins were gathered together the second time, and Mordecai sat in the king's gate— 20 Esther had not yet made known her kindred nor her people; as Mordecai had charged her; for Esther did the commandment of Mordecai, like as when she was brought up with him— 21 in those days, while Mordecai sat in the king's gate, two of the king's chamberlains, Bigthan and Teresh, of those that kept the door, were wroth, and sought to lay hands on the king Ahasuerus. 22 And the thing became known to Mordecai, who told it unto Esther the queen; and Esther told the king thereof in Mordecai's name. 23 And when inquisition was made of the matter, and it was found to be so, they were both hanged on a tree; and it was written in the book of the chronicles before the king.

Esther 3

1 After these things did king Ahasuerus promote Haman the son of Hammedatha the Agagite, and advanced him, and set his seat above all the princes that were with him. 2 And all the king's servants, that were in the king's gate, bowed down, and prostrated themselves before Haman; for the king had so commanded concerning him. But Mordecai bowed not down, nor prostrated himself before him.

3 Then the king's servants, that were in the king's gate, said unto Mordecai: 'Why transgressest thou the king's commandment?' 4 Now it came to pass, when they spoke daily unto him, and he hearkened not unto them, that they told Haman, to see whether Mordecai's words would stand; for he had told them that he was a Jew. 5 And when Haman saw that Mordecai bowed not down, nor prostrated himself before him, then was Haman full of wrath.

6 But it seemed contemptible in his eyes to lay hands on Mordecai alone; for they had made known to him the people of Mordecai; wherefore Haman sought to destroy all the Jews that were throughout the whole kingdom of Ahasuerus, even the people of Mordecai. 7 In the first month, which is the month Nisan, in the twelfth year of king Ahasuerus, they cast pur, that is, the lot, before Haman from day to day, and from month to month, to the twelfth month, which is the month Adar.

8 And Haman said unto king Ahasuerus: 'There is a certain people scattered abroad and dispersed among the peoples in all the provinces of thy kingdom; and their laws are diverse from those of every people; neither keep they the king's laws; therefore it profiteth not the king to suffer them. 9 If it please the king, let it be written that they be destroyed; and I will pay ten thousand talents of silver into the hands of those that have the charge of the king's business, to bring it into the king's treasuries.'

10 And the king took his ring from his hand, and gave it unto Haman the son of Hammedatha the Agagite, the Jews' enemy. 11 And the king said unto Haman: 'The silver is given to thee, the people also, to do with them as it seemeth good to thee.'

12 Then were the king's scribes called in the first month, on the thirteenth day thereof, and there was written, according to all that Haman commanded, unto the king's satraps, and to the governors that were over every province, and to the princes of every people; to every province according to the writing thereof, and to every people after their language; in the name of king Ahasuerus was it written, and it was sealed with the king's ring.

13 And letters were sent by posts into all the king's provinces, to destroy, to slay, and to cause to perish, all Jews, both young and old, little children and women, in one day, even upon the thirteenth day of the twelfth month, which is the month Adar, and to take the spoil of them for a prey. 14 The copy of the writing, to be given out for a decree in every province, was to be published unto all peoples, that they should be ready against that day. 15 The posts went forth in haste by the king's commandment, and the decree was given out in Shushan the castle; and the king and Haman sat down to drink; but the city of Shushan was perplexed.

Esther 4

1 Now when Mordecai knew all that was done, Mordecai rent his clothes, and put on sackcloth with ashes, and went out into the midst of the city, and cried with a loud and a bitter cry; 2 and he came even before the king's gate; for none might enter within the king's gate clothed with sackcloth. 3 And in every province, whithersoever the king's commandment and his decree came, there was great mourning among the Jews, and fasting, and weeping, and wailing; and many lay in sackcloth and ashes.

4 And Esther's maidens and her chamberlains came and told it her; and the queen was exceedingly pained; and she sent raiment to clothe Mordecai; and to take his sackcloth from off him; but he accepted it not. 5 Then called Esther for Hathach, one of the king's chamberlains, whom he had appointed to attend upon her, and charged him to go to Mordecai, to know what this was, and why it was. 6 So Hathach went forth to Mordecai unto the broad place of the city, which was before the king's gate.

7 And Mordecai told him of all that had happened unto him, and the exact sum of the money that Haman had promised to pay to the king's treasuries for the Jews, to destroy them. 8 Also he gave him the copy of the writing of the decree that was given out in Shushan to destroy them, to show it unto Esther, and to declare it unto her; and to charge her that she should go in unto the king, to make supplication unto him, and to make request before him, for her people.

9 And Hathach came and told Esther the words of Mordecai. 10 Then Esther spoke unto Hathach, and gave him a message unto Mordecai: 11 'All the king's servants, and the people of the king's provinces, do know, that whosoever, whether man or woman, shall come unto the king into the inner court, who is not called, there is one law for him, that he be put to death, except such to whom the king shall hold out the golden sceptre, that he may live; but I have not been called to come in unto the king these thirty days.' 12 And they told to Mordecai Esther's words.

13 Then Mordecai bade them to return answer unto Esther: 'Think not with thyself that thou shalt escape in the king's house, more than all the Jews. 14 For if thou altogether holdest thy peace at this time, then will relief and deliverance arise to the Jews from another place, but thou and thy father's house will perish; and who knoweth whether thou art not come to royal estate for such a time as this?'

15 Then Esther bade them return answer unto Mordecai: 16 'Go, gather together all the Jews that are present in Shushan, and fast ye for me, and neither eat nor drink three days, night or day; I also and my maidens will fast in like manner; and so will I go in unto the king, which is not according to the law; and if I perish, I perish.' 17 So Mordecai went his way, and did according to all that Esther had commanded him.

Esther 5

1 Now it came to pass on the third day, that Esther put on her royal apparel, and stood in the inner court of the king's house, over against the king's house; and the king sat upon his royal throne in the royal house, over against the entrance of the house. 2 And it was so, when the king saw Esther the queen standing in the court, that she obtained favour in his sight; and the king held out to Esther the golden sceptre that was in his hand. So Esther drew near, and touched the top of the sceptre.

3 Then said the king unto her: 'What wilt thou, queen Esther? for whatever thy request, even to the half of the kingdom, it shall be given thee.' 4 And Esther said: 'If it seem good unto the king, let the king and Haman come this day unto the banquet that I have prepared for him.' 5 Then the king said: 'Cause Haman to make haste, that it may be done as Esther hath said.' So the king and Haman came to the banquet that Esther had prepared.

6 And the king said unto Esther at the banquet of wine: 'Whatever thy petition, it shall be granted thee; and whatever thy request, even to the half of the kingdom, it shall be performed.' 7 Then answered Esther, and said: 'My petition and my request is— 8 if I have found favour in the sight of the king, and if it please the king to grant my petition, and to perform my request—let the king and Haman come to the banquet that I shall prepare for them, and I will do to-morrow as the king hath said.'

9 Then went Haman forth that day joyful and glad of heart; but when Haman saw Mordecai in the king's gate, that he stood not up, nor moved for him, Haman was filled with wrath against Mordecai. 10 Nevertheless Haman refrained himself, and went home; and he sent and fetched his friends and Zeresh his wife. 11 And Haman recounted unto them the glory of his riches, and the multitude of his children, and everything as to how the king had promoted him, and how he had advanced him above the princes and servants of the king. 12 Haman said moreover: 'Yea, Esther the queen did let no man come in with the king unto the banquet that she had prepared but myself; and to-morrow also am I invited by her together with the king. 13 Yet all this availeth me nothing, so long as I see Mordecai the Jew sitting at the king's gate.'

14 Then said Zeresh his wife and all his friends unto him: 'Let a gallows be made of fifty cubits high, and in the morning speak thou unto the king that Mordecai may be hanged thereon; then go thou in merrily with the king unto the banquet.' And the thing pleased Haman; and he caused the gallows to be made.

Esther 6

1 On that night could not the king sleep; and he commanded to bring the book of records of the chronicles, and they were read before the king. 2 And it was found written, that Mordecai had told of Bigthana and Teresh, two of the king's chamberlains, of those that kept the door, who had sought to lay hands on the king Ahasuerus. 3 And the king said: 'What honour and dignity hath been done to Mordecai for this?' Then said the king's servants that ministered unto him: 'There is nothing done for him.'

4 And the king said: 'Who is in the court?'—Now Haman was come into the outer court of the king's house, to speak unto the king to hang Mordecai on the gallows that he had prepared for him.— 5 And the king's servants said unto him: 'Behold, Haman standeth in the court.' And the king said: 'Let him come in.'

6 So Haman came in. And the king said unto him: 'What shall be done unto the man whom the king delighteth to honour?'— Now Haman said in his heart: 'Whom would the king delight to honour besides myself?'— 7 And Haman said unto the king: 'For the man whom the king delighteth to honour, 8 let royal apparel be brought which the king useth to wear, and the horse that the king rideth upon, and on whose head a crown royal is set; 9 and let the apparel and the horse be delivered to the hand of one of the king's most noble princes, that they may array the man therewith whom the king delighteth to honour, and cause him to ride on horseback through the street of the city, and proclaim before him: Thus shall it be done to the man whom the king delighteth to honour.'

10 Then the king said to Haman: 'Make haste, and take the apparel and the horse, as thou hast said, and do even so to Mordecai the Jew, that sitteth at the king's gate; let nothing fail of all that thou hast spoken.' 11 Then took Haman the apparel and the horse, and arrayed Mordecai, and caused him to

ride through the street of the city, and proclaimed before him: 'Thus shall it be done unto the man whom the king delighteth to honour.'

12 And Mordecai returned to the king's gate. But Haman hasted to his house, mourning and having his head covered. 13 And Haman recounted unto Zeresh his wife and all his friends every thing that had befallen him. Then said his wise men and Zeresh his wife unto him: 'If Mordecai, before whom thou hast begun to fall, be of the seed of the Jews, thou shalt not prevail against him, but shalt surely fall before him.' 14 While they were yet talking with him, came the king's chamberlains, and hastened to bring Haman unto the banquet that Esther had prepared.

Esther 7

1 So the king and Haman came to banquet with Esther the queen. 2 And the king said again unto Esther on the second day at the banquet of wine: 'Whatever thy petition, queen Esther, it shall be granted thee; and whatever thy request, even to the half of the kingdom, it shall be performed.' 3 Then Esther the queen answered and said: 'If I have found favour in thy sight, O king, and if it please the king, let my life be given me at my petition, and my people at my request; 4 for we are sold, I and my people, to be destroyed, to be slain, and to perish. But if we had been sold for bondmen and bondwomen, I had held my peace, for the adversary is not worthy that the king be endamaged.'

5 Then spoke the king Ahasuerus and said unto Esther the queen: 'Who is he, and where is he, that durst presume in his heart to do so?' 6 And Esther said: 'An adversary and an enemy, even this wicked Haman.' Then Haman was terrified before the king and the queen. 7 And the king arose in his wrath from the banquet of wine and went into the palace garden; but Haman remained to make request for his life to Esther the queen; for he saw that there was evil determined against him by the king. 8 Then the king returned out of the palace garden into the place of the banquet of wine; and Haman was fallen upon the couch whereon Esther was. Then said the king: 'Will he even force the queen before me in the house?' As the word went out of the king's mouth, they covered Haman's face. 9 Then said Harbonah, one

of the chamberlains that were before the king: 'Behold also, the gallows fifty cubits high, which Haman hath made for Mordecai, who spoke good for the king, standeth in the house of Haman.' And the king said: 'Hang him thereon.' 10 So they hanged Haman on the gallows that he had prepared for Mordecai. Then was the king's wrath assuaged.

2. *The Book of Ruth: Widowed and Stateless in a Foreign Land*

The second narrative highlighted in this section is a much more quotidian tale that has also often been misunderstood as a "stranger at the gates"[2] story: a stranger whose eventual marriage at the end of the story is the "proof" that all's well that ends well. In fact, while the book of Ruth does deal with strangers and their reception in society, the tone of the book is a much more complex and layered critique of these status quo notions than is normally recognized.

Like Esther, Ruth is estranged, although Ruth voluntarily chooses to accompany her mother-in-law, Naomi, back to Beth-Lehem/Yehudah, leaving the familiarity of her home in Moab. But that does not make the reality of being a stranger any easier: Ruth is virtually ignored by the women of Beth-Lehem, despite her association with their old friend, Naomi. Ruth's ability to work out a new conception of society, which Boaz uniquely recognizes in his conversations with her, foregrounds Ruth's role in founding the future royal family of the Israelites: the house of David.

Contemporary readers may wonder why a stranger, and from the land of Moab at that (see Genesis 19), is chosen as the founder of the monarchy. What does that tell the modern reader about the Hebrew Bible's approach to leadership and difference?

Ruth 1

1 AND IT came to pass in the days when the judges judged, that there was a famine in the land. And a certain man of Beth-lehem in Judah went to sojourn in the field of Moab, he, and his wife, and his two sons. 2 And the name of the man was Elimelech, and the name of his wife Naomi, and the name of his two sons Mahlon and Chilion, Ephrathites of Beth-lehem in Judah. And they came into the field of Moab, and continued there. 3 And Elimelech Naomi's husband died; and she was left,

---

2. This expression appears in Exodus 20:10 and in Deuteronomy 24:14.

and her two sons. 4 And they took them wives of the women of Moab: the name of the one was Orpah, and the name of the other Ruth; and they dwelt there about ten years. 5 And Mahlon and Chilion died both of them; and the woman was left of her two children and of her husband.

6 Then she arose with her daughters-in-law, that she might return from the field of Moab; for she had heard in the field of Moab how that the LORD had remembered His people in giving them bread. 7 And she went forth out of the place where she was, and her two daughters-in-law with her; and they went on the way to return unto the land of Judah. 8 And Naomi said unto her two daughters-in-law: 'Go, return each of you to her mother's house; the LORD deal kindly with you, as ye have dealt with the dead, and with me. 9 The LORD grant you that ye may find rest, each of you in the house of her husband.' Then she kissed them; and they lifted up their voice, and wept. 10 And they said unto her: 'Nay, but we will return with thee unto thy people.' 11 And Naomi said: 'Turn back, my daughters; why will ye go with me? have I yet sons in my womb, that they may be your husbands? 12 Turn back, my daughters, go your way; for I am too old to have a husband. If I should say: I have hope, should I even have an husband to-night, and also bear sons; 13 would ye tarry for them till they were grown? would ye shut yourselves off for them and have no husbands? nay, my daughters; for it grieveth me much for your sakes, for the hand of the LORD is gone forth against me.' 14 And they lifted up their voice, and wept again; and Orpah kissed her mother-in-law; but Ruth cleaved unto her.

15 And she said: 'Behold, thy sister-in-law is gone back unto her people, and unto her god; return thou after thy sister-in-law.' 16 And Ruth said: 'Entreat me not to leave thee, and to return from following after thee; for whither thou goest, I will go; and where thou lodgest, I will lodge; thy people shall be my people, and thy God my God; 17 where thou diest, will I die, and there will I be buried; the LORD do so to me, and more also, if aught but death part thee and me.'

18 And when she saw that she was stedfastly minded to go with her, she left off speaking unto her. 19 So they two went until they came to Beth-lehem. And it came to pass, when they were come to Beth-lehem, that all the city was astir concerning them, and the women said: 'Is this Naomi?' 20 And she said unto them:

'Call me not Naomi,[3] call me Marah;[4] for the Almighty hath dealt very bitterly with me. 21 I went out full, and the LORD hath brought me back home empty; why call ye me Naomi, seeing the LORD hath testified against me, and the Almighty hath afflicted me?'

22 So Naomi returned, and Ruth the Moabitess, her daughter-in-law, with her, who returned out of the field of Moab—and they came to Beth-lehem in the beginning of barley harvest.

At a certain level, some of our basic questions begin to be answered already by the end of the first chapter. By clinging to Naomi, Ruth, a stranger, exhibits a deeper understanding of what it means to be an Israelite and to cling to their faith than do many of the non-welcoming Beth-Lehemite women whom they meet upon their return.

Perhaps paradoxically, Ruth's "clinginess" interacts with a strong sense of individual purpose and morality: significantly, Ruth does not promise Naomi to go exactly on the path that Naomi travels. While Ruth promises to arrive at the same place (Heb.: *el*), she insists that she will take her own road to get there. This sense of moral independence also guides Ruth in the way she fulfills Naomi's commands regarding the night that she spends at Boaz's granary (Ruth 3).

Chapter 2 acquaints us with Ruth's sense of isolation as a stranger within the society of Beth-Lehem. At the same time, as a destitute woman alone with a mother-in-law to support, she figures out how to take advantage of the generous Israelite gleaning laws to keep body and soul together. See Deuteronomy 24 in "Social Justice" in Chapter 7, "Justice."

Ruth 2

1 And Naomi had a kinsman of her husband's, a mighty man of valour, of the family of Elimelech, and his name was Boaz. 2 And Ruth the Moabitess said unto Naomi: 'Let me now go to the field, and glean among the ears of corn after him in whose sight I shall find favour.' And she said unto her: 'Go, my daughter.' 3 And she went, and came and gleaned in the field after the reapers; and her hap was to light on the portion of the field belonging unto Boaz, who was of the family of Elimelech.

4 And, behold, Boaz came from Beth-lehem, and said unto the reapers: 'The LORD be with you.' And they answered him: 'The

---

3. [[That is, Pleasant.—JPS 1917 eds.]]

4. [[That is, Bitter.—JPS 1917 eds.]]

LORD bless thee.' 5 Then said Boaz unto his servant that was set over the reapers: 'Whose damsel is this?' 6 And the servant that was set over the reapers answered and said: 'It is a Moabitish damsel that came back with Naomi out of the field of Moab; 7 and she said: Let me glean, I pray you, and gather after the reapers among the sheaves; so she came, and hath continued even from the morning until now, save that she tarried a little in the house.' 8 Then said Boaz unto Ruth: 'Hearest thou not, my daughter? Go not to glean in another field, neither pass from hence, but abide here fast by my maidens. 9 Let thine eyes be on the field that they do reap, and go thou after them; have I not charged the young men that they shall not touch thee? and when thou art athirst, go unto the vessels, and drink of that which the young men have drawn.'

10 Then she fell on her face, and bowed down to the ground, and said unto him: 'Why have I found favour in thy sight, that thou shouldest take cognizance of me, seeing I am a foreigner?' 11 And Boaz answered and said unto her: 'It hath fully been told me, all that thou hast done unto thy mother-in-law since the death of thy husband; and how thou hast left thy father and thy mother, and the land of thy nativity, and art come unto a people that thou knewest not heretofore. 12 The LORD recompense thy work, and be thy reward complete from the LORD, the God of Israel, under whose wings thou art come to take refuge.' 13 Then she said: 'Let me find favour in thy sight, my LORD; for that thou hast comforted me, and for that thou hast spoken to the heart of thy handmaid, though I be not as one of thy handmaidens.

14 And Boaz said unto her at meal-time: 'Come hither, and eat of the bread, and dip thy morsel in the vinegar.' And she sat beside the reapers; and they reached her parched corn, and she did eat and was satisfied, and left thereof. 15 And when she was risen up to glean, Boaz commanded his young men, saying: 'Let her glean even among the sheaves, and put her not to shame. 16 And also pull out some for her of purpose from the bundles, and leave it, and let her glean, and rebuke her not.' 17 So she gleaned in the field until even; and she beat out that which she had gleaned, and it was about an ephah of barley.

18 And she took it up, and went into the city; and her mother-in-law saw what she had gleaned; and she brought forth and gave to her that which she had left after she was satisfied. 19 And her

mother-in-law said unto her: 'Where hast thou gleaned to-day? and where wroughtest thou? blessed be he that did take knowledge of thee.' And she told her mother-in-law with whom she had wrought, and said: 'The man's name with whom I wrought to-day is Boaz.'

20 And Naomi said unto her daughter-in-law: 'Blessed be he of the LORD, who hath not left off His kindness to the living and to the dead.' And Naomi said unto her: 'The man is nigh of kin unto us, one of our near kinsmen.' 21 And Ruth the Moabitess said: 'Yea, he said unto me: Thou shalt keep fast by my young men, until they have ended all my harvest.' 22 And Naomi said unto Ruth her daughter-in-law: 'It is good, my daughter, that thou go out with his maidens, and that thou be not met in any other field.' 23 So she kept fast by the maidens of Boaz to glean unto the end of barley harvest and of wheat harvest; and she dwelt with her mother-in-law.

Ruth 3

1 And Naomi her mother-in-law said unto her: 'My daughter, shall I not seek rest for thee, that it may be well with thee? 2 And now is there not Boaz our kinsman, with whose maidens thou wast? Behold, he winnoweth barley to-night in the threshing-floor. 3 Wash thyself therefore, and anoint thee, and put thy raiment upon thee, and get thee down to the threshing-floor; but make not thyself known unto the man, until he shall have done eating and drinking. 4 And it shall be, when he lieth down, that thou shalt mark the place where he shall lie, and thou shalt go in, and uncover his feet, and lay thee down; and he will tell thee what thou shalt do.' 5 And she said unto her: 'All that thou sayest unto me I will do.'

6 And she went down unto the threshing-floor, and did according to all that her mother-in-law bade her. 7 And when Boaz had eaten and drunk, and his heart was merry, he went to lie down at the end of the heap of corn; and she came softly, and uncovered his feet, and laid her down.

8 And it came to pass at midnight, that the man was startled, and turned himself; and, behold, a woman lay at his feet. 9 And he said: 'Who art thou?' And she answered: 'I am Ruth thine handmaid; spread therefore thy skirt over thy handmaid; for thou art a near kinsman.' 10 And he said: 'Blessed be thou of

the LORD, my daughter; thou hast shown more kindness in the end than at the beginning, inasmuch as thou didst not follow the young men, whether poor or rich. 11 And now, my daughter, fear not; I will do to thee all that thou sayest; for all the men in the gate of my people do know that thou art a virtuous woman.

12 And now it is true that I am a near kinsman; howbeit there is a kinsman nearer than I. 13 Tarry this night, and it shall be in the morning, that if he will perform unto thee the part of a kinsman, well; let him do the kinsman's part; but if he be not willing to do the part of a kinsman to thee, then will I do the part of a kinsman to thee, as the LORD liveth; lie down until the morning.'

14 And she lay at his feet until the morning; and she rose up before one could discern another. For he said: 'Let it not be known that the woman came to the threshing-floor.' 15 And he said: 'Bring the mantle that is upon thee, and hold it'; and she held it; and he measured six measures of barley, and laid it on her; and he went into the city. 16 And when she came to her mother-in-law, she said: 'Who art thou, my daughter?' And she told her all that the man had done to her. 17 And she said: 'These six measures of barley gave he me; for he said to me: Go not empty unto thy mother-in-law.' 18 Then said she: 'Sit still, my daughter, until thou know how the matter will fall; for the man will not rest, until he have finished the thing this day.'

The narrative of the final chapter seems involved in turgid legalisms that appear to have no bearing on the story of Ruth. Alternatively, some commentators insist that the legal matter referred to in this chapter is the levirate marriage (Leviticus 18), where the brother of a man who dies childless must marry his widow so that the brother's "line" of descendants may continue (or else undergo the ceremony of *halitzah* considered a legal, but shameful, dereliction of duty).

However, as early-modern biblical commentators, such as Isaac Abarbanel, have noted,[5] the requisite elements are not there for this procedure to take place: there are no living brothers of Ruth's dead husband,

---

5. The reference is to Abarbanel's Hebrew biblical commentary on Ruth 4. Biographical information: Isaac Abarbanel (also called Abravanel) (1437–1508) was the Minister of Finance to Ferdinand and Isabella of Spain. When their decree of expulsion regarding the Jews of Spain took effect, Don (an honorific) Isaac Abarbanel was offered an exception: he would be able to stay in Spain and continue his work for the royal court. Abarbanel refused, and eventually wound up in Italy where, journeying among the various Italian city-states, he wrote a commentary on the Hebrew Bible.

and the actual ceremony described in Ruth 4 is not the levirate ceremony of *halitzah*, but a redemption of property (see Deuteronomy 25:25 in "Social Justice and Personal Equality" in Chapter 7, "Justice"), which though laudable is not absolutely mandatory. Thus, Boaz, being second in line in his relationship to Naomi, must allow the closer relative the right of first refusal.

In the end, the story of Ruth is not about the poor girl making the "right" marriage. Rather, it deals with the stranger who, perceiving what the essence of Israelite society ought to be, is instrumental in bringing forth its most enduring symbol of monarchy.

Ruth 4

1 Now Boaz went up to the gate, and sat him down there; and, behold, the near kinsman of whom Boaz spoke came by; unto whom he said: 'Ho, such a one! turn aside, sit down here.' And he turned aside, and sat down. 2 And he took ten men of the elders of the city, and said: 'Sit ye down here.' And they sat down.

3 And he said unto the near kinsman: 'Naomi, that is come back out of the field of Moab, selleth the parcel of land, which was our brother Elimelech's; 4 and I thought to disclose it unto thee, saying: Buy it before them that sit here, and before the elders of my people. If thou wilt redeem it, redeem it; but if it will not be redeemed, then tell me, that I may know; for there is none to redeem it beside thee; and I am after thee.' And he said: 'I will redeem it.' 5 Then said Boaz: 'What day thou buyest the field of the hand of Naomi—hast thou also bought of Ruth the Moabitess, the wife of the dead, to raise up the name of the dead upon his inheritance?' 6 And the near kinsman said: 'I cannot redeem it for myself, lest I mar mine own inheritance; take thou my right of redemption on thee; for I cannot redeem it.'—

7 Now this was the custom in former time in Israel concerning redeeming and concerning exchanging, to confirm all things: a man drew off his shoe, and gave it to his neighbour; and this was the attestation in Israel.— 8 So the near kinsman said unto Boaz: 'Buy it for thyself.' And he drew off his shoe. 9 And Boaz said unto the elders, and unto all the people: 'Ye are witnesses this day, that I have bought all that was Elimelech's, and all that was Chilion's and Mahlon's, of the hand of Naomi. 10 Moreover Ruth the Moabitess, the wife of Mahlon, have I acquired to be my wife, to raise up the name of the dead upon his inheritance,

that the name of the dead be not cut off from among his brethren, and from the gate of his place; ye are witnesses this day.'

11 And all the people that were in the gate, and the elders, said: 'We are witnesses. The LORD make the woman that is come into thy house like Rachel and like Leah, which two did build the house of Israel; and do thou worthily in Ephrath, and be famous in Beth-lehem; 12 and let thy house be like the house of Perez, whom Tamar bore unto Judah, of the seed which the LORD shall give thee of this young woman.'

13 So Boaz took Ruth, and she became his wife; and he went in unto her, and the LORD gave her conception, and she bore a son. 14 And the women said unto Naomi: 'Blessed be the LORD, who hath not left thee this day without a near kinsman, and let his name be famous in Israel. 15 And he shall be unto thee a restorer of life, and a nourisher of thine old age; for thy daughter-in-law, who loveth thee, who is better to thee than seven sons, hath borne him.'

16 And Naomi took the child, and laid it in her bosom, and became nurse unto it. 17 And the women her neighbours gave it a name, saying: 'There is a son born to Naomi'; and they called his name Obed; he is the father of Jesse, the father of David. 18 Now these are the generations of Perez: Perez begot Hezron; 19 and Hezron begot Ram, and Ram begot Amminadab; 20 and Amminadab begot Nahshon, and Nahshon begot Salmon; 21 and Salmon begot Boaz, and Boaz begot Obed; 22 and Obed begot Jesse, and Jesse begot David.

3. The Book of Daniel: Negotiating Survival and Success in a Foreign Court

Like the Book of Esther, the Book of Daniel takes place entirely within the reality of exile: the Israelites are no longer autonomous, and they have been ignominiously exiled. In the ancient world, exile was tantamount to death: no nation had been known to retain its coherence after losing its homeland.

In the case of the Judean kingdom, the process of this exile was a long-drawn out affair: even before the Judean king himself was humiliatingly led into captivity, the best of the Judean youth were colonized and brought to the Babylonian royal court, in an effort to prove to the Israelites that they had no future as a community. In a move of cultural supremacy, the Babylonian royal court even changed the names of these young people. Certainly these "best boys" were under severe pressure to give up their distinctive religious practices, including eating only that food prepared to the standard of their faith practices (in current parlance, this would be referred to as "kosher" food, although this nomenclature does not appear in the Book of Daniel).

a. Negotiating Identity at the Royal Court (Daniel 1)

The Book of Daniel specifically highlights that Daniel and his companions would not eat the king's meat nor drink his wine. Nevertheless, Daniel and his companions flourish at the royal court and are rewarded with high placements in the royal hierarchy. For many twenty-first-century readers, this chapter paints a rosy picture of faith and virtue rewarded.

A closer look at this chapter reveals the slippery path on which Daniel balances to receive positive responses to what must have been perceived as an outlandish request. In the context of making his request, Daniel carefully decides whom to approach: the chief officer in charge of all the Judean captives, who had already exhibited a certain amount of friendliness towards Daniel. Significantly, Daniel frames his petition not as a request, which could have been abruptly refused and, in the context of court etiquette and Daniel's own position as a virtual prisoner, never repeated, but as an experiment.

This is a crucial move. By removing the pressure from the chief officer to agree or to refuse to fulfill their dietary requirements, Daniel avoids the possibility that the chief officer might view Daniel's forthright request as putting the chief officer on the spot. Additionally, from the standpoint of the petitioner, there is another reason to refrain from expressing as an outright request the desire to avoid official court food: Even if the chief officer might be persuaded to agree to Daniel's scheme this particular time, the chief officer's attitude towards Daniel and his companions would henceforth irrevocably change, potentially exposing the young Judean captives to future unimagined perils that they might not be able to withstand without the goodwill of the chief officer, who by then might not be as willing to intercede once again on their behalf. Well aware of his tenuous position at the Babylonian court, Daniel knows that he might have to depend on the favor of the chief officer at some unknown point in the future. At the same time, Daniel deeply believes in his faith practices, and does not want to eat food that he considers religiously forbidden to him.

So Daniel comes up with another way of framing the request. Instead of expressing his bid for kosher food as an entreaty requiring an absolute response—either yes or no—on the part of the chief officer, Daniel broaches the situation in terms of an experiment: Would the chief officer feed them vegetables for a few days, and then check the results? This structures the request in terms of a search for knowledge. Instead of the tense situation that would or could arise if Daniel were openly to demand exceptional treatment, everyone now in the multiethnic makeup of the Babylonian court can potentially be on the same side, because they all are curious to document the results.

Daniel realizes that this experiment might end badly, although the Hebrew biblical text reports that it doesn't. Even in that case, however, in the context of carrying out an experiment, the evaluation of results is not (necessarily) a clear-cut issue, and still allows room for discussion. In essence, Daniel is the example in the ancient world of "getting to yes." As with Joseph, it is no wonder that his adroit handling of the situation leads the king to appreciate his wisdom.

Daniel 1

1 IN THE third year of the reign of Jehoiakim king of Judah came Nebuchadnezzar king of Babylon unto Jerusalem, and besieged it. 2 And the Lord gave Jehoiakim king of Judah into his hand, with part of the vessels of the house of God; and he carried them into the land of Shinar to the house of his god, and the vessels he brought into the treasure-house of his god.

3 And the king spoke unto Ashpenaz his chief officer, that he should bring in certain of the children of Israel, and of the seed royal, and of the nobles, 4 youths in whom was no blemish, but fair to look on, and skilful in all wisdom, and skilful in knowledge, and discerning in thought, and such as had ability to stand in the king's palace; and that he should teach them the learning and the tongue of the Chaldeans.

5 And the king appointed for them a daily portion of the king's food, and of the wine which he drank, and that they should be nourished three years; that at the end thereof they might stand before the king. 6 Now among these were, of the children of Judah, Daniel, Hananiah, Mishael, and Azariah. 7 And the chief of the officers gave names unto them: unto Daniel he gave the name of Belteshazzar; and to Hananiah, of Shadrach; and to Mishael, of Meshach; and to Azariah, of Abed-nego.

8 But Daniel purposed in his heart that he would not defile himself with the king's food, nor with the wine which he drank; therefore he requested of the chief of the officers that he might

not defile himself. 9 And God granted Daniel mercy and compassion in the sight of the chief of the officers.

10 And the chief of the officers said unto Daniel: 'I fear my lord the king, who hath appointed your food and your drink; for why should he see your faces sad in comparison with the youths that are of your own age? so would ye endanger my head with the king.'

11 Then said Daniel to the steward, whom the chief of the officers had appointed over Daniel, Hananiah, Mishael, and Azariah: 12 'Try thy servants, I beseech thee, ten days; and let them give us pulse to eat, and water to drink. 13 Then let our countenances be looked upon before thee, and the countenance of the youths that eat of the king's food; and as thou seest, deal with thy servants.'

14 So he hearkened unto them in this matter, and tried them ten days. 15 And at the end of ten days their countenances appeared fairer, and they were fatter in flesh, than all the youths that did eat of the king's food. 16 So the steward took away their food, and the wine that they should drink, and gave them pulse. 17 Now as for these four youths, God gave them knowledge and skill in all learning and wisdom; and Daniel had understanding in all visions and dreams.

18 And at the end of the days which the king had appointed for bringing them in, the chief of the officers brought them in before Nebuchadnezzar. 19 And the king spoke with them; and among them all was found none like Daniel, Hananiah, Mishael, and Azariah; therefore stood they before the king. 20 And in all matters of wisdom and understanding, that the king inquired of them, he found them ten times better than all the magicians and enchanters that were in all his realm. 21 And Daniel continued even unto the first year of king Cyrus.

b. Negotiating Survival amongst Enemies (Daniel 6)

As the stories of Esther and Joseph amply document, intelligence alone is not enough to guarantee survival in the byzantine corridors of a foreign court. Cabals and intrigues flourish against Daniel, because the king favored him (the narrative of the Book of Daniel spans the reigns of several kings). In one such plot, the enemies of Daniel, knowing that he prays several times a day, persuade the king to sign a decree outlawing prayer directed at anyone but the king himself for the next thirty days.

When Daniel is caught, shortly thereafter, praying to his God, his fate is sealed, and he is thrown into the lions' den. Daniel survives (miraculously, according to the text); but the ease that Daniel's enemies exhibit in manipulating the king leads the modern reader to realize that Daniel's position is not secure, as indeed is made evident throughout Daniel's many adventures in the Book of Daniel. Although the denizens of a royal court seem to be privileged, the lack of rights attached to individuals means that they are constantly honing their wits, not so much to prosper as to survive.

Daniel 6

1 And Darius the Mede received the kingdom, being about threescore and two years old. 2 It pleased Darius to set over the kingdom a hundred and twenty satraps, who should be throughout the whole kingdom; 3 and over them three presidents, of whom Daniel was one; that these satraps might give account unto them, and that the king should have no damage. 4 Then this Daniel distinguished himself above the presidents and the satraps, because a surpassing spirit was in him; and the king thought to set him over the whole realm.

5 Then the presidents and the satraps sought to find occasion against Daniel as touching the kingdom; but they could find no occasion nor fault; forasmuch as he was faithful, neither was there any error or fault found in him. 6 Then said these men: 'We shall not find any occasion against this Daniel, except we find it against him in the matter of the law of his God.' 7 Then these presidents and satraps came tumultuously to the king, and said thus unto him: 'King Darius, live for ever! 8 All the presidents of the kingdom, the prefects and the satraps, the ministers and the governors, have consulted together that the king should establish a statute, and make a strong interdict, that whosoever shall ask a petition of any god or man for thirty days, save of thee, O king, he shall be cast into the den of lions. 9 Now, O king, establish the interdict, and sign the writing, that it be not changed, according to the law of the Medes and Persians, which altereth not.' 10 Wherefore king Darius signed the writing and the interdict.

11 And when Daniel knew that the writing was signed, he went into his house—now his windows were open in his upper chamber toward Jerusalem—and he kneeled upon his knees three times a day, and prayed, and gave thanks before his God, as he did aforetime. 12 Then these men came tumultuously, and

found Daniel making petition and supplication before his God. 13 Then they came near, and spoke before the king concerning the king's interdict: 'Hast thou not signed an interdict, that every man that shall make petition unto any god or man within thirty days, save of thee, O king, shall be cast into the den of lions?' The king answered and said: 'The thing is true, according to the law of the Medes and Persians, which altereth not.' 14 Then answered they and said before the king: 'That Daniel, who is of the children of the captivity of Judah, regardeth not thee, O king, nor the interdict that thou hast signed, but maketh his petition three times a day.'

15 Then the king, when he heard these words, was sore displeased, and set his heart on Daniel to deliver him; and he laboured till the going down of the sun to deliver him. 16 Then these men came tumultuously unto the king, and said unto the king: 'Know, O king, that it is a law of the Medes and Persians, that no interdict nor statute which the king establisheth may be changed.' 17 Then the king commanded, and they brought Daniel, and cast him into the den of lions. Now the king spoke and said unto Daniel: 'Thy God whom thou servest continually, He will deliver thee.' 18 And a stone was brought, and laid upon the mouth of the den; and the king sealed it with his own signet, and with the signet of his lords; that nothing might be changed concerning Daniel.

19 Then the king went to his palace, and passed the night fasting; neither were diversions brought before him; and his sleep fled from him. 20 Then the king arose very early in the morning, and went in haste unto the den of lions. 21 And when he came near unto the den to Daniel, he cried with a pained voice; the king spoke and said to Daniel: 'O Daniel, servant of the living God, is thy God, whom thou servest continually, able to deliver thee from the lions?' 22 Then said Daniel unto the king: 'O king, live for ever! 23 My God hath sent His angel, and hath shut the lions' mouths, and they have not hurt me; forasmuch as before Him innocency was found in me; and also before thee, O king, have I done no hurt.'

24 Then was the king exceeding glad, and commanded that they should take Daniel up out of the den. So Daniel was taken up out of the den, and no manner of hurt was found upon him, because he had trusted in his God. 25 And the king commanded,

and they brought those men that had accused Daniel, and they cast them into the den of lions, them, their children, and their wives; and they had not come to the bottom of the den, when the lions had the mastery of them, and broke all their bones in pieces.

26 Then king Darius wrote unto all the peoples, nations, and languages, that dwell in all the earth: 'Peace be multiplied unto you. 27 I make a decree, that in all the dominion of my kingdom men tremble and fear before the God of Daniel;

For He is the living God,
And stedfast for ever,
And His kingdom that which shall not be destroyed,
And His dominion shall be even unto the end;
28 He delivereth and rescueth,
And He worketh signs and wonders
In heaven and in earth;
Who hath delivered Daniel from the power of the lions.'

29 So this Daniel prospered in the reign of Darius, and in the reign of Cyrus the Persian.

C. Exile Anticipated and Experienced: Views from the Text

Since the Hebrew Bible depicts human exile at the very center of the human experience, it makes sense, even though exile is figured as the ultimate punishment for the Israelites, that exile is portrayed as an (inevitable?) element of their future existence. Moses, in one of his last acts of leadership, transcribes a special copy of the Torah that he places near the Holy Ark so that the Israelites may remember this warning. Moses knows that the Israelites are ever rebellious, and he does not imagine that they will improve upon his death.

1. Exile Anticipated

Deuteronomy 28:64–68

64 And the LORD shall scatter thee among all peoples, from the one end of the earth even unto the other end of the earth; and there thou shalt serve other gods, which thou hast not known, thou nor thy fathers, even wood and stone. 65 And among these

nations shalt thou have no repose, and there shall be no rest for the sole of thy foot; but the LORD shall give thee there a trembling heart, and failing of eyes, and languishing of soul. 66 And thy life shall hang in doubt before thee; and thou shalt fear night and day, and shalt have no assurance of thy life. 67 In the morning thou shalt say: 'Would it were even [evening]!' and at even [evening] thou shalt say: 'Would it were morning!' for the fear of thy heart which thou shalt fear, and for the sight of thine eyes which thou shalt see. 68 And the LORD shall bring thee back into Egypt in ships, by the way whereof I said unto thee: 'Thou shalt see it no more again'; and there ye shall sell yourselves unto your enemies for bondmen and for bondwoman, and no man shall buy you.

Deuteronomy 31:16–30

16 And the LORD said unto Moses: 'Behold, thou art about to sleep with thy fathers; and this people will rise up, and go astray after the foreign gods of the land, whither they go to be among them, and will forsake Me, and break My covenant which I have made with them.

17 Then My anger shall be kindled against them in that day, and I will forsake them, and I will hide My face from them, and they shall be devoured, and many evils and troubles shall come upon them; so that they will say in that day: Are not these evils come upon us because our God is not among us? 18 And I will surely hide My face in that day for all the evil which they shall have wrought, in that they are turned unto other gods.

19 Now therefore write ye this song for you, and teach thou it the children of Israel; put it in their mouths, that this song may be a witness for Me against the children of Israel. 20 For when I shall have brought them into the land which I swore unto their fathers, flowing with milk and honey; and they shall have eaten their fill, and waxen fat; and turned unto other gods, and served them, and despised Me, and broken My covenant;

21 then it shall come to pass, when many evils and troubles are come upon them, that this song shall testify before them as a witness; for it shall not be forgotten out of the mouths of their seed; for I know their imagination how they do even now, before I have brought them into the land which I swore.' 22 So Moses wrote this song the same day, and taught it the children of Israel.

23 And he gave Joshua the son of Nun a charge, and said: 'Be strong and of good courage; for thou shalt bring the children of Israel into the land which I swore unto them; and I will be with thee.'

24 And it came to pass, when Moses had made an end of writing the words of this law in a book, until they were finished, 25 that Moses commanded the Levites, that bore the ark of the covenant of the LORD, saying: 26 'Take this book of the law, and put it by the side of the ark of the covenant of the LORD your God, that it may be there for a witness against thee. 27 For I know thy rebellion, and thy stiff neck; behold, while I am yet alive with you this day, ye have been rebellious against the LORD; and how much more after my death?

28 Assemble unto me all the elders of your tribes, and your officers, that I may speak these words in their ears, and call heaven and earth to witness against them. 29 For I know that after my death ye will in any wise deal corruptly, and turn aside from the way which I have commanded you; and evil will befall you in the end of days; because ye will do that which is evil in the sight of the LORD, to provoke Him through the work of your hands.' 30 And Moses spoke in the ears of all the assembly of Israel the words of this song, until they were finished:

For further reading see Ezekiel 12:1–11.

2. Exile Experienced

This psalm details the tears of the Israelites as they are forced into Babylonian exile; they pledge to remember Jerusalem forever.

Psalm 137:1–6

1 By the rivers of Babylon,
There we sat down, yea, we wept,
When we remembered Zion.
2 Upon the willows in the midst thereof
We hanged up our harps.
3 For there they that led us captive asked of us words of song,
And our tormentors asked of us mirth:
'Sing us one of the songs of Zion.'
4 How shall we sing the LORD's song
In a foreign land?

5 If I forget thee, O Jerusalem,
Let my right hand forget her cunning.
6 Let my tongue cleave to the roof of my mouth,
If I remember thee not;
If I set not Jerusalem
Above my chiefest joy.

Zechariah 12:8–14

8 In that day shall the LORD defend the inhabitants of Jerusalem;
And he that stumbleth among them at that day shall be as David;
And the house of David shall be as a godlike being,
As the angel of the LORD before them.
9 And it shall come to pass in that day,
That I will seek to destroy all the nations
That come against Jerusalem.
10 And I will pour upon the house of David,
And upon the inhabitants of Jerusalem,
The spirit of grace and of supplication;
And they shall look unto Me because they[6] have thrust him
   through;
And they shall mourn for him, as one mourneth for his only son,
And shall be in bitterness for him, as one that is in bitterness for
   his first-born.
11 In that day shall there be a great mourning in Jerusalem,
As the mourning of Hadadrimmon in the valley of Megiddon.
12 And the land shall mourn, every family apart:
The family of the house of David apart, and their wives apart;
The family of the house of Nathan apart, and their wives apart;
13 The family of the house of Levi apart, and their wives apart;
The family of the Shimeites apart, and their wives apart;
14 All the families that remain,
Every family apart, and their wives apart.

---

6. That is, the nations. See verse 9.

CHAPTER 18

REBUILDING THE COMMUNITY: REDEMPTION AND ENVISIONING THE FUTURE

The Hebrew Bible gives a remarkably nuanced picture of what it means to rebuild after exile and destruction. Certainly there are soaring visions of heavenly perfection, most of which are not included in this politically inflected anthology. The selections here emphasize the nuts and bolts of what is involved in reestablishing a society in a location that has been physically devastated, and in which locally transplanted populations do not wish to accept the returning former inhabitants, and therefore libel them to their imperial masters.

These selections examine what it means to reconstruct a society that had been recently exiled in chains into an equitable and (somewhat, given the ubiquity of taxes and political loyalty paid to the Persian Empire) autonomous social order. Are intermarried priests allowed to participate in the newly established Temple service, for example? Does rebuilding a nation imply mandating social exclusivity?

These issues come to the fore with the situation of those intermarried priests (and other Israelites) who have returned to Jerusalem and who cannot, by Hebrew biblical law, serve in the Temple. Ezra reacts to the fact of intermarriage by weeping and fasting. The proposal is made—significantly, not by Ezra himself but by other people (Ezra 10:2–3)—to separate from the non-Jewish wives. Ezra agrees with this proposal, but, importantly, does not force anyone to adhere to it. He merely states his vision of the viable alternatives: priests who want to serve in the Temple must abjure their non-Jewish wives.

Importantly, the Hebrew biblical text does not report further instances of social or religious coercion and consequence: the priests are not forced to divorce their wives (although there is a consequence for not doing so: not serving in the Temple), and there is no record here of those priests who opt to keep their wives being forced out of the new Judean settlement of the land. The tone of the text (Nehemiah 8) seems to indicate an overall voluntary acceptance of these conditions (presumably because it was a known Hebrew biblical regulation; see Leviticus 21:14–15). This situation may not fit twenty-first-century notions of ecumenicism, but it cannot either be adduced as an example of forced conversion by the leadership, or of compelled acceptance of compulsory personal arrangements on the part of the people.

This chapter ends with the hopeful trope of rebuilding, the idea that exile is not a death knell for a proactive population, and the redemptive belief—and hope—that there are second acts[1] in political life.

A. Rebuilding Jerusalem

Haggai 2:1–9, 20–23

1 In the seventh month, in the one and twentieth day of the month, came the word of the LORD by Haggai the prophet, saying: 2 'Speak now to Zerubbabel the son of Shealtiel, governor of Judah, and to Joshua the son of Jehozadak, the high priest, and to the remnant of the people, saying: 3 Who is left among you that saw this house in its former glory? and how do ye see it now? is not such a one as nothing in your eyes?

4 Yet now be strong, O Zerubbabel, saith the LORD; and be strong, O Joshua, son of Jehozadak, the high priest; and be strong, all ye people of the land, saith the LORD, and work; for I am with you, saith the LORD of hosts. 5 The word that I covenanted with you when ye came out of Egypt have I established, and My spirit abideth among you; fear ye not. 6 For thus saith the LORD of hosts: Yet once, it is a little while, and I will shake the heavens, and the earth, and the sea, and the dry land;

7 and I will shake all nations, and the choicest things of all nations shall come, and I will fill this house with glory, saith the LORD of hosts. 8 Mine is the silver, and Mine the gold, saith the LORD of hosts. 9 The glory of this latter house shall be greater than that of the former, saith the LORD of hosts; and in this place will I give peace, saith the LORD of hosts.'

. . . .

20 And the word of the LORD came the second time unto Haggai in the four and twentieth day of the month, saying: 21

---

1. See Chapter 7, "Justice," footnote 1.

'Speak to Zerubbabel, governor of Judah, saying: I will shake the heavens and the earth; 22 and I will overthrow the throne of kingdoms, and I will destroy the strength of the kingdoms of the nations; and I will overthrow the chariots, and those that ride in them; and the horses and their riders shall come down, every one by the sword of his brother. 23 In that day, saith the LORD of hosts, will I take thee, O Zerubbabel, My servant, the son of Shealtiel, saith the LORD, and will make thee as a signet; for I have chosen thee, saith the LORD of hosts.'

For further reading, cf. also Zechariah 1:15–16 and 2:15.

B. "Second Acts" after Exile

The texts in this section show different approaches to rebirth and redevelopment after what looks like the death knell of exile. Jeremiah speaks in the language of history, recalling and recalibrating past events as auguries for the future. In Jeremiah's prophecy, survivors of the sword of exile will be again taken through a wilderness; but this time, instead of complaining (as when they left Egypt), they will recognize it as a place where they can draw a second wind, preparing themselves for the task of rebuilding their national life.

In the next selection, Ezekiel draws his vision not from the common culture of Israelite history, but from the physiological structure of human life. In the famous Valley of the Dry Bones narrative (Ezekiel 37:1–14) Ezekiel utilizes the very stuff of human existence to demonstrate that what is conventionally seen as the hopeless sign of death—dry bones—can instead be viewed as the building blocks of a new structure. Similarly, the liquidity of blood, normally taken as the deadly accompaniment to violence and struggle, is understood by the prophet as the stream of life, reinvigorating a new vision for the future.

1. Jeremiah: Encouraging Hope

Jeremiah 31:1–8, 15–17

1 At that time, saith the LORD,
Will I be the God of all the families of Israel,
And they shall be My people.
2 Thus saith the LORD:
The people that were left of the sword
Have found grace in the wilderness,

Even Israel, when I go to cause him to rest.
3 'From afar the LORD appeared unto me.'
'Yea, I have loved thee with an everlasting love;
Therefore with affection have I drawn thee.
4 Again will I build thee, and thou shalt be built,
O virgin of Israel;
Again shalt thou be adorned with thy tabrets,
And shalt go forth in the dances of them that make merry.
5 Again shalt thou plant vineyards upon the mountains of
Samaria;
The planters shall plant, and shall have the use thereof.
6 For there shall be a day,
That the watchmen shall call upon the mount Ephraim:
Arise ye, and let us go up to Zion,
Unto the LORD our God.'
7 For thus saith the LORD:
Sing with gladness for Jacob,
And shout at the head of the nations;
Announce ye, praise ye, and say:
'O LORD, save Thy people,
The remnant of Israel.'
8 Behold, I will bring them from the north country,
And gather them from the uttermost parts of the earth,
And with them the blind and the lame,
The woman with child and her that travaileth with child together;
A great company shall they return hither.

. . . .

15 Thus saith the LORD:
A voice is heard in Ramah,
Lamentation, and bitter weeping,
Rachel weeping for her children;
She refuseth to be comforted for her children,
Because they are not.
16 Thus saith the LORD:
Refrain thy voice from weeping,
And thine eyes from tears;
For thy work shall be rewarded, saith the LORD;
And they shall come back from the land of the enemy.
17 And there is hope for thy future, saith the LORD;
And thy children shall return to their own border.

2. Ezekiel: Negating Despair

a. The Valley of the Bones

Ezekiel 37:1–14

1 The hand of the LORD was upon me, and the LORD carried me out in a spirit, and set me down in the midst of the valley, and it was full of bones; 2 and He caused me to pass by them round about, and, behold, there were very many in the open valley; and, lo, they were very dry.

3 And He said unto me: 'Son of man, can these bones live?' And I answered: 'O Lord GOD, Thou knowest.'

4 Then He said unto me: 'Prophesy over these bones, and say unto them: O ye dry bones, hear the word of the LORD: 5 Thus saith the Lord GOD unto these bones: Behold, I will cause breath to enter into you, and ye shall live. 6 And I will lay sinews upon you, and will bring up flesh upon you, and cover you with skin, and put breath in you, and ye shall live; and ye shall know that I am the LORD.'

7 So I prophesied as I was commanded; and as I prophesied, there was a noise, and behold a commotion, and the bones came together, bone to its bone. 8 And I beheld, and, lo, there were sinews upon them, and flesh came up, and skin covered them above; but there was no breath in them.

9 Then said He unto me: 'Prophesy unto the breath, prophesy, son of man, and say to the breath: Thus saith the Lord GOD: Come from the four winds, O breath, and breathe upon these slain, that they may live.' 10 So I prophesied as He commanded me, and the breath came into them, and they lived, and stood up upon their feet, an exceeding great host.

11 Then He said unto me: 'Son of man, these bones are the whole house of Israel; behold, they say: Our bones are dried up, and our hope is lost; we are clean cut off. 12 Therefore prophesy, and say unto them: Thus saith the Lord GOD: Behold, I will open your graves, and cause you to come up out of your graves, O My people; and I will bring you into the land of Israel. 13 And ye shall know that I am the LORD, when I have opened your graves, and caused you to come up out of your graves, O My

people. 14 And I will put My spirit in you, and ye shall live, and I will place you in your own land; and ye shall know that I the LORD have spoken, and performed it, saith the LORD.'

Ezekiel 16:6–13

6 And when I passed by thee, and saw thee wallowing in thy blood, I said unto thee: In thy blood, live; yea, I said unto thee: In thy blood, live;

7 I cause thee to increase, even as the growth of the field. And thou didst increase and grow up, and thou camest to excellent beauty: thy breasts were fashioned, and thy hair was grown; yet thou wast naked and bare.

8 Now when I passed by thee, and looked upon thee, and, behold, thy time was the time of love, I spread my skirt over thee, and covered thy nakedness; yea, I swore unto thee, and entered into a covenant with thee, saith the Lord GOD, and thou becamest Mine.

9 Then washed I thee with water; yea, I cleansed away thy blood from thee, and I anointed thee with oil. 10 I clothed thee also with richly woven work, and shod thee with sealskin, and I wound fine linen about thy head, and covered thee with silk. 11 I decked thee also with ornaments, and I put bracelets upon thy hands, and a chain on thy neck. 12 And I put a ring upon thy nose, and earrings in thine ears, and a beautiful crown upon thy head.

13 Thus wast thou decked with gold and silver; and thy raiment was of fine linen, and silk, and richly woven work; thou didst eat fine flour, and honey, and oil; and thou didst wax exceeding beautiful, and thou wast meet for royal estate.

C. Empirical Challenges of Rebuilding

The leaders and prophets of the Hebrew Bible understand that lofty visions alone do not rebuild a country. The excitement of the Israelites to return to their homeland—a nearly incomprehensible project in the context of the realities of the ancient world—is met with resistance on the part of the transplanted residents now in Jerusalem and other parts of the Israelite homeland who, in accordance with Babylonian policy, had been brought in from other parts of the Babylonian Empire to populate the land.

Ezra 4

1 Now when the adversaries of Judah and Benjamin heard that the children of the captivity were building a temple unto the LORD, the God of Israel; 2 then they drew near to Zerubbabel, and to the heads of fathers' houses, and said unto them: 'Let us build with you; for we seek your God, as ye do; and we do sacrifice unto Him since the days of Esarhaddon king of Assyria, who brought us up hither.'

3 But Zerubbabel, and Jeshua, and the rest of the heads of fathers' houses of Israel, said unto them: 'Ye have nothing to do with us to build a house unto our God; but we ourselves together will build unto the LORD, the God of Israel, as king Cyrus the king of Persia hath commanded us.'

4 Then the people of the land weakened the hands of the people of Judah, and harried them while they were building, 5 and hired counsellors against them, to frustrate their purpose, all the days of Cyrus king of Persia, even until the reign of Darius king of Persia. 6 And in the reign of Ahasuerus, in the beginning of his reign, wrote they an accusation against the inhabitants of Judah and Jerusalem.

7 And in the days of Artaxerxes wrote Bishlam, Mithredath, Tabeel, and the rest of his companions, unto Artaxerxes king of Persia; and the writing of the letter was written in the Aramaic character, and set forth in the Aramaic tongue. 8 Rehum the commander and Shimshai the scribe wrote a letter against Jerusalem to Artaxerxes the king in this sort—

9 then wrote Rehum the commander, and Shimshai the scribe, and the rest of their companions; the Dinites, and the Apharesattechites, the Tarpelites, the Apharesites, the Archevites, the Babylonians, the Shushanchites, the Dehites, the Elamites, 10 and the rest of the nations whom the great and noble Asenappar brought over, and set in the city of Samaria, and the rest that are in the country beyond the River:—' And now—

11 this is the copy of the letter that they sent unto him, even unto Artaxerxes the king—thy servants the men beyond the River—and now 12 be it known unto the king, that the Jews that came up from thee are come to us unto Jerusalem; they are building the rebellious and the bad city, and have finished the walls, and are digging out the foundations.

13 Be it known now unto the king, that, if this city be builded, and the walls finished, they will not pay tribute, impost, or toll, and so thou wilt endamage the revenue of the kings. 14 Now because we eat the salt of the palace, and it is not meet for us to see the king's dishonour, therefore have we sent and announced to the king, 15 that search may be made in the book of the records of thy fathers; so shalt thou find in the book of the records, and know that this city is a rebellious city, and hurtful unto kings and provinces, and that they have moved sedition within the same of old time; for which cause was this city laid waste. 16 We announce to the king that, if this city be builded, and the walls finished, by this means thou shalt have no portion beyond the River.'

17 Then sent the king an answer unto Rehum the commander, and to Shimshai the scribe, and to the rest of their companions that dwell in Samaria, and unto the rest beyond the River: 'Peace, and now 18 the letter which ye sent unto us hath been plainly read before me. 19 And I decreed, and search hath been made, and it is found that this city of old time hath made insurrection against kings, and that rebellion and sedition have been made therein. 20 There have been mighty kings also over Jerusalem, who have ruled over all the country beyond the River; and tribute, impost, and toll, was paid unto them. 21 Make ye now a decree to cause these men to cease, and that this city be not builded, until a decree shall be made by me. 22 And take heed that ye be not slack herein; why should damage grow to the hurt of the kings?'

23 Then when the copy of king Artaxerxes' letter was read before Rehum, and Shimshai the scribe, and their companions, they went in haste to Jerusalem unto the Jews, and made them to cease by force and power. 24 Then ceased the work of the house of God which is at Jerusalem; and it ceased unto the second year of the reign of Darius king of Persia.

The resentment of the local adversaries to Judean resettlement is not met with passivity. In the next selection, Nehemiah, a leader of the Judean return, suggests new practices to combat their enmity. With an inventive combination of prayer, self-help, division of labor (Nehemiah 4:16, 21), blending of function (Nehemiah 4:17) and social-class cooperation (Nehemiah 4:22), the rebuilding goes on.

Nehemiah 4:1–17

1 But it came to pass that, when Sanballat, and Tobiah, and the Arabians, and the Ammonites, and the Ashdodites, heard that the repairing of the walls of Jerusalem went forward, and that the breaches began to be stopped, then they were very wroth; 2 and they conspired all of them together to come and fight against Jerusalem, and to cause confusion therein.

3 But we made our prayer unto our God, and set a watch against them day and night, because of them. 4 And Judah said: 'The strength of the bearers of burdens is decayed, and there is much rubbish; so that we are not able to build the wall.' 5 And our adversaries said: 'They shall not know, neither see, till we come into the midst of them, and slay them, and cause the work to cease.'

6 And it came to pass that, when the Jews that dwelt by them came, they said unto us ten times: 'Ye must return unto us from all places.' 7 Therefore set I in the lowest parts of the space behind the wall, in the open places, I even set the people after their families with their swords, their spears, and their bows. 8 And I looked, and rose up, and said unto the nobles, and to the rulers, and to the rest of the people: 'Be not ye afraid of them; remember the Lord, who is great and awful, and fight for your brethren, your sons and your daughters, your wives and your houses.'

9 And it came to pass, when our enemies heard that it was known unto us, and God had brought their counsel to nought, that we returned all of us to the wall, every one unto his work. 10 And it came to pass from that time forth, that half of my servants wrought in the work, and half of them held the spears, the shields, and the bows, and the coats of mail; and the rulers were behind all the house of Judah.

11 They that builded the wall and they that bore burdens laded themselves, every one with one of his hands wrought in the work, and with the other held his weapon; 12 and the builders, every one had his sword girded by his side, and so builded. And he that sounded the horn was by me.

13 And I said unto the nobles, and to the rulers and to the rest of the people: 'The work is great and large, and we are separated upon the wall, one far from another; 14 in what place soever ye

hear the sound of the horn, resort ye thither unto us; our God will fight for us.'

15 So we wrought in the work; and half of them held the spears from the rising of the morning till the stars appeared. 16 Likewise at the same time said I unto the people: 'Let every one with his servant lodge within Jerusalem, that in the night they may be a guard to us, and may labour in the day.' 17 So neither I, nor my brethren, nor my servants, nor the men of the guard that followed me, none of us put off our clothes, every one that went to the water had his weapon.

D. Circumstances of Rebuilding

Even with the goodwill portrayed by the new strategies in the rebuilding of Jerusalem, the Hebrew Bible does not depict this new (and historically unheard of) opportunity as an Edenic enterprise. Instead, the Hebrew Bible shows the contemporary reader the reality of complex initiatives, which, taking place under empirically difficult circumstances, necessarily evoke complicated reactions. In the following selection, the modern reader is witness to the reality of differences among colleagues that threaten the peace of a community that is at the fragile start of its reestablishment.

In this selection, Nehemiah rebukes the upper classes among the returnees for their economic oppression of their less wealthy comrades. By requiring heavy pledges of their poorer compatriots to secure loans that would enable them to survive the hunger and hardships of the years of rebuilding Jerusalem, the wealthy had in effect created a feudal class that was now complaining to Nehemiah to redress this fundamental injustice. What sort of liberation has any meaning politically if it is accompanied by economic enslavement?

Significantly, this argument anticipates the critique that Marx makes of the fundamental injustice of capitalism, in his *Economic and Philosophic Manuscripts of 1844*.[2] For Marx, a system in which the creators of value cannot afford the wealth that they themselves bring into being is morally dissolute and necessarily incoherent; this last, according to Marx, is evidence of the fundamental contradiction that would, he was certain, destroy the system of capitalism both from within (as people begin to recognize this speciousness) and from without (as this incoherence sets off wider contradictions of its own, with empirical international consequences).

---

2. Karl Marx, "Economic and Philosophic Manuscripts of 1844," pp. 66–125 in Robert C. Tucker, ed., *The Marx-Engels Reader*, Second Edition (New York: W. W. Norton, 1978, reprint).

Nehemiah agrees with this logic (Nehemiah 5:5–8) and adds a point of his own: Are not his richer compatriots ashamed of having forgotten the message of the Hebrew Bible, to act kindly and with justice to all human beings? The kind of "pledge" required by the wealthy also smacks of the Hebrew biblical prohibition of usury. Nehemiah's arguments—and, in all likelihood, what Weber later identifies as the persuasive abilities of the "charismatic" leader—carry the day.[3]

Nehemiah 5

1 Then there arose a great cry of the people and of their wives against their brethren the Jews. 2 For there were that said: 'We, our sons and our daughters, are many; let us get for them corn, that we may eat and live.'

3 Some also there were that said: 'We are mortgaging our fields, and our vineyards, and our houses; let us get corn, because of the dearth.'

4 There were also that said: 'We have borrowed money for the king's tribute upon our fields and our vineyards.

5 Yet now our flesh is as the flesh of our brethren, our children as their children; and, lo, we bring into bondage our sons and our daughters to be servants, and some of our daughters are brought into bondage already; neither is it in our power to help it; for other men have our fields and our vineyards.'

6 And I was very angry when I heard their cry and these words.

7 Then I consulted with myself, and contended with the nobles and the rulers, and said unto them: 'Ye lend upon pledge, every one to his brother.' And I held a great assembly against them.

8 And I said unto them: 'We after our ability have redeemed our brethren the Jews, that sold themselves unto the heathen; and would ye nevertheless sell your brethren, and should they sell themselves unto us?' Then held they their peace, and found never a word.

9 Also I said: 'The thing that ye do is not good; ought ye not to walk in the fear of our God, because of the reproach of the

---

3. "The holder of charisma seizes the task . . . and demands obedience and a following by virtue of his mission. . . ." "The Sociology of Charismatic Authority" in Max Weber, *On Charisma and Institution Building*, ed. S. N. Eisenstadt (Chicago: University of Chicago Press, 1968), p. 20.

heathen our enemies? 10 And I likewise, my brethren and my servants, have lent them money and corn. I pray you, let us leave off this exaction. 11 Restore, I pray you, to them, even this day, their fields, their vineyards, their oliveyards, and their houses, also the hundred pieces of silver, and the corn, the wine, and the oil, that ye exact of them.'

12 Then said they: 'We will restore them, and will require nothing of them; so will we do, even as thou sayest.' Then I called the priests, and took an oath of them, that they should do according to this promise. 13 Also I shook out my lap, and said: 'So God shake out every man from his house, and from his labour, that performeth not this promise; even thus be he shaken out, and emptied.' And all the congregation said: 'Amen', and praised the LORD. And the people did according to this promise.

14 Moreover from the time that I was appointed to be their governor in the land of Judah, from the twentieth year even unto the two and thirtieth year of Artaxerxes the king, that is, twelve years, I and my brethren have not eaten the bread of the governor.

15 But the former governors that were before me laid burdens upon the people, and took of them for bread and wine above forty shekels of silver; yea, even their servants lorded over the people; but so did not I, because of the fear of God. 16 Yea, also I set hand to the work of this wall, neither bought we any land; and all my servants were gathered thither unto the work. 17 Moreover there were at my table of the Jews and the rulers a hundred and fifty men, beside those that came unto us from among the nations that were round about us. 18 Now that which was prepared for one day was one ox and six choice sheep, also fowls were prepared for me; and once in ten days store of all sorts of wine; yet for all this I demanded not the bread of the governor, because the service was heavy upon this people. 19 Remember unto me, O my God, for good, all that I have done for this people.

E. Practical Trials of Rebuilding: Coping with Enmity

As we have already seen regarding the leadership experiences of Moses, the Hebrew Bible does not confuse the accuracy of a leader's opinions—or even the fact of being chosen by God—with the people's acceptance of this leader (Moses and Deborah are just two examples of leaders whose instructions are often ignored). Despite the plethora of challenges that Nehemiah meets, and the very real successes that he has, Nehemiah is no exception to this rule. Consequently, he must contend with many rivals to himself and his project of rebuilding.

Ominously, Nehemiah's enemies seek to get him into trouble with the functionaries of empire that continue to hold the ultimate reins of power over the reestablishment of the Second Commonwealth in the ancient Promised Land. As is typical of most power plays, the machinations of plotting and treachery continue long after the particular incident described (building Jerusalem's protective wall) has passed. Politics, as here presented, partakes of both drama and farce, and is always threatening.

Nehemiah 6

1 Now it came to pass, when it was reported to Sanballat and Tobiah, and to Geshem the Arabian, and unto the rest of our enemies, that I had builded the wall, and that there was no breach left therein—though even unto that time I had not set up the doors in the gates—

2 that Sanballat and Geshem sent unto me, saying: 'Come, let us meet together in one of the villages in the plain of Ono.' But they thought to do me mischief. 3 And I sent messengers unto them, saying: 'I am doing a great work, so that I cannot come down; why should the work cease, whilst I leave it, and come down to you?' 4 And they sent unto me four times after this sort; and I answered them after the same manner.

5 Then sent Sanballat his servant unto me in like manner the fifth time with an open letter in his hand; 6 wherein was written: 'It is reported among the nations, and Geshem saith it, that thou and the Jews think to rebel; for which cause thou buildest the wall; and thou wouldest be their king, even according to these words. 7 And thou hast also appointed prophets to proclaim of thee at Jerusalem, saying: There is a king in Judah; and now shall it be reported to the king according to these words. Come now therefore, and let us take counsel together.'

8 Then I sent unto him, saying: 'There are no such things done as thou sayest, but thou feignest them out of thine own heart.' 9 For they all would have us afraid, saying: 'Their hands shall be weakened from the work, that it be not done.' But now, strengthen Thou my hands.

10 And as for me, I went unto the house of Shemaiah the son of Delaiah the son of Mehetabel, who was shut up; and he said: 'Let us meet together in the house of God, within the temple, and let us shut the doors of the temple; for they will come to slay thee; yea, in the night will they come to slay thee.'

11 And I said: 'Should such a man as I flee? and who is there, that, being such as I, could go into the temple and live? I will not go in.' 12 And I discerned, and, lo, God had not sent him; for he pronounced this prophecy against me, whereas Tobiah and Sanballat had hired him. 13 For this cause was he hired, that I should be afraid, and do so, and sin, and that they might have matter for an evil report, that they might taunt me. 14 Remember, O my God, Tobiah and Sanballat according to these their works, and also the prophetess Noadiah, and the rest of the prophets, that would have me put in fear.

15 So the wall was finished in the twenty and fifth day of the month Elul, in fifty and two days. 16 And it came to pass, when all our enemies heard thereof, that all the nations that were about us feared, and were much cast down in their own eyes; for they perceived that this work was wrought of our God. 17 Moreover in those days the nobles of Judah sent many letters unto Tobiah, and the letters of Tobiah came unto them. 18 For there were many in Judah sworn unto him, because he was the son-in-law of Shecaniah the son of Arah; and his son Jehohanan had taken the daughter of Meshullam the son of Berechiah to wife. 19 Also they spoke of his good deeds before me, and reported my words to him. And Tobiah sent letters to put me in fear.

F. Religious Challenges of Rebuilding

As the leaders of the rebuilding of Jerusalem perceive it, the physical rejuvenation of Jerusalem must be accompanied by spiritual renewal. Most specifically, this means that the priestly class who are to serve in the rebuilt Holy Temple must themselves adhere to the strictures of the Torah Commandments. A problematic issue in this regard is the reality of intermarriage, which had accompanied many of the returnees, including the returning priests: according to Israelite religious practice, intermarried individuals are not allowed to serve in the Holy Temple. The following selection presents the proposal to deal with this situation. It is noteworthy that the proposal to "put away the strange wives" comes not from Ezra but from among the people (Ezra 10:2–3). Significant, too, is that not everyone agrees with this proposal, and the disagreement is public and discussed.

Ezra 10:1–17

1 Now while Ezra prayed, and made confession, weeping and casting himself down before the house of God, there was gathered together unto him out of Israel a very great congregation of men and women and children; for the people wept very sore. 2 And Shecaniah the son of Jehiel, one of the sons of Elam, answered and said unto Ezra: 'We have broken faith with our God, and have married foreign women of the peoples of the land; yet now there is hope for Israel concerning this thing. 3 Now therefore let us make a covenant with our God to put away all the wives, and such as are born of them, according to the counsel of the LORD, and of those that tremble at the commandment of our God; and let it be done according to the law. 4 Arise; for the matter belongeth unto thee, and we are with thee; be of good courage, and do it.'

5 Then arose Ezra, and made the chiefs of the priests, the Levites, and all Israel, to swear that they would do according to this word. So they swore. 6 Then Ezra rose up from before the house of God, and went into the chamber of Jehohanan the son of Eliashib; and when he came thither, he did eat no bread, nor drink water; for he mourned because of the faithlessness of them of the captivity. 7 And they made proclamation throughout Judah and Jerusalem unto all the children of the captivity, that they should gather themselves together unto Jerusalem; 8 and that whosoever came not within three days, according to the counsel of the princes and the elders, all his substance should be forfeited, and himself separated from the congregation of the captivity.

9 Then all the men of Judah and Benjamin gathered themselves together unto Jerusalem within the three days; it was the ninth month, on the twentieth day of the month; and all the people sat in the broad place before the house of God, trembling because of this matter, and for the great rain. 10 And Ezra the priest stood up, and said unto them: 'Ye have broken faith, and have married foreign women, to increase the guilt of Israel. 11 Now therefore make confession unto the LORD, the God of your fathers, and

do His pleasure; and separate yourselves from the peoples of the land, and from the foreign women.'

12 Then all the congregation answered and said with a loud voice: 'As thou hast said, so it is for us to do. 13 But the people are many, and it is a time of much rain, and we are not able to stand without, neither is this a work of one day or two; for we have greatly transgressed in this matter. 14 Let now our princes of all the congregation stand, and let all them that are in our cities that have married foreign women come at appointed times, and with them the elders of every city, and the judges thereof, until the fierce wrath of our God be turned from us, as touching this matter.'

15 Only Jonathan the son of Asahel and Jahzeiah the son of Tikvah concerned themselves with[4] this matter; and Meshullam and Shabbethai the Levite helped them. 16 And the children of the captivity did so. And Ezra the priest, with certain heads of fathers' houses, after their fathers' houses, and all of them by their names, were separated; and they sat down in the first day of the tenth month to examine the matter. 17 And they were finished with all the men that had married foreign women by the first day of the first month.

G. Blended Tropes: Redemption and Justice

We end this anthology—but not the discussion—with textual visions of redemption foreseen as a function of justice both transcendent and empirical.

1. Closing the Circle

Deuteronomy 30:1–10

1 And it shall come to pass, when all these things are come upon thee, the blessing and the curse, which I have set before thee, and thou shalt bethink thyself among all the nations, whither the LORD thy God hath driven thee, 2 and shalt return unto the LORD thy God, and hearken to His voice according to all that I command thee this day, thou and thy children, with all thy heart, and with all thy soul;

---

4. JPS 1917: "stood up against."

3 that then the LORD thy God will turn thy captivity, and have compassion upon thee, and will return and gather thee from all the peoples, whither the LORD thy God hath scattered thee. 4 If any of thine that are dispersed be in the uttermost parts of heaven, from thence will the LORD thy God gather thee, and from thence will He fetch thee.

5 And the LORD thy God will bring thee into the land which thy fathers possessed, and thou shalt possess it; and He will do thee good, and multiply thee above thy fathers. 6 And the LORD thy God will circumcise thy heart, and the heart of thy seed, to love the LORD thy God with all thy heart, and with all thy soul, that thou mayest live. 7 And the LORD thy God will put all these curses upon thine enemies, and on them that hate thee, that persecuted thee.

8 And thou shalt return and hearken to the voice of the LORD, and do all His commandments which I command thee this day. 9 And the LORD thy God will make thee over-abundant in all the work of thy hand, in the fruit of thy body, and in the fruit of thy cattle, and in the fruit of thy land, for good; for the LORD will again rejoice over thee for good, as He rejoiced over thy fathers; 10 if thou shalt hearken to the voice of the LORD thy God, to keep His commandments and His statutes which are written in this book of the law; if thou turn unto the LORD thy God with all thy heart, and with all thy soul.

2. Redemption as Fullness and Playfulness: Earthly Bounty and Transcendent Peace

Zechariah 8:4–12

4 Thus saith the LORD of hosts: There shall yet old men and old women sit in the broad places of Jerusalem, every man with his staff in his hand for very age. 5 And the broad places of the city shall be full of boys and girls playing in the broad places thereof.

6 Thus saith the LORD of hosts: If it be marvellous in the eyes of the remnant of this people in those days, should it also be marvellous in Mine eyes? saith the LORD of hosts.

7 Thus saith the LORD of hosts: Behold, I will save My people from the east country, and from the west country; 8 And I will

bring them, and they shall dwell in the midst of Jerusalem; and they shall be My people, and I will be their God, in truth and in righteousness.

9 Thus saith the LORD of hosts: Let your hands be strong, ye that hear in these days these words from the mouth of the prophets that were in the day that the foundation of the house of the LORD of hosts was laid, even the temple, that it might be built. 10 For before those days there was no hire for man, nor any hire for beast; neither was there any peace to him that went out or came in because of the adversary; for I set all men every one against his neighbour.

11 But now I will not be unto the remnant of this people as in the former days, saith the LORD of hosts. 12 For as the seed of peace, the vine shall give her fruit, and the ground shall give her increase, and the heavens shall give their dew; and I will cause the remnant of this people to inherit all these things.

Isaiah 14:1–7

1 For the LORD will have compassion on Jacob, and will yet choose Israel, and set them in their own land; and the stranger shall join himself with them, and they shall cleave to the house of Jacob. 2 And the peoples shall take them, and bring them to their place; and the house of Israel shall possess them in the land of the LORD for servants and for handmaids; and they shall take them captive, whose captives they were; and they shall rule over their oppressors.

3 And it shall come to pass in the day that the LORD shall give thee rest from thy travail, and from thy trouble, and from the hard service wherein thou wast made to serve, 4 that thou shalt take up this parable against the king of Babylon, and say:

How hath the oppressor ceased!
The exactress of gold ceased!
5 The LORD hath broken the staff of the wicked,
The sceptre of the rulers,
6 That smote the peoples in wrath
With an incessant stroke,
That ruled the nations in anger,
With a persecution that none restrained.

7 The whole earth is at rest, and is quiet;
They break forth into singing.

Ezekiel's words use the empirical reality of natural landscape and of physiological human structure to encompass the transcendence of redemption and the bounties, both spiritual and physical, that will come in its train.

Ezekiel 36:1, 6–8, 24–30

1 And thou, son of man, prophesy unto the mountains of Israel, and say: Ye mountains of Israel, hear the word of the LORD.

. . . .

6 therefore prophesy concerning the land of Israel, and say unto the mountains and to the hills, to the streams and to the valleys: Thus saith the Lord GOD: Behold, I have spoken in My jealousy and in My fury, because ye have borne the shame of the nations; 7 therefore thus saith the Lord GOD: I have lifted up My hand: Surely the nations that are round about you, they shall bear their shame. 8 But ye, O mountains of Israel, ye shall shoot forth your branches, and yield your fruit to My people Israel; for they are at hand to come.

. . . .

24 For I will take you from among the nations, and gather you out of all the countries, and will bring you into your own land. 25 And I will sprinkle clean water upon you, and ye shall be clean; from all your uncleannesses, and from all your idols, will I cleanse you.

26 A new heart also will I give you, and a new spirit will I put within you; and I will take away the stony heart out of your flesh, and I will give you a heart of flesh.

27 And I will put My spirit within you, and cause you to walk in My statutes, and ye shall keep Mine ordinances, and do them.

28 And ye shall dwell in the land that I gave to your fathers; and ye shall be My people, and I will be your God.

29 And I will save you from all your uncleannesses; and I will call for the corn, and will increase it, and lay no famine upon you. 30 And I will multiply the fruit of the tree, and the increase of the field, that ye may receive no more the reproach of famine among the nations.

3. Redemption as a Social Movement: Redemption and Justice

Malachi's prophecy figures redemption as the wisdom that brings about philosophical closure (Malachi 3:18): no longer will the wicked prosper while the righteous lay low (Malachi 3:14–16). Along with the reconciliation towards God (Malachi 3:17, 20–21) comes the rapprochement between generations (Malachi 3:24). History and philosophy unite; wisdom is seen in the dynamic functioning of the whole.

Malachi 3:12–24

12 And all nations shall call you happy;
For ye shall be a delightsome land,
Saith the LORD of hosts.
13 Your words have been all too strong against Me,
Saith the LORD.
Yet ye say: 'Wherein have we spoken against thee?'
14 Ye have said: 'It is vain to serve God;
And what profit is it that we have kept His charge,
And that we have walked mournfully
Because of the LORD of hosts?
15 And now we call the proud happy;
Yea, they that work wickedness are built up;
Yea, they try God, and are delivered.'
16 Then they that feared the LORD
Spoke one with another;
And the LORD hearkened, and heard,
And a book of remembrance was written before Him,
For them that feared the LORD, and that thought upon His
   name.
17 And they shall be Mine, saith the LORD of hosts,
In the day that I do make, even Mine own treasure;
And I will spare them, as a man spareth
His own son that serveth him.
18 Then shall ye again discern between the righteous and the
   wicked,
Between him that serveth God
And him that serveth Him not.
19 For, behold, the day cometh,
It burneth as a furnace;
And all the proud, and all that work wickedness, shall be stubble;
And the day that cometh shall set them ablaze,
Saith the LORD of hosts,

That it shall leave them neither root nor branch.
20 But unto you that fear My name
Shall the sun of righteousness arise with healing in its wings;
And ye shall go forth, and gambol
As calves of the stall.
21 And ye shall tread down the wicked;
For they shall be ashes under the soles of your feet
In the day that I do make,
Saith the LORD of hosts.
22 Remember ye the law of Moses My servant,
Which I commanded unto him in Horeb for all Israel,
Even statutes and ordinances.
23 Behold, I will send you
Elijah the prophet
Before the coming Of the great and terrible day of the LORD.
24 And he shall turn the heart of the fathers to the children,
And the heart of the children to their fathers;
Lest I come and smite the land with utter destruction.

4. Redemption as Tranquility, Wisdom, and Play

Similar to what we see in the words of Zechariah 8:4–5, the language of Isaiah also unites the concept of redemption, so often figured as a solemn theological moment, with the carefree notion of play. In this context, play is understood not as mindlessness, but as what is best and most natural among human activities. In this conception, the notion of redemption is that what is natural about human beings is no longer a function of primitive self-absorption, but becomes elevated, enlightened, and full of joy.

Isaiah 11:1–9

1 And there shall come forth a shoot out of the stock of Jesse,
And a twig shall grow forth out of his roots.
2 And the spirit of the LORD shall rest upon him,
The spirit of wisdom and understanding,
The spirit of counsel and might,
The spirit of knowledge and of the fear of the LORD.
3 And his delight shall be in the fear of the LORD;
And he shall not judge after the sight of his eyes,
Neither decide after the hearing of his ears;
4 But with righteousness shall he judge the poor,
And decide with equity for the meek of the land;

And he shall smite the land with the rod of his mouth,
And with the breath of his lips shall he slay the wicked.
5 And righteousness shall be the girdle of his loins,
And faithfulness the girdle of his reins.
6 And the wolf shall dwell with the lamb,
And the leopard shall lie down with the kid;
And the calf and the young lion and the fatling together;
And a little child shall lead them.
7 And the cow and the bear feed;
Their young ones shall lie down together;
And the lion shall eat straw like the ox.
8 And the sucking child shall play on the hole of the asp,
And the weaned child shall put his hand on the basilisk's den.
9 They shall not hurt nor destroy
In all My holy mountain;
For the earth shall be full of the knowledge of the LORD,
As the waters cover the sea.

SELECT BIBLIOGRAPHY

This brief bibliography is offered as a resource for students wishing to expand their acquaintance with aspects of the Hebrew Bible treated in this anthology.

Abarbanel, Don Isaac. *Commentary on the Bible*. Tel Aviv: HaPoel HaMizrahi, 1979.

Alter, Robert. *The Art of Biblical Narrative*. New York: Basic Books, 1981.

———. *The Art of Biblical Poetry*. New York: Basic Books, 1985.

Alter, Robert, and Frank Kermode. *The Literary Guide to the Bible*. Cambridge, MA: Belknap Press of Harvard University Press, 1990.

Bach, Alice, ed. *Women in the Hebrew Bible: A Reader*. New York: Routledge, 1999.

Bakhtin, M. M. *The Dialogic Imagination*. Austin: University of Texas Press, 1981.

Bal, Mieke. *Death and Dissymmetry: The Politics of Coherence in the Book of Judges*. Chicago: Chicago University Press, 1988.

———. *Lethal Love: Feminist Literary Readings of Biblical Love Stories*. Bloomington: Indiana University Press, 1987.

———. "Lots of Writing." In *Ruth and Esther: A Feminist Companion to the Bible (Second Series)*, edited by Athalya Brenner. Sheffield, UK: Sheffield Academic Press, 1999, pp. 212–38.

Bar-Efrat, Shimon. *Narrative Art in the Bible*. Sheffield, UK: Almond Press, 1989.

Baskin, Judith R. *Midrashic Women*. Waltham, MA: Brandeis University Press, 2002.

Berman, Joshua. *Created Equal: How the Bible Broke with Ancient Political Thought*. New York: Oxford University Press, 2008.

Bloom, Harold. *The Anxiety of Influence*. New York: Oxford University Press, 1973, 1997.

Brenner, Athalya, ed. *A Feminist Companion to Exodus to Deuteronomy*. Sheffield, UK: Sheffield Academic Press, 1994; repr. 2001.

————, ed. *A Feminist Companion to Genesis*. Sheffield, UK: Sheffield Academic Press, 1993; repr. 1997.

————, ed. *A Feminist Companion to Samuel and Kings*. Sheffield, UK: Sheffield Academic Press, 1994.

————, ed. *Judges: A Feminist Companion to the Bible (Second Series)*. Sheffield, UK: Sheffield Academic Press, 1999.

————, ed. *Ruth and Esther: A Feminist Companion to the Bible (Second Series)*. Sheffield, UK: Sheffield Academic Press, 1999.

Brenner, Athalya, and Fokkelien van Dijk-Hemmes. *On Gendering Texts: Female and Male Voices in the Hebrew Bible*. Leiden: E. J. Brill, 1996.

Brettler, Marc. "The Book of the Judges: Literature as Politics." *Journal of Biblical Literature* 108, no. 3 (1989): 395–418.

Brettler, Marc Zvi. *The Creation of History in Ancient Israel*. New York: Routledge, 1995.

Brueggemann, Walter. "In Trust and Freedom: A Study of Faith in the Succession Narrative." *Interpretation: A Journal of Bible and Theology* 26, no. 1 (January 1972): 3–19.

Confino, Alon. *The Nation as a Local Metaphor: Württemberg, Imperial Germany, and National Memory, 1871–1918*. Chapel Hill: University of North Carolina Press, 1997.

Cover, Robert M. "Nomos and Narrative." *Harvard Law Review* 97, no. 4 (1983): 4–68.

Dienstag, Joshua Foa. *Dancing in Chains: Narrative and Memory in Political Theory*. Palo Alto, CA: Stanford University Press, 1997.

Elazar, Daniel J. *Covenant and Polity in Biblical Israel*. New Brunswick, NJ: Transaction Publishers, 1998.

————. "Obligations and Rights in the Jewish Political Tradition: Some Preliminary Observations." *Jewish Political Studies Review* 3: 3–4, Fall 1991.

Exum, J. Cheryl. *Fragmented Women: Feminist (Sub)versions of Biblical Narratives*. Valley Forge, PA: Trinity Press International, 1993.

————. *Plotted, Shot, and Painted: Cultural Representations of Biblical Women*. Sheffield, UK: Sheffield Academic Press, 1996.

Fewell, Danna Nolan, and David M. Gunn. *Gender, Power, and Promise: The Subject of the Bible's First Story*. Nashville: Abingdon Press, 1993.

Fishbane, Michael. *The Garments of Torah: Essays in Biblical Hermeneutics.* Bloomington: Indiana University Press, 1989, 1992.

———. *The Exegetical Imagination: On Jewish Thought and Theology.* Cambridge, MA: Harvard University Press, 1998.

Fokkelman, J. P. *Narrative Art in Genesis.* Amsterdam: Van Gorgon, Assen, 1975.

Gottwald, Norman K. *The Hebrew Bible: A Socio-Literary Introduction.* Philadelphia: Fortress Press, 1985.

———. *The Politics of Ancient Israel.* Louisville, KY: Westminster John Knox Press, 2001.

Handelman, Susan A. *The Slayers of Moses.* Albany: SUNY Press, 1983.

Hasan-Rokem, Galit, and David Shulman, eds. *Untying the Knot: On Riddles and Other Enigmatic Modes.* New York: Oxford University Press, 1996.

The Holy Scriptures According to the Masoretic Text. Max Margolis, ed. Philadelphia: The Jewish Publication Society of America, 1917.

Jacobs, Jonathan A., ed. *Judaic Sources and Western Thought.* New York: Oxford University Press, 2013.

Kass, Leon R. *The Beginning of Wisdom: Reading Genesis.* Chicago: University of Chicago Press, 2003.

Kugel, James L. *In Potiphar's House: The Interpretive Life of Biblical Texts.* Cambridge, MA: Harvard University Press, 1990, 1994.

———. *How to Read the Bible.* New York: Free Press, 2007.

Malbim, Rabbi Meir Leibush. *Commentary on the Bible with Mekhilta and Sifrei.* New York: MP Press, 1974 (Hebrew).

Manuel, Frank E. *The Broken Staff: Judaism through Christian Eyes.* Cambridge, MA: Harvard University Press, 1992.

Merkin, Aryeh, ed. *Midrash Rabbah.* Tel Aviv: Yavneh, 1986.

Miller, David L., ed. *Jung and the Interpretation of the Bible.* New York: Continuum, 1995.

Mittelman, Alan. *The Scepter Shall Not Depart from Judah: Perspectives on the Persistence of the Political in Judaism.* Lanham, MD: Lexington Books, 2000.

Morgenstern, Mira. *Conceiving a Nation: The Development of Political Discourse in the Hebrew Bible.* University Park: Penn State Press, 2008.

Naveh, Gila Safran. *Biblical Parables and Their Modern Re-creations*. Albany: SUNY Press, 2000.

Nelson, Eric. *The Hebrew Republic: Jewish Sources and the Transformation of European Political Thought*. Cambridge, MA: Harvard University Press, 2010.

Niditch, Susan. *Folklore and the Hebrew Bible*. Minneapolis: Fortress Press, 1993.

Pangle, Thomas L. *Political Philosophy and the God of Abraham*. Baltimore: Johns Hopkins University Press, 2003.

Pardes, Ilana. *Countertraditions in the Bible: A Feminist Approach*. Cambridge, MA: Harvard University Press, 1992.

Robinson, Marilynne. *When I Was a Child I Read Books*. New York: Farrar, Straus & Giroux, 2012.

Safran-Naveh, Gila. *Biblical Parables and Their Modern Re-creation: From "Apples of Gold in Silver Settings" to "Imperial Messages."* Albany: SUNY Press, 2000.

Schneidau, Herbert N. *Sacred Discontent: The Bible and Western Tradition*. Baton Rouge: Louisiana State University Press, 1976.

Schniedewind, William M. *How the Bible Became a Book*. New York: Cambridge University Press, 2004.

Schochet, Gordon, Fania Oz-Sulzberger, and Meirav Jones, eds. *Political Hebraism: Judaic Sources in Early Modern Political Thought*. Jerusalem: Shalem Press, 2008.

Schwartz, Regina M., ed. *The Book and the Text: The Bible and Literary Theory*. New York: Basil Blackwell, 1990.

Segal, Jerome M. *Joseph's Bones: Understanding the Struggle between God and Mankind in the Bible*. London: Penguin, 2007.

Shamah, Moshe. *Recalling the Covenant*. Jersey City, NJ: Ktav, 2011.

Sheehan, Jonathan. *The Enlightenment Bible: Translation, Scholarship, Culture*. Princeton, NJ: Princeton University Press, 2005.

Trible, Phyllis. *Texts of Terror*. Philadelphia: Fortress Press, 1984.

Walzer, Michael. *Exodus and Revolution*. New York: Basic Books, 1985.

———. *In God's Shadow: Politics in the Hebrew Bible*. New Haven, CT: Yale University Press, 2012.

Walzer, Michael, Menachem Lorberbaum, Noam J. Zohar, and Ari Ackerman, eds. *The Jewish Political Tradition*. Vol. 2. New Haven, CT: Yale University Press, 2003.

Walzer, Michael, Menachem Lorberbaum, Noam J. Zohar, and Yair Lorberbaum, eds. *The Jewish Political Tradition*. Vol. 1. New Haven, CT: Yale University Press, 2000.

Wildavsky, Aaron. *Moses as Political Leader*. Jerusalem: Shalem Press, [1984]; 2005.

Zornberg, Avivah Gottlieb. *Genesis: The Beginning of Desire*. Philadelphia: Jewish Publication Society, 1995.

INDEX OF BIBLICAL PASSAGES

INDEX OF MAJOR NAMES

Variant spellings used in this volume, as well as different names for the same character or thing, are given following a slash. Names that may refer to more than one personage in the Hebrew Bible are disambiguated by a parenthetical gloss following the name.